REGNUM STUDIES IN MISSION

Developing Just and Inclusive Communities

Series Preface

Regnum Studies in Mission are born from the lived experience of Christians and Christian communities in mission, especially but not solely in the fast growing churches among the people of the developing world. These churches have more to tell than stories of growth. They are making significant impacts on their cultures in the cause of Christ They are producing 'cultural products' which express the reality of Christian faith, hope and love in their societies.

Regnum Studies in Mission are the fruit often of rigorous research to the highest international standards and always of authentic Christian engagement in the transformation of people and societies. These are for the world. The formation of Christian theology, missiology and practice in the twenty-first century will depend to a great extent on the active participation of growing churches contributing biblical and culturally appropriate expressions of Christian practice to inform World Christianity.

Regnum is supported by the generosity of EMW

Developing Just and Inclusive Communities

Challenges for Diakonia / Christian Social Practice and Social Work

Hans Morten Haugen, Benedicte Tveter Kivle, Tony Addy, Terese Bue Kessel, John Klaasen (eds)

First published 2022 by Regnum Books International

Regnum is an imprint of the Oxford Centre for Mission Studies
St. Philip and St. James Church
Woodstock Road
Oxford OX2 6HR, UK
www.regnumbooks.net

09 08 07 06 05 04 03 7 6 5 4 3 2 1

British Library Cataloguing in Publication Data
A catalogue record for this book is available from the British Library

ISBN: 978-1-5064-9736-5
eBook ISBN: 978-1-5064-9737-2

Typeset by Words by Design
Cover image Courtney Smith. www.unsplash.com

Published with the support of

Digni VID

Distributed by Fortress Press in the US, Canada, India, and Brazil

Contents

Foreword
Dr Isabel Apawo Phiri

The *Developing Just and Inclusive Communities: Challenges for Diakonia/ Christian Social Practice and Social Work* is a much-needed publication today when one reads the signs of our times. The Russian invasion of Ukraine in 2022 has increased the need for guidance on how the ecumenical movement and local churches in the affected countries (and globally) can respond verbally and through action against armed conflict, the domination of the powerful countries and racism and take care of the internally displaced people and refugees. This war has brought to mind what is said in the World Council of Churches *Together Towards Life* document paragraph 43 which says:

> The affirmation of God's mission (*missio Dei*) points to the belief in God as One who acts in history and in creation, in concrete realities of time and contexts, who seeks the fullness of life for the whole earth through justice, peace and reconciliation. Participation in God's ongoing work of liberation and reconciliation by the Holy Spirit, therefore, includes discerning and unmasking the demons that exploit and enslave. For example, this involves deconstructing patriarchal ideologies, upholding the right to self-determination for Indigenous peoples, and challenging the social embeddedness of racism and casteism.

Another section in *Together Towards Life,* which I find helpful to discern the direction taken by the book *Developing Just and Inclusive Communities: Challenges for Diakonia/Christian Social Practice and Social Work* and is also helpful in reading the signs of our times is paragraph 46. It says:

> The good news of God's reign is about the promise of the actualization of a just and inclusive world. Inclusivity fosters just relationships in the community of humanity and creation, with mutual acknowledgement of persons and creation, and mutual respect and sustenance of each one's sacred worth. It also facilitates each one's full participation in the life of the community. Baptism in Christ implies a lifelong commitment to give an account of this hope by overcoming the barriers in order to find a common identity under the sovereignty of God (Galatians 3:27-28). Therefore, discrimination of all types against any human being is unacceptable in the sight of God.

The World Council of Churches document *Together Towards Life* made the above affirmations in the context of mission from the margins, which is a key theme in this new book. The key advantage of this book over *Together Towards Life* is that it contains well researched qualitative and quantitative essays that give visions of inclusive and just diaconal communities rooted within particular contexts.The concrete examples come from both the global south and global north, reminding the reader of the importance of context in understanding sustainable community development.

As the essays highlight the link between the United Nation Sustainable Development Goal 16 *Promote just, peaceful and inclusive societies* and target 7, which says: *Ensure responsive, inclusive, participatory and representative decision-making at all levels*, one also perceive the need to constantly read the signs of times of our times, reflect theologically on them and act accordingly. Some of the essays in this publication have taken this approach and provide the reader a thick description and analysis of what is happening locally and how it affects the global and vice versa.

As this book goes to the press, at the World Council of Churches we are celebrating the long-awaited approval of the *Called to Transformation Ecumenical Diakonia Resource Document.* Both this book and this document affirm that the diaconal and development issues have not changed over the years but have become more complex. Under such circumstances, ecumenical diakonia must not ignore the root causes of the suffering of those who we seek to serve. Diakonia cannot be detached from peace, justice and transformation. Furthermore, when we say that the world sets the agenda for ecumenical diakonia at global and local level, we affirm that our service to our neighbours in the context of systemic disdain for life has to speak to the full dimension of our context. We cannot serve locally ignorant of or detached from the global context knowing as we do that every local situation is shaped and impacted by the global forces. Nor can we respond in faith only to the global and systemic realities without authentic compassion for those who suffer and for those who dare to create islands of hope in the global ocean of despair.

This book has also highlighted the importance of diakonia to be prophetic. Its goal is concrete presence of God on earth in the service to vulnerable men and women, children and the earth. Diakonia is the sign of God with and among us, Immanuel (Isaiah 7:14). And this sign is given through the action of God there, where life is threatened. Amidst this reality, it is necessary to act with words and actions.

I therefore recommend this book as a very important resource to future researchers who want to develop further the issues raised here. It is a must read for students, educators, church leaders and practitioners of diakonia and development who want to take seriously the vision of an inclusive and just communities.

Dr Isabel Apawo Phiri, Deputy General Secretary World Council of Churches

Editors' Foreword

Hans Morten Haugen, Benedicte Tveter Kivle, Tony Addy, Terese Bue Kessel and John Klaasen

The background for this book is the common interest of the authors in the ideas of inclusion and participation in the context of churches and community organisations.

The Agenda 2030 provides the overall framework for the book. Whilst various ways of affirming this Agenda were available, the editors chose the United Nations sustainable development goal (SDG) 16 and its SDG Target 16.7: 'Ensure responsive, inclusive, participatory and representative decision-making at all levels.' Such decision-making processes will promote collective and individual empowerment and lead to just and inclusive communities.

This book draws on the insights and experiences from three previous books initiated by VID Specialized University and published by Regnum books, in the frame of diaconal reflection and practice: *Diakonia as Christian Social Practice* (2014), *Diakonia in a Gender Context* (2016) and *The Diaconal Church* (2019). It brings together experiences and perspectives from several continents, providing transnational insights. Compared to the three previous books, this book stands out by more explicitly including perspectives from community organisations and community work, in addition to churches and church-based organisations.

We express our acknowledgement to all contributors who have invested time, intellect and insight in writing their chapters, and to two anonymous reviewers for their most constructive feedbacks to the chapters.

Also, acknowledgement is expressed to VID Specialized University, whose impetus for the book came from its master programme in community development and social innovation (MACOMM), its research group on community development (CODE) and its leading role in ReDi, the International Society for the Research and Study of Diaconia and Christian Social Practice.

Finally, acknowledgement is given to the Norwegian organisation Digni – an umbrella organization for 20 Christian organizations working against poverty and for dignified lives – for funding the book, and to Regnum for another experience of excellent cooperation.

The Roles of Churches and Community Organisations

Hans Morten Haugen, Benedicte Tveter Kivle, Tony Addy, Terese Bue Kessel and John Klaasen

The ambition for this book is reflected in the title *Developing Just and Inclusive Communities. Challenges for Diakonia/Christian Social Practice and Social Work*. The authors hope to engage students, practitioners and researchers in a reflection to influence practices that imply exclusion or injustice of some sort, in order to change direction within the context of the church and other social agents in local communities. We understand communities as relational practices which emphasise common being, and as spaces where there is common decision-making and where issues of power are handled, but does not depend on a shared, common identity. Despite numerous attempts by actors at international, national and local levels to ease human suffering, reverse polarisation and fight injustice, the challenges for community organisations and churches are ever present and demand action. To act wisely, there is a need for more understanding of structural and societal processes within and amongst actors at community level.

The authors represent the practice field as well as academia, hence the stories that evolve are often first-hand experiences unwrapped with relevant theoretical perspectives to understand the essence of what it means to be a 'just' or 'unjust', 'exclusive' or 'inclusive' community. The authors write from different parts of the world with experiences on how decision-making on a community level can be for the best or worse. It has been important within these pages to include both practitioners and academics to reflect practically and theoretically on some selected challenges in diaconal and secular social contexts to develop a diverse perspective on the issue of just and inclusive communities.

The first part of the title, *Developing Just and Inclusive Communities*, reflects one target from United Nations sustainable development goal (SDG) 16 which is to 'promote peaceful and inclusive societies for sustainable development, provide access to justice for all and build effective, accountable and inclusive institutions at all levels'.[1] Amongst the many important SDG targets, we would like to point out Target 16.7: 'Ensure responsive, inclusive, participatory and

[1] UN 2015, Sustainable Development Goal 16.

representative decision-making at all levels'. This target highlights the quality of the decision-making process that is often invisible and embedded in community life; hence it is an important meta-perspective in the discussion on how to develop a just and inclusive community.

The discussion about sustainable societies and sustainable communities is rooted within the ecumenical movement. Although the Institute for Environment and Development (founded in 1971) was probably the first organisation to use the word sustainability,[2] the first international organisations to work with this concept related to society and community was the World Council of Churches (WCC) in the meetings held in preparation for the Assembly that took place in Nairobi in 1975.[3] Prior to this, a series of meetings had prepared the ground and, in the deliberations, the concept of sustainability was directly related to justice and participation. The WCC launched a thematic programme after the Assembly which created a unifying theme for the Council, working towards a Just, Participatory and Sustainable Society (JPSS).

Communities, with an emphasis on social practice, develop continuously by the efforts of institutions – private, public or church-related – or by efforts of community organisations. Every day, decisions are made that influence the lives of community members in one way or another. A relevant consideration is whether decision-making and social processes within these institutions and organisations are inclusive or not, and whether their practices result in more just and inclusive communities. Throughout this book the authors seek different answers to this question from different positions and within a variety of contexts.

Regardless of the contexts and the specificities of churches and faith-based or secular organisations, we are convinced that SDG 16 and SDG Target 16.7 represent crucial insight into what changes are necessary, as reflected in the last part of the title: *Challenges for Diakonia/Christian Social Practice and Social Work*. Many denominations depend on a church structure that by nature is both hierarchical and patriarchal, hence preventing women from participating in important decision-making processes. Such systematic exclusion of more than half of its churchgoers hampers gender inclusive reflection where decisions are taken for the benefit of the entire community. In some parts of the world, these structures remain relatively unaltered but elsewhere changes are taking place.

In some parts of the world, where the infrastructure of the government does not secure basic human rights, churches and non-government organisations (NGOs) play a crucial role. They are often amongst the most important societal actors in the community in terms of human resources as well as moral and financial resources, often termed 'assets': a term that will be reviewed and

---

[2] J. A. Du Pisani, 'Sustainable development – historical roots of the concept', *Environmental Sciences* 3:2 (2006), 83-96, 91.

[3] N. Lossky, et al. (Eds), *Dictionary of the Ecumenical Movement* (Geneva: WCC Publications, 1991), pp. 550-552.

criticised in this book. On the other hand, in areas where material conditions are to a large extent fulfilled, churches and faith-based organisations may play an important social role with regard to loneliness, and the seeking of meaning in life. Churches in these parts of the world are less important overall as societal actors, also due to the multitude of other organised societal actors.

The book also seeks to foster a better understanding of social work, defined by the International Federation of Social Workers as (extract):

> A practice-based profession and an academic discipline that promotes social change and development, social cohesion, and the empowerment and liberation of people. Principles of social justice, human rights, collective responsibility, and respect for diversities are central to social work. Underpinned by theories of social work, social sciences, humanities and indigenous knowledge, social work engages people and structures to address life challenges and enhance wellbeing.[4]

Additional insight into the definition is provided under the headings Core Mandates, Principles, Knowledge, and Practice. Whilst the dimensions of 'profession' and 'academic discipline' are highlighted, there is no mentioning of 'volunteers', neither in the definition nor under the various headings. Rather than focusing on what is left out, we will focus on what is included, and what we see as a considerable overlap between this definition and SDG 16 and SDG Target 16.7, as well as the social efforts of a wide range of churches and diaconal organisations.

In this book the authors highlight the transformative process of inclusion, which is never-ending and acknowledge the present realities of power abuse, exclusion and marginalisation also seen within the life of Christian churches and other community organisations. In line with three previous books initiated by VID Specialized University and published by Regnum books, in the frame of diaconal reflection and practice – *Diakonia as Christian Social Practice* (2014), *Diakonia in a Gender Context* (2016) and *The Diaconal Church* (2019) – we affirm that diakonia is integral to all churches. Diaconal and Christian social practice strive to implement in the churches processes to enhance just and inclusive communities within the church and its societal surroundings. In this fourth book we include the broader context, including community organisation alongside the church, when describing and analysing the work for inclusion and justice within local communities.

Community organisations and churches are in various ways concerned with human dignity, societal justice, and fighting greed and destructive forces. We emphasise, however, that only those churches and church leaders that are concerned with the transformative potential in diaconal approach can promote SDG 16 and SDG Target 16.7. This does not mean that community organisations should start dismantling their structures and abolish their privileges. The crucial

---

[4] International Federation of Social Workers, *Global Definition of Social Work* (2014).

question is rather: How can the church and community organisations be challenged to become more responsive, inclusive and participatory, and secure representative decision-making at all levels? And what does inclusive and just communities mean? In the following, we will point at the four concepts, 'responsive', 'inclusive', 'participatory' and 'representative'.

Responsive: The term here refers to a deliberate analysis of societal structures that impede certain persons and groups of persons from fulfilling their God-given potential. Persons with disabilities have for too long been impeded in their participation and whilst we have witnessed new attention and stronger acknowledgment of their overall contributions, there is still a way to go to ensure real equality.[5] Whilst changes have happened through processes of legal recognition, in domestic law and through the Convention on the Rights of Persons with Disabilities (adopted in 2007; 182 state parties), churches have contributed to affirming their dignity and creation in the image of God. Most notably is the document *The Gift of Being*,[6] linking diversity, community, and vulnerability into a novel anthropology.

Inclusive: New approaches of social work, embedded in Christian faith, are found in the document *Seeking Conviviality. Re-forming Community Diakonia in Europe*.[7] In emphasising the core concepts of dignity, justice and vocation, the approach is inclusive: 'Who are or could be your allies in this work?'[8] These allies could be other churches or congregations, or it could be grassroots movements or organisations that are not formally related to a church. The allies could be certain organisations and movements within a church body. This being a transcontinental research project, concepts such as Ubuntu and community are critically analysed. Ubuntu is a widely used concept for the meaning of personhood within the context of community. In the various chapters, the authors seek to identify who are recognised and who are excluded in the decision-making processes in given communities.

Participatory: Substantial social analysis and inclusive involvement to identify the right responses necessitates that all relevant groups of persons, whether formally organised or not, are able to contribute with their abilities to create community. If the purpose is to change political priorities, participatory processes are crucial. Advocacy by churches and other social actors are

[5] Inger Marie Lid and Anna Rebecca Solevåg (eds), *Religiøst medborgerskap. Funksjonshemming, likeverd og menneskesyn* (Oslo: Cappelen Damm Akademisk, 2020).

[6] World Council of Churches, *The Gift of Being. Called to Be a Church of All and for All* (2016).

[7] Lutheran World Federation and interdiac, *Seeking Conviviality. Re-forming Community Diakonia in Europe* (2013).

[8] Lutheran World Federation and interdiac, *Seeking*, 42.

embedded in such experiences, often allowing the persons affected to formulate the demands, including what is termed Local to Global Advocacy (L2G).[9]

Representative: A minority of churches in the world are democratic, understood to imply that all members can regularly give their views on who are the right persons to decide within the churches. Moreover, many diaconal organisations, even when having elected boards, are overseen by churches who own these organisations. Acknowledging these realities, what role – if any – should churches and church-related organisations have in promoting representative decision-making? First, theological justifications for certain forms of decision-making within the church should not translate into decision-making principles in the societal realm. Second, enabling less-represented groups to be involved in decision-making is the most effective way to reduce overall dissatisfaction, as non-represented persons feel alienated from those in power. Representing persons in decision-making will also enhance overall accountability, implying that those in power are held to account for their use of power.

Power and Fostering Participation

Power is only implicitly recognised within SDG 16 and SDG Target 16.7, but all relevant elements highlighted above have obvious power dimensions. Diaconal actors, inspired by the simple and challenging question 'What do you want me to do for you?' (Matt 20:32; Mk 10:51; Lk 18:41), must be more attentive to the power asymmetries that are inherent in any giving–receiving relationship. In order to facilitate processes of change, community development initiatives must start with the question: 'What do we want us to do?'

Awareness of the internal and external impediments for a real and inclusive development process within a place-based community – and how to overcome these – can be assisted by the so-called power cube.[10] The power cube consists of three dimensions: *Forms* of power (visible, hidden and invisible), *places* of power (global to local; not forgetting the household level), and *spaces* of power (closed, invited, created). The editors emphasise that power is always involved in processes of community development. Even if none of the chapters have applied the power cube, the emphasis on non-discrimination, participation, accountability and empowerment are central in all chapters.

---

[9] Lutheran World Federation, *LWF Advocacy Handbook. A Guide for Member Churches and Country Programs* (2018).

[10] Gaventa, John, *Reflections on the Uses of the 'Power Cube'. Approach for Analyzing the Spaces, Places and Dynamics of Civil Society Participation and Engagement CFP evaluation series 2003-2006: no 4* (2005).

Social Innovation and Learning

Communities are never status quo and are always in a developing process. No community is the same year after year. People move in and out and affect the community by their mere presence or absence. Economic and political factors impact the dimension of justice and inclusion within the community.

The changes may not be noticeable from one day to another. However, even repetitive routines and rites will develop and change. Inclusive and just decision-making is not set once and for all but must be continuously assessed and adjusted to the current situation.

In the book authors pinpoint how churches, NGOs and public services continuously face challenges that push communities in the direction of exclusion and inequality. Amongst the many topics is the challenge of extreme poverty whilst striving for inclusiveness, or the processes of inclusion of newcomers in specific geographical communities, and how silenced topics influence the lives of individuals and, therefore, the community. Most chapters imply a discussion on how agents can redirect the development of their community into becoming more just and inclusive. Sometimes the initiatives are radical, sometimes they are incremental. But they share the vision of an inclusive and just community. This insight connects learning and innovation intrinsically to the everyday practices in communities.

Personhood and Inclusion

The church stands with other institutions, disciplines and communities in a long tradition of identity formation. The concept of personhood is investigated for its contribution towards inclusion and more participatory community development. Theological and philosophical perspectives of personhood are analysed to identify markers for inclusive community development. Classical doctrinal formulations such as imago Dei and African philosophical notions of identity formation are juxtaposed and contrast to provide principles for innovation and creativity towards inclusivity and development.

Outline of the Book's Five Parts and Each Chapter

As the book brings up diverse topics, we introduce five parts to seek to integrate the various chapters under a common theme and display the overall thematic content of the book.

The first part is titled *Overall Approaches*. In the first chapter, titled *Approaches to Community Development*, Tony Addy acknowledges community development work as a diverse field; therefore, it is important when discussing this field to be able to situate the approach that is being described or advocated within the overall field. This chapter maps the various understandings so that practitioners can situate their work and the work of an organisation within the proposed typology. These various understandings have been used by different types of organisations, including churches and faith-based organisations. The different types of community development work express a diversity of approaches to the purpose and process of the activity, the role of the worker and participants, and to the question of power and politics. The chapter is relevant to a discussion of community development as it relates to SDG 16 and SDG Target 16.7, which aim at achieving responsive, inclusive, participatory and representative decision-making.

John Klaasen's chapter, *Personhood and Inclusive Communities: Access to Justice for All*, identifies the role of personhood in taking responsibility for community development. Personhood is conceptualised from the perspectives of both theology and philosophy to give a comprehensive and critical analysis of the entanglement of personhood as being and doing. Four interrelated yet divergent notions of personhood are critically described and applied to community development. As a constructive contribution, markers for inclusive community development are identified and described in relation to the sustainable development goals of inclusive communities.

In the last chapter of the three introductory chapters, Hans Morten Haugen discusses *Human Rights as Inclusionary and Empowering Tools*. The chapter specifies development as encompassing control and reducing power asymmetries. This is a broader understanding than previous understandings of development. Embedding the chapter in social constructivism, and applying the collective dimensions of human rights, the chapter identifies the weaknesses and strengths of three models of organising societies: state-centred, market-centred and community-centred. Inclusive and empowering development will be achieved by building on the positive aspects of these three models. Whilst human rights are essential for just and inclusive development – specifying the content of decision-making processes – certain human rights and aspects of human rights remain controversial amongst churches. Norwegian Church Aid illustrates how relevant terms appear in strategic documents of a strongly church-based non-governmental organisation (NGO).

Three chapters are found under the heading *Approaches to Community Development and Diakonia*. In the chapter *A Critical Evaluation of Ubuntu Principle for Just and Inclusive Communities in a Contemporary Africa*, Benson Onyekachukwu Anofuechi analyses the term 'Ubuntu'. This term, expressing African humanism, has been and still is subject to criticism in African society. In African literature, philosophy, ethics, anthropology and theology, Ubuntu does play a role and scholars in Africa and beyond find the concept a contested one. This study uniquely contributes towards demonstrating that the Ubuntu principle prima facie contributes to building a peaceful community through just and inclusive processes across cultures. It unpacks Ubuntu philosophy of Augustine Shutte and Kwame Gyekye by critically juxtaposing the commonalities and contestation of developing just and inclusive communities to enhance sustainable development goals (SDGs) 16. It is proposed that the

Ubuntu principle extensively contributes to making any society thrive by aiding people of a nation to become more socially interconnected across the globe.

In the chapter *Seeking Conviviality as a Core Concept for Community Development*, Tony Addy introduces the concept and practice of seeking conviviality as a core concept for community development work. It proposes a rethinking of the International Association for Community Development's definition of community development. Problems arise from diverse understandings of community, especially in contexts of migration and super diversity. The concept of 'development' is explored in terms of the aims of work in localities. Seeking conviviality is proposed as a new perspective in community development work and implications for practice and training are elaborated. The roots of convivial thinking and practice are explored as they relate to everyday life and to professional practice. Diversity is addressed as a key issue, and a fresh approach to community practice is outlined. The 'service model' for professional practice and the implications for the planning and implementation of local projects are discussed.

Stephanie Dietrich's chapter is titled *A Diaconal Approach to Community Development in The Light of the Sustainable Development Goals: 'Leaving No One Behind' through Exploring Religious Resources for Creating Just and Inclusive Communities*. The 'Leaving no one behind' is key to linking a faith-based approach with the global development agenda as expressed through the SDGs. She discusses critically what we mean when we underline that diakonia, in the same way as the SDG agenda, takes its starting point 'from the margins', and that it seeks to reach 'the furthest behind' first. Marginalisation is discussed in relation to the SDGs, drawing on the theory of intersectionality. The chapter elaborates on a theological and diaconal basis which is relevant for the development of an inclusive approach to the role Christian actors can play in such community development activities, with a critical focus on the notion of a 'perspective from the margins' and its background within liberation theology. Dietrich affirms that theological approaches correspond with a rights-based understanding as underlying the SDGs, and that all people of good will, regardless of their religious or ideological background, should cooperate actively and jointly in the creation of just and inclusive communities.

Under the heading *Social Practice and Diakonia* we find four chapters. Silje Kivle Andreassen and Kjersti Gautestad Norheim's chapter is titled *In What Ways Can the Church Function as a Generator for Inclusive and Sustainable Communities? A Case Study on What Role the Local Congregation Plays in Two Different Urban Communities*. The chapter, based on a field study of two different congregations within the Church of Norway (CoN), analyses how they interact with the local community and how they participate in building inclusive and sustainable communities. In Norway, there are approximately 1,000 different local communities. Some of the communities are populous, whilst others are less so. But one thing they have in common is that they all have a church in their proximity. At the same time as Norway has become gradually more urbanised, the role of the church has also been through great changes. The chapter identifies ways through which congregations within CoN actively take part in community formation in urban, local communities.

The chapter *Lifezone Sport International: A Narrative of Diaconia Viewed through the Lens of Tangible Hope* by Jeremy Wyngaard emanates from semi-structured interviews that took place in 2020. These were conducted with persons with diverse relationships to the Faith Based Organisation (FBO) Lifezone Sport International (LSI), working in the historically underprivileged dual suburb of Factreton and Kensington in Cape Town. The interviews found that tangible hope is experienced by people who are engaged in any form of diaconal work. This phenomenon can best be articulated through the theoretical lens of reflexive thematic analysis, a method popularised and continually evolved by Braun and Clarke within a broader phenomenological qualitative research methodology that relies strongly on the lived experiences of volunteers, coaches, networking partners, parents and players who have been associated with LSI.

Contemporary Mizuko Ritual in Japan for Aborted Children: A Proposal to Pastoral Counselling in The Christian Church is a chapter by Terese Bue Kessel. *Mizuko* means 'water child' and refers to an aborted or miscarried child. The sorrow that follows an abortion is recognised at a memorial service in Japanese temples. Scholars who have tried to interview women who attended a *mizuko kuyo* ritual have had difficulty accessing their personal narratives. Whilst the Christian faith is held in relatively high esteem in Japanese society, the topic of abortion is not discussed, including in the church. A relevant question to ask, therefore, is 'What can the Japanese memorial service for aborted children suggest to pastoral counselling?' Also pertinent is entering the issue into dialogue with pastoral counselling and the practice of listening, which is traditionally part of diaconal work. The concepts embedded in this chapter are the church's contribution to community development and building gender inclusive communities.

Silje Hole Hirsch's chapter *Parenting Strategies to Prevent Risks for Adolescents in Urban Neighbourhoods* investigates the parenting strategies that parents with immigrant backgrounds use to protect their teenage children from risks in their neighbourhoods. The chapter is based on an empirical project with parents from immigrant backgrounds who are parenting teenagers in three local communities in Oslo, Norway, and parents on a parenting guidance course. The findings are investigated using theories of parenting strategy, social cohesion, and conviviality. The parents' strategies to navigate the identified risks are presented according to two sub-strategies: strategies for *setting boundaries* and strategies for *participation in the community*.

Three chapters are included under the heading *Learning, Social Innovation & Leadership*.

In the chapter *Ministerial Formation of Former 'Mission Churches' in South Africa: 'Missional Consciousness' as an Enabler for Community Development*, Eugene Baron finds that the ministerial formation processes in the former 'mission churches' within the Reformed church family in South Africa can represent a challenge to community development. He responds to the problem and argues that it can only be addressed through the establishment of a 'missional consciousness' of prospective ministers. The chapter elaborates on how the engendering of a 'missional consciousness' is necessary to form and empower such prospective Christian ministers to initiate and steer such community development projects in their respective communities. Baron argues that a commitment of the former mission Churches should include nurturing a 'missional consciousness' in ministerial formation.

The chapter *Faith-based Organisations and Social Innovation for Just and Inclusive Communities? A Scoping Review* by Dag Håkon Eriksen and Annette Leis-Peters stands out by its method and length. Based on an extensive literature search of four databases, this chapter presents a scoping review of the empirical research field at the intersection of faith-based organisations, community development and innovation. The current state of empirical knowledge in this field exploring the empirical data being studied and the concepts used are presented. This chapter presents the external and organisational factors that influence innovation. It also describes how the relationship between faith and innovation is characterised. Leadership factors are also addressed. This chapter ends with a focus on the different innovation processes and their results, and a model of the factors is presented.

Benedicte Tveter Kivle and Beate Jelstad Løvaas' chapter *Leading towards Inclusion in Communities: Unity and Diversity when Leading towards Inclusiveness* presents a theoretical framework for community leaders to better understand how to lead towards inclusive communities. They combine known indicators of inclusion in organisations with theoretical elements of leadership and place them according to the theoretical divide between diversity and unity. They suggest specific leadership strategies that can make inclusion a reality for participants and members in community organisations by balancing the need for unity and diversity.

Under the heading *Social Inclusion, Gender, Disability & Diversity*, three chapters are included. In *Ruth the Moabite: A Story About an Immigrant and Her Struggle for Identity*, Tiana Bosman explores how a critical, in-depth reading of an Old Testament narrative text can uncover the injustice and exclusion that the immigrant woman Ruth faced when she tried to assimilate into a host culture. Faith communities are challenged not to use the narrative of Ruth as an exceptional case study that should be applied to contemporary communities as an example of how immigrants could be included in their host communities, but rather as an example of how not to treat immigrants. Readers who are engaged in diaconal work are challenged to learn from the wrongful treatment of Ruth and to find new, life-affirming ways of treating immigrants.

In *Gender Responsive Organisations and the 2030 Agenda*, Marit Breen provides a case study on how to bring about gender responsive organisational change, seeking to build inclusive communities in terms of women's representation and gender justice. Data are gathered from the Free Pentecostal Fellowship of Kenya (FPFK) and their Tuinuane Women's project, which is a development project that seeks to improve access to savings and loans for women in Kenya. By investigating which role the project had on women's voice and representation in FPFK, the case study shows how the gendered context, unequal gendered power relations, and women empowerment mutually influence intended outcomes concerning gender equality in an organisation and thus its ability to be a change actor in civil society.

Amos Ounsoubo's chapter, *The Use of Asset-based Approach as a Tool for the Inclusion of Persons with Disabilities: Case Study of HANDICARE in Ngaoundéré – Cameroon*, studies the inclusion of persons with disabilities (PwD) using asset-based methods. Rather than addressing the issue from the perspective of the vulnerability of PwD, the chapter discusses the matter from the perspective of the abilities of PwD. An illustration of a twin-track framework will be given from HANDICARE, which is working for the inclusion of the hearing-impaired youth. By analysing the method used by HANDICARE through two diaconal asset-based approaches, Use Your Talents (UYT) (the main concept) and Seeking Conviviality, as well as the concepts of empowerment, social innovation, and disability-inclusive development are applied. Ounsoubu finds that applying UYT enhances the hearing-impaired youths' skills, giving them confidence to consider themselves as full members of the community.

We end the book with a brief concluding chapter seeking to identify common challenges and responses.

Bibliography

Du Pisani, J. A. 'Sustainable development – historical roots of the concept', *Environmental Sciences*, 3:2 (2006), 83-96.

Gaventa, John. *Reflections on the Uses of the 'Power Cube'. Approach for Analyzing the Spaces, Places and Dynamics of Civil Society Participation and Engagement CFP Evaluation Series 2003-2006: no 4* (2005); https://www.participatorymethods.org/sites/participatorymethods.org/files/reflections_on_uses_powercube.pdf.

International Federation of Social Workers. *Global Definition of Social Work* (2014); https://www.ifsw.org/what-is-social-work/global-definition-of-social-work.

Lid, Inger Marie and Anna Rebecca Solevåg (eds), *Religiøst medborgerskap. Funksjonshemming, likeverd og Menneskesyn*, Cappelen Damm Akademisk, https://doi.org/10.23865/noasp.100.

Lossky, Nicholas, José Míguez Bonino, John S. Pobee, Geoffrey Wainwright, Tom F. Stransky and Pauline Webb (Eds), *Dictionary of the Ecumenical Movement* (Geneva: WCC Publications, 1991).

Lutheran World Federation and interdiac, *Seeking Conviviality. Re-forming Community Diakonia in Europe* (Geneva: LWF, 2013).

Lutheran World Federation, *LWF Advocacy Handbook. A Guide for Member Churches and Country Programs* (2018); https://www.lutheranworld.org/sites/default/files/2018/documents/advocacy_handbook.pdf.

UN (2015). *Sustainable Development Goal 16*; https://www.un.org/ruleoflaw/sdg-16.World Council of Churches, 'The Gift of Being. Called to Be a Church of All and for All', *The Ecumenical Review*, 68:2-3 (2016), 316-343.

Part One

Overall Approaches

Approaches to Community Development

Tony Addy

Introduction

This chapter sets the scene for the discussions of community development in the later sections of the book. It addresses one of the biggest problems confronting people writing about community development, which is the lack of any agreed common understanding of what it might be. In fact, community development is defined in a myriad of ways, each of which expresses the experience, viewpoint and interest of the person or organisation which wishes to invoke the term.[1] Therefore, it is helpful to create a framework which will assist in analysing the field and the contributions to this book. The chapter proposes a typology of community development approaches, each of which have been used by development agencies, churches, and civil society organisations. The typology explores the process of community development work and the generalised understandings of power which lie behind each approach.

A second problem which besets the discussion of community development work is the fact that the contexts in which community development is practised are extremely diverse. However, there has been a marked internationalisation in the theory and practice of community development which in some cases may be creative. Nevertheless, in many cases, practice from one context, for example in the global north, is imposed on another context in the global south. It is therefore very important to relate the community development approach to the specific political and economic realities faced by local communities and actors for community development.

The third problem to be faced is that community development is usually described from the point of view of a person who is or who will be a community development worker or of an organisation which wants to use a community development approach. This raises the knotty question of power and decision-

---

[1] For a discussion of the diverse understandings of 'community' and 'development' see T. Addy, 'Seeking Conviviality' as a Core Concept for Community Development in H. M Haugen et.al., Eds.. *Developing Just and Inclusive Communities. Challenges for Diakonia as Christian Social Practice and for Social Work* (Oxford, Regnum, 2022), 79-94.

making and the accountability of the organisations or churches which espouse a community development approach.

Furthermore, the book is linked to the UN sustainable development goal 16, which is aiming for a just, peaceful and inclusive society and within that, SDG Target 16.7, which focuses on achieving responsive, inclusive, participatory and representative decision-making. Each understanding of community development relates to this goal, but the differences between the various approaches are quite substantial. Some approaches to community development are based on developing a participatory democracy. Others are seen as a way of strengthening decision-making by representative structures, which are seen to be deficient in terms of inclusion and representativeness. Still others have no real understanding of the relation between local community development and the exercise of political or economic power.

Developing a Typology

Before introducing the typology, it is important to recognise that here we are talking about 'approaches' and that these are 'ideal types'. Practitioners and organisations often make an eclectic mix of elements from different approaches. Furthermore, here we are concentrating on approaches which are implemented by using different methods of work and specific tools. The three elements of approach, methods and tools should be integrated, but very often there is 'mixing' of the methods and tools used in the various approaches. Sometimes the methods and tools used fit with the chosen approach, sometimes not. It may seem obvious, but it is also important to note that in this discussion we are focusing on the role of the person or organisation which wishes to implement a community development approach. One important point to bear in mind, therefore, is the way in which the description of the approach situates and understands the people with whom the community development worker will be engaged. Almost all the language surrounding each approach assumes there is a kind of deficit in the people or situation which the approach aims to address. This is one of the classic problematic questions of intervention in any context.

I have divided the field of community development into four main approaches:

The first approach I have called 'participatory & inductive community development'. This type of community development emphasises working with local people with an approach which is concerned with a process of development understood as inductive. This group of approaches can be divided into two subgroups:

The first subgroup is rather pragmatic and builds on the everyday experience of people and their own perceptions. It can further be divided into an approach which is basically 'needs based' or it may be 'asset' or 'strengths based'.

The second subgroup of participatory and dialogical approaches is 'participatory, critical community development and participatory learning'. This may use some elements of the inductive process, but it emphasises the fact that local phenomena are rooted in a wider structural context. The work process includes an analysis of the wider context through a participatory learning process and builds a strategy which takes a more critical and wider perspective, even whilst engaging in local action.

The second approach is called 'organising as an approach to community development'. It is focused on the specific grievances people have and on building a powerful organisation for change. The aim is to build an organisation which will start very close to the issues people feel are important for them in their everyday life. A process of organising based in a locality builds on contacts with people which rely on focused discussions around specific issues. The aim is to redefine 'problems' as public issues which are the result of the operation of economic or political power. A key objective is to build a democratic organisation that aims to unite people in a series of 'actions' to change the interests of an institution, which has the power and which is the cause of the issue, so that it responds to the issues. This approach has also been used by churches and other religious groups often in an alliance with trade unions and other organisations. It works to change the policies of the institutions which affect peoples' housing or working conditions, for example. I have divided this approach into two sections which reflect different traditions of community organising, working with local organisations such as churches and trade unions, and working directly with residents.

The third approach is institutional, in that it is related to working on the interests of relatively powerful organisations which impact on localities or on the priorities of funding bodies. This is an approach which is often linked to social planning. The strategy is to work with local people to create better outcomes, often from a new development or stemming from a change of policy or even cuts to spending on social and health care. The aim may be to secure a consensus for change or to open a space where people make their own contributions to resolving a particular problem. This approach often follows a problem-solving process, in that it is assumed that in a locality where, for example, the municipality or the police perceive a problem, the local community should be mobilised to address that problem. This can be related to social care, criminality or other institutionally identified problems. In this case a positive outcome is sought, and the community development approach focuses on this target in a way which can often be quantified.

Fourthly, there is what could be termed a 'market' approach to community development. Especially in North America, community development corporations have been financed by government and large foundations to build up assets in a locality. The assets may be housing and enterprises or facilities of different kinds. The involvement of the 'local community' is through representation on the board of such a 'community development corporation'. The organisation has a mixture of finance from public sources but may also borrow money and trade. This implies that the other ways people become involved is as workers or as consumers of goods and services, very often of housing. Community development corporations may arise from community development processes or may also use community development as a complementary part of their activities.

Type	Description	Process	Power
Participatory & Inductive Community Development	Participatory, Inductive Community Development	Working in a non-directive, participatory way, prioritising process over outcome. Includes strengths-based or asset-based approaches. (Can, however, tend towards identifying the 'problem' as belonging to the identified group)	Pluralist/Neoliberal: No specific view on the issue of power and the influence of the wider political context
	Participatory, Critical Community Development, Participatory Learning	Working with local groups to analyse their situation critically and develop strategy, which may be for resistance, political change, or innovation	Pluralist/Transformative: Critical perspective on political and economic powerholders. Often build on a rights-based approach
Organising as an approach to Community Development	Community Organising (Neighbourhood Based, Organisation Based or Hybrid)	Building an organisation based on local block/street/neighbourhood organising or on local organisations and faith communities or on both	Pluralist: Achieve the resolution of an issue by altering the interests of powerful actors
Institution Based Community Development	Problem Focused/Outcome Based Community Development	Using a community development process to involve people in solving a local 'problem', which has usually been identified by a key institution	Pluralist/Neoliberal: Solve a problem by mobilising community interests and resources

	Social Planning and Community Development (Sozialraum entwicklung)	Merging institutional interests, local organisations and groups in a planning and development process	Pluralist: Achieve better outcomes by involving a wider range of stakeholders
Market Focused Community Development	Investment Based Community Development (mainly USA)	Usually creating a community development company which holds assets and investments	Pluralist/Neoliberal: Assume the main issue is investment via market or subsidised market mechanisms

Table 1. Typology of approaches to community development

Participatory and Inductive Community Development

(i) Participatory and Inductive Community Development

The first approach to community development which we will examine is often called the 'non-directive' approach. It is based on several assumptions relating to the motivation of those who promote this approach. Two key words pepper the discussion of the texts which show this very clearly. The first word is 'development' which implies that the people and/or the context is in some significant way 'underdeveloped' and needs bringing up to some standard which exists somewhere else. The second word, linked to development, is 'betterment', which also has a normative ring to it.[2] It implies change of two main kinds – change for the 'better' in the environment in which people live, and change for the 'better' in the people themselves. This implies that people need more competence in decision-making and implementing those decisions. It is not surprising, therefore, that the practices of community development following this model were first developed for work in the Global South and in work with marginalised communities in the USA.[3]

This approach arose in response to 'directive' approaches to local communities which had proved to be ineffective in producing long-term change in people and context. In the global south, it was related to preparation for 'independence' and 'self-government' and in the north to the continuance of

---

[2] For example: W. W. Biddle and L. J. Biddle, *The Community Development Process: The Rediscovery of Local Initiative* (New York: Holt, Rinehart & Winston, 1965) pp 76-79 on development; and R. T. Batten, and M. Batten, *The Non-Directive Approach in Group and Community Work* (London: Oxford University Press, 1967) p 30 on betterment.

[3] For example, T. R. Batten worked as an educator in Nigeria and Uganda before returning to Britain and initiating community development projects and community development learning at the University of London Institute of Education.

poverty and social exclusion and the perceived erosion of 'community'. Community development work was intended to promote self-organisation and this approach was applied to the creation of autonomous groups in neighbourhoods or villages as well as by organisations such as churches and non-governmental organisations to develop their work.[4]

The kernel of the approach is summed up in the word 'process' and the positive strength of this idea was that it does not espouse any particular expected outcome. Rather, the idea was to use a 'non-directive' leadership model to enable the group to work on its own problem analysis and action plan, and to carry out the actions. The community development worker or the sponsoring organisation should not decide for people or persuade them to follow a particular course of action. But the approach is also very firmly 'needs based' because the process centres on people being involved in deciding what their 'needs' are and how they should be met. Thus, the worker aims to promote participation and self-determination. The actions could be some material improvement in the locality carried out by the group or the creation of initiatives of mutual aid or self-help. It could also lead to representations to relevant authorities for changes in public policy or for new provision for specific needs.

The 'non-directive approach' is rooted in the pluralist theory that assumes a society and a polity made up of different interest groups and that by supporting and encouraging participation, services will become more responsible, and relevant authorities more conscious of the impacts of their decisions.

This approach is often criticised because it is often based on a view of the person and the 'community', which are painted in a negative light. The idea of starting with the 'negative' is not a strong motivational approach. Consequently, community development work using this approach began to use the phrase 'starting from strengths'. This positive approach was more constructive and tapped into people's energy and creativity. Later, in the context of the run-down of welfare services in the United States and the more economically liberal environment, the phrase 'Asset-Based Community Development' (ABCD) came into prominence and has since been adopted by community development workers in many contexts worldwide. ABCD processes, including asset mapping and community relationship building, came into prominence through the work of Kretzmann and McKnight.[5]

A key step in this approach is so-called 'asset mapping' which, as well as individual skills and organisational capacities, focuses on assets such as public services and public space, businesses in the locality and environmental assets

---

[4] For an approach adapted to churches see: G. Lovell and C. Widdicombe, *Churches & Communities: An approach to the development of the local church* (London: Search Press, 1978).

[5] J. P. Kretzmann and J. L. McKnight, *Building Communities from the Inside Out: A Path Toward Finding and Mobilizing a Community's Assets* (Skokie, IL: ACTA Publications, 1993).

such as land and water. The aim is to mobilise these assets collectively to build a 'better community' and even a stronger community economy. The main actors are the residents who, through their strengthened relationships, can mobilise talents and assets in new initiatives related to addressing perceived problems. This approach has been used by development NGOs and churches in many contexts.[6]

ABCD, whilst being a well-known approach which uses many different methods and tools, has attracted criticism for its pragmatism. It is weak on its analysis of power, in terms of powerful actors in local communities which may co-opt the process for their own organisational, economic, or personal ends. It also eschews a structural analysis of the context which would address the fundamental issue of the causes of the problems and issues which people and localities face. Because it arose in the context of neighbourhood problems in the USA it locates many problems in the dependency which state services allegedly foster and thereby the positive role of local and national government tends to be denigrated or ignored. This may not seem to be an immediate issue in places where the state is not functional, but justice and the provision of adequate services are essential to a well-functioning community and this issue should not be side-lined. In western contexts, it has been alleged that ABCD is well matched with the neo-liberal emphasis on a minimal state.[7]

(ii) Participatory, Critical Community Development, Participatory Learning

We now turn to a second 'inductive' approach to community development which also relies on learning processes with local people. The difference is that in this case the approach takes a critical stance towards politics and economics and the impact of powerful actors on local communities. However, it also starts close to peoples' everyday life. This approach is both participatory and dialogical, but it recognises that people are 'silenced' by oppressive structures which disempower them and undermine their agency. These forces operate on people and communities, especially on those who are vulnerable or marginalised. This is seen as a global phenomenon which subordinates people through the operation of economic power, and which impacts different subordinate groups according to their identity. It means that the impacts in any specific place are experienced differently by diverse groups, and this is one of the most important factors which community development work must take seriously. It implies that the wider

---

[6] For example: B. Peters et.al., *Applying an Asset-Based Community Development Approach in Ethiopia* (Antigonish: Coady International Institute and Oxfam, Canada, 2009), S. Haus, *Use Your Talents: The Congregation as Primary Development Agent* (Digni, Oslo 2017) and A. Barrett, *Asset Based Community Development: A Theological Reflection* (London: Church Urban Fund, 2013).

[7] See, for example: M. MacLeod and A. Emejulu, *Neoliberalism with a Human Face? A Critical Analysis of Asset Based Community Development in Scotland*, Journal of Community Practice, 22:4 (2014), 430-450.

structures of the political economy also create or support divisions in localities. This further implies that it is not sufficient to work with local communities to find solutions to local problems. The power distribution in the local community, which reflects and is legitimised by wider structures, means that the process of empowerment, complex though it is, is vital to community development.[8]

Paulo Freire is a key thinker for this approach to community development and he emphasised the importance of starting with people's stories which are shared in a trustful and deep, questioning dialogue. People tell and retell stories which are meaningful to them, but stories are told in different ways to different audiences. When a person meets a professional, they tell their story in a way which is intended to get the professional to act in a certain way – for example, to give a subsistence allowance. People who often have to 'tell their story' to officials find a way to do it which limits the hurtfulness of their experience. But in a trustful and dialogical setting, where the worker may also share their story, it is possible to dig for the deeper meaning and develop trust and action. Stories shared can also become the basis of a 'community narrative'.[9] Personal story and community narrative are told and retold, and a positive community narrative may be celebrated as part of a process of empowerment.

This approach to community development through sharing stories and developing 'generative themes' depends on a facilitator who can formulate the questions for the group work and accompany the processes of action and reflection. The criticism of this approach, as for other inductive approaches, relates to the fact that the outcome and outputs of the work are open. These approaches intrinsically do not start with highly specific objectives which are defined 'externally', therefore the criticism is often made that the focus is on 'process' not 'product'! However, the impacts of these processes are long term and may lead to fundamental change.[10]

In some contexts, long-term participatory community development work has led to the creation of community enterprises or community development trusts which become in themselves important local economic actors. They may have started community enterprises or cooperatives, launched initiatives for food production or have become owners of buildings and land which may have previously been owned by a municipality.[11] They often organise community

---

[8] M. Ledwith, *Community Development: A Critical Approach* (Bristol: Policy Press, 2021) p. 41.

[9] An example of this approach is explored in: J. Porkka and M. Pentikäinen (eds), *Community of the Future: New Approaches to Community-based Work, Social Service and Diaconia – Challenges to and from the CABLE Approach* (Helsinki: Diaconia University of Applied Sciences, 2013).

[10] See for example: A. E. Hope and S: J. Timmel (eds.), *Training for Transformation in Practice* (Rugby: Practical Action, 2014).

[11] M. van Ham, D. Reuschke, R. Kleinhans, C. Mason and S. Syrett (Eds.), *Entrepreneurial Neighbourhoods: Towards an Understanding of the Economies of Neighbourhoods and Communities* (Cheltenham: Edward Elgar Publishing, 2017).

development processes in their area to continue the work, evaluate the projects and continue the critical analysis of the context. Very often these economic initiatives are inspired by the need to transform the economy because of the crisis of global heating and the importance of transforming the way the economy instrumentalises the environment. There are many examples of community-based solidarity economic initiatives across the world.[12]

Organising as an Approach to Community Development

The tradition of community organising has its roots in labour union organising and in the work of the pioneer of this approach, Saul Alinksy.[13] It has also been used by churches and ecumenical organisations in different world regions. In many cases, churches have been sponsors of community organising efforts. Community organising is based on the fundamental equality of all people and is firmly committed to the idea of empowerment, based on the understanding that to produce positive change for marginalised groups and communities, people must be organised into a powerful organisation which can effect change by changing the interests of people and organisations that have power. The basic understanding is that change only comes through actual or perceived power effectively applied on an identified powerful interest, whether it be economic or political.

The basic tenet of community organising is that a broad-based people's organisation should be built as a long-term vehicle for working for change and for holding power holders accountable for their actions. The process of organising is not built on idealism or on an overarching vision but has a focus on specific issues which affect a community. A platform can be created where different interests of various groups are worked on in a kind of 'trade off' where one or two key issues are worked on at once. There is a plurality of 'heirs' to the Alinsky tradition in the USA and in other countries.[14]

The community organising strategy can be seen to have two strands, each of which has the same objective. One strand relies more heavily on building an organisation street by street, or block by block and the other is based on creating an organisation built on existing organisations, although each uses similar methods. There are several key 'rules' for community organising and one is that

---

[12] Esteves, A. M., Solidarity Economy Markets as "Mobilizational Commons": Re-signifying the Market through the Lens of Cooperation, *Community Development Journal*, 56. 3 2021, 470-486. For Transition Network see: https://transitionnetwork.org; Accessed 16.09.21 For Social Solidarity Economy Network see: http://www.ripess.org/?lang=en (Paris: International Network for the Promotion of Social Solidarity Economy; accessed 16.09.21).

[13] See: S. D. Alinsky *Reveille for Radicals* (Chicago: University of Chicago Press, 1946) and S. D. Alinsky, *Rules for Radicals* (New York: Vintage Books, 1971).

[14] A. Schutz and M. Miller, Mike (eds.), *People Power: The Community Organising Tradition of Saul Alinsky* (Nashville: Vanderbilt University Press, 2015).

the organisation should be independent and not in the pay of any powerful actor in the local context (although churches and faith communities as well as foundations have funded organising efforts in different contexts). The second is that the organisation exists to produce change and not to produce services or become a substitute for the state or municipality. Community organisations are not spontaneous, single-issue groups nor are they advocacy organisations. They are a vehicle through which people speak and act for themselves. Community organisations do not address 'problems' as such, they work to turn 'problems' that people and communities face into 'issues' which can be addressed publicly.

Community organising is based on building relationships and bringing people together across diversities to work on agreed issues. The key task of the organiser is to connect deeply with the experience of people in the locality where they work. They should listen and reflect on the experience of local people without pretending to be 'one of them' and should provoke and challenge received wisdom by asking 'disruptive' questions. Through these processes relationships are built and, in some cases, common value statements adopted.

The basic building block of community organising is the so-called 'one on one' conversation which aims to identify a person's specific commitments and willingness to be involved in specific actions. This is 'in essence a strategic interview... which is vital to identify(ing) a person's self-interest'.[15] Particularly, the interview aims to identify potential leaders for specific actions. The organiser follows up interviews which seem promising in order to build a relationship between the organiser and the person. Therefore, the interview has a qualitative difference to dialogue in the inductive processes of community development. Community organising may also depend on listening exercises and neighbourhood meetings as well as meetings with faith communities which are designed to elicit their understanding of salient issues. When the issues have been identified, the organising team works to analyse the issues and research it and its causes. This analytic work will also identify possible allies and targets. The prioritising of issues and the accountability for the action plan and its implementation are decided in a citizen's assembly. In these processes there is a clear distinction between the community organiser or the team of organisers who run the process and carry out the analysis, and leaders of the actions and the organisation, who 'emerge' through the organising process.

In terms of working for change, the key idea is to carry out public actions which are often targeted on specific persons and institutions and can often mobilise large numbers of people. The kinds of action may range from traditional public meetings to demonstrations outside specific offices or even the homes of specific people deemed to hold the power to make change.

The strength of community organising rests on the ability to mobilise large numbers of people around issues which are relevant to their lives. Resources may be pooled to campaign on an issue which is relevant to one group or one locality

[15] C. Shannahan, *A Theology of Community Organising* (London, Routledge, 2014), 21.

or which is relevant to all the residents in an area. The dangers which arise are related to the power of the organising team despite the processes of accountability, and related to the need to keep actions rolling and varied, fun and surprising. There are also criticisms related to the value base and the intentional focus on self-interest (which is not, however, the same as selfishness). Another weakness of the approach is the lack of a guiding vision for social transformation, although protagonists defend this by pointing out that if an organisation wins a 'victory' in the field of planning or living wage, it contributes to social change objectives. A second weakness is that without reflection, the skills and tactics learnt by community organising processes can be used by the participants to disadvantage other perhaps newly marginalised people, for example, immigrants. In a nutshell, the organising process works pragmatically to achieve gains within the 'world as it is' but it has no goal for the long-term transformation of society and economy.[16]

Institution Based Community Development

In addition to the approaches to community development identified so far, community development has permeated the work of many institutions and organisations. It has been seen as an approach to youth work, social work, education, planning or health care. In these cases, it has either been an approach to 'inductive' community work which has been adopted or this approach has been a part of a service system which wants to use community resources to address a particular issue or group of issues. One contradiction in this approach is that very often non-participative, externally led organisations are attempting to build participatory action and democratically controlled initiatives. Institution based community development can be divided into two main streams of thinking and practice:

(i) Problem Focused/Outcome Based Community Development

In many contexts, especially where services are being reduced, community development has been brought into play as a part of the response to political and economic change. A problem may be identified, for example, a rise in juvenile crime or the isolation and lack of care for elderly people. Organisations responsible for health care, social services and the police often recognise that 'the community' may hold resources and perhaps even the 'answer' to some of the problems they face. In fact, in many western countries, community development work funding is now tied to limited time frames and defined

[16] M. Martinson, and C. Su, 2012 Contrasting Organizing Approaches in M. Minkler (ed.), *Community Organizing and Community Building for Health and Welfare* (New Brunswick: Rutgers University Press, 2012) 59-77 and Shannahan, *A Theology of Community Organising*, 86-111, and 167-168.

objectives. The difficulty with this approach is that the long-term processes of inductive community development do not easily 'fit' to these specific demands.

There are many examples of the application of community development approaches to address problems in a locality. These could more accurately be described as locally based mutual aid or self-help initiatives, because they lack the inductive perspective where the problems and issues are defined within the locality and where the action might be to call for institutional change. Some of the methods and tools of community development may be used and the outcomes can be creative and positive, but the narrow focus and often the short timescale militates against more comprehensive action.

For these reasons it is preferred that organisations and institutions take a longer-term perspective and support processes of community development because within these processes there can be dialogue with significant actors where there can be a reciprocal exchange of ideas and issues.

(ii) Social Planning and Community Development (and Sozialraum entwicklung)

Community development work has been of importance in the field of planning and social planning. Community development has a natural input into planning processes because place-based groups have a concern for different planning issues related to, for example, traffic, land use, housing policy and the environment. Planning may be critiqued or improved by the input of local groups. Normally, planners aim for public consultation on their proposals but where there is a community development process, groups can have a much more formative influence.

Securing a 'community input' and contribution has also become a key focus of processes of Sozialraumentwicklung (the development of the social space), which has become a feature of German and Austrian planning and development processes.[17] The idea is to engage all the actors in a specific place ('Sozialraum') in long-term processes of developing a locality and the services within it. One of the key approaches used in this process is community development which may lead to the promotion of new forms of mutual aid and self-help groups. Churches and faith communities are involved in this overall process in many places. The development of links between church-based providers of health and social care such as diakonia and caritas, who may run institutional services in a locality, and the local parishes is part of the process. 'Sozialraumentwicklung' has also become a key aspect of the work of parishes and deaneries which aim to relate to the 'social space' in which they are set.[18]

---

[17] R. Fürst, and W. Hinte (eds.), *Sozialraumorientierung 4.0* (Vienna: Facultas Verlag, 2020).

[18] U. F. Schmälzle, S. Schürmeyer, T. Gunnemann, M. Therre and A. Honnacker, *Menschen, die sich halten – Netze, die sie tragen: Analysen zu Projekten der Caritas im lokalen Lebensraum* (Münster: LIT Verlag, 3rd edition, 2018).

Market Focused Community Development

There is a strand of community development which is funded and supported by private funds and by other economic interests, for example, the pension funds of churches in the USA. The meaning of community development in this context is often less related to processes of working with people and more in the direction of investing in communities which are marginalised in different ways. Investment can be in enterprises, housing or amenities. The impetus for the involvement may have been community action and there may be possibilities for participation in decision-making but the most usual form of participation is a 'customer' or 'consumer'. These initiatives are also often supposed to make a return on the capital invested and are embedded within the normal market economy, even if their target is marginalised people and communities.[19] It may also be that organisations which have emerged from community development processes become involved in owning or operating privatised assets or running community or social enterprises and other economic initiatives.

In some contexts, long-term community development work has led to the creation of community enterprises or community development trusts which become in themselves important local economic actors. They may have started community enterprises or cooperatives, launched initiatives for food production or have become owners of buildings and land which may have been owned previously by a municipality.[20] They often organise community development processes in their area to continue the work, evaluate the projects and continue the critical analysis of the context.

Conclusion

As is evident from this survey, there is no universally agreed definition of community development. The theory and practice of the different 'types' are based on diverse understanding of aims and approaches. All have worked with diverse faith communities and to a greater or lesser extent been open to diversity. The differences relate to the way in which the main purpose of the approach is elaborated with regard to the prevailing social, political, and economic conditions. Differences also relate to the way in which the approach identifies the problem or issue to be addressed and they take different views on the position and agency of the participants in the processes.

The most fundamental difference relates to two factors. Firstly, an understanding of power and change. Community organising assumes that the main issue relates to the fact that those who face issues of injustice lack power

---

[19] G.P. Green and A. L. Haines, *Asset Building & Community Development* (Thousand Oaks: Sage Publications, 2015).

[20] M. van Ham, D. Reuschke, R. Kleinhans, C. Mason and S. Syrett (Eds.), *Entrepreneurial Neighbourhoods: Towards an Understanding of the Economies of Neighbourhoods and Communities* (Cheltenham: Edward Elgar Publishing, 2017).

and the main aims are therefore to hold power accountable and change the balance of power. It is based on dramatising the conflict within the system. On the other hand, institutional and targeted community development is largely framed within the understanding of the major institutions and their perception of what should be tackled from a position of power – at least power to 'define'. Market based approaches aim to improve the position of marginalised groups within the existing economic structure. Participatory approaches, on the other hand, relate to processes of 'betterment' within the context and start from the perceptions and strengths of the participants. The approach sees the wider structures as possible holders of assets and the understanding that they may also be supporters of the process.

Therefore, most approaches to community development aim to be 'game changers'. The exception is participatory, critical community development, which aims for transformation. Participatory approaches in general have the strength that they start with the perceptions (stories) of people and the community narrative. This means that although they are interventions in marginalised communities, they do not begin with a pathology of the people. However, without the critical approach, there is a possibility that community development ameliorates a situation and ignores the powerful actors, who may even co-opt the process for their own purposes. Participatory, critical community development starts with the everyday life of diverse people and works with them, recognising the impact of powerful social, cultural, and economic structures on their lives and possibilities. It seeks to work for transformation by encouraging analysis of the context starting from 'story' but recognising the need to work on strategies which may influence the wider context.

Bibliography

Participatory and Inductive Community Development

Barrett, A., *Asset Based Community Development: A Theological Reflection*, Downloaded from: https://cuf.org.uk/resources/a-theological-reflection-on-asset-based-community-development (London: Church Urban Fund, 2013, accessed 17.08.21).*

Batten, R. T. and Batten, M., *Communities & Their Development* (London: Oxford University Press, 1957).

Batten, R.T. and Batten, M., *The Non-Directive Approach in Group and Community Work* (London: Oxford UniversityPress, 1967).*

Biddle, W. W. and Biddle, L. J., *The Community Development Process: the Rediscovery of Local Initiative* (New York: Holt, Rinehart & Winston, 1965).*

Haus, S., *Use Your Talents: The Congregation as Primary Development Agent* (Digni, Oslo 2017).*

Kretzmann, J. P. and McKnight, J. L., *Building Communities from the Inside Out: A Path Toward Finding and Mobilizing a Community's Assets* (Skokie, IL: ACTA Publications, 1993).*

Lovell, G., *The Church & Community Development* (London, Chester House Publications, 1972).

Lovell, G. and Widdicombe, C., *Churches & Communities: An Approach to the Development of the Local Church* (London, Search Press, 1978).*

MacLeod, M. A. and Emejulu, A., Neoliberalism with a Human Face? A critical Analysis of Asset Based Community Development in Scotland *Journal of Community Practice* (22:4 2014).*

Peters, B., Gonsamo, M., Molla, S. and Mathie, A., *Applying an Asset-Based Community Development Approach in Ethiopia*, Downloaded from: https://coady.stfx.ca/wp-content/uploads/pdfs/resources/publications/research/ABCD-approach-Ethiopia.pdf (Antigonish: Coady International Institute and Oxfam, Canada, 2009, accessed 17.08.21).*

Participatory and Critical Community Development, Community Learning

Addy, T., 'Seeking Conviviality' as a Core Concept for Community Development, Haugen, H.M., Kivle, B. M. T., Addy, T., Kessel, T.B. and J. Klaasen, Eds. *Developing Just and Inclusive Communities. Challenges for Diakonia as Christian Social Practice and for Social Work* (Oxford, Regnum, 2022) pp 79-94.

Addy, T., *Seeking Conviviality. Re-forming Community Diakonia in Europe* (Geneva: Lutheran World Federation, 2014).

Alinsky, S.D., *Reveille for Radicals* (Chicago: University of Chicago Press, 1946).

Esteves, A. M., Solidarity Economy Markets as "Mobilizational Commons": Re-signifying the Market through the Lens of Cooperation, *Community Development Journal*, 56. 3 2021 pp 470-486.*

Hope, A. E. and Timmel, S. J. (eds.), *Training for Transformation in Practice* (Rugby: Practical Action, 2014).*

Ife, J., *Community Development in an Uncertain World* (Sydney: Cambridge University Press, 2016).

International Network for the Promotion of Social Solidarity Economy: http://www.ripess.org/?lang=en (Paris: International Network for the Promotion of Social Solidarity Economy, accessed 16.09.21).

Ledwith, M., *Community Development: A Critical Approach* (Bristol: Policy Press, 2021).*

Mayo, M. and Shaw, M. (eds.), *Class, Inequality & Community Development* (Bristol: Policy Press 2016).

Porkka, J. and Pentikäinen, M. (eds.), *Community of the Future: New Approaches to Community-based Work, Social Service and Diaconia: Challenges to and from the CABLE Approach* (Helsinki: Diaconia University of Applied Sciences, 2013).*

Social Solidarity Economy Network: http://www.ripess.org/?lang=en (Paris: International Network for the Promotion of Social Solidarity Economy, accessed 16.09.21).*

Transition Network: https://transitionnetwork.org (Totnes: Transition Network, accessed 16.09.21).*

Westoby, P. and Dowling, G., *Theory and Practice of Dialogical Community Development: International Perspectives* (London: Routledge, 2013).

Community Organising

Alinsky, S. D., *Reveille for Radicals* (Chicago: University of Chicago Press, 1946).*

Alinsky, S. D., *Rules for Radicals* (New York: Vintage Books, 1971).*

Kahn, S., *Organising: A Guide for Grassroots Leaders* (New York: McGraw Hill, 1982).

Martinson, M. and Su, C., Contrasting Organizing Approaches in Minkler, M. (Ed.) *Community Organizing and Community Building for Health and Welfare* (New Brunswick: Rutgers University Press, 2012).*

Schutz, A. & M. Miller, M. (eds.), *People Power: The Community Organising Tradition of Saul Alinsky* (Nashville: Vanderbilt University Press, 2015).*

Shannahan, C., *A Theology of Community Organising* (London, Routledge, 2014).*

Institution Based Community Development

Alisch, M. and May, M. (eds.), *Kompetenzen im Sozialraum – Sozialraumentwicklung – und organisation als Transdiziplinäres Projekt* (Opladen: Barbara Budrich, 2008).

Bestmann, S., *Die Kirche im Dorf lassen? Das Fachkonzept Sozialraumorientierung und die Rolle der Kirchengemeinden,* Downloaded from: https://www.sozialraum.de/die-kirche-im-dorf-lassen (Düsseldorf: sozialraum.de, 1/2012. Accessed 16.09.21).

Douglass, M. and Friedman, J. (eds.), *Cities for Citizens* (Chichester: John Wiley, 1998).

Fürst, R. & Hinte, W. (eds.), *Sozialraumorientierung 4.0* (Vienna, Facultas Verlag, 2020).*

Perlman, R. and Gurin, A., *Community Organisation & Social Planning* (New York: John Wiley & Sons, 1972).

Schmälzle, U. F., Schürmeyer, S., Gunnemann, T., Therre, M. and Honnacker, A. *Menschen, die sich halten – Netze, die sie Tragen: Analysen zu Projekten der Caritas im lokalen Lebensraum* (Münster: LIT Verlag, 3rd edition, 2018).*

Wegner, G. and Lämmlin, G. (eds.), *Kirche im Quartier: Die Praxis: Ein Handbuch* (Leipzig: Evangelische Verlagsanstalt, 2nd edition 2020).

Investment Based Community Development

Green, G. P. and Haines, A. L., *Asset Building & Community Development* (Thousand Oaks: Sage Publications, 2015).*

Social Investment Forum Foundation (n.d.), *Community Investing: A Toolkit for the Faith Communities,* Downloaded from: https://www.cdfifund.gov/sites/cdfi/files/documents/(15)-community-investing-toolkit-for-the-faith-community.pdf (London: Church Urban Fund, accessed 17.08.21).

US Department of Housing and Urban Development (2001), *Faith-Based Organisations in Community Development*, downloaded from: https://www.huduser.gov/portal/publications/faithbased.pdf (Washington: US Department of Housing and Urban Development, 2001, accessed 17.08.21).

Van Ham, M., Reuschke, D., Kleinhans, R., Mason, C., and Syrett, S. (eds.), *Entrepreneurial Neighbourhoods: Towards an Understanding of the Economies of Neighbourhoods and Communities* (Cheltenham: Edward Elgar Publishing, 2017).*

Sources referred to in the text are marked with a *

Personhood and Inclusive Communities: Access to Justice for All

John Klaasen

Introduction

My interest lies with the connection of personhood and inclusive communities. The question that elicits my interest is to what extent the influential Christian models and African philosophical models of personhood correlate with inclusive communities. I am interested in the complex process through which people come to accept responsibility for addressing their situations and forming relationships of mutual enrichment and reciprocal nourishment. How do we ensure access to justice for all? This question is based on the intuition that personhood may well be crucial for any notion of development and inclusive communities, precisely in impoverished contexts. Even where people are made aware of their opportunities and capabilities (rights based development) and where the obstacles thwarting development are removed (development from below and empowerment theories) or where the skills and talents of local communities are acknowledged (Asset Based Development and Use Your Talents), such things would not necessarily translate into accepting responsibility for development. There is a discontinuity between knowing what is right and doing what is right.

The notion of personhood does not refer to the development of a distinct personality in each person (developmental psychology). In this instance the focus is on the development of a particular identity that distinguishes an individual human being from others or a particular community from other communities.

Dignity and integrity as two core values of what it means to be human undergirds the accepting of responsibility for development. In this study the category of personhood will be used to describe such an understanding of being human. This would include at least a notion of human distinctiveness but not separateness, of being related to others, of human dignity, respect for the otherness of others and a sense of a common humanity. On this basis the crucial question for an adequate notion of development with specific reference to inclusive communities may be revisited. Moreover, the question is therefore not only what such a notion of personhood entails but also how individuals and communities take responsibility for others within the setting of communities that are undergirded with access to justice for all.

In order to address this dual question a constructive contribution is required and may be developed with conversation partners such as the author of *Being as Communion,* Orthodox theologian John Zizioulas, born in 1931; the author of *Catholicity and Emerging Personhood: A Contemporary Theological Anthropology*, Daniel P. Horan, born in 1983; African philosophers such as Kwame Gyekye (1939–2019), author of *Tradition and Modernity: Philosophical Reflections on the African Experience*; and Ifeanyi Menkiti (1940–2019), author of *Person and Community in African Traditional Thought*. Hence the chapter builds on gour notions of personhood, linking them to four markers of community development, discussing whether these foster inclusive development.

The context for this research is Sustainable Development Goal 16 on 'justice, peace and inclusive communities'. More specifically, the study is situated within SDG Target 16.7 which is about ensuring 'responsive, inclusive, participatory and representative decision-making at all levels'. The goal is to ensure justice for all. This study investigates personhood as an approach to taking responsibility for justice for all.

Theoretical Framework

Poverty, Personhood and Development

There has been a shift from institutions and organisations to people and agency in the discourse of development and community development. It is worth mentioning the conferences of the World Council of Churches such as the World Conference on Church and Society in Geneva (1966), Uppsala (1968), the Society, Development and Peace (SODEPAX) and the Commission on the Churches' Participation in Development (CCPD) (1970).[1] Within the secular perspectives are David Korten's four generation approach and Sen's capabilities approach. With community development, the Asset Based approach and Use Your Talents approach take the persons and agency as a more prominent factor for sustainable development.

Concepts such as well-being, livelihood, capability, equity and sustainability form the development approach by Robert Chambers. 'For Chambers, the objective of development is *responsible well-being* for all. He describes well-being as quality of life; its opposite is ill-being. This moves him beyond the limiting categories of wealth and poverty.'[2] Responsible well-being includes

[1] J. Klaasen, 'The Ecumenical Movement and Development', *Missionalia*, Vol 43, No 3 (November, 2015), 323-35.

[2] B.L. Myers, 1999, *Walking with the Poor: Principles and Practices of Transformational Development*, Maryknoll: Ohio books.

livelihood security such as meeting basic needs, rights and access to opportunities to enjoy resources to live a secure life, and to withstand risks and unforeseen disasters. Responsible well-being also includes the formation of capabilities to live a life of well-being. 'He includes what people are capable of being as well as what they are capable of doing'. Coupled with livelihood security and capabilities are equity and sustainability. Equity translates into the movement of the poor and vulnerable from the margins to the centre, and sustainability refers to the long-term economic, institutional and environmental impact on the change of persons' livelihood.[3]

'Community development is about the interdependence of the meaning of the two terms. Community is the fluid substantive nature of the persons as a solid interactive organism'. 'Organism' refers to the 'complex structure of interdependent and subordinate elements whose relations and properties are largely determined by their function in the whole.'[4] This view of identity can be contrasted and compared with African notions of community asserted by influential African philosophers such as Menkiti and Gyekye, as well as European theologians Zizioulas and Horan.

> Community development is about cultivating and nurturing the potentially transforming agency…It is a process of mutual and reciprocal growth toward our humanity… [5]

Personhood as a concept is the most used reference for what it means to be a person or, differently put, it is the most used answer for the question 'who am I?' Within theology and philosophy personhood dominates the African conception of human being. Doctrines of Christian anthropology such as 'The image of God' (Catholic) and 'The likeness of God' (Eastern Orthodox) have dominated the Christian understanding of what it means to be human. The normativity of community (Mbiti) is the substance of African philosophical notions of personhood.

De Gruchy adds an interesting dimension to what it means to be a person. De Gruchy relates the 'who' or being and the 'vocation' or doing of persons. De Gruchy asserts that within the development discourse the 'being' or 'knowing' part of what it means to be human is neglected. He adds Genesis 1:18 and 2:15 to the traditional Christian formulation of 'Image of God' and 'Like of God'.[6]

---

[3] Myers, *Walking with the Poor*, 105.

[4] "Organism," from Merriam Webster Dictionary [Online]. Retrieved from https://www.merriam-webster.com/dictionary/organism (accessed 20.2.19).

[5] J. Klaasen, 'Theology and Development: Taking Personal Responsibility for Community Development', *HTS Teologiese Studies/Theological Studies*, 75(2) (2019), 1-7.

[6] S. De Gruchy, 'Of Agency, Assets and Appreciation: Seeking some Commonalities between Theology and Development', *Journal of Theology for Southern Africa*, 117 (November 2003), 20-39.

From a secular perspective Korten's social transformation, people and agency coupled with the interaction with the environment and the ecumenical movement's shift from institutions to the poor resonates with De Gruchy's approach.[7]

I will briefly outline what personhood entails in African notions by drawing from African philosophy. I will also draw from western theology in order to broaden the scope of personhood and engage critically for the emergence of correlations or divergence of personhood and inclusive communities. I will also refer to western concepts of personhood because African personhood is both aligned with the western concepts of personhood (Gyekye) and opposed to such personhood (Menkiti). In African philosophy there are different concepts of personhood. I will only refer to two concepts – those of Menkiti and Gyekye. These two concepts are different in so far as the former is normative and the latter is based on morality. In conclusion, a number of markers for community development will be briefly described.

Menkiti and a Normative Conception of Personhood

Menkiti is widely regarded as the person who established the notion of personhood within African philosophy. Menkiti draws from Tempels' 'force' thesis and Mbiti's dictum which is also referred to as a 'communalist' thesis[8] to formulate the influential conceptualisation of what it means to be a human being in an African context. Menkiti refers to Mbiti when he asserts that an African view of person can be summed up in this statement: 'I am therefore we are, and since we are, therefore I am… it is in rootedness in an ongoing human community that the individual comes to see himself as man… the community defines the person as person'.[9]

Differentiating between the single intrinsic characteristic or possession such as reason or memory that constitutes what it means to be a person from a western perspective, Menkiti propagates that the community attributes personhood in the African view. This raises the second assertion of how and when personhood is acquired. With regard to the first assertion, Menkiti propounds that the community takes precedence over the individual both ontologically and epistemically.[10] It is the language, values, roles, power relations, identities and other social aspects of the community that the individual comes to accept as determinant of his or her personhood.[11] Community does not constitute a

---

[7] Klaasen, 'The Ecumenical Movement', 331-32.

[8] B. Matolino, 'The (Mal) Function of "It" in Ifeanyi Menkiti's Normative Account of Person', *African Studies Quarterly*, Volume 12 Issue 4 (Fal 2011), 23-37.

[9] I.A. Menkiti, 'Person and Community in African Traditional Thought', in Wright R.A. (ed.), 1984, *African Philosophy: An Introduction*, Maryland: Lanham, 171-181.

[10] Menkiti, 'Person and Community', 171.

[11] Menkiti, 'Person and Community', 172.

collection of individuals with individual precedence over the collective. It is also not a conglomerate of individuals who cooperate for functionality or commonality. In both such notions community is temporal and disintegrates after a short period.

Within the scope of community as a source of personhood there are three modes: 'collectivities', 'constituted' and 'random collection of individuals'. According to Menkiti the first mode is the African view. This mode is 'assumed to be an organic dimension to the relationship between the component individuals'.[12] Molefe asserts that Menkiti's 'talk of an environment refers to the whole gamut of a culture that serves as an incubator in the process of socialisation (humanisation) and also of forming personal identity. More explicitly, he tells us that self-identity is possible only by reference to these collective (cultural) facts'.[13] Matolino contends that three interrelated elements can be identified from this radical community. The existence of the individual is bound with that of the community; rites and rituals transform the individual through different social stages into personhood; and the growth of the community and that of the individual intersects.[14]

Personhood through social formation is a process that relates to the social–physical and not so much to the biological and psychological importance. The interaction of individuals within the common community accounts for the development of personhood. This process takes years and is bound in the common values, roles, habits, beliefs, customs and morality of a community. Menkiti refers to the process as a development from 'it' to 'it'. The first 'it' refers to a 'non-living' being who has been through a social process to learn from persons the commonalities of the community. The second 'it' refers to the progression beyond the formation of personhood when the person declines in her or his ability to uphold, perform and act their personhood in accordance with the norms of the community. This stage of depersonalisation happens after death.

> For the ancestral dead are not in the world of the spirits, nor are they dead in the memory of the living men and women who continue to remember them, and who incessantly ask their help through various acts libation and sacrificial offering. …. Later after several generations, the ancestors cease to be remembered by personal non-existence, and lose all that they once possessed by way of personal identity ….[15]

People are 'it' at birth, until they can uphold and act the norms of the community, and after death.

---

[12] Menkiti, 'Person and Community', 179-180.

[13] M. Molefe, 'Personhood and Rights in an African Tradition', South African Journal of Political Studies 45.2 (June, 2017), 1-15.

[14] B. Matolino, 'Radicals Versus Moderates: A Critique of Gyekye's Moderate Communitarianism', *South African Journal of Philosophy*, 28(2) (2009), 160-170.

[15] Menkiti, 'Person and Community', 174.

Menkiti compares and contrasts the existentialist view of Jean-Paul Sartre by drawing commonalities and fundamental differences between existentialism and African acquired personhood. Whilst existentialism also propagates a movement towards (from existence to essence) the manner of progression, choice leads to individualism and eccentricity. Choice is a prerequisite for freedom and every individual who can choose is free and every free being has personhood. This contrasts the African view on fundamental epistemological grounds. In African communalism an infant or child does not have personhood because he or she does not have the capacity to learn from culture or the community the traits that accounts for personhood. The difference between existentialism and the African view of acquiring person lies within the place of the individual and the community.[16]

Within this notion of personhood there is an overemphasis on the community above the individual to the extent that the individual is only a means to the end of the community. The role of the individual diminishes within the norms of culture and the individual loses its critical voice.

Gyekye and Moral Being

The community normative approach to personhood raises serious questions about social aspects such as relationships, power, status and development. What kind of persons are socialised in community normative formation when relationships are unequal, power relations are unequal, persons are divided into hierarchical and material categories, and development is absolutely subjected to communal rituals and rites? Onyowe asserts that the 'founders' of African philosophy – Tempels, Mbiti and Menkiti – can be identified as using negritude as a protest and contest against the western view of personhood. He identifies gaps in the logic of community normative personhood and concludes that the motivation of the African view of personhood is itself a social power issue. In the process of freeing the African persons from colonialism, the drive for power has increased. For Onyowe the problem does not lie so much with the validity of the claim of those who propagate community normative personhood, but with the uncritical manner in which this has spread throughout the African notions of personhood.[17]

One important philosopher who holds a different African view of personhood from the normative view is Gyekye. Gyekye opts for a moral basis of personhood. His view is well captured in the following:

> Thus, a moral conception of personhood is held in African thought; personhood is defined in terms of moral achievement. Personhood conceived in terms of moral

[16] Menkiti, 'Person and Community', 174.

[17] A.O. Oyowe, 2013, 'Personhood and Social Power in African hought', *Alternation,* 20,1, 203-228.

> achievement will be most relevant to the communitarian framework that holds the ethic responsibility in high esteem: the ethic that stresses sensitivity to the interests and well-being of other members of the community; though not necessarily to the detriment of individual rights.[18]

For Gyekye the African view of community for personhood is not normative but, rather, the extent to which the person lives a moral life that is judged by the community to be ethical. It is the way the person lives their life in the community instead of what the community projects on the individual. The choices that the person makes, the kinds of interactions with other members of the community, and the actions of the person determine the value that the person brings to the community. 'The moral foundation of a person, to a large extent, links the individual with the community. For the one described as a "person" does not act with total disregard for the well-being of the community'.[19]

Personhood on the basis of morality gives community a less normative role and Gyekye refers to community as 'moderate community'.[20] (Gyekye 1995:154). This implies that the community does not usurp the individual and consequently does not deny the individual their rights.

> Moderate communitarianism is the idea that although the African society is communitarian in character, it also grants some individuality and/or individual rights. And that African communitarianism is not, thus, unrestricted. Gyekye understood Mbiti and Menkiti as presenting what he called 'radical or unrestricted communitarianism' because of these scholars' failure to account for individual rights in the African social setting.[21]

'Moderate community' has three components, namely, social structure, social relationships and common good. The social structure of a community which is symbolically presented by sayings such as 'One tree does not constitute a forest' depicts how people are conceived, respected and viewed by the community. The structure of the society embeds specific moral norms which the individual adheres to and lives out. Persons are social beings and relate to each other in mutuality and reciprocity. To operate in a community the individual holds common goals and values with others in the community in order for the individual to flourish and grow in personhood. Common good is defined as 'good that is common to individual human beings – at least those embraced within a community, a good that can be said to be commonly, universally shared by all

---

[18] K. Gyekye, 1997, 'Tradition and Modernity: Philosophical Reflections on the African Experience', Oxford University Press.

[19] H.M. Majeed, 2017, 'The Nexus between "Person", Personhood and Community in Kwame Gyekye's Philosophy', *Unizik Journal of Arts and Humanities* (*UJAH*) 18(3), 26-45.

[20] K. Gyekye, *An Essay in African Philosophical Thought: The Akan Conception Scheme (*Philadelphia: Temple University Press, 1995).

[21] Majeed, The Nexus between, 32.

human individuals, a good the possession of which is essential for the ordinary or basic functioning of the individual in a human society'.[22] According to Gyekye the influence of the community on personhood is limited because the individual characteristics, such as reason, enable the person to achieve personhood.[23]

Gyekye has come under criticism because of his inconsistencies in the logic of his view of personhood. Whereas Menkiti's communitarian/normative conception of personhood is consistent to the point that it is the community that confers personhood, Gyekye moves between the community and specific qualities that individuals possess such as reason or moral ability. For example, whilst Gyekye is communitarian he leaves room for personal rights such as property rights and involvement in enterprise.[24]

Gyekye is also not clear whether personhood is innate or processual. Hajeed points out this inconsistency by asserting that:

> First, Gyekye regards the innate dimension as a given, yet it reaches 'its full actualization in community'. While he seeks to make this dimension stable or static, it is difficult to understand how personhood, conceived this way, could begin to actualise and culminate in 'full actualisation' without entailing a process. But if it entails a process, then, it is not static as Gyekye supposes.[25]

Hajeed also points out Gyekye's view that reason is a quality possessed by individuals which distinguishes them as human beings according to the Akan philosophy; reason is a quality that distinguishes human beings from non-human beings but it does not translate into personhood. Another related uncertainty is that reason capacitates individuals to think about moral and non-moral issues and even to choose moral or non-moral actions, but that does not necessarily translate into action.[26]

In both conceptions of personhood the community has a central role in its development. The question is what kind of community is conducive for personhood? Communitarian or normative conceptions of personhood run the risk of motivating African views of personhood on the basis of the struggle for power and not the epistemic. African personhood is a counter-colonialism effort to assert personhood outside of the view of the west. Both Menkiti and Gyekye seek to conceptualise personhood against the Cartesian view of a specific character (reason). Despite Menkiti comparing Jean-Paul Sartre's existentialism with the African view of requiring personhood and Gyekye's use of reason as ontological for personhood, both seek to dismiss the view of personhood of the west. Another power struggle includes the cultural norms, values and rituals that dominate the individual rights. Although Gyekye is less radical than Menkiti, the

[22] Gyekye, Tradition and Modernity, 45.
[23] Gyekye, Tradition and Modernity, 53.
[24] Gyekye, Tradition and Modernity, 149-157.
[25] Majeed, The Nexus Between, 39.
[26] Majeed, The Nexus Between, 39-40.

inconsistencies in Gyekye's view of personhood leaves him open to unequal power relations between the individual and the community. The third difficulty relates to personhood that is engendered socially, and takes place in a social space that defines human beings in binaries such as men and women, child and adult, on the basis of social and cultural status. Another power related phenomenon that should be questioned is the power imbalances of the rituals or cultural processes that human beings must go through as part of processural attaining of personhood. One cannot ignore the imbalances of power in rituals and cultural processes that is associated with gender.[27]

Catholicity and Personhood

Whereas the above perspectives are philosophical, the next two perspectives are theological. Horan's notion of personhood seeks to keep the universal and particular in tension. Horan dismisses the absolute uniqueness of persons. He is critical of the classical use of creation, created in the image of God, as the foundations of Christian theological anthropology. In a second breakaway, and what is a more radical divergence from traditional conceptions of personhood, Horan rejects the essentialist notion of humanity in favour of particularity and individuation.

Drawing from the medieval Franciscan philosopher and theologian John Duns Scotus's haecceitas, the principle of individuation, Horan places humanity in a different but not superior position to the rest of creation. Haecceitas has two principles: distinction from common nature despite its unity with specific nature; and that individuals with the same nature differ.

> According to Scotus's principle of individuation (*entitas individualis* or *haecceitas)*, what makes an individual an individual is identical with the thing's very existence or being. It is not an external, accidental, or material modification of an eternal idea or of universal substantia but a real, positive, unique, unalienable, and unrepeatable principle. This principle, *haecceitas*, is absolutely intrinsic to that which it individuates within creation – including both material and nonmaterial things – and *really* identical with such an individual thing's very *being.*[28]

Particularity presumes individual over the community. The human person is positive and not negative as found in the notions of mediaeval scholars such as Thomas Aquinas. Human is 'a this' and not a 'not that'.[29] Another significance

[27] For a detailed discussion of the power and personhood as socially gendered see Oyowe, O.A., 2013, Personhood and Social Power in African Thought, *Alternation,* 20,1, 203-228.

[28] D.P. Horan, 'Beyond Essentialism and Complimentarity: Toward a Theological Anthropology Rooted in Haecceitasi', *Theological Studies*, 75(1) (2014), 94-117.

[29] D.P. Horan, *Catholicity and EmergingPpersonhood: A Contemporary Theological Anthropology (*New York: Orbis Books. 2019).

of haecceitas for theological anthropology is the innate 'relationality, dignity and value of *each* person over and above the depersonalising elevation of *humanity* in a general and essentialist sense'.[30] Horan's notion of individuating also goes beyond the human person and states that every part of the created order has value 'according to the divine act'.[31]

Haecceitas also challenges the traditional notion of imago Dei that passed on the idea that human persons are the culmination of creation, that human persons alone possess imago Dei, and that human persons have absolute uniqueness in a hierarchical created order.[32] On the other hand, different notions of human persons are found when we view the creation narrative in terms of spatial rather than linear. Horan asserts that 'a renewed sense of the text actually provides an unexpected resource for recalling our origins and recognizing the kingship of creation. For example, there are numerous parallels presented and continuity seen between human beings and nonhuman creation within the narrative'.[33]

Horan criticises the use of person that has dominated the Christian tradition for more than five centuries. Community goes beyond the human community and whilst the person is best described as individuation, the rest of creation takes its place in the centre with humans. The rest of creation is not dominated or alienated by the absolute uniqueness of the individual, but the environment and non-human living beings have been created by God equally.

The use of haecceitas by Horan raises important questions for community development and the sustainability of development efforts. How is the relationship between humans and the environment, between living and non-living beings, and between creation and God?

Zizioulas and Personhood

Zizioulas is widely regarded as the most important Orthodox theologian of recent times. Zizioulas's theology is built on two theological convictions. The first is that anthropology is fundamentally rooted in the ontology of personhood. What it means to be human is essentially found in the church as the visible display of God's nature. The second theological conviction is that his trinitarian theology is not based on divine ousia but on divine personhood, diverting from the Greek Fathers' influential doctrine of the divine substance as oneness of God. In his formulation the divine substance, through the lens of the Trinity, refers to the otherness of God or Threeness. Communion and relationship are not linear or one-way but perichoretic.[34]

---

[30] Horan, *Catholicity,* 138.
[31] Horan, *Catholicity,* 138.
[32] Horan, *Catholicity,* 238.
[33] Horan, *Catholicity,* 140-141.
[34] J. Micallef, 'Communion and Otherness in John Zizioulas' Theology of Personhood as Basis for True Otherness, Identity and Unity', *Sophia XI,* 2 (2019), 221-245.

Two terms explain the concept of personhood according to Zizioulas. 'Ekstasis' is a term used in the mystical writings of Pseudo-Dionysius, Maximus, etc, 'and etymologically means standing out from, a movement towards communion, a movement of affirmation of the other, a freedom from the whole, a freedom for oneself in one's own particularity as bearer of the whole' (Zizioulas 1975:408 as in Mecallief 2019: 228).[35] This means that whilst one always has a sense of particularity, one always transcends the boundaries of oneself. The boundaries become blurred with that of the other. 'Hypostasis' means the particular being. Particular in the sense that Zizioulas's use of the concept is distinguished from individualised nature or personality. Whereas nature and personality exist within itself, person is absolutely unique (Zizioulas 106-107 in Mecallief 2019:229).[36] Person is not just particular and individual or universal or communion. Ekstasis and hypostasis illustrate that personhood is about the particular and communion in a manner of existence. This mode of being is found in the ecclesia and derives from God, Father, Son and Holy Spirit.

Communion

Zizioulas distinguished between a human community and an ecclesial communion. The ecclesial community is the community that is called by God to be the image and likeness of God in the world. Through the sacrament of baptism, people are initiated into the community and they take on a new mode of existence. The ecclesial community is based on the person of Christ and Christ's relationship with the Father and with his family and friends. This is different from the biological community's disposition of love that excludes the other. Love, according to the ecclesial community, is inclusive because personhood means to be connected with a range of relationships without exclusivity.[37]

Another sacrament, the Eucharist, keeps the creative tension between the biological community and the ecclesial community. 'Zizioulas introduced a new ontological category of Sacramental or Eucharistic hypostasis to express the authentic personhood which is offered historically and experientially by the Holy Eucharist which provides a locus where man experiences transcendence of the ontological necessity and exclusiveness entailed by the biological hypostasis'.[38] The eschatological nature of the Eucharist extends and intersects the biological hypostasis and the ecclesial hypostasis. Persons are not only historical beings but the Eucharist re-enacts the narrative of the present and the 'not yet' as a continuum.

---

[35] Micallef, 'Communion and Otherness', 228.
[36] Micallef, 'Communion and Otherness', 229.
[37] Micallef, 'Communion and Otherness', 234.
[38] Micallef, 'Communion and Otherness', 235.

Zizioulas asserts that the true nature of the ecclesia is 'maximalistic, ecclesiology with a maximalistic anthropology – and even cosmology – resulting from it. Orthodox ecclesiology, by stressing the holiness of the Church, does not and should not lead to triumphalism but to a deep sense of compassion and metanoia'.[39] This implies that personhood leaves no space for exclusion apart from exclusion itself.

Zizioulas's type of community can be criticised as essentialist because of the sharp distinction he draws between a human community and a church community. His normative notion of community for personhood attempts to keep the tension between the individual and the community. However, his use of Otherness and difference as enriching, transforming and meaning-making suggest that the barriers are blurred amongst persons. Zizioulas's notion of community is that the ecclesia is not only about particularity or the universal. Otherness and difference synthesise uniqueness and relationship in personhood that is situated in community. Otherness is coupled with relationship in the sense that the other is truly and freely other. God is absolutely other from creation and persons are free to be other not because of their nature but because of their mode of existence. The mode of existence is the relationship that the self has with a unique other.

Personhood and Inclusive Communities

It is within the sense of inclusive communities that personhood contributes to development. Taking responsibility for development and particularly community development is part of being human. At least when human beings are viewed from the perspective of personhood the relationship between humans, and that between humans and the rest of creation is of such a nature that individual development is inextricably connected with the development of others. The development is best expressed within interdependent relationships. Notions of personhood from African perspectives prioritise relationships for the development of persons and communities. This kind of relationship varies in degree within the different notions, but it nevertheless takes a priority.

There is a direct link between personhood and inclusive communities. Where personhood overemphasises communitarianism, inclusivity is limited to status and power (Menkiti). This kind of approach influences decision-making, rights, dignity of persons and capabilities. In the cases of Gyekye and Horan, the individual is less dependent on the community and the connection between the community and individuals is more equal than in the communitarianism of Menkiti. This kind of relationship between individuals and community is more inclusive than the communitarian approach that makes the community essentialist. Decision-making, rights, dignity of persons and non-human beings,

[39] J.D. Zizioulas, 'Communion and Otherness', Orthodox Peace Fellowship, Occasional paper no. 19, 1-9.

and capabilities are prioritised over alienation, domination and exclusion. Zizioulas's notion of personhood is about a movement towards the other and difference with a sense of responsibility towards personhood. This refers both to the essence of being and doing of a person.

There are different conceptions of personhood and how it relates to community development. Instead of placing one view of personhood above the other, it is best to point out markers for inclusive and just communities based on notions of personhood.

1. The tension between the individual and community needs to be kept in a creative manner. When an individual develops, the community also grows. A just and peaceful community is as important as just and peaceful individuals because of the interaction between community and individuals.

> With regard to community, I refer to the formation of the individual self in relationships. The self is never in isolation, but as a social being develops through interaction. The self is neither above the community nor suppressed to subordination or coerced into an identity that is alien to the self. The self becomes in relation to other selves and chooses the good as the self in relationship with other selves.[40]

2. Inclusive and just communities are the responsibility of each person. This responsibility also includes care for the environment. An ethic of responsibility (Gyekye) is intrinsic to what it means to be human. Despite the differentiations in status within the notions of personhood, persons have a relationship with other persons and with non-living beings. The Eucharist, as described by Zizioulas, is the context where non-living elements such as wine and bread take on a life-giving nature. Community development must take seriously the life-giving nature of the environment and its resources. Inclusive and just communities assume that individuals and communities take responsibility for sustainable development. Taking responsibility is a vocation and is coupled with 'being' (De Gruchy).

3. Personhood presupposes relationships. Relationships are not of the suppressive, alienating or marginalisation types. Relationships are of a kind that fosters mutual enrichment and reciprocal growth. Relationships do not differentiate in order to marginalise or alienate, but are of a 'different but not separate' nature. This means that there is an acknowledgement of difference in skills, gifts, physique, ability and resources. However, differentiation does not result in separation within personhood.

4. Power relations within personhood is balanced with the stages of development. No one or group of resources, abilities or elements of development should be placed above the other skills or possessions. Power should be placed

[40] J. Klaasen, 'Open ended narrative for moral formation', *ACTA Theologica*, Vol.32 (December 2012), 104-117.

within agency and persons should have the freedom to exercise their various and diverse abilities for inclusive and just communities. Marginalised groups such as those with disabilities, women, children and historically disadvantaged persons should, particularly, be included in the decision-making processes.

Bibliography

de Gruchy S., 'Of Agency, Assets and Appreciation: Seeking some Commonalities between Theology and Development', *Journal of Theology for Southern Africa*, 117 (November 2003), 20-39.

Gyekye, K., *An Essay in African Philosophical Thought: The Akan Conception Scheme,* Philadelphia: Temple University Press, 1995.

Gyekye, K., *Tradition and Modernity: Philosophical Reflections on the African Experience,* New York: Oxford University Press, 1997.

Horan D.P., 'Beyond Essentialism and Complementarity: Toward a Theological Anthropology Rooted in Haecceitas', *Theological Studies*, 75(1) (2014), 94-117.

Horan, D.P. *Catholicity and Emerging Personhood: A Contemporary Theological Anthropology,* New York: Orbis Books, 2019.

Klaasen, J., 'Open Ended Narrative for Moral Formation', *ACTA Theologica*, Vol.32 (December 2012), 104-117.

Klaasen, J., 'The Ecumenical Movement and Development', *Missionalia*, Vol 43, No 3 (November, 2015), 323-35.

Klaasen, J., 2017, 'The Role of Personhood in Development: An African Perspective on Development in South Africa', *Missionalia,* 45-1, 29-44.

Klaasen, J., 'Theology and Development: Taking Personal Responsibility for Community Development', HTS Teologiese Studies/Theological Studies, 75(2) (2019), 1-7.

Majeed, H.M., 2017, 'The Nexus between "Person", Personhood and Community in Kwame Gyekye's Philosophy', *Unizik Journal of Arts and Humanities* (*UJAH*), 18(3), 26-45.

Matolino, B., 2011, 'The (Mal) Function of "It" in Ifeanyi Menkiti's Normative Account of Person', *African Studies Quarterly,* Vol 12, Issue 4, 23-37.

Menkiti, I.A., 'Person and Community in African Traditional Thought', in Wright R.A. (ed.), 1984, *African Philosophy: An Introduction*, Maryland: Lanham, 171-181.

Merriam Webster Dictionary [Online]. Retrieved from https://www.merriam-webster.com/dictionary/organism (accessed 20.2.19).

Myers, B.L., *Walking with the Poor: Principles and Practices of Transformational Development,* Maryknoll: Orbis books, 1999.

Micallef, J., 'Communion and Otherness in John Zizioulas' Theology of Personhood as Basis for True Otherness, Identity and Unity', *Sophia X1,* 2 (2019), 221-245.

Molefe, M., 'Personhood and Rights in an African Tradition', *South African Journal of Political Studies*, 45.2 (June, 2017), 1-15.

Oyowe, O.A., 2013, Personhood and Social Power in African Thought, *Alternation,* 20,1, 203-228.

Zizioulas, J.D., 'Communion and Otherness', Orthodox Peace Fellowship, Occasional paper no. 19, 1-9.

Human Rights as Inclusionary and Empowering Tools

Hans Morten Haugen

Introduction

This chapter will provide arguments for why human rights are the best tools for empowerment and for impacting political priorities towards inclusive development, and what prevents these potentials of human rights to be fully realised. The chapter identifies both opposition by religious leaders – due to the substantive content of some human rights and the way they are promoted – and by political leaders, who want to maintain *status quo*.

In their book *Social Policy for Development*, Anthony Hall and James Midgley present three major models or value systems decisive for social policies in diverse countries and contexts: (i) the statist, institutional-welfarism model; (ii) the individualist, free market enterprise model; and (iii) the populist or community development model.[1] I will argue that the optimal model that can be replicated in diverse contexts, also in those with weak states and institutions or with weak traditions of democracy, is a model that takes the best elements from all of these. This model can best be perceived through seeing human rights as the most effective tools for fostering inclusive development.

This model is embedded in an understanding that struggles over development having to take place at several levels: international, national, local, and in the households. Too often, persons are excluded from participating in decision-making, and not provided with adequate opportunities to be in control of their own lives. I therefore endorse this definition, provided in a Norwegian white paper:

> A key element [of development policy] is control – at individual, social and state level. It is important to create a situation where people can control their own

---

[1] Anthony Hall and James Midgley, *Social Policy for Development* (London: Sage, 2004), 33-36.

> resources and claim their rights, where they enjoy a minimum of economic and human security, and are thus able to make choices that will improve their future.[2]

This definition clearly reflects the shift from philanthropy via welfare to livelihoods. Inclusive development is a human-centred development, and human rights presuppose mechanisms to hold those with power to account for their exercise of power.

I will first embed my analysis in social constructivism, and then explain more about the inadequacies of the three models. I will then provide more insight into the human rights as tools for holding those with power to account and empower persons, households and communities. Moreover, after identifying tensions and highlighting diaconal values, I review some efforts of church-based actors within international diakonia using human rights in order to change policies, showing how these church-based actors can be useful partners in certain situations. Finally, I will analyse why human rights-embedded struggles have not been able to live up to their potential, before concluding. My choice of church-based actors as examples should not be read as an ignorance of the contribution towards community development from other faith traditions,[3] but space disallows a wider discussion.

Social Constructivism

Social constructivism, emphasising how norms, knowledge, and culture developed through human interaction forms 'collectively held or intersubjective ideas and understanding on social life.'[4] This understanding acknowledges norms as being rooted in communities, as well as how knowledge is crucial for allowing change towards a more inclusive development.

The term 'human interaction' is also a part of this definition. People learn and norms develop through interactions of various forms. The term 'human interaction' is wide enough to encompass unequal power distributions that exist in any society. Hence, a social constructivist approach adds dimensions that are not present in an idealist approach – being primarily concerned with norms – or a realist approach – being primarily concerned with power.

Moreover, Social constructivism says that how we understand the social world is shaped by our objective conditions, experiences and subjective perceptions. Subjective perceptions about our own lives are positively affected

---

[2] Norwegian government, *Report No. 13 (2008–2009) to the Storting. Climate, Conflict and Capital. Norwegian Development Policy Adapting to Change* (Oslo: Norwegian government 2009).

[3] Chandra Muzaffar, *Rights Religion and Reform* (Abingdon, UK: Routledge, 2013).

[4] Martha Finnemore and Kathryn Sikkink, 'Taking Stock: The Constructivist Research Program in International Relations and Comparative Politics', in *Annual Review of Political Science*, 4:1 (2001), 391-416, 393.

by having a high religious involvement.[5] The explanations given are both the social network that religious involvement generates and the higher individual coping abilities that come with religious involvement. Having relatively higher life satisfaction does not imply complacency but might make persons of faith less desperate and more hopeful when facing hardships, which is a good basis from which committed action can develop.

The Three Models

As for any models, the state-centred, market-centred and community-centred models might not necessarily exist in a pure form. For pedagogical purposes, these models might nevertheless be useful. After presenting each of them, I will argue that they miss out certain important dimensions.

The state-centred model embeds power with the entity that has the potential to do the ultimate good but also do the ultimate evil towards human beings. The central characteristic of the state is that it has monopoly on the legitimate exercise of violence, including to wage war to defend itself and to punish and keep persons in confinement. A developmentalist state or a equality-promoting state is the ideal state, and a good state is a strong state that promotes accountable institutions,[6] and allows persons to use their creativities and abilities.[7] Hence, the state should facilitate so that industrious persons and enterprises can flourish. However, large extraction or infrastructure projects might impact negatively on the livelihoods of certain communities, and those who are most dependent on harvesting from nature will be most affected. Ensuring that the diversity that exists in a state is adequately reflected in the decision-making bodies of the state, and that no minority is systematically excluded, has been found to be the best guarantor of inclusive and peaceful development.[8]

The market-centred model built on a capitalist production system has at its core the fostering of predictable societal conditions that enable persons to take

---

[5] Ingrid Storm, 'Does economic insecurity predict religiosity? Evidence from the European Social Survey 2002-2014', in *Sociology of Religion*, 78:2 (2017), 146-172. Both national and personal difficult economic situations generate less dissatisfaction amongst religiously active persons, according to European Social Survey 2002-2014.

[6] The three success criteria identified by Francis Fukuyama are strong states, accountable institutions and rule of law; see Francis Fukuyama, *The Origins of Political Order. From Prehuman Times to the French Revolution* (New York: Farrar, Straus and Giroux, 2011) and Francis Fukuyama, *Political Order and Political Decay. From the Industrial Revolution to the Globalization of Democracy* (London: Profile Books, 2014).

[7] Carl Henrik Knutsen, *The Economic Effects of Democracy and Dictatorship* (PhD dissertation) (Oslo: University of Oslo, 2011) shows that the decisive difference between the democracies and dictatorships in terms of economic outcomes is that the former allows persons to think freely and creatively, hence being innovative.

[8] Lars-Erik Cederman, Kristian Skrede Gleditsch and Halvard Buhaug, *Inequalities, Grievances and Civil War* (Cambridge: Cambridge University Press, 2013).

risks and invest in new production technologies. The new production system emerging through the industrial revolution was made possible when the Christian norm of sharing gradually became challenged in the centuries following the Reformation, that fostered norms of individual freedom and responsibility. These new norms were seen, for instance, amongst the English Puritans, that were also the first colonisers of North America. Without willing investors, the industrial revolution might not have taken place in England in the second part of the 18th century.[9] What characterises modern global capitalism is oligopolies, but in most countries people survive in an informal economy, with weak public social protection systems, trade unions, insurance systems or predictability.[10] Whilst social and environmental problems – first in England and then globally – that followed should never be ignored, most persons agree that the industrial revolution has benefitted humanity. The fruits of the industrial revolution have not, however, benefitted other species of animals and plants that God cares for (Gen 1:30).

The community-centred model says that the response to the challenges facing the communities should be community-wide. The asset-based community development approach seeks to identify the resources within the community and foster strategies that utilise these resources for the overall benefit of the community. Community-based approaches termed 'populist' are endorsed by Hall and Midgley.[11] By this, they refer to bottom-up processes of decision-making that can be said to belong to the political left.[12] This understanding implies a substantively different notion of the term 'populist' than the common usage of the term, namely right-wing, national-chauvinist populism. To avoid being misunderstood, the term 'from below' might be better than the term 'populism'.[13] The term 'communitarianism' has also been proposed to be linked with populism.[14] Communitarianism tradition emerged in the USA in the 1980s to fill the lacunae of a social democratic tradition to challenge the prevailing

[9] The importance of frugality and not displaying one's wealth, that was also a central element amongst the Puritans, is emphasised in Hans Morten Haugen, *Kampen om utviklingen. Teorier, strategier og globale utfordringer* (Oslo: Cappelen Damm, 2016a), 29-30.

[10] For interesting figures and proposals, see Commission on Legal Empowerment of the Poor, *Making the Law Work for Everyone* (2008) 139, stating that 71 and 72 per cent, respectively, of all workers in Asia and Sub-Saharan Africa work in the informal economy.

[11] Hall and Midgley, *Social Policy*, 33, defining populism as an 'ideology that emphasises the involvement of 'the people' and their common values, beliefs and culture in social welfare.'

[12] For an account of populism as inclusive decision-making from below, see Thomas Frank, *The People, No. A Brief History of Anti-Populism* (New York: Metropolitan Books, 2020).

[13] Jim Ife, *Human Rights from Below: Achieving Rights Through Community Development* (Cambridge: Cambridge University Press, 2009).

[14] Hall and Midgley, *Social Policy*, 33.

influence of liberalism. Whilst one definition emphasises 'communally defined norms for politics and society …',[15] one author studying various welfare models links communitarianism to market-based social care.[16] Whilst communitarianism is said to represent a 'very important normative perspective… particularly in… the South',[17] adherence to the norms might imply too much conformism,[18] not allowing constructive challenging of oppressive norms.

We see that all three models have both strengths and weaknesses or risks. The risks can be summarised as follows: The state might be too intrusive, not adequately able to protect the rights of the most affected, and the power inherent in the state might easily lead to power abuse. The market might not serve the interests of the most vulnerable persons, not being able to include the social and ecological costs, termed 'externalities', and not able to self-regulate itself in a proper way. The community might maintain strong power bias and exclude certain groups of persons from the decision-making process and foster too strong societal conformity. Communitarianism is conceptually neither adequately clear nor adequately addressing local power asymmetries, and hence not able to effectively challenge those benefitting from *status quo*.[19]

Above, I gave certain characteristics of states, such as developmental, good and strong. The reality is that many states of the world are relatively weak states, and an increasing number of states are considered as not free or undemocratic.[20] Weak states might lead to corruption, inability to regulate market actors in a proper way, or inability to facilitate inclusive and participatory approaches to overcome exclusionary and oppressive practices within certain communities.

---

[15] Craig Calhoun (ed.), *Dictionary of the Social Sciences* (Oxford: Oxford University Press, 2002).

[16] Lars Trägård, 'Religious Civil Society and the National Welfare State. Secular Reciprocity Versus Christian charity', in Synnøve K.N. Bendixen and Trygve Wyller (eds), *Contested Hospitalities in a Time of Migration* (London: Routledge, 2019), pp. 19-37, 32.

[17] Hall and Midgley, *Social Policy*, 33.

[18] Ife, *Human Rights*, 14-16; on the distinctions between community and inclusive community, see Benedicte Tveter Kivle and Beate Jelstad Løvaas, 'Leading towards Inclusion in Communities – Unity and Diversity when Leading towards Inclusiveness', in Hans Morten Haugen, Benedicte Tveter Kivle, Tony Addy, Terese Bue Kessel and John Klaasen (eds), *Developing Just and Inclusive Communities. Challenges for Diakonia as Christian Social Practice and for Social Work* (Oxford: Regnum, 2022), 215-230.

[19] For an acknowledgement of the contribution of communitarianism as one of the sources from which human rights originates, but without justifying this further, see Kathryn Sikkink, *Evidence for Hope: Making Human Rights Work in the 21st Century* (Princeton: Princeton University Press, 2017), 231.

[20] Freedom House, *Freedom in the World 2020* (Washington D.C: Freedom House, 2020), 1, noting that there have been 14 consecutive years with less freedom and specifying that '[e]thnic, religious, and other minority groups have borne the brunt of government abuses ….'

Human Rights – Highlighting the Collective Dimension

Human rights as defined in international treaties provide a minimum level of a life with dignity and freedoms. Moreover, human rights principles, understood as the minimum requirements of conduct for any decision-making process, can foster inclusive approaches, irrespective of whether the decision-maker is a public, a non-profit or a for-profit actor. The UN specialised agencies, funds and programmes agree that both substantive human rights and human rights principles are to 'guide all development cooperation and programming in all sectors and in all phases of the programming process.'[21]

Whilst only one international treaty, the Convention on the Rights of Persons with Disabilities (CDPR), lists – in Article 3 – the relevant human rights principles that apply to this convention, the UN Food and Agricultural Organization (FAO) has specified seven human rights principles that apply generally:[22] dignity, non-discrimination, rule of law, accountability, transparency, participation and empowerment. By observing these, inclusive decision-making will result in the empowerment of individuals, households and communities.

Decision-making by applying the principle of free, prior and informed consent (FPIC) is emerging framework for adequate decision-making processes.[23] Indigenous peoples, international courts and non-governmental organisations argue that the C must read *consent* – including the right to give or not give a consent – and not merely *consultation*. The reality is, however, that only one state, the Philippines in its 1997 Indigenous Peoples Rights Act, explicitly acknowledges that indigenous peoples have a right to *consent*. The consultation process must have as the objective that indigenous peoples' consent is obtained, for instance by down-scaling or moving the proposed project, so that it becomes acceptable for the affected community.

One international treaty applies the term 'consent', namely, the 1989 ILO Convention 169 on indigenous peoples, which states in Article 16.2 (extract): 'Where the relocation of these peoples is considered necessary as an exceptional measure, such relocation shall take place only with their free and informed consent.' Only 23 states have ratified the ILO 169. Moreover, two non-binding UN sources have applied the C as consent. First, the UN Declaration on the

---

[21] UN Development Group, *The Human Rights Based Approach to Development Cooperation. Towards a Common Understanding among UN Agencies* (New York: UN Development Group, 2003).

[22] For one example, see FAO, *A Right to Food Based Approach to Enhance the Contribution of Non-Wood Forest Products to Food Security and Nutrition: Background Paper for the International Conference on Forests for Food Security and Nutrition, No. 3* (Rome: FAO, 2013).

[23] For a more detailed assessment of the requirements of FPIC, see Hans Morten Haugen, 'The Right to Veto or Emphasising Adequate Decision-Making Processes? Clarifying the Scope of the Free, Prior and informed Consent (FPIC) Requirement', in *Netherlands Quarterly of Human Rights*, 34:3 (2016b), 250-273.

Rights of Indigenous Peoples specifies the FPIC requirement.[24] Second, the outcome document of the 2014 UN World Conference on Indigenous Peoples requires that states shall 'consult and cooperate in good faith with the indigenous peoples concerned through their own representative institutions in order to obtain their free, prior and informed consent.'[25] Hence, states are willing to include the term 'consent' in non-binding declarations, but not in their own laws.

Moreover, three so-called treaty bodies of the United Nations, and the Inter-American Court of Human Rights (IACHR) have applied the FPIC as consent, and understood it as being derived from the right to culture and the right to property, respectively.[26] These have criticised the states for permitting harmful activities by public or for-profit actors and not adequately complying with the FPIC requirement.[27]

The above examples illustrate three important clarifications about how human rights operate. First, human rights aim to protect vulnerable groups of persons rather than promoting a neo-liberal economic agenda. Second, human rights have strong collective dimensions, not promoting individualism. Third, human rights monitoring bodies are to take account of a given peoples' cultural norms and representative institutions. Human rights norms emphasising inclusive and collective decision-making can, however, lead to the effective exclusion of women or adolescents, contrary to human rights.[28]

---

[24] UN General Assembly, *A/RES/61/295* (2007); the strongest wording – 'no… shall take place without their… consent' – is found in Article 10 (relocation of persons) and 29.2 (storing of hazardous material).

[25] UN General Assembly, *A/RES/69/2* (2014), paras. 3 and 20.

[26] Article 15(1)(a) of the 1966 International Covenant on Economic, Social and Cultural Rights (ICESCR) and Article 27 of the 1966 International Covenant on Civil and Political Rights (ICCPR) both recognise the right to enjoy one's culture, the latter explicitly for members of minorities. Consent for indigenous peoples as one way of protecting cultural rights is recognised by the Committee for Economic, Social and Cultural Rights in its General comment 21: Right of everyone to take part in cultural life, E/C.12/GC/21 (2009), paras. 36 and 37. The right to collectively owned property is recognised in the 1965 Convention on the Elimination of All Forms of Racial Discrimination Article 5(d)(v). The 1969 American Convention on Human Rights does not include a collective right to property, but the IACtHR has nevertheless interpreted Article 21 to have a collective dimension.

[27] For some examples, see Haugen, 'The Right', 250-251, n 2,5,7.

[28] See Hans Morten Haugen, 'Diakonia as Rights-Based Practice', in Stephanie Dietrich, Knud Jørgensen, Kari Karsrud Korslien and Kjell Nordstokke (eds), *Diakonia as Christian Social Practice. An Introduction* (Oxford: Regnum, 2014), pp. 123-138, 131 n 38 and accompanying text; see also ILO 169 Article 8.2 (extract): 'These peoples shall have the right to retain their own customs and institutions, where these are not incompatible with fundamental rights defined by the national legal system and with internationally recognised human rights.'

Some Tensions between Christian Dogmatics and Human Rights

The UN specialised agencies, funds and programmes, as well as some bilateral donor agencies have, since the 1990s, formulated human rights policies. Church-based agencies within the realm of international development now embed their emergency, development and advocacy efforts in a rights-based approach, linking rights-claims by communities and the accountability of public authorities.[29] Nevertheless, there are conflicting relationships between church dogmatics and human rights.

A minority of churches globally endorse women's reproductive rights and human rights for LGBT (lesbian, gay, bisexual and transgender) persons. Churches which – due to their dogmatic positions – cannot endorse rights can nevertheless be important actors within their own communities. They can speak up for viewing everyone as equal in dignity and worth simply by having been created in the image of God. Hence, these churches can contribute to eliminating prejudices and traditional and harmful stereotypes of women and LGBT persons and affirming the equal dignity and full integrity of all human persons.[30] Churches and diaconal actors *can* – and *should* – fight any harassment and affirm everyone's dignity without having to adjust their dogmatic position.[31]

In summary, the conflicts between human rights and church dogmatics can be mediated by what can be termed 'diaconal values'. Engaging with patriarchal and hierarchical churches for promoting equality for women or LGBT persons should, however, be done only after identifying the promoters and preventers within the churches, as there might be diverse opinions, tensions and exclusionary practices within these churches.

Diaconal Actors Embedded in Human Rights

Rather than identifying examples of community development, I will identify the potential of joining forces, sometimes internationally. Local, national and international church-based actors can achieve more together than by acting on

---

[29] Act Alliance, ACT Alliance Advocacy strategy (2016); Act Alliance EU, *Rights-based Development from a Faith-based Perspective* (Brussels: Act Alliance EU, 2009) 6, emphasising 'root-causes of poverty and exclusion.'

[30] The 1979 Convention on the Elimination of All Forms of Discrimination against Women, obligated in Article 5(1), states to take all appropriate measures to 'achieving the elimination of prejudices and customary and all other practices which are based on the idea of the inferiority or the superiority of either of the sexes or on stereotyped roles for men and women.' On LGBT persons, no human rights conventions explicitly refer to LGBT persons, and whilst the European Court of Human Rights has not specified that states have to legislate for LGBT, this is specified by the Inter-American Court of Human Rights, Opinión Consultiva OC-24/17 (2018), paras. 197, 224 and 228.

[31] Haugen, 'Diakonia', 132, concluding after an assessment of NCA's values that there are '*no contradictions between human rights principles and diaconal principles*' (emphasis in original).

their own. I will identify five characteristics of how diaconal actors embed their advocacy work: i) identifying powerful actors to hold to account; ii) linking local and global challenges; iii) seeking wide cooperation; iv) having an understanding of potential tensions between local community members; and (v) applying a general rights-based rhetoric. Following a previous analysis of Norwegian Church Aid (NCA),[32] I will identify how just and inclusive communities are promoted in NCA's recently adopted global strategies, merely identifying how certain terms appear. I will also include certain efforts of its largest owner, Church of Norway (CoN).

First, one must identify political or other actors which can be held accountable and identify irregularities in the practices of these actors affecting communities. In 2012, the CoN Synod asked (then) Statoil to withdraw from a tar sand extraction project in Alberta, Canada, that is harmful for local communities, more specifically the Dënesųłiné ('Dene') first nation.[33] This was reiterated by the Norwegian Church Endowment at several General Assemblies in (then) Statoil. CoN's Sami Church Council joined the 'We own Statoil!' campaign, and invited Dene Elder, François Paulette, to address the (then) Statoil's General Assembly.[34] What is today Equinor withdrew in 2016.

Second, it is important to link an advocacy effort for an affected community, as in the tar sand case, to wider policy issues, in this case climate change. Other examples could be fair trade, tax justice or human trafficking. One element of fair trade promotion has been the strengthening of producer cooperatives to enhance farmers' negotiation position. Advocacy efforts for tax justice have been linked to advocacy efforts for a more accountable mining industry for instance in Tanzania. Combatting human trafficking is about making those paying for the goods and services able to understand what forces persons to become victims of traffickers, supporting prevention, and reintegration.

Third, the Tanzania example is interesting because it also illustrates the importance of cooperation with other actors. In Tanzania it was NCA that brought together the National Church Council, the Catholic Bishops' Conference and the National Muslim Council of Tanzania to present joint messages to national mining authorities and the mining companies, ending the poisoning of water and soil and the dangers of accidents in these mines.

Fourth, there is a presumption that those who speak on behalf of the affected communities actually speak on behalf of the whole communities. This is in line with the approach of FPIC as specified above. This is not always the case, as some see new opportunities because of the presence of new investments. Intra-community tensions might be an outcome of these disagreements.

---

[32] Haugen, 'Diakonia'.

[33] Church of Norway, KM 04/12, Skaperverk og bærekraft, revidert prosjektplan (2012), 4.

[34] On the importance of enabling community members to speak for themselves, see Ife, *Human Rights*, 174.

Fifth, the rhetoric emphasises rights and not the more precise term 'human rights'. One simple comparison can illustrate this for NCA, with the three last multiyear global strategies as illustrations.

Horizontally: Applied terms Vertically: NCA Strategies	Rights	Human rights	Humanitarian	Justice	Pages with substantive texts
2011–2015[35]	122	35	19	51	42
2015–2019[36]	22	6	24	18	13
2020–2024[37]	27	8	25	21	13

Table 1. Appearance of selected terms in NCA's last multiyear strategies

Whilst the frequency of terms does not directly explain how the NCA and its partners work for just and inclusive communities, the frequency of the term 'rights' is astonishing. We see that the 2011–2015 strategy is a long document, and that the term 'rights' is applied on average three times on each page. As some of the pages have relatively little text, this is even more noticeable. The most recent global strategy applies the term 'rights' on average twice per page, and the content is in many ways similar to the strategy for the period 2015–2019. One of the new formulations in the 2020–2024 strategy is 'to reframe religious narratives that harm and hold girls and women back from realising their human rights.'[38] This implies challenging patriarchal religious authorities and oppressive practices and promoting just and gender-inclusive communities.

We also see that the term 'justice' featured prominently in the 2011–2015 global strategy, whilst the term 'humanitarian' is increasingly applied. It is important to stress that these figures are shown for illustrative purposes, and it is beyond the scope of the chapter to provide a detailed assessment of NCA's actual work. Whilst all NCA's global strategy documents have a few references to diakonia, only the most recent global strategy has one explicit reference to biblical narratives or ethics, taken from Isaiah 58.[39]

[35] NCA 2011, 'Global Strategy'.
[36] NCA 2015, 'Global Strategy'.
[37] NCA 2019, 'Global Strategy'.
[38] NCA 2019, 'Global Strategy', 11.
[39] NCA 2019, 'Global Strategy', 6. The biblical basis is clearer in NCA, *Together for a Just World. Statement of Principles* (Oslo: NCA, 2008), 6-7.

In summary, being embedded in a Christian tradition does not imply that Christian terminology is frequently applied, but that a language that has general appeal is sought. Moreover, religious authorities are identified as crucial to promote a shift away from exclusion and oppression – intended or not – and towards just and inclusive development.

States Restricting Human Rights-Embedded Struggles

Empowerment should be seen as the objective of any intervention aiming at development. If the rights or human rights-based approach is fostering inclusion and empowerment of individuals, households and communities, should public authorities not be expected to endorse this?

It is important to acknowledge that human rights as part of international law have been negotiated, adopted, signed, ratified and, in some cases, even made part of national legislation by conscious decisions by public authorities. Nevertheless, human rights are not necessarily endorsed as a basis for furthering changes towards just and inclusive communities. I will give three explanations for why states place restrictions on the use of human rights terminology and programmes, characterised by the NCA as 'a political crisis, where human rights, civil society space and international cooperation is under pressure.'[40]

First, applying a human rights-based approach is seen as fostering changes that might threaten the societal order that those in power actually benefit from, at least in the short term. Wanting to control foreign financing is not wrong in itself but labelling anyone who receives money from abroad as a 'foreign agent' – a term used in Russian legislation and practiced by several other states – is wrong.

Second, attempts of fostering human rights promotion through traditional values was seen in the UN Human Rights Council in 2010–2013. The merger of nationalism and traditional religion in many states represents a forceful counterforce against human rights, wrongly perceiving human rights as an instrument for promoting foreign values, individualism and alleged immoral behaviour.

Third, growing authoritarianism and stronger appeal of 'strong men' and the reduction of democracies globally does not resonate well with greater emphasis on human rights, which seeks to hold those who exercise power to account.

Conclusion

There are conflicting and complementary roles of the state, market and local community in fostering just and inclusive communities, in accordance with SDG

---

[40] NCA 2019, 'Global Strategy', 6; see also Haugen, 'Diaconia', 136, n 55 and accompanying text.

16, and I have also demonstrated how international networking involving churches and agencies can be important.

Whilst some aspects of human rights might still be problematic for some churches, I have shown how one church-owned agency, NCA, has chosen human rights, in addition to other terms, in its three recent multi-year strategies. Emphasising norms development, social constructivism appears to be a relevant theoretical approach for explaining this shift. Whilst not analysed in this chapter, I know that NCA has extensive networks – to international and domestic authorities and business actors, in addition to international church organisations, church partners and other partners.

Amongst the 12 targets under SDG 16, this book has chosen to highlight SDG 16.7: 'Ensure responsive, inclusive, participatory and representative decision-making at all levels', as further demonstrated in the introductory chapter. In line with SDG 16.7, I have highlighted the strengths and potential pitfalls of community-based decision-making. By facilitating such decision-making, this will also enable the development of wider norms in line with social constructivism.

The one element of SDG 16 that is not brought up in this chapter is the term 'peaceful'. It is relevant that human rights improvement and new policies resulting from social struggles – with new groups of persons making demands and claiming their rights – will not necessarily be a harmonious and peaceful process. The aim, however, of these struggles is better-functioning institutions, where those with power are held to account for their exercise of this power.

Human rights can serve as a tool for shifting power relations. The struggle for human rights and inclusive development will not succeed unless individuals, communities, organisations and movements that include churches do unite, share experiences, learn and make demands, and by this empower themselves. This applies irrespective of whether the given country has weak institutions and weak or no democracy. Working for change under such conditions will be hard but promoting the good news about justice and God's unconditional love for all was never promised to be convenient.

Bibliography

Act Alliance, *ACT Alliance Advocacy Strategy* (2016); https://actalliance.org/wp-content/uploads/2018/01/AA_advocacy-strategy-english-final.pdf.

Act Alliance EU, *Rights-based Development from a Faith-based Perspective* (Brussels: Act Alliance EU, 2009).

Calhoun, Craig, *Dictionary of the Social Sciences* (Oxford: Oxford University Press, 2002).

Cederman, Lars-Erik, Kristian Skrede Gleditsch and Halvard Buhaug, *Inequalities, Grievances and Civil War* (Cambridge: Cambridge University Press, 2013).

Church of Norway, KM 04/12, *Skaperverk og bærekraft, revidert prosjektplan* (2012); https://kirken.no/globalassets/kirken.no/migrering/km_4_12_skaperverk_merknad_vedtak.pdf.

Commission on Legal Empowerment of the Poor, *Making the Law Work for Everyone Volume 2* (2008); https://www.un.org/ruleoflaw/files/Making_the_Law_Work_for_Everyone.pdf.

FAO, *A Right to Food Based Approach to Enhance the Contribution of Non-Wood Forest Products to Food Security and Nutrition: Background Paper for the International Conference on Forests for Food Security and Nutrition, No. 3* (Rome: FAO, 2013).

Frank, Thomas, *The People, No. A Brief History of Anti-Populism* (New York: Metropolitan Books, 2020).

Finnemore, Martha and Kathryn Sikkink, 'Taking stock: The Constructivist Research Program in International Relations and Comparative Politics', *Annual Review of Political Science*, 4:1 (2001), 391-416.

Freedom House, *Freedom in the World 2020. A Leaderless Struggle for Democracy* (Washington D.C: Freedom House, 2020).

Fukuyama, Francis, *The Origins of Political Order. From Prehuman Times to the French Revolution* (New York: Farrar, Straus and Giroux, 2011).

Fukuyama, Francis, *Political Order and Political Decay. From the Industrial Revolution to the Globalization of Democracy* (London: Profile Books, 2014).

Hall, Anthony and James Midgley, *Social Policy for Development* (London: Sage, 2004).

Haugen, Hans Morten, 'Diakonia as Rights-Based Practice'. *Diakonia as Christian Social Practice. An Introduction.* Stephanie Dietrich, Knud Jørgensen, Kari Karsrud Korslien and Kjell Nordstokke Eds. (Oxford: Regnum, 2014), 123-138.

Haugen, Hans Morten, *Kampen om utviklingen. Teorier, strategier og globale utfordringer* (Oslo: Cappelen Damm, 2016a).

Haugen, Hans Morten, 'The Right to Veto or Emphasising Adequate Decision-Making Processes? Clarifying the Scope of the Free, Prior and Informed Consent (FPIC) Requirement', *Netherlands Quarterly of Human Rights*, 34:3 (2016b), 250-273.

Ife, Jim, *Human Rights from Below: Achieving Rights Through Community Development* (Cambridge: Cambridge University Press, 2009).

Inter-American Court of Human Rights, Opinión Consultiva OC-24/17 (2018).

Kivle, Benedicte Tveter and Beate Jelstad Løvaas, 'Leading towards Inclusion in Communities – Unity and Diversity when Leading towards Inclusiveness'. *Developing Just and Inclusive Communities. Challenges for Diakonia as Christian Social Practice and for Social Work.* Hans Morten Haugen, Benedicte Kivle, Tony Addy, Terese Bue Kessel and John Klaasen Eds. (Oxford: Regnum, 2022), 215-229.

Knutsen, Carl Henrik, *The Economic Effects of Democracy and Dictatorship* (PhD dissertation) (Oslo: University of Oslo, 2011).

Muzaffar, Chandra, *Rights, Religion and Reform* (Abingdon, UK: Routledge 2013).

NCA, *Together for a Just World. Statement of Principles* (2008); https://www.kirkensnodhjelp.no/globalassets/strategiske-dokumenter-og-foringer/kn_prinsippdok_en_2011.pdf.

NCA, *Global Strategy 2011-2015* (2011); https://www.kirkensnodhjelp.no/globalassets/strategiske-dokumenter-og-foringer/global_strategy_2011-2015_nca.pdf.

NCA, *Global Strategy. Faith in Action* (2015); https://www.kirkensnodhjelp.no/globalassets/strategiske-dokumenter-og-foringer/globalstrategy-2015.pdf.

NCA, *Global Strategy. Faith in Action* (2019); ttps://www.kirkensnodhjelp.no/contentassets/aa5fdabbb9ca418ca60830df9fb36ab9/global-strategy-2019.pdf.

Norwegian government, *Report No. 13 (2008–2009) to the Storting. Climate, Conflict and Capital. Norwegian Development Policy Adapting to Change* (Oslo: Norwegian government, 2009).

Sikkink, Kathryn, *Evidence for Hope: Making Human Rights Work in the 21st Century* (Princeton: Princeton University Press, 2017).

Storm, Ingrid, 'Does Economic Insecurity Predict Religiosity? Evidence from the European Social Survey 2002-2014', *Sociology of Religion*, 78:2 (2017), 146-172.

Trägård, Lars, 'Religious Civil Society and the National Welfare State. Secular Reciprocity Versus Christian Charity'. *Contested Hospitalities in a Time of Migration*. Synnøve K.N. Bendixen and Trygve Wyller Eds. (London: Routledge, 2019), 19-37.

UN Committee for Economic, Social and Cultural Rights, *General Comment 21: Right of Everyone to Take Part in Cultural Life, E/C.12/GC/21* (2009).

UN Development Group, *The Human Rights Based Approach to Development Cooperation. Towards a Common Understanding among UN Agencies* (New York: UN Development Group, 2003).

UN General Assembly, *A/RES/61/295, UN Declaration on the Rights of Indigenous Peoples* (2007).

UN General Assembly, *A/RES/69/2, Outcome Document of the High-level Plenary Meeting of the General Assembly Known as the World Conference on Indigenous Peoples* (2014).

Part Two

Approaches to Community Development and Diakonia

A Critical Evaluation of Ubuntu Principle as Just and Inclusive Communities in a Contemporary Africa

Benson Anofuechi

Introduction

The concept of Ubuntu, as developing just and inclusive communities, denotes a multi-faceted African worldview that embraces the values of human interconnectedness. Although Ubuntu is defined in a variety of ways, it remains a contested phrase, worldview, value system and ethic. It is commonly understood through the South African (Xhosa) maxim 'Ubuntu ungamuntu ngabanye abantu', which basically means that 'people are people through other people.'[1]

According to Archbishop Emeritus Desmond Tutu, Ubuntu is a belief and a powerful tool to strengthen a community, to communicate through community support, dignity, and identity achieved through interdependence, reciprocity, empathy, generosity, and community commitment.[2] Indeed, the roots of this philosophy came from the ancient African village, where for centuries tribes have lived in harmony together to knit individuals, partners, villages, and communities for the benefit of the society. Thus, Ubuntu has strongly produced inclusive communities, where humans behave with respect towards one another, to bind and link them together to result in a better co-existence in communities nationally and hence, given time, a better globe.

Ubuntu has also made its way to various dimensions of everyday practical life, including religion, education, politics, business management, moral renewal, the truth and reconciliation process, environmental preservation, community development and nation-building. The term is not absolute in nature, as individuals generally define it based on their own perceptions and experiences. By implication, Ubuntu finds itself subject to overuse, misuse or even abuse, which in turn provokes many critics. Ubuntu as an African

---

[1] Johann Broodryk, *Ubuntu. Life-coping skills from Africa* (Johannesburg: Knowres Publishing, 2006), 22.

[2] Desmond Tutu. *God Has a Dream: A Vision of Hope for Our Time (*Johannesburg: Rider, 2004), 27.

worldview is defined by its values including, amongst others, caring for the well-being of others, respecting them for who they are, sharing one's possessions with the needy, being moved by compassion, and always acting in loving kindness. However, this notion has often been gradually erased by modernisation across African culture. Ubuntu has considerable value for people of sub-Saharan Africa and serves as a common point of reference, shaping their attitudes and behaviour and, as a philosophy of social and humane living, promotes buen vivir[3] and conviviality.[4]

My study explores Augustine Shutte's perspective of Ubuntu philosophy, as the author of Ubuntu*: An ethic for a new South Africa* (2001). Shutte postulates that the African traditional understanding of humanity in a just and inclusive community could only be expressed through African humanism, termed Ubuntu. His conceptualisation of Ubuntu could be applied in every sphere of everyday life such as religion, and education.

Similarly, a Ghanaian philosopher, Kwame Gyekye's perspective on the Ubuntu principle for achieving inclusive communities and his concept of Akan philosophy led him to produce the book, *Person and Community*: *In Defense* of *Moderate Communitarianism* (1997). Gyekye's concept of moderate communitarianism sees a person as inherently a communal being, rooted in a context of social relationship and interdependence. Also, an Austria-Israeli thinker (Martin Buber), in his philosophy of dialogue, put forward a form of existentialism centred on the distinction between an I-Thou relationship and an I-It relationship of people to each other and to nature. An I-Thou relationship is akin to the African concept of Ubuntu, because it recognises the importance of the relationship to the 'other' in every person's existence.[5]

Therefore, it is in the practice of Ubuntu that African nations will find their relevance in the global village and in achieving the SDG 16 emphasis on promoting peaceful and inclusive societies for sustainable development. This chapter critically explores the fundamental question of the connection between Ubuntu principle and the sustainable development goals by engaging the

---

[3] *Buen Vivir*, or Full of Life is the *Sumak Kawsay*, Ecuadorian concept of a community based local approach to organise harmonious social relations around the idea that the surrounding eco-systems has similar rights to those of human beings. See Natasha Chassagne, *Buen Vivir as an Alternative to Sustainable Development: Lessons from Ecuador* (London: Routledge, 2000), 4.

[4] Conviviality simply means art of practice and living together. For the distinction between conviviality and community development, see Tony Addy, 'Seeking Conviviality' as a Core Concept for Community Development', in Haugen, Hans Morten; Kivle, Benedicte Tveter; Addy, Tony; Kessel, Terese Bue; Klaasen, John (eds). *Developing Just and Inclusive Communities: Challenges for Diakonia as Christian Social Practice and for Social Work* (Oxford: Regnum, 2022), 79-94.

[5] John, Elijah and Maurice Akpabio. 'Martin Buber's Dialogue and the Possibility of Peaceful Co-existence in a Plural Society,' *Nnamdi Azikiwe Journal of Philosophy*, 11:3:(2019), 5.

historical aspect of this development, the scholarly views, and the application of this basic principle in everyday practices.

A Brief Definition and Historical Development of Ubuntu

It is significant to note that definitions and perceptions are closely connected and may also be controversial at times. Ubuntu may be defined in a large variety of ways, which is influenced by the different insights and encounters of persons. Yet, the basic principles remain the same.[6] According to Shutte, Ubuntu means 'humanity'.[7] It fundamentally represents an understanding of what it is to be human, and also of what is indispensable for people to grow and find fulfilment. Ubuntu should not be confused with the idea of 'western humanism', as these distinct concepts address two different perceptions of, and perspectives on reality or being. In contrast to that, Ubuntu as humanness is essentially African, although with contested viewpoints or context but in basic principles the understanding remains the same.[8]

Also, Prinsloo argues that western humanism implies that man (sic) is the element by which all things are measured; that is, the human being relying on observation, logic and reason. This kind of humanism eliminates the supernatural aspect of being, as it is driven by intellect and individualism. The self-reflecting person is regarded to be the possessor of human nature. In this instance, the definition of a human being is 'static'; perhaps in contrast to that, Ubuntu as humanness is essentially African. Prinsloo further maintains that African humanism is deeply spiritual and emotional. The African worldview of Ubuntu is therefore religious, expansive, transcendental and also centrifugal, suggesting that there are degrees or modifications of human nature. As opposed to some western views, a person is defined dynamically and in relational terms (constructivist perspective).[9]

Etymologically, the term 'Ubuntu' is derived from the Bantu languages of Africa. In this regard, Munyaka and Motlhabi cite the work of Bantu Mfenyana, a socio-linguist who displays a special interest in the African way of life. He maintains that understanding the original meaning of Ubuntu requires a separation of the prefixes and suffixes surrounding the root 'Ntu'. 'Ubu', the prefix, pertains to the abstract, and 'Ntu' is an ancestor who modelled the way of life for human beings. The two authors also state that most common definitions of Ubuntu regard it as being derived from the term 'Muntu', which

---

[6] Johann Broodryk, *Ubuntu. Life Lessons from Africa* (Pretoria: Ubuntu School of Philosophy, 2002), 21.

[7] Augustine Shutte, *Ubuntu. An Ethic for a New South Africa* (Pietermaritzburg: Cluster Publications, 2001), 2.

[8] Johann Broodryk, *Ubuntu. Management Philosophy* (Randburg: Knowres, 2005), 1.

[9] Erasmus, Prinsloo, 'Ubuntu Culture and Participatory Management', In Coetzee, Pieter and Roux, Abraham (eds). *Philosophy from Africa. A Text with Readings* (Cape Town: Oxford, 2000), 46.

implies a person or human being. In addition to that, Ubuntu finds recognition in the different languages all over Africa. For example, in isiZulu it is 'Ubuntu'; in seSotho it is 'Botho'; in shiVhenda it is 'Vhuthu'; in Akan (Ghana) it is 'Biakoye'; in Yoruba (Nigeria) it is 'Ajobi'; in Shangaan it is 'Numunhu'; in xiTsonga it is 'Bunhu'; in Shona (Zimbabwe) it is 'Nunhu'; inKiswahili (Tanzania) it is 'Ujamaa' or 'family-hood'; in Swahili (Kenya) it is 'Utu'; in Uganda, it is translated as 'Abantu'; in English it is 'Humanness'; and in Afrikaans 'Mensheid/Medemenslikheid'.[10]

Ethics of the Application of Ubuntu

The various practical applications of an African worldview (Ubuntu) are developing just and inclusive communities in Africa, including education, religion, politics, business management, moral renewal, the truth and reconciliation process, environmental preservation, community development and nation-building. In this section we will focus on the ethics of the application of Ubuntu. We will draw on the work of Augustine Shutte and others to highlight applications in the fields of education and religion.[11]

Education is regarded as the key to community development in all areas of society, whether human capital, modernisation, social reproduction, environmental conservation, religion or even politics.[12] Venter argues this because the educational system in Africa is often marked by western curricula, labels and methods, instead of the more concrete African philosophy of education which holds more relevance and meaning to its African students. Venter refers to the work of Mkabela and Luthuli in South Africa who discuss the criteria for such a system.[13] In their view, the African philosophy of education should, amongst other things, address the influence of modernisation on African culture; explore African traditional thought and its impact on educational issues; actively attempt the principles of thinking critically; overcome the notion that Africans are inferior by starting to formulate a new history of themselves; investigate the basis of moral thinking; and reflection on education challenges arising in contemporary Africa.

In the African worldview of Ubuntu, learning is seen as a lifelong process, where education starts (in the family) from early childhood, throughout primary, secondary and tertiary levels, continuing for the rest of a person's life. Therefore,

---

[10] Mluleki Munyaka and Mokgethi Motlhabi, 'Ubuntu and its Socio-moral Significance', In Munyaradzi Murove (ed). *African Ethics. An Anthology of Comparative and Applied Ethics* (Scottsville: University of KwaZulu-Natal, 2009), 63-84.

[11] Shutte, *Ubuntu: An Ethic*, viii.

[12] Clive Harber and Jeff Serf, *Exploring Ubuntu: Education & Development: an Introduction to Theories and Debates* (Birmingham: Tide-Centre, 2004), 6-7.

[13] Elza Venter, 'The Notion of Ubuntu and Communalism in African Educational Discourse', *Studies in Philosophy and Education*, 23:2 (2004), 155.

incorporating the concept of Ubuntu into informal as well as into formal education embraces the essential values within individuals, ultimately enabling them to become better human beings.[14] Naude argues that through the lens of Ubuntu, various students' calls for the transformation and decolonisation of education in South Africa have been imminent. The resistance to colonial or western philosophies and traditions being portrayed as the foundation stones of learning and professional success (known as 'coloniality') is not unique to African countries. Yet given that most African countries have a long history of colonial rule and still-lingering after-effects, the 'decolonisation project' has gained momentum.[15]

Broodryk highlights examples of everyday applications of Ubuntu in the education system in South Africa. According to him, Ubuntu is being taught in a variety of schools as part of the subject 'guidance'. Its distinct values are captured into the framework of national education. Also, it forms part of the curriculum of many tertiary institutions in a number of academic fields. In addition, a series of television programmes, 'Heartlines' (broadcasted since 2006), showcases real-life situations which illustrate the practical implementation of Ubuntu, reminding South Africans about the importance of honouring its typical Ubuntu values. Similarly, the 'Ninth Educational Management Association International Conference' on Ubuntu held in 2006 proposed the teaching of Ubuntu as part of the formal education system in all African countries. Also, Ubuntu was introduced in the policies of the department of education of South Africa after 1994 through the policy of *Batho Pele* (people first) to promote accountability and a friendly environment. Ubuntu values and principles embedded in *Batho Pele* principles are used by teachers to improve school leadership, thus providing quality teaching, care and courtesy for students.[16]

Furthermore, the Ubuntu global network held the second Ubuntu leaders' world E-summit on 16 May 2021 in celebration of the United Nations international day of living together in peace. It sought to inspire and commit the participants to the great objectives set by the UN through the promotion of peace, tolerance, inclusion and solidarity. Leaders from South Africa – the cradle of Ubuntu where it is applied to inspire the creation of a 'rainbow society' in the words of Nelson Mandela – and from Latin America, a land of wisdom, shared with the world insights and lessons gained from overcoming challenges.[17]

We look at the field of religion because Africans, by and large, are a religious people. Religion is freely practised in all its diversity, including the Muslim,

---

[14] Shutte, *Ubuntu: An Ethic,* 109-126.

[15] Piet Naude. 'Decolonising knowledge: Can Ubuntu Ethics Save Us from Coloniality?' *Journal of Business Ethics,* 159:1 (2019): 23-37: 24.

[16] Broodryk, *Ubuntu: Life-coping,* 25-26.

[17] Ubuntu Global Network, ubuntusummit.org/index.php/en/ubuntu-summit-en, 2021.

Hindu, Buddhist, Bahai, Jewish and African Traditionalist faiths.[18] Shutte highlights the significance of making the worldview of Ubuntu central to religious convictions. He argues that Ubuntu, as African humanism, will do justice for all humanity and ensure an authentic fulfilment of the deepest desires to become better persons.[19] Being present in everyone, it cuts through any divisive barrier and is experienced when a person empowers others to grow, and when others empower them to grow. This limitless and infinite transcendental power is then the focus of a religion within the Ubuntu concept. This belief is repeated by Conradie and Sakuba who refer to P. Tempels' *Bantu Philosophy*.[20] Tempels holds that in African thought, a human being is a vital force, influencing and being influenced by other forces. This vital force originates from God and is therefore sacred. Based on this argument, the actions of Ubuntu as an African practice are a manifestation of that vital force which is intrinsic to the human nature and sustainable community development.

A significant model that takes the Ubuntu religious approach to heart is the Ubuntu theology of Desmond Tutu. He combines the values of the Christian faith with that of Ubuntu philosophy, and as a result Christianity is 'Africanised.'[21] This method also proved very useful in the truth and reconciliation (TRC) process in South Africa where perpetrators and victims from different cultures came face to face. Christianity has often, and is still in many cases, perceived as 'the imposed western religion' that merged within African soil as a product of colonialism. Ubuntu principle contributes to a peaceful and inclusive religious community for intercultural dialogue, especially in a multi-racial, multi-religious society or where there is a crisis because of ethnic diversity or tribalism. Current literature shows that Ubuntu is consistent with a pluralistic attitude,[22] for instance, Louw maintains that in terms of religion, the Ubuntu worldview inspires people to expose themselves to others, and to meet the difference of their humanity so as to inform and enrich their own, and to acknowledge the diversity of humanity.[23]

---

[18] Piet Meiring, 'The Baruti Versus the Lawyers: The Role of Religion in the TRC Process', in Charles Villa – Vicencio and Wilhelm Verwoerd (eds). *Looking Back Reaching Forward. Reflections on the Truth and Reconciliation Commission of South Africa* (Cape Town: UCT Press, 2000), 125.

[19] Shutte, *Ubuntu: An Ethic,* 195-202.

[20] Ernst Conradie and Xolani Sakuba, 'Sin and Evil in African Christian Theologies: A Classification'. In P. Coertzen (ed). *Ned Geref. Theologiese Tydskrif* (Stellenbosch: Sun Press, 2006), 59.

[21] Hanna, Eklund. 'Ubuntu: An Analysis of the Political Rhetoric of a Traditional Concept in Contemporary South Africa' (2008), 29.

[22] Nisbert Taringa, 'Possibilities and Limitations for Intercultural Dialogue from the Perspective of Ubuntu Philosophy', *Swedish Missiological Themes*, 95:2 (2007), 195.

[23] Dirk Louw, *Ubuntu and the Challenges of Multiculturalism in Post-apartheid South Africa* (Utrecht: Zuidam and Uithof, 2002), 13.

Furthermore, Ubuntu resonates with the idea of church being essentially about solidarity, struggle for justice and peace, as a congregational description of the social responsibility of the church community. The church as the Ubuntu community is expected to be a community of sharing and interdependence. This, however, requires a reinterpretation and theological enrichment (through scripture) of negative forms of solidarity such as those based on essentialist notions of identity whether that is in the form of race, ethnicity or even religion. In that way, Ubuntu becomes a congregational socio-ethical vision of inclusion. The contribution in the community called Ubuntu entails solidarity not only within the community but also towards others. Archbishop Tutu underscores the inalienable dignity of perpetrators of some unthinkable violations of human dignity, such as apartheid; both the oppressor and the oppressed are created in the image of God.[24]

Person and Community

The African notion of person is made up of three distinct entities: the *okra* (the soul), *sunsum* (spirit) and the *nipadua* (body). The *okra* aspect is believed to be given by God (*Onyame*) and also bears the destiny of the human being. The *sunsum* is assumed to be the foundation of one's personality. The *nipadua* is the substantial component of the person. A person is embedded within the ontological and epistemic community.[25] Akan philosophy informs a variety of social practices and judgements about personal identity, moral responsibility, and relationship amongst persons' within the community. There is a sense in which a person is understood in terms of their moral or normative being.[26] In this section we will draw on the understanding of moderate communitarianism as elaborated by Kwame Gyeke.[27]

The relationship between Kwame Gyekye's concept of moderate communitarianism,[28] could be compared to Augustine Shutte's concept of radical defenceless communitarianism. The concepts of person, personhood and communitarianism are not the same in some African traditions. The main contention in the debate on personhood is whether or not the communal focus of African society undermines the autonomy and identity of the individual person.

[24] Desmond Tutu. *God Is Not a Christian and Other Provocations* (London: Harper Collins, 2011), 28.

[25] Hasskei Majeed. The Nexus between 'Person', Personhood, and Community in Kwame Gyekye's Philosophy. *UJAH: Unizik Journal of Arts and Humanities*, 18:3 (2017), 26.

[26] Majeed, *The Nexus*, 27.

[27] Kwame Gyekye. *Tradition and Modernity: Reflections on the African Experience* (New York: Oxford University Press, 1997).

[28] Kwame Gyekye, *Tradition.* Moderate communitarianism is the idea that the African society is communitarian in character, it also grants some individuality or individual rights.

Political leaders such as Senghor and Kenyatta observed the communal structure of African life and society. Kenyatta asserts that '… individualism and self-seeking was ruled out.'[29] This statement does appear too strict in its understanding of communitarianism. From a communitarian point of view, the person is essentially social or communal, not an isolated individual. The community therefore consists of people who are interconnected through common values, goals and interests. They also have intellectual and ideological goals and moral values; as long as they cherish them, they are ever ready to pursue and defend them.

Gyekye's concept of communitarianism is different from that of Shutte. Gyekye accuses other philosophers of failing to accommodate the rights and freedom of individuals within the community. In his moderate communitarianism, Gyekye views the community as a reality in itself and not as a mere association of individuals. However, he argues that individual capacities should be recognised for they define who a person is in moral or Ubuntu principle. At the core of Gyekye's concept of moderate communitarianism lies aspects such as the common good, community of mutuality, the principle of reciprocity and the notion of rights. These aspects together contribute to an understanding of a person in the traditional African thought of just and inclusive community. Gyekye, in his version of moderate communitarianism, sees the person as an inherent communal being, embedded in a context of social relationships. For him, a community refers to a particular social setting and networks characterised by sharing an overall way of life.[30]

Klaasen's approach to the African view of development of personhood maintains that effective development of a person can only be achieved by filling the gap between rich and poor. Also, less dependence and exploitation can emerge from 'theological markers such as the Trinitarian God, relationship with others and vulnerability' within the community. He further adds that the role of personhood as a source of sustainable community development should encompass personal responsibility for self-development of both the person and others in the community.[31] The development of a person in a community benefits the whole community. The traditions of the community bring the person to the point where they are ready to be fulfilled further as a complete human being. Moreover, a person is born a human being, and the traditions of the community help them to create intercommunal relationships based on and promoting harmony. In turn, this will lead to a general wish for well-being inside the community. It is the harmony in an inclusive community that is the ultimate goal

[29] Gyekye. 'Person and Community in African Thought'. In Coetzee, Pieter and Roux, Abraham (eds.), *Philosophy from Africa* (International Thomson Publishing: Johannesburg, 2003): 298-299.

[30] Gyekye, *Tradition and Modernity,* 49.

[31] Klaasen, John. The Role of Personhood in Development: An African Perspective on Development in South Africa. *Missionalia, 45*:1 (2017), 35.

of Ubuntu and peaceful co-existence for the sake of justice for all.[32] Ubuntu is in all people, actions and thoughts, and supports and maintains harmony in the community.

As previously mentioned, Martin Buber puts forward the notion of people living together with nature within inclusive communities and this, as with Ubuntu, requires constant practice to foster peaceful co-existence of people. This philosophy uniquely identifies with Africans because of their culture of accommodation, communalism, hospitality and brotherhood. Regrettably, these are gradually being swept away through the infiltration and adulteration of African culture due to modernisation. The African culture of diversity in the traditional background is relational to the communal and accommodating spirit of Ubuntu.[33] It is through dialogue and peaceful co-existence that a just community begins to develop towards inclusivity and sustainability.

A Critical Application of Ubuntu for a Just and Inclusive Community

Just and inclusive communities working towards fulfilling sustainable developmental goals should be based on continuous interaction and the practical application of Ubuntu philosophy in everyday life and professional practices. Due to the ever-changing cultural settings, the Ubuntu philosophy requires ongoing contact and interaction. Yet, this is not the case, and in many societies this African way of life is being erased gradually by modernisation. There is no contemporary forum or mechanism to continuously resuscitate and foster Ubuntu values, as new ways of thinking often replace the old ones. Thus, without concrete practice, Ubuntu might disappear.[34] In this section I explore the problems associated with critical application of Ubuntu.

Kamwangamalu is of the opinion that Ubuntu is especially practised in Southern Africa. He argues that it will not be of benefit to people if it is not practically reflected in their daily life. The notion of Ubuntu is by no means intended to be used as a commodity, yet it has become something largely taken for granted by the business sector. He queries: 'Is Ubuntu really about profit-making. Isn't the basic point of departure for Ubuntu the view of man as a social being?'[35] Eklund, referring to for-profit companies such as Canonical Limited who developed the Ubuntu desktop system, states that they are guilty of carrying people further away from the philosophy and bringing them closer to the capital market. In addition to that, she argues that in the event of such a company going

[32] For further reading, see John Klaasen 'Personhood and Inclusive Communities: Access to Justice for All', in *Developing Just and Inclusive Communities: Challenges for Diakonia as Christian Social Practice and for Social Work,* ed. Haugen, Hans Morten, *et al. (*Oxford: Regnum, 2021), 33-48.

[33] Elijah and Akpabio, *Martin Buber's Dialogue*, 5.

[34] Eklund, *Ubuntu*, 37.

[35] Nkonko, Kamwangamalu. 'Ubuntu in South Africa: A Sociolinguistic Perspective to a Pan-African Concept.' *Critical Arts*, 13:2 (1999): 24-41.

bankrupt, the value of Ubuntu will most probably vanish because it has been linked to a capitalist idea.[36] More than that, Venter believes that in the world of competition, integrating the values of Ubuntu into profit-making is more likely to be an obstacle than a help.[37]

Another aspect of Ubuntu in the business practice needs to be addressed, and that is the adoption of an Ubuntu-style management. Prinsloo deems that this management approach cannot solve all of an organisation's problems. He says that limited attention is frequently devoted to consensus procedures. Because Ubuntu culture is practised at the various organisational levels, the implications thereof should be fully understood and agreed upon beforehand. It is believed that this management approach requires greater consensus and an extensive decision-making process. Furthermore, he holds that whereas this style might imply an increase in work prospects, it should not entail decreased remuneration.[38]

Ubuntu in the context of interfaith dialogue has also attracted criticism. It is generally argued that the Ubuntu worldview tends to be pluralistic, and therefore embraces all religions. However, in practice this does not seem to be the case. Taringa states that Ubuntu in pluralistic dialogue signifies mere tolerance instead of genuine pluralism. Ubuntu has a tendency to deny the otherness of truth claims of all religions and cultures. In claiming to be pluralistic, in reality it favours the African traditional cultures and religions.[39]

In the political landscape, Ubuntu also faces condemnation. Kamwangamalu questions the worldview of Ubuntu, by saying that if a country such as South Africa – part of Africa – where this way of life supposedly thrives, has allowed an evil such as the apartheid system to become the order of the day, what is the significance of Ubuntu? In addition to that, one of the TRC analysts, Richard Wilson, argues that 'Ubuntu should be recognized for what it is: an ideological concept with multiple meanings which conjoins human rights, restorative justice, reconciliation and nation-building within the populist language of Pan-Africanism.'[40] Tambulasi and Kayuni conclude a discussion on this matter by stating that Ubuntu in politics is worth nothing if it is not tied with good governance.[41] It is believed that whilst Ubuntu may be a given, it remains a task. It may be part and parcel of our African heritage, but it needs to be revitalised in our minds and hearts towards achieving the sustainable development goals agenda.

---

[36] Eklund, *Ubuntu*, 36.
[37] Venter, *The Notion,* 150.
[38] Prinsloo, *Ubuntu Culture*, 49.
[39] Taringa, *Possibilities and Limitations*, 192.
[40] Kamwangamalu, *Ubuntu in South Africa*, 40.
[41] Richard Tambulasi and Happy Kayuni, 'Ubuntu and Democratic Good Governance in Malawi', In Munyaradzi Murove (ed) *African Ethics. An Anthology of Comparative and Applied Ethics* (Scottsville: University of KwaZulu-Natal, 2009), 438.

The Relationship between Ubuntu and Sustainable Development

Ubuntu is a living concept and not merely a utopian vision, and it has implications for societal, economic and environmental development. The notion of SDGs comes close to Ubuntu with its idea of mutual responsibility and forms of cooperation in the spirit of Ubuntu. The Ubuntu principle cultivates interdependence in all areas of life. The western idea of a social contract maintains the competitive human being and homo 'economicus' whereas the African concept of Ubuntu portrays a cooperative human being. Examples of cooperation in Ubuntu are *shosholoza* ('work as one', team work) and collective enterprises, *stokvels*, in which profits are equally shared and may never be gained at the expense of another.[42]

For the emergence of a just and sustainable economy, the 2009 Ubuntu declaration (with the support of Desmond Tutu and Cherie Blair) underlines the issues of, inter alia, financial system reform, green economy, women's economic empowerment, growth and jobs as well as climate change and sustainability, calling for a holistic response.[43] It is believed that the concept of Ubuntu, the spirit of cooperation, is vital in tackling these global issues. However, Ubuntu emphasises our interconnectedness as humans (and nature) and hence development in Africa is intrinsically related with that of other parts of the globe. For example, the South African Vukani-Ubuntu community development project is a non-profit organisation, empowering communities in the country and it has existed for decades in the skilled jewellery-making industry. By the use of 'Integrated Sustainable Development', this grass-root development project has improved the lives of previously disadvantaged communities.[44] Also, the Ubuntu Touch Project (Medi-Spa's flagship upliftment project), the Ubuntu Projekt, a development project (Masiphumelele of Cape Town), and the Ubuntu Building Project, all based in South Africa, are designed to help in developing sustainable communities.[45]

Therefore, Ubuntu can significantly enhance just, inclusive and peaceful communities and promote the achievement of sustainable development through the recognition that our embeddedness in the human community is not merely in the present community, but also in past and future communities. An Ubuntu sustainable development would, therefore, have significantly greater leverage in interventions focused on promoting inclusive, peaceful, social, economic and environmental development across the board.

---

[42] Louw, *Ubuntu*, 13.

[43] Dorine Eva Van Norren, 'The Nexus between Ubuntu and Global Public Goods: Its Relevance for the Post 2015 Development Agenda.' *Development Studies Research. An Open Access Journal*, 1:1 (2014), 255-266.

[44] Vukani-Ubuntu is a community development organisation formed in 1998, generating interest and injecting a wind of positive change in the jewellery sector in South Africa. It has established 11 community development projects in one decade. During the 10-year period, Vukani-Ubuntu also trained over 400 students (Vukani.org).

[45] See, 'Ubuntutouch.co.za', 2021.

Conclusion

This chapter has made a critical assessment of Ubuntu as a source of inspiration for a just and inclusive community in present-day Africa. The scholarly views of Shutte and Gyekye of Ubuntu understanding and core perspectives have been explored. A brief definition and historical background of this African worldview and its practical application in professional and everyday life have been discussed. Ubuntu has also contributed to the African moral culture of humanity and has resonance with conviviality and buen vivir. The chapter concluded that the Ubuntu concept could lead to positive attributes and provide continuity for attributes such as mutuality, relatedness and reciprocity as core contributors in the work towards SDG 16.7. For the future, this chapter advocates the further study of the Ubuntu philosophy of social inclusion and peaceful living in Africa as an instrument for sustainable development and justice for all.

Bibliography

Addy, Tony, 'Seeking Conviviality as a Core Concept for Community Development', in *Developing Just and Inclusive Communities: Challenges for Diakonia as Christian Social Practice and for Social Work*, Haugen, Hans Morten; Kivle, Benedicte Tveter; Addy, Tony; Kessel, Terese Bue; Klaasen, John (Eds). (Oxford: Regnum, 2022), 79-94.

Broodryk, Johann, *Ubuntu: Life Lessons from Africa* (Pretoria: Ubuntu School of Philosophy, 2002).

Broodryk, Johann, *Ubuntu Management Philosophy: Exporting Ancient African Wisdom into the Global World* (Ranburg: Knowres Publishing, 2005).

Broodryk, Johann, *Ubuntu: Life Coping Skills from Africa* (Johannesburg: Knowres Publishing, 2006).

Chassagne, Natasha, *Buen Vivir as an Alternative to Sustainable Development: Lessons from Ecuador* (London: Routledge, 2000).

Conradie Ernst and Xolani, Sakuba, 'Sin and Evil in African Christian Theologies: A Classification', in P. Coertzen (ed). *Ned Geref. Theologiese Tydskrif* (Stellenbosch: Sun Press, 2006), 59-71.

Eklund, Hanna, 'Ubuntu: An Analysis of the Political Rhetoric of a Traditional Concept in Contemporary South Africa.' (Thesis 2008), 29-36.

Elijah, John and Akpabio, Maurice, 'Martin Buber's Dialogue and the Possibility of Peaceful Co-existence in a Plural Society,' *Nnamdi Azikiwe Journal of Philosophy*, 11:3 (2019): 1-14.

Kamwangamalu, Nkonko, 'Ubuntu in South Africa: A Sociolinguistic Perspective to a Pan-African Concept.' *Critical Arts*, 13:2 (1999): 24-41.

Klaasen, John, The Role of Personhood in Development: An African Perspective on Development in South Africa. *Missionalia*, *45*:1 (2017): 29-44.

Klaasen, John. 'Personhood and Inclusive Communities: Access to Justice for All', in *Developing Just and Inclusive Communities: Challenges for*

Diakonia as Christian Social Practice and for Social Work, edited by Haugen, Hans Morten, *et al.* (Oxford: Regnum Books, 2022), 33-48.

Munyaka, Mluleki and Motlhabi, Mokgethi, 'Ubuntu and its Socio-moral Significance', in Munyaradzi Murove (ed). *African Ethics. An Anthology of Comparative and Applied Ethics* (Scottsville: University of KwaZulu-Natal, 2009), 63-84.

Gyekye, Kwame, *Tradition and Modernity: Reflections on the African Experience* (New York: Oxford University Press, 1997).

Gyekye, Kwame, 'Person and Community in African Thought', in Coetzee, Pieter and Roux, Abraham (eds*.), Philosophy from Africa* (International Thomson *Publishing:* Johannesburg, 2003).

Harber, Clive, and Jeff Serf, *Exploring Ubuntu: Education & Development: An Introduction to Theories and Debates* (Birmingham: Tide-Centre, 2004).

Louw, Dirk, *Ubuntu and the Challenges of Multiculturalism in Post-apartheid South Africa* (Utrecht: Zuidam and amp: Uithof, 2003).

Majeed, Hasskei, The Nexus between 'Person', Personhood, and Community in Kwame Gyekye's Philosophy. *UJAH: Unizik Journal of Arts and Humanities*, 18:3: (2017): 26-27.

Meiring, Piet, 'The Baruti Versus the Lawyers: The Role of Religion in the TRC Process', in Charles Villa-Vicencio and Wilhelm Verwoerd (eds). *Looking Back Reaching Forward. Reflections on the Truth and Reconciliation Commission of South Africa* (Cape Town: UCT Press, 2002): 123-133.

Naude, Piet, 'Decolonising knowledge: Can Ubuntu Ethics Save Us from Coloniality?' *Journal of Business Ethics,* 159:1 (2019): 23-37.

Prinsloo, Erasmus, 'Ubuntu Culture and Participatory Management', in Coetzee, Pieter and Roux, Abraham (ed). *Philosophy from Africa. A Text with Readings* (Cape Town: UCT Press, 2000).

Shutte, Augustine, *Ubuntu: An Ethic for a New South Africa* (Pietermaritzburg: Cluster Publications, 2001).

Tambulasi Richard and Happy Kayuni, 'Ubuntu and Democratic Good Governance in Malawi', in Munyaradzi Murove (ed) *African Ethics. An Anthology of Comparative and Applied Ethics* (Scottsville: University of KwaZulu-Natal, 2009), 438.

Taringa, Nisbert, 'Possibilities and Limitations for Intercultural Dialogue from the Perspective of Ubuntu Philosophy.' *Swedish Missiological Themes*, 95:2 (2007): 185-196.

Tutu, Desmond, *God Is Not a Christian and Other Provocations* (Allen J, ed.). (London: Harper Collins, 2011).

Tutu, Desmond, *God Has a Dream: A Vision of Hope for Our Time* (Johannesburg: Rider, 2004).

Tutu, Desmond, *No Future without Forgiveness* (New York: Doubleday, 1999).

Ubuntu Global Network (2021). http://ubuntusummit.org/index.php/en/ubuntu-summit-en 2021 pdf.

Van Norren, Dorine Eva, 'The Nexus between Ubuntu and Global Public Goods: Its Relevance for the Post 2015 development Agenda.' *Development Studies Research. An Open Access Journal*, 1:1 (2014): 255-266.

Venter, Elza, 'The Notion of Ubuntu and Communalism in African Educational Discourse' *Studies in Philosophy and Education*, 23:2 (2004): 149-160.

‘Seeking Conviviality’ as a Core Concept for Community Development

Tony Addy

Introduction

‘Seeking Conviviality’ as a core concept for community-based work and work for structural change emerged from discussions with groups of local community and diaconal workers in Central and Eastern Europe. It is a concept which is rarely used in relation to community practice in most contexts. One advantage of this is that it promotes reflection and provides a new approach to working in localities. The concept and practice have been further developed in a pan-European group of around thirty local practitioners, organised under the auspices of the Lutheran World Federation and with interdiac acting as a continuous consultant.[1] Through this process the concept of ‘Seeking Conviviality’ has gradually been shaped to focus on issues of diversity and work in localities, and on the structural issues which affect local contexts, such as work and economy and social policy. The process has also considered the role of the churches and diaconia in the face of new challenges. In this chapter we will consider some of the issues this raises for the practice of community development work.

The word ‘conviviality’ implies ‘living together’ and it has in more recent years been used more widely in the social sciences to describe experiences of everyday life in superdiverse cities in Europe.[2] The concept has also informed a great deal of social research in cities in several world regions, and some have spoken of a ‘convivial turn’ in social research itself.[3] Therefore, coincidentally church-based actors and secular social scientists and practitioners have begun to use the convivial lens to understand the context and practice, particularly in cities. The bibliography is now extensive, and the concept is operative in other

[1] interdiac is the International Academy for Diaconia and Christian Social Action, Central and Eastern Europe (www.interdiac.eu).

[2] A. Wise and G. Noble, ‘Convivialties – an Orientation’. *Journal of Intercultural Studies*, Vol 37.5 (August 2016).

[3] M. L. Berg and M. Nowicka, ‘Introduction: Convivial Tools for Research & Practice’, in M. L. Berg, and M. Nowicka (eds.), *Studying Diversity and Urban Multiculture* (London: UCL Press, 2019).

S. Neal, K. Bennett, A. Cochrane and G. Mohan, ‘Community *and* Conviviality? Informal Life in Multicultural Places’. *Sociology*, Vol 53.1 February 2019.

world regions than Europe, including Africa and Latin America. It also has resonance with other concepts which inform analysis and practice, notably 'buen vivir'[4] and 'Ubuntu'.[5]

In this chapter we will explore the meaning of convivial thinking as it can be seen in the practice of critical community development.[6] However, we will start with a short introduction to community development within which convivial thinking about community development can be situated. It will become clear how this relates to the UN sustainable development goals and especially those related to participation, diversity, and inclusion.[7]

Rethinking Community Development

There is a need to rethink community development because of the changing context, particularly in large cities, but also because both words in the phrase are subject to multiple interpretations. Starting with the word community itself, in a well-known book Colin Bell and Howard Newby analysed 94 sociological definitions of community and they found that the only common element across the field of sociology was that community is about people and relationships.[8]

In more recent definitions of community development, such as that put forward by the International Association for Community Development, the focus is on people within a common place or with a common identity.[9] This begs as many questions as it answers because it is no longer clear that having a common place leads to common interests and it raises the question of who gets to define common identity and common issues. Because of economic change and migration, interests in one place can, at the extreme, even be diametrically opposed. Common identity is also problematic because for different people,

---

[4] A. Acosta, *Buen Vivir: Vom Recht auf ein gutes Leben* (Munich: oekom, 2015).

[5] B. O. Anofuechi, 'A Critical Evaluation of the *Ubuntu* Principle as Just and Inclusive Communities in Contemporary Africa'. H.M. Haugen, B. M. T. Kivle, T. Addy, T.B. Kessel and J. Klaasen (eds.), *Developing Just and Inclusive Communities. Challenges for Diakonia as Christian Social Practice and for Social Work* (Oxford, Regnum, 2022), 65-78.

[6] T. Addy, 'Approaches to Community Development'. H.M. Haugen, B. M. T. Kivle, T. Addy, T.B. Kessel and J. Klaasen (eds.), *Developing Just and Inclusive Communities. Challenges for Diakonia as Christian Social Practice and for Social Work* (Oxford, Regnum, 2022), 15-32.

[7] The full description of the Goals can be accessed here:
United Nations Department of Economic and Social Affairs: UN Sustainable Development Goals: n.d., https://www.un.org/ga/search/view_doc.asp?symbol=A/RES/70/1&Lang=E; accessed 13.9.21.

[8] C. Bell and H. Newby, *Community Studies: An Introduction to the Sociology of the Local Community'* (London: HarperCollins, 1972).

[9] International Association for Community Development, 2020, *'Towards International Shared Standards for Community Development'* (Glasgow: IACD 2020):8.

different aspects of identity are more or less important. Therefore, there is a need for a concept which can handle diversity and fluidity.

The second problem arises because community can be used as an analytic or descriptive term or as a normative term. This issue was explored in a UK context by Raymond Plant, who pointed out that great confusion is caused by this dual use.[10] Its normative use is of course exploited by policy makers who refer to community when describing some idealised past, or who draw on these idealised images to humanise policies or institutions by implying that they in fact embody the attributes people have lost in the process of economic, political, and cultural change.

The third problem, which directly relates to SDG Target 16.7: 'Responsive, inclusive, participatory and representative decision-making', is that community is usually defined by boundaries which are either chosen or imposed! We might even say that the boundary decision, who is 'in' and who is 'out', is one of the key functions implied when we use the word community.[11] Being 'in' or 'out' may be chosen or imposed because, whilst one function of community boundaries is to identify who is included, simultaneously it may also identify which people are excluded. In terms of communities based on 'identity', following the International Association for Community Development (IACD) definition, in Britain people often talk about 'the black and minority ethnic community' or in faith terms, 'the Moslem community'.[12] The danger here is that an externally imposed identifier may be devoid of meaning, except as a policy signifier. It may also be divisive when one part of the identified group feels excluded. When the UN document speaks about decision-making it is referring to governance. 'Seeking Conviviality' as an approach to community development has a contribution to make because it is about strengthening the agency of people who are not normally involved in decision-making or even engaged in (formal) participatory processes, without placing people in an ascribed category.

Talja Blokland, in an insightful and creative book, has tried to circumvent this problem by talking about 'community as urban practice'. Her book explores the fact that everybody seems to know what the concept 'community' means, and it remains a focus of longing as conditions of everyday life become more stressed due to austerity and more challenging due to increasing diversity. She concludes that community signifies the search for relatedness and belonging but in the 'modern' context we need to go beyond community as a fixed, stable entity and see it as, to coin a phrase, 'fluid'.[13]

---

[10] Raymond Plant, *Community and Ideology* (London: Routledge & Kegan Paul, 2009).

[11] United Nations Department of Economic and Social Affairs, Sustainable development Goal 16. n.d., https://sdgs.un.org/goals/goal16 (accessed 18.7.21).

[12] International Association for Community Development, 2020, 8.

[13] Talja Blokland, *Community as Urban Practice* (Cambridge: Polity Press, 2017).

If we want to go on using the word ‘community’, we need to be clear what we mean, not only contextually but also in terms of ‘practice’ and Talja Blokland gives a pointer in this direction, towards a solidarity which does not depend on a shared, common identity. Therefore, community can be understood as performative, as a relational practice which emphasises common being. To extend this to the field of community development work, ‘community’ also signifies a space where there is common decision-making and the issue of power is handled both in practice, between the worker and the diverse groups in the locality, and towards power-holding institutions and organisations which shape life for good or ill. In this chapter I am mainly going to focus on local place-based work.

The second word in this defining pair is ‘development’ which is equally problematic. We could limit the use of the word to mean a ‘practice’ which supports the development of ‘community’ in the sense referred to above. However, development is a word with its own ambiguous meaning and imperative. The reason is that it has its roots in colonialism and in ideas of progress, both of which flourished at the end of the 19th century. It was not only enlightenment thinking and idealism that foregrounded the concept of ‘progress’ but also economic forces and technology. So ‘development’ tied to the idea of progress and the development of the economy and society under the influence of science-based technology is somehow implied by community development. As it is often said, we cannot be against ‘development'. This leads directly to the conceptualising of former colonised countries as underdeveloped, and of poor and disadvantaged communities in the Global North as needing ‘development’ to reach some implied or expressed normative standard. As a side comment, community development in Great Britain was given a boost by people who were engaged in ‘enlightened colonial administration’ during the 1950s at the time of the independence movements. The idea was to ‘prepare people for self-government’![14]

Definitions of community development have struggled with (or avoided) the use of one or other of these terms but the most widely held definition of community development is as follows:

> Community Development is a practice-based profession and an academic discipline that promotes participative democracy, sustainable development, rights, economic opportunity, equality and social justice, through the organisation, education and

[14] T. R. Batten with M. Batten, *‘The Non-Directive Approach in Group and Community Work’* (London: Oxford University Press, 1967), 27–29. See also: George Lovell, 2007, ‘T. R. (Reg) Batten and Madge Batten: Their Worldwide Contributions to the Non-directive Approach to Community Development’. The Encyclopaedia of Pedagogy and Informal Education. Downloaded from: www.infed.org/thinkers/batten.htm (London: infed, n.d., accessed 18.07.21).

> empowerment of people within their communities, whether these be of locality, identity or interest, in urban and rural settings.[15]

As can be seen, this definition is bound to professional practice, but it does have a very close relevance to SDG Target 16.7: Responsive, inclusive, participatory, and representative decision-making.[16] In the following parts of this chapter, I will develop the use of the phrase 'Seeking Conviviality' to ground an approach to local work, particularly with diverse communities and marginalised people.

Roots of Convivial Thinking and Practice

'Seeking Conviviality' has been developed as an approach to local diaconal practice in the work of the Lutheran World Federation process on 're-forming community diakonia in Europe' and by interdiac. The roots of the concept have been described more fully in the publications related to this process and in several book chapters.[17]

The first point to highlight is that 'convivial life together', in distinction to 'community', does not presuppose a bounded entity but refers to a process of relationship building. It implies crossing boundaries which are implicit in the traditional understanding of community and even in the IACD definition mentioned previously.

The second point is that it is not primarily professional practice – it refers to everyday life and the role of the professional is to facilitate processes and spaces where convivial life together can be supported and experienced. It also implies a concern with the social, political, and economic structures which prevent convivial life together.

Thirdly, behind the concept are four specific ideas related to personhood:

- Persons are formed through the relationships with others, throughout life, including with institutions. Therefore, these relationships are taken seriously in professional practice. (Belonging depends on relationships.)
- People express their identity through the story they tell about their life and the story may change through new experiences and reflection. Therefore, creating a safe space where people can share their story is a basis for professional practice. Empowerment implies changing the narrative which people tell about themselves and/or their situation.
- Identity should not be ascribed from 'outside' nor can the way in which people themselves want to identify be ascribed; similarly, problems cannot

[15] International Association for Community Development, 2020.

[16] United Nations Department of Economic and Social Affairs, Sustainable Development Goal 16.

[17] For a bibliography see: the interdiac online space: https://www.online-space.eu/conviviality-as-a-core-concept-for-diaconia (Český Těšín n.d. Accessed 17.09.21).

be defined from outside. All kinds of labelling – even well-meaning categorisations and not only stereotyping – tend to disempower people and destroy convivial life together. A conviviality-based approach also relates to intersectionality because it takes seriously the self-identity of diverse participants.[18]

- Conviviality implies reciprocity between people – all are givers and receivers. This understanding of person and society is derived from the work of Marcel Mauss which has been very influential in the movement centred around, 'The Convivialist Manifesto – A Declaration of Interdependence' and its subsequent redrafting.[19]

Fourthly, convivial life together assumes diversity and recognises it – this is very important for an approach to community development, especially if one group perceives itself to be the 'mainstream'. This is related to the issue of power in processes of group decision-making, where one group may assume a normative position without reflection. The process of working together should be designed so that all can begin to see the particularity of their perspective as rooted in their diverse life experiences.

A further point related to convivial life together is that the economy, technology, and work are taken seriously as aspects of creating identity. This aspect draws on the inspirational work of Ivan Illich who, in a seminal book called 'Tools for Conviviality', drew attention to the fact that not only does the economic model create a highly unequal society, which is hardly conducive to convivial life together, but also that the very 'tools' of an industrialised society tend to undermine convivial life together. Illich uses 'tools' to mean not only physical tools and computers but also institutions and even methods of working with people. As well as the impact on people, the industrialised economy also affects people's relationship to the environment. Therefore, to seek a convivial economy implies a critique of economic systems in terms of their impact on relationships between people and technology, and people and the environment, as well as between people.

---

[18] For a fuller discussion see: T. Addy and U. Siirto, 'Conviviality as a Vision and Approach for a Diaconal Society'. Ampony, G. et.al. (eds.), *International Handbook on Ecumenical Diakonia* (Oxford: Regnum Books, 2021).

[19] Marcel Mauss, *The Gift – The Form and Reason for Exchange in Archaic Societies* (Abingdon: Routledge, 2nd Ed, 2002).
'Convivialist Manifesto: A Declaration of Interdependence'. *Global Dialogues 3* (Duisburg: Käte Hamburger Kolleg /Centre for Global Cooperation Research KHK/GCR21, 2014).

Conviviality – Crossing Borders and Boundaries

Most of the literature about community development focuses attention on the role of the professional and concentrates on knowledge and skills for practice.[20] This means that there is often an implicit subordination of the experience and neglect of the agency of the people the professional will work with. Conviviality, however, is not a mark of professional practice in the first place, it is an aspect of everyday life.[21] This idea was first opened up by Paul Gilroy who contrasted the everyday lived reality of communities marked by extreme diversity – which he termed convivial – and the melancholic lives of people in majority traditional white localities in the UK.[22] We can relate this idea to the discussion by Zygmunt Bauman of the everyday negotiation of shared meanings in spaces in large, diverse cities.[23]

Increasingly, people from many different backgrounds are 'thrown together' in one place – especially, but not only, in cities.[24] People living in one place may inhabit different 'life worlds' and therefore have diverse values or interests. They may have been forced to move or may be forced to stay in the same place and yet others may have chosen to live there. Education and socio-economic backgrounds may be very different and people may have important life connections to other places in the world, which will also affect everyday life. Conflicts rooted in other places across the world may influence everyday events in a locality. In the face of such diversity, we need to ask in what ways it is possible to create a shared, liveable space. This is an even more complex problem because it is not only an interpersonal or intergroup issue. Economic forces and political policies are also important factors in supporting or undermining convivial life together. Therefore, anyone starting to do community development work, especially in an urban neighbourhood, faces a locality which can often be characterised as 'super-diverse'.[25]

Everyday encounters between people in a neighbourhood can create informal opportunities for people to step over their boundaries and borders but they can also create 'walls', intentionally or otherwise. If we want to work for conviviality, we soon recognise that we cannot overcome borders and create conviviality by good will, positive thoughts, and warm feelings! It is also important to recognise that conviviality is not built on the absence of conflict between and within different groups, but that it requires work to understand diverse perspectives, transform conflicts and find a common horizon for change. However, building on and supporting everyday conviviality can build a powerful

---

[20] Akwugo Emejulu, *'Community Development as Micropolitics: Comparing Theories, Policies and Politics in America and Britain'* (Bristol: Policy Press, 2016).

[21] Paul Gilroy, *After Empire: Melancholia or Convivial Culture* (London: Routledge, 2004).

[22] Gilroy, *After Empire….*

[23] Zygmunt Bauman, *Liquid Love* (Cambridge: Polity Press, 2013).

[24] Doreen Massey, *For Space* (London: Sage, 2005).

[25] Steven Vertovec, *Super-Diversity* (London: Routledge, 2021).

basis for social action and work for social change. This means we also need to think carefully about the position of the worker between powerful organisations and the different groups in the locality.

Turning our attention to purposeful action to create and support conviviality we must reflect on the practice of crossing borders or boundaries. It is important to recognise that the service models of previous social workers, priests, diaconal workers and so on have created a distinct set of expectations and if the aim is to transform practice, this should be borne in mind. Maybe the expectations people have of us are also formed byprevious experiences of the organisation or church for which we work. These, plus our own socialisation and professional training create one side of the boundary.

When a worker meets the 'other', it is important that they recognise the need to negotiate the boundary between themselves and those they work with, and the related power differentials. How they do that determines the possibility for trust-building and work for change. Crossing borders or boundaries can be likened to crossing the *threshold* between one world and identity, and another world and its identity.

This threshold can be high or low, but it always exists, and the space of the threshold is critical, because it is a liminal space where the meanings each ascribes to the other are not yet clear. Whenever we meet another person, we tell a 'story' about ourselves, and the content and way of telling the story is shaped by expectations and power differentials. This is true for everyday life and for the meeting between professionals and those they work with. However, opening a space of trust and open 'storytelling' in a creative way may lead to unexpected change.

In the present context, this form of cooperation is becoming more important yet more difficult for two reasons. Firstly, in the present turbulent and unpredictable social, political, and economic context people feel very insecure and at risk, so they tend to withdraw and seek security, often in a strong leader or a previous imagined 'pure' community. The second reason is that we are living in a time where there is support for a very individualistic, meritocratic culture with a strong focus on happiness through consumption. The one who is not successful is responsible for their own failure to succeed, and vice versa. An approach through Seeking Conviviality aims to address these two kinds of 'mental prison' – that of a person seeking security in a received or re-imagined communitarian identity, and that of the person who sees themselves as a lonely decision-maker who makes their identity through consumption.

Outline of a Convivial Approach to Professional Practice

Seeking Conviviality as an approach to professional diaconal or social and community work or as voluntary social action requires critical reflection. This approach contrasts with that found in many of the manuals and toolkits for social and community development work. Many community work and diaconal projects are based on an 'off the shelf diagnosis' and a prescriptive, protocolled approach to intervention. In the worst case, the work is project based and focused on time-bounded processes and clear steps for working with people for already prescribed outcomes. We could call this 'reproductive work' because the model it represents reproduces the approach of systems that are excluding some people, and which do not allow for creativity. Seeking Conviviality aims for 'productive work', which means work that builds on the reflected understanding of the participants, who may have diverse interests and backgrounds, and which may produce new meaning and a new sense and practice of agency leading to change or innovation.[26] Therefore, in Seeking Conviviality the aim is to support an inductive, participatory, bottom-up approach that recognises and handles difference, including the differences between people and between the worker and the 'other'. It requires taking the time to build up the convivial culture of everyday life. Because the process is productive, and the situations are complex and ambiguous it has been called an 'art' and a 'practice'.[27]

When we focus attention on professional practice, which aims at transformation, it is important to reflect on a person's professional identity or 'habitus' and not only to think about 'knowledge and skills'. This is related to the previous discussion about the way in which Seeking Conviviality approaches crossing borders and boundaries. If the aim is to work for sustainable change which is deeper than simply securing practical improvements in the given situation, then reflective practice is a key factor. Community development, which aims for empowerment and transformation, is dealing with the question of meaning and story.[28] It involves changes in the way people think about themselves and even their belief and value system. To support this process and essential first step, the professional has reflected on the motivation for their work, their expectation for the outcome, and how the approach they take supports this outcome. *Each worker has their own deep service model*, which is constructed from their socialisation, faith or world view, motivation, and expectation. This service model must be clarified because it is the basic resource out of which people work. Of course, through critical incidents and reflexivity a worker's service model may change; therefore, this is ongoing work.

Secondly, through professional training, workers have, most probably, incorporated another service model, which may have a critical relationship to the personal service model.

---

[26] M. Larson and E. Wikström, 'Relational Interaction Processes Project Networks: The Consent and Negotiation Perspectives'. *Scandinavian Journal of Management*, 23, September 2007, 333.

[27] Tony Addy, *Seeking Conviviality: Re-forming Community Diakonia in Europe* (Geneva, Lutheran World Federation, 2013).

[28] T. Addy, 'Approaches to Community Development', in H.M. Haugen, B. M. T. Kivle, T. Addy, T.B. Kessel and J. Klaasen. (eds.), *Developing Just and Inclusive Communities. Challenges for Diakonia as Christian Social Practice and for Social Work* (Oxford, Regnum, 2022), 15-32.

Thirdly, to make matters more complicated, the personal and professional service model may or may not be similar to the service model of the employing organisation or church. Furthermore, these three dimensions may or may not match the expectations of the people that the professional works with. We could picture it like this:

Figure 1. Motivation and Expectation for a Community Development Worker

Each corner of this triangle has its own motivation and expectation, and the three service models may be synchronous or in tension! In each context the overlapping motivations and expectations will shape practice, which means shaping the relationship between the worker and the different 'other'.

Furthermore, when the worker meets the different 'other' they are, in effect, crossing a boundary between themselves and a person from a different 'life world'. In any context, there will be several distinct or overlapping life worlds and in a Seeking Conviviality approach, the community worker has to pay attention to this diversity and construct spaces for trusted communication in order to build up a shared perspective and a common basis for action together. The worker has the aim to build up and support the agency of people, based on their own understanding of their situation and their chosen goals as this is the basis for sustainable change.

Professional community workers usually find themselves 'in between' the people they are working with and the institutions which shape the people's lives in large or small ways. These organisations may also have their own goals related to the local context and the worker's employing organisation may be one of these organisations. Therefore, as in the diagram below, the worker is in an 'in-between position' and all these dimensions come into play. Therefore, a worker has to be clear about their position and their service model, or they will create confusion and suspicion in the 'other'. The temptation is to use the 'in-between position' to become a spokesperson or a go-between on behalf of the people in the locality.

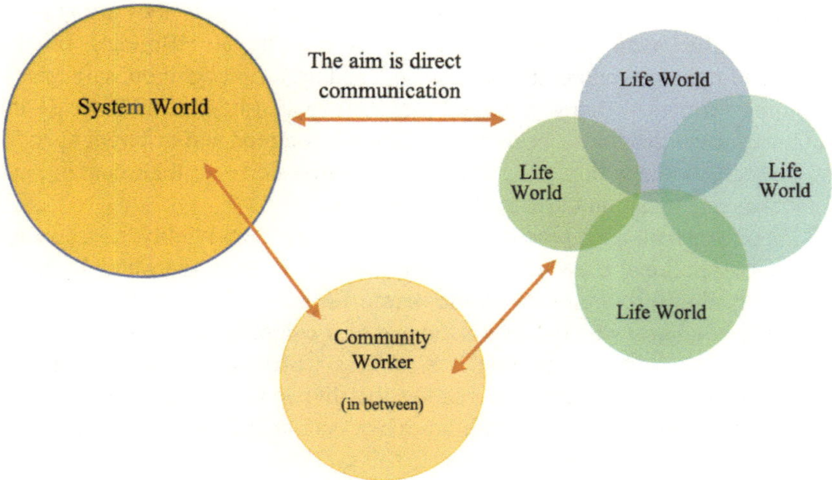

Figure 2. The position of a community development worker in between system and life worlds

Looking more deeply, Seeking Conviviality is an approach built on a process of reflection and learning which disturbs normal patterns and expectations and which creates new practices for professional work. The point is that we all live out of the narrative, which is our biography, and on this basis, we communicate with other people, including those with whom we work. To follow this approach, professionals must work this out and not bypass it with techniques. It is out of the resources and strengths of our biography that we, as a worker or an activist, can begin to work for change.[29] Working on this basis is a key to developing horizontal ('eye-to-eye') communication rather than 'strategic' communication with the different 'other', which in turn is sensitive to the power inherent in our own position.

In relation to professional social or diaconal work practice, this approach to the 'other' recognises that the 'threshold' or liminal space between the worker and those from diverse other life worlds is an important space for transforming

---

[29] For a fuller description of this approach to learning see: Tony Addy, 'Reflections on Community Based Work, Social Service and Diaconia' in Jouko Porkka & Marja Pentikäinen (eds), *'Community of the Future- Challenges and New Approaches to Community Based Work and Diaconia' (*Helsinki: Diaconia University of Applied Sciences, 2013) and Oksana Prosvirnina and Tony Addy, 'interdiac Pedagogy an Introduction and Guide' (Český Těšín: interdiac, 2020).

practice. Care must be taken not to fill up this space with ready-made identification and interpretation. The recognition that workers occupy an 'in-between' position is critical. They are different to the people they work with in all their diversity and, if they are working for 'transformation' they are also not to be identified with the 'system world' of institutions.[30] Building on this understanding, a new interstitial space is opened up for recognition, self-esteem and empowerment.[31] Being open and receptive to sharing personal stories and group narratives provides a basis for working on common and different agendas and through shared action, the stories and narratives change their content, and this makes an impact on the identity of the actors.

This understanding of practice underpins Seeking Conviviality, as a concept based on a relational view of the person. It points to the understanding of the deeper meaning of community as the search for an ethical, relational practice that builds solidarity which does not depend on a common shared identity.[32] We could otherwise suggest that this is a process which aims to build empathy between people rather than exacerbating the divisions. For the practitioner it means being close to the diverse life-worlds of people and not to have a focus on specific predefined problems or projects. This closeness enables the professional to be open to the reality of everyday life for different people and groups, and to work with them on the agendas which are important to them. It means having a receptive approach which embodies the possibility of creating a double learning model whereby all learn together and create new knowledge. It is no longer a matter of the professional defining agendas and outcomes as well as structures and processes. Through a common learning process, the normally excluded 'other' contributes to the surprising gift of innovation. This process of sharing stories and reflecting on them enables a diverse group to find ways of working together for change in their common and specific situations. The trust-building process is the basis of building sustainable organisations for resistance, innovation, and transformation because it is not called into being by finance alone.[33]

---

[30] Jürgen Habermas describes the way in which various system worlds aim to colonise the life world(s) of people and the danger is that professionals take on part of this role because usually they are employed, or their work is financed by a system world institution. Jürgen Habermas (trans. Thomas McCarthy), 'Theory of Communicative Action, Vol. 2: Lifeworld and System: A Critique of Functionalist Reason' (Boston: Beacon Press, 1987).

[31] Rasmus H. Birk and Mia A. Fallov, 'Between a Rock and Hard Place: State Led Territorial Stigmatization, Informal Care Practices and the Interstitiality of Community Workers in Denmark', *Community Development Journal*, Vol 56.2 2021, pp 286–282.

[32] T. Blokland, *Community as Urban Practice*.

[33] A more detailed of this approach to work on biography, story, meaning and empowerment for transformation can be further explored in: Margaret Ledwith, *Community Development: A Critical and Radical Approach* (Bristol, Policy Press 3rd edition 2020) and Titus Schlattman, and Rob van Waarde, *That's the Name of the Game* (Tubbergen: van der Ross Verlag 2015).

'Seeking Conviviality' is not narrowly focused on problem solving or on meeting needs but on processes which can create the energy where the problems and issues can be addressed in new and creative ways, whether they be local or the consequence of unjust structures and systems. It represents a further development of the participatory critical approach analysed previously and it links to the SDG Target 16.7 by supporting a process which ensures 'responsive, inclusive, participatory and representative decision-making'.[34] It is based on a reflected understanding of professional power, recognises the diversity of identity and implies an approach which enhances communication to build trust and strengthen agency.

Bibliography

Acosta, A., *'Buen Vivir: Vom Recht auf ein gutes Leben'*. (Munich: oekom, 2015).

Addy, T., 'Approaches to Community Development', in Haugen, H.M., Kivle, B. M. T., Addy, T., Kessel; T. B. and Klaasen, J. (eds.), *Developing Just and Inclusive Communities. Challenges for Diakonia as Christian Social Practice and for Social Work* (Oxford, Regnum, 2021), 15-32.

Addy, T., 'Reflections on Community Based Work, Social Service and Diaconia', in Porkka, J. & Pentikäinen, M. (eds), *'Community of the Future: Challenges and New Approaches to Community Based Work and Diaconia'* (Helsinki: Diaconia University of Applied Sciences, 2013).

Addy, T., *Seeking Conviviality: Re-forming Community Diakonia in Europe* (Geneva: Lutheran World Federation, 2013).

Addy, T and Siirto, U., 'Conviviality as a Vision and Approach for a Diaconal Society', in Ampony, G. et.al., *'International Handbook on Ecumenical Diakonia'* (Oxford: Regnum Books, 2021).

Anofuechi, B. O., 'A Critical Evaluation of the *Ubuntu* Principle as Just and Inclusive Communities in Contemporary Africa'. Haugen, H.M., Kivle, B. M. T., Addy, T., Kessel; T. B. and Klaasen, J. (eds.), *Developing Just and Inclusive Communities. Challenges for Diakonia as Christian Social Practice and for Social Work* (Oxford, Regnum, 2022), 65-78.

Batten, T. R. with Batten, M., *The Non-Directive Approach in Group and Community Work* (London: Oxford University Press, 1967).

Bauman, Z., *Liquid Love* (Cambridge: Polity Press, 2013).

Bell, C & Newby, H., *Community Studies: An Introduction to the Sociology of the Local Community* (London: HarperCollins, 1972).

Berg, M.L. and Nowicka, M., 'Introduction: Convivial Tools for Research & Practice', in Berg, M.L. and Nowicka, M (eds.), *Studying Diversity and Urban Multiculture* (London: UCL Press, 2019).

[34] United Nations Department of Economic and Social Affairs, *UN Sustainable Development Goals* and T. Addy, *Approaches to Community Development*.

Birk, R.H & Fallov, M.A. 2021. 'Between a Rock and Hard Place: State Led Territorial Stigmatization, Informal Care Practices and the Interstitially of Community Workers in Denmark', in *Community Development Journal*, Vol 56.2.

Blokland, T., *Community as Urban Practice* (Cambridge: Polity Press, 2017).

'Convivialist Manifesto: A Declaration of Interdependence', *Global Dialogues 3* (Duisburg: Käte Hamburger Kolleg /Centre for Global Cooperation Research KHK/GCR21, 2014).

Emejulu, A., *Community Development as Micropolitics: Comparing Theories, Policies and Politics in America and Britain* (Bristol: Policy Press, 2016).

Gilroy, P., *After Empire: Melancholia or Convivial Culture* (London: Routledge, 2004).

Habermas. J. (tr. McCarthy, T.), *Theory of Communicative Action, Vol. 2: Lifeworld and System: A Critique of Functionalist Reason* (Boston: Beacon Press, 1987).

International Association for Community Development, *Towards International Shared Standards for Community Development* (Glasgow: IACD, 2020).

interdiac online space: https://www.online-space.eu/conviviality-as-a-core-concept-for-diaconia (Český Těšín n.d., accessed 17.09.21).

Larson, M. & Wikström, E.,
'Relational Interaction Processes Project Networks:
The Consent and Negotiation Perspectives.' *Scandinavian Journal of Management*, 23, 2007, 333.

Ledwith, M., *Community Development: A Critical and Radical Approach* (Bristol, Policy Press 3rd edition, 2020).

Lovell, G., 2007, 'T. R. (Reg) Batten and Madge Batten: Their Worldwide Contributions to the Non-directive Approach to Community Development', The Encyclopaedia of Pedagogy and Informal Education. (London, infed, n.d.). Downloaded from: www.infed.org/thinkers/batten.htm (accessed 18.07.21).

Massey, D., *For Space* (London: Sage 2005).

Mauss, M., *'The Gift: The Form and Reason for Exchange in Archaic Societies'* (Abingdon: Routledge 2nd Ed., 2002).

Neal, S., Bennett, K., Cochrane, A. & Mohan, G., 2019, 'Community *and* Conviviality? Informal Life in Multicultural Places, in *Sociology*, Vol 53, Issue 1.

Plant, R., *'Community and Ideology'* (London: Routledge & Kegan Paul, 2009).

Prosvirnina, O. and Addy, T., *interdiac Pedagogy: An Introduction and Guide* (Český Těšín: interdiac, 2020).

Schlattman, T. and van Waarde, R, *That's the Name of the Game* (Tubbergen: van der Ross Verlag, 2015).

United Nations Department of Economic and Social Affairs: Sustainable Development Goals n.d., https://www.un.org/ga/search/view_doc.asp?symbol=A/RES/70/1&Lang=E; (accessed 13.09.21).

United Nations Department of Economic and Social Affairs: Sustainable Development Goal 16 n.d., https://sdgs.un.org/goals/goal16; accessed 18.07.21.

Vertovec, S., Super-Diversity (London: Routledge, 2021).

Wise, A. and Noble, G, 'Convivialties: An Orientation', *Journal of Intercultural Studies* (Vol 37, Issue 5, 2016).

A Diaconal Approach to Community Development in the Light of the Sustainable Development Goals: 'Leaving No One Behind' through Exploring Religious Resources for Creating Just and Inclusive Communities

Stephanie Dietrich

Introduction

The United Nation's (UN's) sustainable development goals (SDGs) seek to support a global development which ends 'poverty in all its forms and everywhere' (SDG1) by 2030. Meanwhile, one wonders whether it is meaningful to formulate goals which obviously will not be achieved by 2030, perceived as either utopia or sand in the eyes of those who are living under conditions of extreme poverty all around the world. As one of my students from an African context underlined: 'The global agenda sounds like heaven on earth – but we have never seen any signs of its arrival. The situation in our countries is just as disastrous as before, or even worse.' What can we meaningfully say when we speak about 'reaching the furthest behind first', and what might this mean in practice?

The UN's overarching target for the achievement of the SDGs is 'Leaving no one behind'.

> Leave no one behind (LNOB) is the central, transformative promise of the 2030 Agenda for Sustainable Development and its Sustainable Development Goals (SDGs). It represents the unequivocal commitment of all UN Member States to eradicate poverty in all its forms, end discrimination and exclusion, and reduce the inequalities and vulnerabilities that leave people behind and undermine the potential of individuals and of humanity as a whole.[1]

The Introduction to the Declaration states:

---

[1] https://unsdg.un.org/2030-agenda/universal-values/leave-no-one-behind (accessed 15.3.2021).

> As we embark on this great collective journey, we pledge that no one will be left behind. Recognizing that the dignity of the human person is fundamental, we wish to see the Goals and targets met for all nations and peoples and for all segments of society. And we will endeavour to reach the furthest behind first.[2]

As this chapter will show, this UN goal corresponds well with the normative basis of Christian social practice, *diakonia*. Within a Christian tradition one typically emphasises that the poor and marginalised are at the heart of diaconal practice; they are not recipients of charity, but actors, right-holders and the owners of their own life and the development of their communities.[3] Christian anthropology emphasises that every human being is created in the image and likeness of God, notwithstanding its status and abilities, nationality, age, sex, etc. Therefore, all life is equally valuable and to be fully respected and protected. Thus, just and inclusive communities can only be developed when everyone is welcome and everybody's voice counts – and no one is left behind.

This chapter seeks to explore the contribution of a faith-based, diaconal approach to developing just and inclusive communities and 'leaving no one behind'. Its focus is community development within international development work and global aid. The discussion here seeks to indicate the large degree of overlap between values developed within the framework of diakonia/Christian social practice and the value system behind the SDGs, thereby underlining the need that all people of good will, regardless of their religious or ideological background, should *cooperate* actively and jointly in the creation of just and inclusive communities.

I will discuss critically what we mean when we underline that diakonia, in the same way as the SDG agenda, takes its starting point 'from the margins', and that it seeks to reach 'the furthest behind' first. I deliberate 'marginalisation' in relation to the SDGs and draw on the theory of intersectionality as a theoretical tool to encounter the complexity of the issues addressed. The discussion includes an elaboration on a theological and diaconal basis which is relevant for the development of an inclusive approach to the role Christian actors can play in such community development activities, with a critical focus on the notion of a '*perspective from the margins*' and its background within liberation theology. I will also show how these theological approaches might correlate with a *rights-based* understanding as underlying the UN's SDGs.

---

[2] https://sdgs.un.org/2030agenda (accessed 5.5.2021).

[3] Stephanie Dietrich, 'Reflections on Core Aspects of Diaconal Theory', in: Dietrich, S. et.al. *Diakonia as Christian Social Practice: An Introduction*. (Oxford: Regnum, 2014), 13-27.

Diakonia from the Margins as Basis for Just and Inclusive Communities

Many religious organisations, institutions, and local faith entities, such as congregations and churches, engage in sustainable development and humanitarian assistance. Much of this engagement from diaconal actors has its normative basis in a theological understanding of the equal value and dignity of every human being as created in the image and likeness of God (Christian anthropology). Diaconal actors often refer to the biblical tradition of 'prophetic diakonia', renouncing injustice and speaking up for the poor and marginalised. Reference is given to Jesus as a model for radical engagement for supporting people in need and empowering them to create a better life for themselves and their communities.[4]

In recent diaconal studies, one frequently finds underlined that diakonia has, or at least should have, a perspective 'from the margins'. According to this understanding reality needs to be defined, and power structures revealed from the perspective of those 'at the margins'. The World Council of Churches' (WCC) Conference in Colombo, Sri Lanka 2012 emphasised that 'the world may tend to see the margins as places of disgrace and powerlessness; however, the biblical witness points towards God who is always present in the struggles of those unjustly pushed to the margins of society.'[5] The main objective lies in understanding 'the marginalised' as actors and subjects, not as recipients and objects of development imposed by 'the global North'. This plays into the discourse on post-colonialism and international development practices as a way of replacing earlier colonialism through new approaches creating dependencies through development practice.[6] Nevertheless, one might ask what this means in practice for the marginalised.

The Colombo conference opted for a new approach in endeavouring 'to re-imagine diakonia from the vantage point of those who are, in many cases, traditionally considered as recipients or objects of churches' diakonia – the vulnerable and marginalized communities.' Thus, according to this understanding, diakonia is not action *for* the marginalised, but it is the diakonia *of* the marginalised people. Taking a starting point in this perspective on diakonia includes depending on the insights of 'the margins' and acknowledging its faith and agency. Practically, churches and development actors in the Global North are asked to move from patronising top-down projects to finding new ways of accompaniment, cooperation, support for self-governed transformation and real partnership. Based on a biblical understanding which emphasises God's restorative action in uplifting the poor and marginalised and resisting injustice

[4] Brian Myers, *Walking with the Poor: Principles and Practices of Transformational Development* (Maryknoll: Orbis 2011), 72-76.

[5] Carlos Ham, 'Ecumenical Chronicle Colombo: Theological Perspectives on Diakonia in the Twenty-First Century', *The Ecumenical Review*, 64:3 (2012), 383-392, 387.

[6] Cf. Corrie Decker and Elisabeth McMahon, *The Idea of Development in Africa: A History* (Cambridge: Cambridge University Press 2021).

and oppression, this approach is based on New Testament stories of Jesus acting amongst and for the marginalised people of his time.

This perspective 'from the margins' is also emphasised in the WCC study document on Ecumenical Diakonia,[7] following the Colombo statement. The focal point, the diakonia *of* the marginalised, implies challenging both local communities and churches, and larger church bodies and development actors to implement an understanding of themselves as diaconal bodies with the potential and power to contribute to a paradigm shift. Such a paradigm shift is more than the claim for a participatory approach; it seeks to turn traditional power structures and mechanisms and the power to define reality upside down.

Historical Roots within Liberation Theology

Putting the 'marginalised' at the centre is not new, neither in global development, community development or diakonia. Ideologically, it can be traced back to the justice movement emerging in the 1970s. Liberation theology has had and still has a major impact on the understanding of the marginalised as being at the Church's centre and a bottom-up perspective, and on modern diaconal approaches, through emphasising social concern for the poor and political liberation for oppressed people. This theology, evolving in the Latin American Roman Catholic context beginning in the 1960s, was characterised by what Jon Sobrino and Gurtavo Gutiérezz said is the 'preferential option for the poor'.[8] The language of 'preferential option for the poor' comes from the Latin American Bishops' Conferences held in Medellin, Colombia, in 1968[9], and in Puebla, Mexico, in 1979.[10] The Medellin Conference called upon the Catholic Church in Latin America to become a church *of* the poor: 'to be the evangelizer of the poor and one with them, a witness to the value of the riches of the Kingdom, and the humble servant of all our people'. In their description of the term, the bishops stated that 'this option does not imply exclusion of anyone, but it does imply a preference for the poor and a drawing closer to them'.[11] Liberation theology has had a decisive role, not only in a Latin American Roman Catholic context, but also in other contexts of oppression and political mis-leadership, such as the

---

[7] https://kirken.no/globalassets/kirken.no/smm/dokumenter/2019/wcc-ecumenical-diakonia-study-document.pdf (not formally adopted by WCC Central Committee).
[8] Gustavo Gutiérezz, et al., *A Theology of Liberation: History, Politics and Salvation* (London: SCM Press,1974), 150.
[9] The Bishops of Latin America, 'The Medellin Statement', in: *New_Blackfriars* (1968), 50:582),59-111.
[10] O.P. A.C. (2016) Puebla Conference (CELAM III), in: Gooren H. (eds) *Encyclopedia of Latin American Religions*. Springer, Cham. https://doi.org/10.1007/978-3-319-08956-0_215-1.
[11] For a broad description of the Medellin and the Puebla Conference, see Gustavo Gutiérrez, *The Power of the Poor in History: Selected Writings* (Eugene, Or.: Wipf & Stock, 2004).

apartheid regime in South Africa or the struggle for justice in the Middle Eastern region. Core aspect of this theology is to understand the poor and vulnerable not only as people to be cared for, or 'included' by the powerful, but rather as the centre of the community and society. Salvation is not just an eternal issue, to comfort people to hope for a better life after death, but rather a motivation to fight for a better life now, including the fight against injustice and oppression. Jesus is seen as the eternal liberator and as the one who encourages the oppressed to fight for liberation and against oppression.

An influential philosopher for the development of a diaconal approach to community development was the Brazilian educator and philosopher Paulo Freire, who was the leading mind behind 'critical pedagogy', and the influential work *Pedagogy of the Oppressed.*[12] Freire's work goes far beyond a pedagogy; it implies a paradigm for social change and development, as Freire on the one hand emphasises a normative vision of a 'utopian aspiration for change,'[13], and on the other hand the need to develop concrete methods and practices of communication and social interaction through his liberating pedagogy.

Does this mean that there is a shift of power, from the oppressors to the oppressed, from the Global North to the global South, from those who consider themselves to be the centre to the marginalised?

Freire himself emphasised the need for a broad and all-encompassing conscientisation, based on the idea that there will be no end to oppression if domination just changes sides. Rather, through humility, empathy, love, hope and dialogue,[14] the relationship oppressed–oppressor and the power asymmetry of this relationship are addressed and changed, empowered by utopia/hope, but still aware of the harsh reality of life and all the hindrances and obstacles for change. Not at least, this implies a change of practice.

Who are the Marginalised, and Who is Defining Them?

We take our starting point in Nissen's definition of the marginalised as various groups 'that social discrimination processes have excluded from the decision-making processes'.[15] Building further on Nissen's definition, I want to accentuate that the discrimination processes are not only social, but also economic and political.

---

[12] Paolo Freire and Donaldo Ramos, *Pedagogy of the Oppressed* (New York: Continuum, 2000).

[13] Suzina, A. C. and T. Tufte. 'Freire's Vision of Development and Social Change: Past Experiences, Present Challenges and Perspectives for the Future', *International Communication Gazette*, 82:5 (2020), 411-424.

[14] For a description of Freire's five principles; cf. Suzina/Tufte: Freire's Vision, 2020.

[15] Johannes Nissen, 'Creating a Space for the Others. The Marginalized as a Challenge to Diaconia and Church: A Theological Perspective', *Diaconia. Journal for the Study of Christian Social Practice*, 5:1 (2014), 31-46, 32.

Marianne Rodriguez Nygaard underlines that an ecclesiology which puts 'the suffering of people… in the centre of the church' will radically challenge and change the church in its self-understanding:

> If people who suffer are placed at the center, the church can only reflect its identity with respect to the margins. A father can only be a father if he has a child. Likewise, the church can only be a church if it is in relationship with the margins. The church must be identified through its relationships.[16]

Nygaard asks for a redefinition of the church overcoming the dichotomy of word and action by placing *interaction* in the centre of what it means to be church. Diakonia is thus to be understood as the gospel in *interaction*, and not, as the Church of Norway currently defines it, as 'gospel in action'.[17] This understanding might also be helpful when addressing the dichotomies between word and deed; witness, evangelisation and social action; and the separation between the spiritual and the material realms, which have been core aspects of a modern worldview.

There are further dilemmas when addressing the understanding of marginalisation. Speaking about the marginalised from the position of a white professor in the Global North might in itself be self-contradictory. Who are 'the marginalised', and what is this marginalisation about? Through the concept 'diakonia *of* the marginalised', one seeks to emphasise that it is the marginalised *themselves* who are speaking, defining themselves and having the power to define their lives. Yet, it is left somehow unclear what this means in practice. It also brings to the table the discussion about the identity of community, the challenging aspects of defining community borders through terms such as 'exclusion' and 'inclusion' (who is inside, who is outside, and who decides?), and different aspects of power distribution in global cooperation.

Building on the term 'marginalised' as being excluded from decision-making processes, one can distinguish between levels of marginalisation and different types of marginalisation, since there are always people of different, and maybe more severe, marginalisation, also within wider groups, that are perceived to be marginalised. Examples include people within the category 'marginalisation caused by poverty', 'marginalisation caused by gender', and again within this category, 'marginalisation caused by disability'. A woman living in poverty, that is, below the poverty level in her context who, in addition to her life-condition and identity as a woman is also disabled – having a physical handicap, for example – would thus belong to three different groups of potential marginalisation. Below, the multidimensionality of marginalised identity will be

---

[16] Marianne Rodriguez Nygaard, 'Reflective Practice of Diaconia from the Margins: Ecclesiological and Professional Implications', *Diaconia. Journal for the Study of Christian Social Practice*, 8:2 (2017), 166-187.

[17] Church of Norway, *Plan for Diakonia* (2007); for 2020 plan (not available in English); see Church of Norway, Plan for diakoni 2020.

reflected upon by drawing on intersectionality theories as a potential tool to address and discern this issue. Based on the idea that the marginalised themselves are the subjects and actors, and that one needs to take a starting point in their already existing agency, one might nevertheless ask whether this understanding somehow is tending to hide the disastrous conditions of power imbalances and injustice on both local and global levels. It is therefore important to reflect in which way concepts of marginalisation, precariousness[18] or 'leaving no one behind/the furthest behind first' are in need of accentuation and further exploration.

No Simple Answers – In Need of Intersectionality

A theory which might be helpful when trying to address this field in its complexity is the theory of intersectionality.[19] Intersectionality seeks to support critical understandings of social inequity and structures of oppression by focusing on the interplay of different social categorisations such as race, gender, class, sexuality, age, ability, and citizenship status. It does not classify groups or people as being 'at the margins' but rather serves as a tool to distinguish and concern the multi-layered factors at work in assigning people to positions of relative advantage or disadvantage. In terms of intersectionality, the description of the multiple relations and power structures becomes more nuanced and complex. The 'marginalised' and 'poor' suits the social categories of the (privileged) donor, but also categories of individuals in positions of different relative power. Intersectionality helps to describe and understand the interconnected nature of social categorisations, which are regarded as creating overlapping and interdependent systems of power. The theory of intersectionality emerges from the scholarship and activism of black feminist thinkers, who introduced it as an analytical tool to define, understand, and challenge the multiple forms of oppression that simultaneously impede the value and freedoms of black women's everyday lives.[20] Thus, it can possibly be extended to describe the complexities of marginalised positions through a series of categories that reveal the overlapping and thus intersecting logics of different

[18] Guy Standing, 'The Precariat: Why it Needs Deliberative Democracy' (2012) (accessed at https://www.opendemocracy.net/en/precariat-why-it-needs-deliberative-democracy/# 5.5.2021).

[19] Gabriele Winker and Nina Degele, *Intersektionalität. Zur Analyse sozialer Ungleichheiten*. 2. unveränderte Auflage. (Bielefeld: Transcript Verlag, 2010). Ilse Lenz, 'Intersektionalität: Zum Verhältnis von Geschlecht und sozialer Ungleichheit'. In: Becker, Ruth & Kortendiek, Beate (Hrsg.): *Handbuch Frauen- und Geschlechterforschung: Theorie, Methoden, Empirie*. Band 35. (Wiesbaden: Springer, 2010).

[20] Kimberle Crenshaw, 'Demarginalizing the Intersection of Race and Sex: A Black Feminist Critique of Antidiscrimination Doctrine, Feminist Theory and Antiracist Politics', in: *University of Chicago Legal Forum*, Issue 1, Article 8 (1989), 139-167.

forms of social domination and exploitation. In this way, intersectionality might guide our understandings of how systemic inequities are maintained across a variety of social and political demographics, also in the context of international development and community development.

An awareness of the complexity of power relations between people globally, within countries, civil societies, local communities and within close personal relations, family structures and different groups within societies is decisive when trying to cope with global and local inequalities and the search for sustainable development, where no one is left behind. Nevertheless, the fact that intersectionality allows and calls for an awareness of complexity and the abandonment of any form of oversimplification might be both helpful and harmful, when it potentially becomes impossible to critique multiple intersections of oppression or injustice because of their complexity.[21]

Partnership and Power Imbalance/in Balance

For organisations which are resource holders, the search for partnership amidst all imbalances and mechanisms of global injustice obviously causes dilemmas and obstacles. There is a need to avoid simplistic diagnosis and easy answers to complex situations. On the one hand, global actors underline that they are *partners* in development, that their relationship should be shaped by equality, mutuality and reciprocity. Today's understanding of international development reflects the move from a needs-based to a rights-based understanding, a paradigm shift which is often referred to also within diaconal studies. On the other hand, knowing that there is an unequal distribution of material resources and power, *partnership* in relations of cooperation between different actors needs to be discerned and defined thoroughly. The question needs to be posed who has the power to define a good life, which remedies are needed to achieve access to such life for all, and who has the decision-making power. When it comes to power distribution, it is decisive to analyse who has the material resources, and how they are distributed and shared. When addressing policies and practices of international cooperation within a rights-based approach, global actors need to keep in mind the responsibility of states and governments as primary duty-bearers.

One basic step towards *partnership* in development is the creation of a joint framework of values and understanding, and the creation of good frameworks for mutual respect and trust where there is space for all who are involved. Only where there is mutual trust there can be a solid basis for real partnership on an eye-to-eye level. This applies to all who are involved in community development and international development. Thus, an important aspect of community development lies in the strengthening of civil society actors through mutual

[21] Liam Kofi Bright, Daniel Malinsky and Morgan Thompson, 'Causally Interpreting Intersectionality Theory', in: *Philosophy of Science*, 83:1 (2016), 60–81.

support and empowerment, so that these actors can play constructive roles within their respective societies and contexts, and enhance the level of trust, good governance and partnership between different actors as mutually empowered partners become more equal.

Links between the SDGs and Diaconal Community Development

The SDGs are developing further what was emphasised in the Millennium Development Goals (MDGs). But whilst the MDGs mainly addressed the situation in the global South, where the Global North is perceived as the 'donating actor', the SDGs take a different approach. The SDGs apply to everyone, and one emphasises that the global challenges only can be addressed through cooperation and partnership. All nations and all people are asked to join into the global community addressing the challenges as global. Thus, the SDGs are taking a very different starting point to earlier development strategies developed by the global community and UN institutions; namely, the idea that we are all partners striving to achieve the global development agenda.

There are two aspects I want to stress in this context: The SDGs' emphasis on all people being interdependent and relying on each other, globally, with the obligation to work together, to support one another and to work together towards a joint goal; and secondly, the SDGs' emphasis that all goals are interconnected, and that everyone and every community and nation needs to reflect where it can contribute individually, locally, nationally, and globally.

Rights-based approaches are shared by most development actors and non-governmental_organisations (NGOs) to achieve a positive transformation of power relations. There are two stakeholder groups in rights-based community development – the rights holders and the duty bearers (the institutions obligated to fulfil the holders' rights). The starting point is the global recognition, linked to the Universal Declaration of Human Rights in 1948, that all human beings inherently have certain rights. From a diaconal viewpoint, this can be linked easily to the theological understanding of all humankind being created in the image and likeness of God, having equal value and dignity, and thus deserving to be treated well. In a diaconal context, this basic anthropology results in the idea that we are all equal in God's eyes, and we are obliged to care for each other as God has cared for humankind.

Rights-based approaches work to shift the paradigm away from charity and towards moral duties according to the international consensus on human rights. This includes an emphasis on governments as duty bearers towards their citizens, and advocacy towards official political authorities, demanding them to fulfil their legal obligations. Thus, people living under conditions of poverty and marginalisation are not simple recipients of help and support, but right-holders and actors. This change from a needs-based to a rights-based understanding has been decisive for both secular and diaconal community development. The question to be posed is whether a rights-based approach can overcome the dichotomy between the partners involved in the development process. What change does naming the 'marginalised and poor' as 'right-holders' – where the former 'donors' become 'duty bearers' instead of charitable actors – actually bring for the people affected?

Taking a starting point in a rights-based approach supports the idea that all humankind is sharing joint values and joint goals, and supports sustainable development for all through cooperation, interconnectivity, and mutuality. The joint values relate to the unique value of every human being and all creation, clearly linked to the humanistic basis, lying behind the global human rights and SDG agenda. Based on such a value evolves the *goal* of 'leaving no one behind' which, in the context of diakonia, includes fight for justice, care for creation and neighbourly love.[22]

Rights-based community development practice integrates advocacy and political work with the goal of empowering and supporting poor and marginalised people to become agents and active citizens participating in the development both on an individual and a communal basis. Scholars such as Amartya Sen have nevertheless emphasised that increasing human agency and promoting human rights is not enough.[23] There is also a need for supportive social environments, such as economic facilities and social opportunities, political freedom and access to health and education, which are needed *before* people can exercise their individual freedom. Civil society actors, such as churches and faith communities, have the potential to be important partners for the establishment and maintenance of such a 'civic space', where people are being empowered and experience supportive social environments. Although partnership on all levels is underlined by the SDG agenda, little reference is given towards civil society and non-profit actors and religious actors as potential partners in achieving the global goals. The SDG focus is on governments, trade, technology and finance actors. Only SDG Target 16.7 explicitly names civil society actors as potentially relevant partners.

The Value and Contribution of a Diaconal Approach to Creating 'Just and Inclusive Communities'

There is an increasing affirmative attitude towards religious actors by national and international authorities,[24] based on a fairly instrumental understanding of

---

[22] Church of Norway, *Plan.*

[23] Amartya Sen, *Development as Freedom* (New York: Alfred Knopf, 1999).

[24] Cf. United Nations, United Nations Inter-Agency Task Force on Engaging Faith-Based Actors for Sustainable Development (2021) and PaRD (International Partnership on Religion and Sustainable Development) (2021). More than 80 % of the global population affiliate with a religion, and religious actors contribute significantly to sustainable development around the world. Cf. Rudelmar Bueno de Faria, Diakonia as Public Service and Public Witness', in: In: Dietrich, S., et al., *The Diaconal Church* (Oxford: Regnum Books, 2019), 27-40.

religion. Over and above such an instrumental understanding of the role faith and religion can play, I want to delve into a few aspects of religious/diaconal agency which in themselves, intrinsically, can be valuable for the development of just and inclusive communities, and thereby contribute to the achievement of the SDGs. The term 'added value' is sometimes used when it comes to the description of community development driven by faith-based actors, where the religious identity, motivation, or way of performing the respective activity is connected to the religious identity of the organisation or actor. It is difficult to define precisely, and even more so to measure, what such an 'added value' might imply. The term can be misleading when it suggests that diaconal/faith-based action is better than similar action performed by non-diaconal actors. I would therefore suggest replacing the term 'added value' with the term 'intrinsic values', helping to outline some of the main aspects and specificities of faith-based actors and diaconal service.

Diaconal Actors as Grass Root Actors

In times when NGOs and externally funded development projects come and go, governments often are unstable, and religious actors often remain part of the communities, enduring hope and shared purpose. 'Faith-based organisations often reach deep into inaccessible or remote populations. In many places, communities trust religious authorities who have credibility, strong moral influence, and the ability to influence how people think and act. Based on this trust and credibility, religious leaders and institutions have a strong convening and mobilising power amongst communities, which is critical for education and promoting social cohesion.'[25] Especially during the pandemic in 2020 and 2021, political and governmental authorities realised that cooperating with civil society organisations, as churches and other religious stakeholders, is decisive to reach those who are 'furthest behind'. Faith-based local actors have been present during the whole pandemic, close to the needs and struggles of the people and, at times, have the possibility to adjust long-term development projects into acute humanitarian help when the crisis hits the people, since they are already present and established with infrastructures and services, locally. Thus, churches and faith-based organisations on the one hand have the potential to contribute, under difficult circumstances and conditions where other actors strive or fail, as grass-root actors with knowledge of the local people and situation. On the other hand, we know that sometimes the same actors are part of structured power and thus carry the risk to become part of the problem. Therefore, education and cooperation for good governance need to be a part of all cooperation.

[25] Chad Rimmer and Julia Brümmer, 'Diakonia and the Sustainable Development agenda: Trends and Crucial Concerns', in: *International Handbook on Ecumenical Diakonia*, Godwin Ampony et.al. (eds.) (Oxford: Regnum, 2021), 372-377, 373.

Strengthening of Civil Society through Strengthening of Faith-based Actors' Contribution to Social Capital

Institutions such as NORAD, the Norwegian Agency for Development Cooperation, have assured their strengthened support to civil society organisations,[26] emphasising that intensive engagement of civil society is decisive to reach the sustainable development goals of 'leaving no one behind' and 'realising human rights for all'. This reflects an awareness that the SDGs can be achieved only if nations and governments, all groups within societies, and individuals join hands in this endeavour.

The German evangelical church, EKD, has discussed critically the role of the churches when it comes to the fulfilment of the SDG agenda, also questioning a predominantly materialistic understanding of how the Agenda 2030 can be fulfilled.[27] The EKD raises profound questions about the need for a value basis when it comes to development, and the demand for a fundamental change of culture and values within societies 'in which attentiveness to creation, the needs of other people and future generations, as well as reflecting upon the value of life above and beyond economic growth and consumption, gain importance.'[28]

Holistic Approach to Development

One of the most significant characteristics of the SDGs, compared to the Millenium Goals, is the Agenda's emphasis that all the goals are connected and integrated, interdependent and cross-cutting. This implies a recognition that social, economic and environmental development cannot happen without addressing issues of gender equality, poverty elimination, quality education, climate and good governance.

Such a holistic approach easily connects with a diaconal approach, highlighting that diakonia means 'serving the whole human person'.[29] From a theological viewpoint, one is also constantly reminded to remember that

---

[26] In the preface to Norad, *Norad's Support to Civil Society: Guiding Principle* (2018), 1, this is highlighted: 'A strong civil society is a key feature of any democratic social order and a goal in its own right. Civil society is key to ensuring public engagement in defining, implementing and monitoring strategies at all levels, for achieving sustainable development targets. Civil society plays a key role in monitoring and holding authorities accountable, in challenging power structures, setting the agenda and developing policy, and bringing people together around a common agenda to exert influence for a democratic society. Not least, civil society plays an important role in delivering services to marginalised groups and individuals, who are subject to discrimination or live in fragile or humanitarian settings. This work is demanding and takes time.'

[27] EKD (2018), *"Lent to Us is the Star on Which We Live". The Agenda 2030: A Challenge to the Churches* (Hannover: EKD, 2018).

[28] EKD (2018), 25.

[29] Kjell Nordstokke, *Serving the Whole Person: The Practice and Understanding of Diakonia* (Minneapolis: Lutheran University Press, 2010).

diakonia is not primarily a human achievement or obligation, but also a part of God's mission, and God's plan to reconcile humankind and the whole cosmos. 'The trend towards integrated indivisibility affirms that the SDGs can be a pathway for people of faith to live out their vocation in civil society within the horizon of shalom, or sustainable peace.'[30]

Engaging in sustainable development is not something new for the churches and diaconal actors. Nevertheless, the Agenda 2030 offers the possibility for churches and church-related actors to have a fresh look at their own sustainable development goals and perceptions.[31]

Conclusion

In this chapter, I have tried to show the close relationship between the SDG agenda and the way diaconal actors understand their identity and mission. I have also elaborated on some of the dilemmas and challenges of diaconal and sustainable development theories and practices.

Diaconal stakeholders can make visible the potential that lies in a cooperation with faith-based actors locally and remind duty bearers and all other stakeholders that people should have the right themselves to define what is a good life. Faith-based actors should also remind other actors that not all development necessarily can be counted and measured numerally, but that it is also experienced and perceived individually and communally, in a holistic way.

This chapter did not focus especially on the link between the diaconal goal of 'care for creation', and the SDGs focus on eliminating climate change. This would be the task of a separate chapter. To join all our efforts to 'leave no one behind', to create a better world- together-, there is a need to think in terms of an ecologically interdependent work. All humankind and all creation are interdependent and interwoven, and the global crisis can only be addressed jointly. The 2020 pandemic and the climate crisis, leading into natural disasters and catastrophic living conditions for people all over the world, serve as a reminder that leaving no one behind implies care for the whole creation.

---

[30] Rimmer and Brümmer, 'Diakonia', 374.

[31] Within the Lutheran World Federation, the project 'Waking the Giant' is an interesting example of how churches encounter and get inspired through the SDGs. Cf. LWF: https://wakingthegiant.lutheranworld.org/ (accessed 5.5.2021). 'Waking the giant' works on the provision of tools and materials and exchange of experiences between churches through relating their work to the SDG agenda. The project helps to give an overview and to assess how faith-based actors carry out activities which contribute directly to the achievement of the global Agenda 2030.

Bibliography

Bright, Liam Kofi; Malinsky, Daniel and Thompson, Morgan, 'Causally Interpreting Intersectionality Theory', *Philosophy of Science*, 83:1 (2016), 60–81.

Church of Norway, *Plan for Diakoni* (2020). https://kirken.no/globalassets/kirken.no/om-kirken/samfunnsansvar/diakoni/plan-for-diakoni_rev2020.pdf.

Church of Norway, *Plan for Diakonia* (2007). https://kirken.no/globalassets/kirken.no/church-of-norway/plan_diakonia2_english.pdf.

Crenshaw, Kimberley, 'Demarginalizing the Intersection of Race and Sex: A Black Feminist Critique of Antidiscrimination Doctrine, Feminist Theory and Antiracist Politics', *University of Chicago Legal Forum,* Issue 1, Article 8 (1989), 139-167.

Decker, Corrie and McMahon, Elisabeth, *The Idea of Development in Africa: A History* (Cambridge: Cambridge University Press, 2021).

De Faria, Rudelmar Bueno, 'Diakonia as Public Service and Public Witness', in: S. Dietrich, S, K. Jørgensen, K. K. Korslien and K Nordstokke (eds.), *The Diaconal Church* (Oxford, Regnum Books (2019), 27-40.

Dietrich, Stephanie, 'Reflections on Core Aspects of Diaconal Theory', in: S. Dietrich, K. Jørgensen, K. K. Korslien and K Nordstokke (eds.), *Diakonia as Christian Social Practice: An Introduction* (Oxford: Regnum, 2014), 13-27.

EKD, '*Lent to Us is the Star on Which We Live'. The Agenda 2030: A Challenge to the Churches.* A Discussion Paper authored by the Advisory Commission of the EKD on Sustainable Development (Hannover: EKD, 2018).

Ham, Carlos, 'Ecumenical Chronicle Colombo: Theological Perspectives on Diakonia in the Twenty-First Century', *The Ecumenical Review*, 64:3 (2012), 383-392.

Myers, Brian, *Walking with the Poor: Principles and Practices of Transformational Development*, 2nd d. (Maryknoll: Orbis, 2011).

Nissen, Johannes, 'Creating a Space for the Others. The Marginalized as a Challenge to Diaconia and Church: A Theological Perspective', *Diaconia. Journal for the Study of Christian Social Practice*, 5:1 (2014), 31-46.

Nordstokke, Kjell: *Serving the Whole Person: The Practice and Understanding of Diakonia* (Minneapolis: Lutheran University Press, 2010).

Norad, *Norad's Support to Civil Society: Guiding Principles* (Oslo: Norway, 2018). https://www.norad.no/om-bistand/publikasjon/2018/norads-support-to-civil-society-guiding-principles.

Nygaard, Marianne Rodriguez, 'Reflective Practice of Diaconia from the Margins: Ecclesiological and Professional Implications', *Diaconia. Journal for the Study of Christian Social Practice*, 8:2 (2017), 166-187.

PaRD, International Partnership on Religion and Sustainable Development (2021), https://www.partner-religion-development.org.

Rimmer, Chad and Brümmer, Julia, 'Diakonia and the Sustainable Development Agenda: Trends and Crucial Concerns'', *International Handbook on Ecumenical Diakonia*, Godwin Ampony, Martin Büscher, Beate Hofmann, Félicité Ngnintedem, Dennis Solon, Dietrich Werner (eds.) (Oxford: Regnum, 2021), 372-377.

Sen, Amartya, *Development as Freedom* (New York: Alfred Knopf, 1999).

Standing, Guy, 'The Precariat: Why it Needs Deliberative Democracy' (2012). https://www.opendemocracy.net/en/precariat-why-it-needs-deliberative-democracy/#.

United Nations, United Nations Inter-Agency Task Force on Engaging Faith-Based Actors for Sustainable Development (2012). https://jliflc.com/organizations/united-nations-inter-agency-task-force-on-engaging-faith-based-actors-for-sustainable-development.

Winker, Gabriele and Degele, Nina, *Intersektionalität. Zur Analyse sozialer Ungleichheiten*. 2. unveränderte Auflage (Bielefeld: Transcript Verlag, 2010).

Part Three

Social Practice and Diakonia

In What Ways Can the Church Function as a Generator for Inclusive and Sustainable Communities? A Case Study on What Role the Local Congregation Plays in Two Different Urban Communities

Silje K. Andreassen and Kjersti G. Norheim

Introduction

Norway is a long-stretched country with 5.3 million inhabitants. As much as 82% of the population lives in some sort of community or *tettsted*.[1] There are approximately 1,000 different communities in Norway, and one thing they all have in common is that they have a church in their proximity.

Church of Norway (CoN) is the Evangelical-Lutheran majority church in Norway. It is constitutionally defined as a nationwide 'folk church', geographically divided into 1,205 parishes. In 2017, CoN went from being a state church to becoming a legal entity separated from the state administration.[2] This, in addition to a more secular and multicultural population, has led CoN to recreate its role.

CoN's Plan for diakonia[3] was revised in 2020, and the plan now highlights the 2030 Agenda for Sustainable Development, with its 17 sustainable development goals (SDGs). The SDGs function as a useful framework to understand the church's role and responsibility in the local and nationwide community, and to develop CoN's interaction with public services, organisations, and institutions. In the context of this book SDG 16, that aims to 'build effective, accountable and inclusive institutions at all levels',[4] is highlighted and is the inspiration also for this article.

According to the plan for diakonia, CoN aims at working together with *all people of good will* to make both sustainable and inclusive communities. But

---

[1] Statistics Norway, Population and land area in urban settlements (2020). A *tettsted* in Norway is understood to be a place with at least 200 inhabitants within a certain geographical area; United Nations Statistics Division, Definition of "urban" (2005).

[2] For a brief overview (in Norwegian) see Government of Norway, Den norske kirke (2021).

[3] Church of Norway, Plan for Diakoni (2020).

[4] United Nations Department of Economic and Social Affairs: The 17 Goals (2015).

what part *does* the congregation play in urban communities today? We wanted to see *how* the interaction between congregations and other actors takes place in urban settings with the purpose of building inclusive and sustainable communities.

This chapter is based on an empirical qualitative study lasting from May through December 2020, in two different CoN congregations.[5] Both public and private actors were seen as relevant partners, and our informants referred to partners such as school leaders, a leader of a volunteer centre, a leader of a local history association, and a musician. In both places the church seemed to play a vital role in defining the identity of the community and, fascinatingly enough, several of the partners with whom the church interacted also pointed out that the worship played an important role locally. This last finding led us into a discussion of how space may be produced when different actors are participating with their variety of expressions in a worship.

After presenting the method we have used in the study, we will give a short presentation of the data material before presenting two main findings. In the last part of the article, we will discuss the findings in the light of theories on linking social capital, that are derived from Robert Putnam's theory on social capital, and a spatial theory based on Henry Lefebvre's Production of Space, further developed by Kaia Rønsdal and Edward Soja.

What Did We Do?

The question that led us into the project, was this: In what ways do local churches interact with the local partners in building inclusive and sustainable communities in urban villages? To find out more about that we used the method of best practice. We started out by asking the Bishops' Conference to point us in the direction of congregations where the church and the local community interact well. We received more than 30 candidates. We then narrowed them down to two by using selection criteria such as geography, demography, gender and the minister's time of employment. We wanted to interview ministers who had been working for at least two to three years, because the ministers were our starting point in mapping out relations between the church and other local actors. We finally decided on two congregations that we have given the fictitious names Dal and Berg. The interviewees in the study are anonymous and the names of the places and congregations are, therefore, anonymised.

Visiting Dal and Berg we first interviewed the main ministers using semi-structured interviews.[6] We made an interview guide with open ended questions

---

[5] The data collection and analysis was done with funding from the Olavstipend (scholarship for priests); see Church of Norway, Olavstipend til forskning på urbane kirker (2019).

[6] Trine Anker, *Analyse i praksis. En håndbok for masterstudenter* (Oslo: Cappelen Damm Akademisk, 2020), 38.

so that during the interview we could follow up with new questions when the interviewee introduced topics that we found relevant to the research. In these interviews we mapped local institutions and individuals, both volunteers and professionals, that were important partners for the ministers in their work. By also interviewing public and private partners from the local society, we aimed at getting a broader and fuller description of how the church works to build inclusive and sustainable communities locally. These interviews also taught us more about how the local community perceives the interaction with the local church.

In Berg, we interviewed the principal at the local school and two volunteers: a local musician and a person from the local history association. In Dal, we interviewed the principal of the local primary school, the leader of the volunteer centre and a colleague of the minister recently employed in the congregation. We ended each field trip by interviewing the main ministers a second time. This gave us the opportunity to dig deeper and broaden our understanding. Altogether, we did ten interviews. In addition, we have observation notes, material from the homepages of the two congregations and other written material that we collected whilst there. All interviews were conducted in Norwegian. We have translated the citations used in this chapter into English.

After collecting the material, we entered the process of analysing the data material using an abductive approach.[7] In order to get a better understanding of the material, we searched for theories that could help us deepen the understanding of the topic under investigation and extract meaning from the data.[8] In this last phase of the project we also met with both of the main ministers again. Finally, we met with the two ministers to reflect on the findings from the material. This last step was inspired by the method of action research as at this point we, both being ministers within CoN, stepped out of the role of a researcher and took part in the conversation.

---

[7] Alan Bryman, *Social Research Methods* (Oxford University Press, 2012), 401.

[8] Abductive analysis is to move back and forth between theory and data. We did not have a fixed theory when we started up but after analysing the data, we investigated different theories that could help us interpret our findings. We then listened again to recorded interviews with new theoretical insight to see if there were important data we had missed. We then considered the theory again. The method is also related to pragmatism according to Tavory and Timmermanns: 'Inspired by early American pragmatism, and especially the work of Charles S. Peirce, we view research as recursively moving back and forth between a set of observations and a theoretical generalization.' Iddo Tavory and Stefan Timmermans, *Abductive Analysis: Theorizing Qualitative Research,* Available by: VitalSource Bookshelf (The University of Chicago Press, 2014).

The Context of the Two Local Churches

Berg and Dal are situated in different parts of Norway, and they are both suburbs to a city. Berg is part of a city of about 200,000 inhabitants, and Dal is part of a city of about 50,000 inhabitants. The two congregations belong to different dioceses. About 75% of the population in Berg and about 65% of Dal's population are members of CoN. In comparison, 68% of the Norwegian population as a whole were members of CoN in 2020.[9]

Both Berg and Dal have gone through considerable changes during the last 30 years as they have developed from rural to urban areas. According to the musician in Berg, 'It has been a huge change. The area is not recognizable.' Berg and Dal contain a mixture of detached houses, townhouses, and apartment buildings. Our interviewees point to the fact that within the population of both places you can find people from the wealthy middle class and the working class, meaning that in both places you will find rich and poor living in the proximity, yet they are separated.

Finding 1: 'We Aim at the Same Goal'

Both local communities were characterised by the fact that they had developed from a rural to a highly urbanised context in a short amount of time. It was almost as if they had gone through a metamorphosis. The leader of the volunteer centre at Dal said: 'This used to be a rural area, but now everything is turned upside-down.' To our confusion, despite these changes, both places seemed to have a strong identity. The colleague of the minister at Dal underlined this by saying she 'liked communities [like this], communities with such an identity.' She added: 'Where I grew up we didn't have such an identity'. The church worker at Dal led us in the direction of theories on the *local character* of a place[10] and *place-identity*. The *local character* refers to features that make it possible to distinguish this specific place from another. The *identity* of a place somehow seems to be a variable that might differ in strength.

The notion that the identity of the place, its local character, can affect the way we interact with partners in the local community, was first pointed out to us by the minister at Berg. The first time we met him, he introduced himself as a minister by telling us about the different *places* he had served. It became clear

---

[9] Statistics Norway, Den norske kirke (2021).

[10] Place-identity of the place might be the most exact term when it comes to describing local character. It is to be understood as 'those features of nature, culture and people that are used in the discourses and classifications of science, politics, cultural activism, regional marketing, tourism, governance and political or religious regionalization to distinguish one place from others.' See Jianchao Peng, Dirk Strijker and Qun Wu, 'Place Identity: How Far Have We Come in Exploring its Meaning?' *Frontiers in Psychology*, 11:294 (2020), 1-19. Although place-identity of the place is a more accurate term, we will in the following replace it with the term that has a wider understanding, namely: *local* or *urban character*.

that the different places had both formed him as a minister and led him into different networks. It seemed important for the ministers to learn as much about the local character as possible. The minister at Dal told us how he tried to *tune in*. This expression originates from a time when you had to tune in the radio to a specific wavelength in order to get the right signals. The minister at Dal used the expression to explain how he seeks to *tune in* to both the place and the people where he serves to find the right wavelength, so to speak. The minister at Berg described something similar when he told us: 'It is about loving the people and the identity of the place'. The minister at Dal added: 'We are called to love the place where we are, not to save it. That is our primary calling.'

The strength of the local character seemed to play an important role, also, in the interaction between the church and the local community. It was as if the identity of the place created some sort of common ground for the interaction. There seemed to be a correlation between the strength of the identity and the strength of the common ground to interact from.

Whilst the local character seemed strong both at Berg and Dal, there still seemed to be some tension within the communities. This became clear to us whilst visiting the local schools. Both principals made it clear that there was a tension between those who were well off when it comes to economic and material resources, and those less resourceful in terms of material resources. There also seemed to be a tension between different ethnicities and backgrounds. The kids seemed to be divided into *them* and *us*. The leader of the volunteer centre at Dal underlined the importance of creating meeting places for adults with different cultures as well, so there is reason to assume that this division also takes place in the community at large. Therefore, on meeting representatives from these multicultural communities we were curious about how they saw the church as a partner in building both inclusivity and sustainability.

Both principals talked about the differences they identified within the group of pupils. 'We are the district with the most public housing and the most child-welfare cases' said the principal at Dal, whereas at Berg the principal said: 'in this area there are a lot of families with low income, little or no education and no family around.' Then she added: 'The church has met these families in a good way.' She did not explain exactly what the church had done to meet these families, but she focused on how the church lent out rooms so that they could have school assemblies and she also underlined how the minister talked about social issues in his sermons.

The principal at Berg underlined that 'our focus is on the safety for the vulnerable families' and 'cooperation [with other local organisations such as the church] is crucial, especially for the single-parent families'. The principal at Dal said, 'Exclusion has huge expenses.' After explaining how the school focuses on inclusion he added: 'I feel the school and the church aim at the same goal.' Both principals seemed to consider the church as an important local partner when it comes to preventing exclusion and building inclusive communities. This corresponds with Principle 2 in the Universal Values behind the SDGs called *Leave No One Behind.*[11]

One of our main questions when entering the study was: How does the church interact with the local community? And since meeting points are important in building social networks, we were also curious about where the church and representatives of the local community met. To our surprise, the church and the actual church building seem to play a much more important role than we expected. 'The church is our neighbour', said the principal at Berg. 'We get to use the room. We get to use the equipment. It is great', she added. The musician at Berg and his band also wanted to use the church for their concerts. He said: 'It was obvious that I had to go there [to the church], because it is *my* church. I used to play here before the church was built.' At Dal, the location of the church played an important role. 'I was fascinated by the location of the church', the church worker said, adding: 'It is central to a lot of what is happening at Dal.' In Dal, the leader of the volunteer centre invites other local leaders – including the principals, the minister, the leader of the sports club and the leader of the scout group – to a forum for the local community where they share challenges and joys, and discuss common causes.

As we saw earlier the interaction between different actors in the local community could be strengthened if they found common ground and that common ground could be created by a strong local character. Another important factor to promote interaction is to create meeting places. We found that the interaction with actors from the local community both at Berg and Dal seemed to consist of formal and informal interaction. We also found that, especially when it comes to informal interaction, there seemed to be a need for someone to initiate interaction between the partners. At Berg, we saw that the minister was the one who often initiated interaction. He worked to a pattern that reminded us of the children's game connect-the-dots. For instance, when the lead singer of the local band asked to have their concert in the church the minister, shortly after, invited the band to a yearly service. Similarly, he introduced the leader of the history association to the lunch meeting for the elders in church, and so on. The minister at Dal was a different type altogether. 'I am not one to start up things', he said. There already existed a defined meeting place at the forum for the local community at Dal, and both the principal at the local school and the leader of the volunteer centre seemed to be taking a lot of initiative. Therefore, the minister could live by what he called his rule, saying that the most important thing for the church is to simply show up.

Even if there were variations in who initiated the interaction, the church building seemed to play an important role. To sum up, we found that the interaction between the church and the local community seemed to be both formal and informal. In both cases we saw that there was a need for common

---

[11] United Nations Sustainable Development Group, Universal Values. Principle Two: Leave No One Behind (2021).

ground, and we also found that a strong local character could function as common ground for the interaction. The church building also enabled the church to function as a facilitator for the interaction. The local character, the church building and different initiators and participators made the church a partner in counteracting exclusion and enhancing inclusivity.

Finding 2: 'Without the Church Something is Missing'

The worship on Sunday morning is essential for most congregations within CoN. It is open for everyone, but still many people seem to find it difficult to participate. It is a common habit in Norwegian society that only the most eager Christians attend Sunday worship on a regular basis. The worship is often criticised for being boring and hard to understand with its old, liturgical language. When we started this study, asking in what way does the church interact with the local community, we did not expect the worship to play a key role. But we were wrong. In both Berg and Dal worship brings together the church and groups from the local community.

In Berg, the local history association and the congregation celebrate worship together outdoors once a year. This yearly worship is a fundamental part of the interaction between the church and the history association, along with the history association's contribution to the church magazine on a regular basis. The location of the open-air worship is an old farm in a forest nearby. The farm is owned and maintained by the history association. At the open-air worship the regular church seats are replaced by free seating in the grass, on rocks and on old chairs that are carried out from the buildings. The distinctions between host and guests are repealed. The organ is replaced by an accordion. The accordion is chosen with an intention of being more inclusive, as many might relate the organ with classic church music. Moreover, the psalms are chosen with the intention of being familiar for most of those attending. They celebrated baptism in this open-air worship once and volunteers from the history association made a baptismal font. The pastor brought hot water from the church and mixed it with colder water from a nearby lake, so the water was at a perfect temperature for the baby.

In Dal, a fundamental part of the interaction between church and a local elementary school is a yearly worship in December. School worship in church during December has a long tradition and is common in Norway. Parents may ask for exemption for their children due to religious freedom.[12] From time to time a debate arises on how the tradition of school worship is contributing to increased differences and creating distance between children in classes and neighbourhoods. Those who support the school worship tradition often emphasise the school's responsibility to facilitate occasions for learning and experiencing elements from the Norwegian Christian cultural heritage.

[12] Utdanningsdirektoratet, Skolegudstjenester (2019).

According to the principal at Dal elementary school only half of the student group attended the December worship some years ago when he started as a principal. His perception was that the worship lacked enthusiasm amongst teachers and children, and many had exemption. The principal wanted to make the December worship an occasion for building community and tolerance and to share joy and creativity. First, he asked the minister if they could remove the word 'worship' and rename 'school worship' to 'Christmas gathering'. The minister agreed on this. Secondly, they invited the municipal music and cultural school to participate in the Christmas gathering. The municipal music and cultural school offers teaching in music and dance to the school's students free of charge. Including the municipal music and cultural school allowed more children to be involved in the Christmas gathering preparations, and the gathering was more influenced than before by the children's creative gifts. The Christmas gathering is still located in the church and the minister is sharing the gospel of Christmas, leading a prayer and the blessing. There are still a few parents asking for exemption for their children. But far more children are participating and far more parents than before show up in church to see their children perform, although many of them are not members of the church. The principal says: 'When people are good at cooperating it is a benefit for the local community. Because then different things are better linked.' And he underlines the role of the church when he says:

> In a community where people are constantly moving in and moving out it is important to have a fundament of stability that helps us focus. There is a need for structure and cooperation. Without the church something is missing.

The principal finds that in a local community every organisation, governmental and non-governmental, needs to interact to make the community sustainable and inclusive for all. He says the school's interaction with the church is one of many interactions that builds this local community by increasing knowledge and tolerance amongst citizens with different cultural and religious backgrounds. The interaction between school and church would most likely have died within a matter of years had the minister not held a dialogue with the school to recreate school worship into something new and viable.

Acting as Partners – Building Social Capital

Our initial research question was: In what way does the church interact with the local community to help build inclusive and sustainable communities? At the two places we visited we found that the church and the local community interacted in different ways. In each place the church seemed to play a different yet equally important role. The identity of a place seemed to play a role in creating common ground in both places. At Berg, the minister worked with a local musician who told us how the place where the church now stood used to be his playground as a child and that this played an important role in why and how his interaction with the minister and the church started. The place and the church seemed to be intertwined for him, and he expressed a sense of belonging to both. The leader of the history association also focused on the place, the history of the place and the identity of it. Again, we saw that the local character seemed to create the common ground for the interaction to build on. We did not find, however, whether the identity of the place was strong because of the interaction, or if the interaction was made possible by the fact that the identity of the place was strong.

Another of our findings, especially by the schools, was that the church seemed to be perceived as a fitting partner to help prevent exclusion. None of the principals elaborated *how* the church worked to prevent exclusion, but one of them pointed to what the minister said in his sermons. Another great asset to the church was the church building which made it possible for the church to facilitate meeting places both for the local schools, and also for the entire local community. Creating meeting places so that people in the local community gather is of great importance when it comes to building sustainable and inclusive societies.

In trying to get a better understanding of what we learnt from the two places we visited, we examined theory on social capital and, in particular, what has been called linking social capital. It was the lead social scientist in the World Bank's Development Research Group, Michael Woolcock, who introduced the term 'linking social capital'.[13] Linking social capital builds on Robert Putnam's theory on social capital and refers to 'relations between individuals and groups in different social strata in a hierarchy where power, social status and wealth are accessed by different groups.'[14] Linking social capital then, introduces the importance of how institutional power can both impede and facilitate networking amongst persons with different backgrounds. Robert Putnam and David E. Campbell found – with data from the USA – that religious involvement is positively correlated with social trust and active citizenship.[15] A study using Norwegian data found correlation between religious commitment and some forms of voluntary work, particularly social and health-related work, including international involvement.[16] Rogers and Konieczny, drawing upon a wide range of studies from around the world, found that a congregation's conscious orientations of bridging social and other divides are crucial in order to overcome the individual's class unconsciousness. This unconsciousness implies that one

[13] Tristan Claridge, 'Functions of Social Capital – Bonding, Bridging, Linking', *Social Capital Research* (2018).
[14] Claridge, 'Functions'.
[15] Robert Putnam and David Campell, *American Grace. How Religion Divides and Unites Us* (New York: Simon & Schuster, 2012).
[16] Dag Wollebæk, *Religion og sosial kapital: Hva viser internasjonale spørreundersøkelser?* (Oslo/Bergen: Senter for forskning på sivilsamfunn og frivillig sector, 2013), 113.

prefers relating to one's own kind. Congregations without adequate consciousness – and corresponding ways of working – might reinforce various forms of stratification in their communities.[17]

When meeting places are created and individuals meet, they might get a better understanding of one another and power differences might weaken. If the church, then, is able to facilitate meeting places for people with different backgrounds, and different social and economic resources, it might play an important role in building linking social capital and in so doing, help to develop the local community, empower those with fewer material resources, and help weaken power differences. We saw signs that this might be happening both at Dal and at Berg. What intrigued us the most, though, was witnessing how important the worship seemed to be in achieving this.

Acting as Partners – Worship as a Space of Inclusion

We found it helpful to use spatial theory to understand worship as a place and tool for interaction between the church and the history association in Berg and the school in Dal. Kaia Rønsdal has developed the use of spatial analysis based on Henry Lefebvre's production of space, and shows how this method is useful in diakonia.[18] Basically, she uses Lefebvre's three levels of space: The first level, perceived space, focuses on how each one of us perceives our social surroundings. The second level, conceived space, describes how a space is understood and represented, for instance, by a map, a picture, a plan, or an image. The third level, lived space, is the wide range of how the space is experienced; what happens in the encounter of different individuals or groups in this space. In our research we also looked to Edward Soja, a postmodern political geographer who, like Rønsdal, builds on Lefebvre's three levels of space whilst analysing space and society during urbanisation of cities on the west coast of the US. Soja uses the terms 'Firstspace', 'Secondspace' and 'Thirdspace'.[19]

In the open-air worship in Berg, the place – the specific location, Firstspace – is more open than in the church, and limits between guests and hosts are weaker. The history association's connection to the old houses and the surrounding area, their restoration and love and future hope for this place – Secondspace – meets the worship, singing, praying, and the gospel of the church. And when these two

---

[17] Megan Rogers and Mary Ellen Konieczny, *Does Religion Always Help the Poor? Variations in Religion and Social Class in the West and Societies in the Global South,* Palgrave Communications.

[18] Kaia S. Rønsdal, 'Adressing the Spatial Turn in Diaconia', in: Godwin Ampony, Martin Büscher, Beate Hofmann, Félicité Ngnintedem, Dennis Solon and Dietrich Werner (eds.), *International Handbook on Ecumenical Diakonia* (Oxford: Regnum Books International, 2021), 515-519.

[19] Edward Soja, 'Thirdspace: Expanding the Scope of Geograghical Imagination', in: Alan Read (ed.), *Architecturally Speaking: Ppractices of Art, Architecture, and the Everyday* (London: Routledge, 2000), 13-30.

worlds meet and blend in with each other, when they equally affect each other and own the space together, a Thirdspace may happen. The baptism water becomes a symbol of the Thirdspace that happens in the open-air worship. Water from the church building is mixed with water from the lake. When the water is mixed you cannot separate the hot church water from the cold lake water, but they are both in there and have reached the perfect, not too hot and not too cold, temperature.

In the December gathering in Dal, the children's dance and music meet the holy place of the church with its altar and altarpiece; the church liturgy with gospel, prayer and hymns; and the minister wearing his special liturgical garment and preaching of Jesus. The children bring with them not only singing and dancing but also their different family backgrounds and religions, and their thoughts and images of the church. When the children's (and the teacher's) Secondspace meet the minister's (and the church musician's) Secondspace in the December gathering and blend in together, a new space, a Thirdspace, may happen. Borders between hosts and guests are removed. The children own the room and are responsible for what fills the gathering to the same extent as the minister. In the frame of the gathering it is possible for the children to act on a more equal basis.

A key to open a Thirdspace is that those involved are acting as partners. Each partner needs to be aware of how power and resources are distributed, and strive to balance out the inequality. This idea of even partnership corresponds to the idea behind the SDGs. In order to reach the goals, we all, privileged and marginalised, need to act as partners and cooperate.[20] We find that the church contributes to an inclusive and sustainable community when it, in partnership with the school, invites children from the local community – with their different backgrounds and religions, some with many resources and some with fewer – to bring their creative gifts to a meeting together with the cultural and poetic gifts of the old church tradition. We find that the church contributes to an inclusive and sustainable community when it joins with the local history association and brings worship to the old farm, a place that carries important parts of the community's history, represents maintenance of historic buildings, and is in the middle of nature and God's creation.

Bibliography

Anker, Trine, *Analyse i praksis. En håndbok for masterstudenter* (Oslo: Cappelen Damm Akademisk, 2020).

[20] Stephanie Dietrich, 'A Diaconal Approach to Community Development: Exploring Religious Resources for Creating Just and Inclusive Communities', in Haugen, Hans Morten; Kivle, Benedicte Tveter; Addy, Tony; Kessel, Terese Bue and Klaasen, John (eds.), *Developing Just and Inclusive Communities. Challenges for Diakonia and Social Work* (Oxford: Regnum, 2022), 95-110.

Bryman, Alan, *Social Research Methods* (Oxford: Oxford University Press, 2012).

Claridge, Tristan, 'Functions of Social Capital: Bonding, Bridging, Linking', *Social Capital Research* (2018); https://www.socialcapitalresearch.com/wp-content/uploads/2018/11/Functions-of-Social-Capital.pdf.

Church of Norway, Olavstipend til forskning på urbane kirker (2019); https://kirken.no/nb-NO/om-kirken/aktuelt/olavstipend%20til%20forskning%20p%C3%A5%20urbane%20kirker.

Church of Norway, Plan for Diakoni (2020); https://kirken.no/globalassets/kirken.no/om-kirken/samfunnsansvar/diakoni/plan-for-diakoni_rev2020.pdf.

Dietrich, Stephanie, 'A Diaconal Approach to Community Development: Exploring Religious Resources for Creating Just and Inclusive Communities', in: *Developing Just and Inclusive Communities. Challenges for Diakonia and Social Work*, Haugen, Hans Morten; Kivle, Benedicte Tveter; Addy, Tony; Kessel, Terese Bue; and Klaasen, John (eds.) (Oxford: Regnum, 2022), 95-110.

Government of Norway, Den norske kirke (2017); https://www.regjeringen.no/no/tema/tro-og-livssyn/den-norske-kirke/id1217.

Hauge, Åshild Lappegard, 'Identity and Place: A Critical Comparison of Three Identity Theories', *Architectural Science Review*, 50:1 (2007), 44-51.

Peng, Jianchao, Dirk Strijker and Qun Wu, 'Place Identity: How Far Have We Come in Exploring its Meaning?', *Frontiers in Psychology*, 11:294 (2020), 1-19; https://doi.org/10.3389/fpsyg.2020.00294.

Putnam, Robert and David Campbell, *American Grace. How Religion Divides and Unites us* (New York: Simon & Schuster, 2012).

Rogers, Megan and Mary Ellen Konieczny, *Does Religion Always Help the Poor? Variations in Religion and Social Class in the West and Societies in the Global South,* Palgrave Communications; https://www.nature.com/articles/s41599-018-0135-3.pdf.

Rønsdal, Kaia S., 'Addressing the Spatial Turn in Diaconia', in: *International Handbook on Ecumenical Diakonia,* Godwin Ampony; Martin Büscher; Beate Hofmann; Félicité Ngnintedem; Dennis Solon and Dietrich Werner (eds.) (Oxford: Regnum Books International, 2021), 515-519.

Soja, Edward, 'Thirdspace: Expanding the Scope of Geographical Imagination', in: Alan Read (ed.), *Architecturally Speaking: Practices of Art, Architecture, and the Everyday* (London: Routledge, 2000), 13-30.

Statistics Norway, Population and Land Area in Urban Settlements (2020); https://www.ssb.no/en/befolkning/folketall/statistikk/tettsteders-befolkning-og-areal.

Statistics Norway, Den norske Kirke (2021); https://www.ssb.no/kultur-og-fritid/religion-og-livssyn/statistikk/den-norske-kirke.

Tavory, Iddo and Timmermans, Stefan, *Abductive Analysis: Theorizing Qualitative Research*, Available by: VitalSource Bookshelf (The University of Chicago Press, 2014).

United Nations Department of Economic and Social Affairs, The 17 Goals (2015); https://sdgs.un.org/goals.

United Nations Statistics Division, Definition of 'urban' (2005); https://unstats.un.org/unsd/demographic/sconcerns/densurb/Defintion_of%20Urban.pdf.

United Nations Sustainable Development Group, Universal Values. Principle Two: Leave No One Behind (2021); https://unsdg.un.org/2030-agenda/universal-values/leave-no-one-behind.

Utdanningsdirektoratet, Skolegudstjenester (2019); https://www.udir.no/regelverk-og-tilsyn/skole-og-opplaring/saksbehandling/skolegudstjenester.

Wollebæk, Dag, *Religion og sosial kapital: Hva viser internasjonale spørreundersøkelser?* (Oslo/Bergen: Senter for forskning på sivilsamfunn og frivillig sektor, 2013).

Lifezone Sport International: A Narrative of Diaconia Viewed through the Lens of Tangible Hope

Jeremy Wyngaard

Introduction

The aim of this chapter is to illustrate the essence of the term 'tangible hope' – a phrase previously used by me at The Fifth Biennial Conference for the International Society for the Research and Study of Diaconia and Christian Social Practice (ReDi) in Stockholm in 2014.[1] The title of the article was 'Diaconia under Pressure: The Church, Economics and Christian Social Practice'. Previously, I introduced the term in an article in the journal *Missionalia*, in 2015.[2] For me, the notion of tangible hope is deeply connected to human personality, character, identity and community, and it is undeniably relational. One can only serve others better in giving of oneself time, energy and resources to those who are in need.

Method

This chapter is grounded in reflexive thematic analysis (reflexive TA), 'an approach that is flexible enough to be compatible with both experiential and critical qualitative research'.[3] Central to a reflexive TA approach is the notion of reflexivity, or the importance of my clarification of the data. Within reflexive

---

[1] There are no accessible weblinks to the 'Program Paper Sessions' of the 2014 ReDi Conference.

[2] Jeremy Wyngaard, 'Missio Dei and Youth Ministry. Mobilizing Young People's Assets and Developing Relationships', *Missionalia*, 43:3 (2015), 410-424, 419.

[3] Virginia Braun and Victoria Clarke, 'One Size Fits All? What Counts as Quality Practice in (Reflexive) Thematic Analysis?', *Qualitative Research in Psychology*, 18:3 (2021), 328-352; see also Virginia Braun and Victoria Clarke, 'Using Thematic Analysis in Psychology', *Qualitative Research in Psychology*, 3:2 (2006), 77-101; and Virginia Braun and Victoria Clarke, 'Reflecting on Reflexive Thematic Analysis', *Qualitative Research in Sport, Exercise and Health*, 11:4 (2019), 589-597.

TA, analysis transpires because of, rather than despite, my subjectivity – my values, background, decisions, and interests.[4]

The reflexive TA approach for this chapter is based on completed questionnaires collected from twenty-three mostly former and some current coaches and volunteers connected with Lifezome Ministries International (LSI/LMI).[5]

There were four categories of informants:

- Coaches/volunteers (Informants 1 to 7)
- Networking partners (Informants 8 to 15)
- Parents (Informants 16 to 19)
- Players (Informants 20 to 23)

The questionnaires were divided into three main sections:[6]

- Questions on experiences
- Questions on motivations
- Questions on social impact

The main question that I will focus on and discuss is also a strategic question that I posed in the extensive questionnaires that I emailed to the twenty-three informants: 'How would you describe the notion of hope in relation to LMI's work?' In order to articulate the essence of tangible hope as a nuanced concept in diaconal studies, it was important to analyse each informant's responses, especially their responses to the main question.

During the coding and reflexive TA process, I compiled two tables, the first of which was based on where the word 'hope' appeared in answers to questions other than the main question. The second table of codes and themes was created to capture all responses to the main question.

Context

My voluntary community work is primarily done through LMI, the FBO that I founded in 1997. The organisation is still very active in the twin-suburb of Factreton-Kensington in Cape Town and currently has a sports-based ministry at one primary school (Wingfield Primary) where it facilitates the physical education programme for approximately 800 students per week. In 2006, LSI became the niche ministry of LMI, who tried to address the many challenges that our community was facing. We tackled issues such as hunger and education as a

[4] G Terry and N Hayfield, 'Conceptual Foundations of Thematic Analysis', in: *Essentials of Thematic Analysis*, ed. by Clara E. Hill and Sarah Knox (American Psychological Association, 2021), 4.

[5] Lifezone Ministries International (LMI) is synonymous with LSI.

[6] Michael J. Sup, *Sport and Development Volunteerism: A Phenomenological Inquiry of Volunteers' Experiences in a Salvadorian Program, PhD dissertation* (Ohio: The Patton College of Education of Ohio University, 2019), 19, demonstrated that questions of experiences, motivations and impact are vital for obtaining a holistic appreciation for community development sports-based research.

way to support destitute children in our neighbourhood until we started using sport, especially soccer, as a medium to promote the well-being of youth in primary schools in Factreton-Kensington.

This location was previously known as Windermere, a mixed area of informal home dwellers, sub-economic housing, and middle-class housing for mixed race people.[7] Most of the Factreton-Kensington schools struggle financially and have extremely limited, if any, resources to improve the physical condition of these learning institutions due to apartheid segregationist policies.[8] This is evidenced by 'no-fees' schools, such as WD Hendricks and the nearby Garden Village primary schools.[9]

Some of the informants confirm LSI's ministry context; notably, a Dutch volunteer from Nijmegen (worked 4.5 months in 2014):

> Sometimes I was really happy to see kids playing with a smile on your face but sometimes I heard about shootings and gangs which gave me anger. I realize how difficult it is to not fall into crime or a gang and thinking about that really makes me sad. A lot of those kids did not have a choice as for them it is normal to use violence to survive. I am happy I could contribute to a smile on their face and hopefully a better person.

This was also confirmed by a young Swedish volunteer (worked 3 months in 2015): '… I felt like what I did mattered to other people. It was also tough at times because the area where LSI operates is an area where a lot of people are experiencing hardships.' The assertion by the deputy principal of one of the schools (being in a collaboration with LSI since 2006) that 'Our area is saturated with gangsterism and drugs' is affirmed by scholarly literature.[10] Facing this situation, another Dutch youth (short-term volunteer in 2014) affirmed: '… it is important that young people from problem areas, through sport, can escape from their daily problems and have a view of a better life.'

It can be argued that the observed contextual phenomena as experienced by these informants, show that they understood the context of poverty[11] and violence within which they volunteered and where LMI does its daily ministry. Their lived experiences in our community create an important link in helping one to analyse many themes emanating from the research data. The research that

---

[7] Steffen Jensen, *Gangs, Politics & Dignity in Cape Town* (Johannesburg: Wits University Press, 2008), 46.

[8] Don Pinnock, *Gang Town* (Cape Town: Tafelberg, 2018), 12.

[9] Department of Basic Education, Western Cape no fee schools 2021 (2021), 18, 21; see also Department of Basic Education, School fees (2020).

[10] Pinnock, *Gang Town*, 89.

[11] Jeremy Gregory Wyngaard, *In Search of Root Causes of Poverty: Testing a Theological Perspective in Development Dialogues, PhD dissertation* (Stellenbosch: University of Stellenbosch, 2013) engages the root causes of poverty and also highlights some of the existential challenges that people in Cape Town face, especially the people in the Factreton-Kensington community where LSI is based.

follows here will principally focus on some of the essential comments made by most of the informants in each of the respective categories, in the quest to create codes and build relevant themes that would contribute to an investigation into the possible *isness* or essence of tangible hope.

Tangible Hope in a Context of Hopelessness

Informants (a local coach, a foreign volunteer, a parent, and two players) pointed to poverty, inequality, unemployment, and many other societal problems[12] that produce a sense of hopelessness. According to the survey, some informants from South Africa, Sweden, and the Netherlands could perceive a sense of hopelessness in the lives of some children in the schools or in the broader community where they were coaching. This does not mean that everyone or the entire community is in a hopeless position. However, what it really means is that some volunteers/coaches were able to interpret and internalise this experience of hopelessness of many children in the community where they served. Some of the answers from the survey discuss hopelessness in this way:

> [Hope is] the one thing that LMI offers. So many of the kids that the project reaches out to are without hope. LMI provided an opportunity for these kids to dream, to experience love and hope for a better tomorrow. (Local coach who is now a full-time teacher at one of our partnering schools.)

This point of moving from hopelessness to hope was reiterated by other informants: 'I think at that point, [in] the communities [that] we served, there was a lot of hopelessness due to many factors.' (Informant 3, a local volunteer.) Another used the term 'hopeless' when describing those that LSI sought to reach out to: 'I grew in love and compassion for the poor, marginalized and hopeless.' (Project coordinator.)

What these experiences demonstrate is that the reality of hopelessness opens up a consciousness and solidarity for those in need, whilst it also contributes to changing hopelessness into hope. In real terms, one could argue that this can lead to tangible hope. Such experiences also add to the personal development of coaches/volunteers and show how one's personhood could be positively affected when one responds, in hope, tp the seemingly hopeless condition of individuals or the broader community.[13] The tension between the individual and community needs to be kept in a creative manner. When an individual develops, the

---

[12] Watch the video trailer of hope of one of the LSI players who lives in tough conditions, highlighting the history of inequality in South Africa, at https://www.youtube.com/watch?v=xwwKgk7aS98.

[13] John Klaasen, 'Personhood and Inclusive Communities: Access to Justice for All', in Hans Morten Haugen, Benedicte Tveter Kivle, Tony Addy, Terese Bue Kessel and John Klaasen (eds), *Developing Just and Inclusive Communities. Challenges for Diakonia as Christian Social Practice and for Social Work* (Oxford: Regnum, 2022), 33-48.

community also grows. A just and peaceful community is as important as just and peaceful individuals because of the interaction between community and individuals. With regard to community, I refer to the formation of the individual self in relationships, and the notion of personhood is important in this regard. The self is never in isolation, but as a social being develops through interaction. The self is neither above the community nor suppressed to subordination or coerced into an identity that is alien to the self. The self develops in relation to other selves and chooses the good as the self in relationship with other selves.[14] This understanding of personhood resonates well with the notion of tangible hope which, I argue, is inherently relational. This might inspire everyone who responds, in hope, to the seemingly hopeless condition of individuals or the broader community.

What Is Hope?

Through the data coding process of the informants' returned questionnaires, I will present some of their perspectives where the word 'hope' was mentioned but where the questions did not directly ask anything related to the conceptualisation or their understanding of hope (Table 1 in my reflexive TA process). A brief analysis of the selected informants' comments, provides valuable insight into the task of trying to understand the essence of tangible hope. The lived experiences of the informants in relation to LMI, project strongly through their selection of words and emotions expressed in the questionnaires. Therefore, as one examines these comments, glimpses of the essence of tangible hope begin to appear. The following section will highlight some of the codes that support this essence of tangible hope.

I will now present some of their interpretations.

Two informants, a couple who are members of one of the networking partners, stated the following about their experiences when participating in the LMI project, and what they would tell others about LMI:

> There is a great feeling of purpose and hope. How it is possible to improve daily life for children. The importance of working together both within communities, but also between countries and people very far away. Very positive feelings, joyful and hopeful.
>
> It would be a great life opportunity for an organization and for individuals to grow and to share hope and joy, and to be a part of the work filled with purpose.

It would appear that this couple's responses of 'hope' show that there is synergy between purpose and hope, and that this contributes to the well-being ((SDG 3) of children and the exercising of their bodies and minds. There is also

[14] John Klaasen, 'Personhood'.

a communal spirit of working together locally and internationally, and the international cooperation is joyful and hopeful. They would recommend others to volunteer with LMI in order that volunteers grow and experience a sense of purpose, hope and joy at the organisation.

In her responses to the question, 'How would you describe the purpose and the impact of the work that LMI/LSI does?', a young Swedish networking partner (Informant 10) contributed the following:

> To help those who need help in any possible way, to help young people grow into the best versions of themselves and to spread hope. The impact on those who have met and been involved with the LMI project is clearly visible. The hope shining in the eyes of the children while they're running down the field chasing the ball. The impact I would describe is confidence encouraging, spreading hope and to see all persons' value and to help one another to build up each other from spirit to the full potential of a soccer player.

Tangible hope can be visualised or perceived when we interpret this young Swedish lady's response when describing the purpose and impact of LMI. Her response shows that LMI lends support to young people, provides opportunities for personal development and the fulfilment of one's potential, whilst it also requires volitional commitment and participation by others (coaches) to produce the hope that shines in the eyes of children who play sport at LMI. Another aspect of tangible hope drawn from her feedback implies that hope is contagious and encourages others to also be hope-givers. Hope has a distinct nature of being outward-looking and shared; it is about dreaming that anything is possible even in very difficult environments such as those within which LMI serves.

In addition, she described how she understood LMI, based on her encounters with the FBO since 2012:

> It is much more than just a project or an organisation. It is much more than just soccer or sports. LMI is hope, LMI is dreams and LMI is relations. Every time I've visited SA or a soccer team has visited Sweden I've felt something special and I know a lot of people can agree with me. It's like an atmosphere. No matter what language you speak, or don't speak and no matter how good you are at sports or soccer. You are welcomed and you are needed. LMI is impressive.

The essence of tangible hope is further observed in the feedback of Informants 10 and 11 to the question regarding how she would describe LMI. She noted that 'LMI is hope'. By this, one can construe that the DNA or identity of LMI is hope. Its ethos is based on a relational approach and helps people to dream that anything is possible (tangible). The fact that Informant 11 observed a sense of the organisation's valuing of others and that she felt 'welcomed and… needed' says something about the personhood and human dignity that are entrenched in LMI/LSI's 'being'.

A parent (Informant 19) of one of LSI's players, emphasised: 'The purpose is to change lives and instilling hope that in life nothing is impossible.'

This parent's assertion that LMI's purpose is about changing lives and instilling hope would seem to indicate that tangible hope is transformative, is people-centred, and that it is linked to making the 'impossible' things possible. This people-centred nature of LMI is further articulated by a player's (Informant 21) comments that LSI helps others 'by giving them hope'. Informant 1 (coach, who is now a full-time teacher) also reinforces this point that LMI helps others by giving them 'a sense of hope and belonging'. This suggests that tangible hope is outward-looking, is accepting, embraces others, acknowledges, affirms, and is deeply connected to having compassion for others.

Lastly, an ex-coach (Informant 4; now a trainee minister in the Anglican Church) responded to 'How would you describe the purpose and impact of the work that LMI does?', as follows:

> I'd describe it as a trajectory. The work of transformation is not instantaneous and there will be disappointments but the moments of hope and success stories that filter in during and after one's times at LMI is beautiful. LMI is about grafting and seeing the goal while in the thick of the game (sorry a soccer analogy). Some games/days are awesome, and everything goes right and other days you just got to put in the hard work.

This informant's response to the question, 'How would you describe the purpose and the impact of the work that LMI does?', is quite informative regarding the ambivalence connected to the notion of transformation. This is because, whilst transformation is like a 'trajectory' and 'not instantaneous', it is also ambivalent in nature. This ambivalence is felt because the vision of transformation often comes with disappointment when things sometimes go wrong at the organisation or when projects do not run as planned. There is this ambivalence between disappointments, failures, and success. This leads one to explore the meaning and relevance of hope (tangible hope) for diaconal practice.

What Does Tangible Hope Mean for Diaconal Practice?

In my survey, I asked the question to all of the informants: 'How would you describe the notion of *hope* in relation to LMI's work?' It was anticipated that this question would serve as an important hermeneutical key in the discussion to determine the essence of tangible hope as experienced in the diaconal practice of LMI.

Through reflexive TA of the data, I tabulated the information because it was possible to recognise many descriptors of tangible hope expressed by all four categories of informants: people-centredness, belonging, selfless giving, participatory, well-being, experiential, relational empowering, spiritual, contextual and well-being. These descriptors helped in giving tangible hope some sort of essence or meaning.

To make it easier to understand the essence of tangible hope, I have grouped the descriptors under three significant headings, namely:

- Tangible hope as outward-looking (missional, contextual, outward-looking, missional, selfless, caring);
- Tangible hope as personhood (relational, affirmation, well-being, belonging, poverty, gangsterism, drugs, etc.);
- Tangible hope as pragmatic (intentional, purposeful, experiential, empowering).

Further extensive research will be conducted to contribute an even more concrete understanding of the essence or isness of tangible hope, and this categorisation could possibly attract other academics to take this nuanced concept further.

Tangible Hope as Outward-looking

Keeping in mind the preceding subjectivity,[15] and taking into account the limitations just mentioned, I argue, firstly, that tangible hope is outward-looking. All of the coaches, players, networking partners, and some parents experienced tangible hope as outward-looking (for example Informants 1 to 7; and Informants 20 to 23). This outward-looking focus means that the organisation goes to where the people are. It goes to where there is poverty, hopelessness, hardship, and other socio-economic challenges. It is an inclusive approach that contributes to human well-being. Speaking of poverty, one of the parents of an LSI player (Informant 19) thought that LMI is '… one of the cornerstones that gives hope to children from poor backgrounds; it gives them hope, [that], with dedication and discipline, they can overcome any obstacle.'

Hope is also referred to by LMI coaches who are serving the community's marginalised children, youth, and schools. Two examples of this are an informant who, as an unemployed teacher, was offered a full time teaching post at one of our partnering schools because of his excellent volunteerism, and an informant who came to South Africa as a refugee and who, after obtaining coaching qualifications, found a new job as a football coach with a big football company. For both coaches, who were unemployed before they joined LMI, the organisation itself was outward-looking, intentionally seeking to attract unemployed youth and adults to the organisation so that they could gain some experience in order for them to later find meaningful employment elsewhere.

---

[15] Citing Braun and Clarke, David Byrne, 'A Worked Example of Braun and Clarke's Approach to Reflexive Thematic Analysis', *Quality & Quantity* (2021), 2, encourages the researcher 'to embrace reflexivity, subjectivity, and creativity as assets in knowledge production.'

Hence, tangible hope for LMI is outward-looking in more ways than one. It is more than just giving marginalised children hope through our sports activities and international football tours, it is also outward-looking in terms of addressing poverty, unemployment, and hopelessness, whilst addressing the personhood of the individual in relation to the community.

Tangible Hope as Personhood

Not only can tangible hope be seen as outward-looking, it can also be seen as personhood. Several of the coaches, volunteers and international partners in my survey recorded how their own perspectives of their personal lives have been transformed. A coach from the Netherlands (Informant 6) spoke of his experiences in this way:

> I really appreciate my own (privileged) life more. I have seen how hard life can be in the slums and how it affects kids. On the other hand, I have met amazing people who were the poorest people on earth (money or belonging-wise) but were most likely happier than most rich people in the world. It made me think about my own life and I have been way more appreciative about the luxurious position I grew up in compared to a lot of South Africans.

Amongst the responses to the question, 'How would you describe the notion of hope in relation to LMI's work?', a coach (Informant 2) from South Africa (originally from the Democratic Republic of Congo) answers:

> LMI is a wonderful project which not only brings hope to those who are part of it but also brings a sense of comfort and belonging to them. The project makes you feel like you're a part of something and that you matter, and it brings that kind of feeling to the kids as well and that is what the project is all about. Making sure everyone feels like they are worth something and are capable of reaching their goals if they believe and work hard enough.

Many informants interpreted their experiences of being a volunteer as positively impacting their person or *personhood*. Klaasen's notion of personhood emphasises that 'inclusive and just communities are the responsibility of each person. Despite the differentiations in status within the notions of personhood, persons have a relationship with other persons and with non-living beings'.[16] Such relational dynamism is clearly linked to personhood and tangible hope. I therefore argue that, so far, this research shows that people need each other to prosper or thrive. People need people in order to find their purpose and meaning in life.

It is evident that the theme of positive self-esteem and/or self-actualisation is a strong feature emanating from the comments of most of the informants. It

[16] Klaasen, 'Personhood', 8-9.

appears that these experiences were a direct result of the coaches'/volunteers' service to students at primary schools or with youth in the LSI programme. Other volunteers also mentioned how tough it was for them to experience the hardship of others and LSI's perceived lack of resources. Here it seems that at least two volunteers (from the Netherlands and Sweden) experienced empathy as well as sympathy for the problems that our community faced, as they volunteered in LMI's programmes for four and three months respectively. Therefore, it is important to note that, not only is tangible hope about positive experiences, it also necessitates feelings of disappointment (Informant 4), sadness, anger (Informant 6) and other experiences that cause some sort of personal discomfort.

Nevertheless, most coaches' (Informants 1 to 7) and players' (Informants 20 to 23) feedback showed that tangible hope could also mean the improvement of their personal well-being. One of the questions in the survey asked, 'In which way (if any) did LMI contribute to your overall well-being as a person?' Amongst the replies to personal well-being, there appears to be many different descriptions. From South Africa, a LSI employee, referring to his own personal development, replied: 'While in the thick of running programmes and doing the work, one doesn't recognise the growth and development.'

Also from South Africa, an informant who had been unemployed before joining LMI responded that it '[h]elped me to develop in a well-rounded manner. The ability to meet and interact with so many people from different cultures. Truly broadened my horizons and understanding of the world and people.' The coach originating from tanother African country indicated that 'It made me a better and responsible person and molded me into what I believe to be a leader.' LMI's affirmation of this volunteer as a human being and not as a refugee or foreigner, is representative of its goal to promote human dignity for all people. In summary, the foregoing analysis shows how tangible hope as personhood crosses all boundaries, is pragmatic, as well as inclusive of people from anywhere in the world.

Tangible Hope as Pragmatic

Tangible hope ought also to be seen as pragmatic in its essence. To begin this discussion on the correlation between tangible hope and pragmatism, a Dutch former volunteer (Informant 14) noted: 'LMI offers hope to young people. In this way they may be able to make something of their lives and escape the situation they are in.' Additionally, this former volunteer, also responding to the question regarding how his short time at LMI helped him as a student and in his new job, replied that 'I can use my experiences in Cape Town well. Healthy body and mind are very important. Working in a team is also useful.'

These comments demonstrate the emphasis of well-being and the pragmatic nature of tangible hope. Unemployed people who have time and energy to offer are not seen as unemployed but instead are regarded as assets who are available to serve society. Such a pragmatic approach calls for affirming the Godgiftedness of each person and attempts to include all people in meaningful service to fellow human beings.

From South Africa, a football player (Informant 20) who first toured Sweden with LSI in 2011 and 2012 as an eleven-year-old boy, and who is now a professional footballer in Varberg, Sweden, commented:

> Some of my teammates back then had it much worse off than me, which I gathered from discussions with them. I'm referring to family and household circumstances. But once we stepped onto the field that would all disappear. Football, and Lifezone, was a source of hope and inspiration. An opportunity for many to forget all [of] the sad and bad [things], and just enjoy life!

This informant also represented South Africa at all of the age group levels (under-17, under-20, and under-23) and captained the under-17s and under-20s on a few occasions. LSI assisted his development through our diaconal-focused work and managed to refer him to the best football academy in Cape Town at the time, Ajax Cape Town Football Club.

Commenting on the immense personal value of LSI's football tours to Sweden since 2009, another informant – who has also played semi-professional football – expresses hope in this way:

> With the tours to Sweden, the idea of hope is written all over it. Making dreams possible for kids who never thought it was possible surely gives hope to the next.

It is also worth noting that this informant was privileged to have toured Sweden on at least six occasions with LSI as a player, and he gained plenty of experience in international travel from a very early age. Therefore, when he received an invitation in 2019 to play football in New Zealand, he was able to travel independently at the age of nineteen.

Lastly, a senior teacher and deputy principal (Informant 8) at one of the primary schools where LMI is still actively conducting physical education classes for all of their grades, writes of his experience of *trust* with LMI:

> I was the contact person for LMI's programme manager at our school. Our close communication led to a partnership of trust and confidence being developed which has lasted to this day.

This teacher's view places the focus on the nature of LMI's ethos – trust. For an educational institution that is usually saddled by laborious government 'red tape' and education department laws to agree to have a young FBO as a partner, implied that the trust factor was critical in establishing the relationship. This helped to instil confidence in an on-going partnership development process between LMI and the school, for the well-being of hundreds of school children per year since 2006.

The fact that this professional relationship 'has lasted to this day' says something about LMI's tangible presence at the school and also that it is a consistent source of hope for the learners and staff alike.

Some of the ways LMI has demonstrated this tangible hope through diaconia in the school are:[17]

- 2006: Used the school's unkempt, open fields as a base for creating a football facility, and started a football programme for ten primary schools in Factreton, Kensington and Maitland, before relocating it to the nearby municipal sports field.
- 2006 to 2013: Sourced football gear and sports equipment donations for all ten primary schools on a regular basis.
- 2013: Facilitated the donation and installation of a five-a-side artificial football pitch which we have called 'The Dream Pitch' (worth nearly one million South African Rands). Here, an informant from the networking organisation The Dreamfields Project played the main role.
- 2014: Recognised by the City of Cape Town for having the second-best sports recreational programme in its three sub-councils.
- 2013-2022: Conducting physical education classes for, on average, 800 children per week. (This corresponds extremely well with SDG 3 on good health and well-being.)[18]
- 2006 to 2022: Attracting international volunteers (from South America and Europe) to the school and to LMI in general.
- 2009 to 2019: Facilitated ten 'Dreampossible' football-cultural tours to Sweden for dozens of learners from different schools in the LMI programme. (New tours in collaboration with our main international networking partner, ACCESS have been placed on hold due to the COVID-19 pandemic.)

These are modest, concrete accomplishments for an under-resourced grassroots community development organisation such as LMI, and show that these activities are only possible through building healthy relationships, and by faith and pragmatism. People who were unemployed or under-employed, and who do not consider themselves to be rich financially but who are rich in time, energy and dedication, made these achievements possible. Their motivation to (tangibly) participate in the well-being of others, creates hope. Not only does it create hope, but it is also at the heart of understanding the essence of tangible hope.

---

[17] A list of results and films documenting the achievements is included after the Bibliography.

[18] The Global Goals for Sustainable Development; 2020a; www.globalgoals.org.

Conclusion

In this chapter I have presented some results from a qualitative study amongst twenty-three volunteers, coaches, players, parents, and networking partners. The study was undertaken during 2020 in preparation for the completion of a chapter on diaconal practice in relation to building just and sustainable communities. The twenty-three informants, from Sweden, the Netherlands, and South Africa, have all participated in some way in LMI's community development (diaconal work) in South Africa, and/or in Sweden since 2006. The answers show that they contributed immensely to understanding the essence of tangible hope. I have categorised their answers into the following three main headings:

- Tangible hope as outward-looking
- Tangible hope as personhood
- Tangible hope as pragmatic

Each category shows that tangible hope is experienced differently by different informants, but that there are a number of similar experiences and reflections connected with it. Although some informants were aware of challenges (such as when things went wrong with a project), they very much underlined the point that they remained hopeful because they had also experienced the joys of success (such as the tours to Sweden or the installation of 'The Dream Pitch' that made it possible for LSI to introduce a physical education programme for hundreds of students at a primary school). The tangible, practical work of the informants (and many others) was always complemented by a sense of hope, the underlying ethos of LMI's work in the community. Volunteers, coaches, players and networking partners often connected their experiences, and the recipients of LMI's work, to well-being, hope and a range of other values such as love, joy, and a sense of belonging.

The pragmatic nature of tangible hope widens the traditional understanding of diaconia particularly when experienced in a (South) African context where poverty, hopelessness, and other social problems seem to dominate the lives of masses of people.

Bibliography

ACCESS Sverige-Sydafrika (2021); https://access-sydafrika.org/.

Braun, Virginia and Clarke, Victoria, 'Using Thematic Analysis in Psychology', *Qualitative Research in Psychology*, 3:2 (2006), 77-101.

Braun, Virginia and Clarke, Victoria, 'Reflecting on Reflexive Thematic Analysis', *Qualitative Research in Sport, Exercise and Health*, 11:4 (2019), 589-597.

Braun, Virginia and Clarke, Victoria, 'One Size Fits All? What Counts as Quality Practice in (Reflexive) Thematic Analysis?', *Qualitative Research in Psychology*, 18:3 (2021), 328–352.

Byrne, David, 'A Worked Example of Braun and Clarke's Approach to Reflexive Thematic Analysis', *Quality & Quantity* (2021), 1-22. https://doi.org/10.1007/s11135-021-01182-y.

Department of Basic Education, Western Cape No Fee Schools (2021). https://www.education.gov.za/Portals/0/Documents/Publications/No%20fee%20schools/WC%20No%20Fee%20Schools%202021%20list.pdf?ver=2021-01-20-120726-817.

Department of Basic Education, School Fees (2020). https://www.education.gov.za/Informationfor/ParentsandGuardians/SchoolFees.aspx.

Emiliussen, Jakob; Soren, Engelsen; Regina, Christiansen; and Soren, Harnow Klausen, 'We Are All In It! Phenomenological Qualitative Research and Embeddedness', *International Journal of Qualitative Methods*, 20 (2021), 1-6.

Jensen, Steffen, *Gangs, Politics & Dignity in Cape Town* (Johannesburg: Wits University Press, 2008).

Klaasen, John S, 'Personhood and Inclusive Communities: Access to Justice for All'. *Developing Just and Inclusive Communities. Challenges for Diakonia as Christian Social Practice and for Social Work* (eds.) Hans Morten Haugen, Benedicte Tveter Kivle, Tony Addy, Terese Bue Kessel and John Klaasen (Oxford: Regnum, 2022).

Pinnock, Don. *Gang Town* (Cape Town: Tafelberg 2018).

Reggie the Boy Who Carries a Dream upon His Shoulders, trailer (2013); 2020a; https://www.youtube.com/watch?v=xwwKgk7aS98.

Sup, Michael J. 2019, *Sport and Development Volunteerism: A Phenomenological Inquiry of Volunteers' Experiences in a Salvadorian Program* (PhD). Ohio: Patton College of Education: Ohio University, 2019).

Terry, Gareth and Hayfield, Nikki, *Conceptual Foundations of Thematic Analysis: Essentials of Thematic nalysis*, ed. by Clara E. Hill and Sarah Knox (American Psychological Association, 2021), 4.

The Global Goals for Sustainable Development (2020); 2020a; www.globalgoals.org.

Wyngaard, Jeremy Gregory, *In Search of Root Causes of Poverty. Testing a Theological Perspective in Development Dialogues* (PhD dissertation) (Stellenbosch: University of Stellenbosch, 2013).

Wyngaard, Jeremy, 'Missio Dei and Youth Ministry. Mobilizing Young People's Assets and Developing Relationships', *Missionalia*, 43:3 (2015) 410-424.

To get an impression of the achievements see note 257 and accompanying text; see:

Lifezone KSOH S8E06 e tv Dream Centre 2013 (2015); https://www.youtube.com/watch?v=JszqKjwhPqk&t=9s.

Welcome to Life Zone Soccer: 1996 to 2018 (2018); https://lifezonesoccer.co.za.

Lifezone Soccer (2011); https://www.youtube.com/watch?v=YE70vjXJrfY
Lifezone Soccer Cape Town 2008 (2008); https://www.youtube.com/watch?v=RItzVP6GNS8&t=139
Lifezone Soccer Dream Possible3 Sweden 2012 (2013); https://www.youtube.com/watch?v=wypxaUXmWFU
Lifezone Soccer International (LSI) DreamPossible4 (2014); https://www.youtube.com/watch?v=8Bs_AAj9dfU&t=6s
LifeZone Soccer International (LSI) Under 17 (2017); https://sifcup.se/2017,en,wrap=clean/result/team/10536088/info.
LifeZoneSoccer Wins Storsjocupen Boys Under 12 (2012); https://www.youtube.com/watch?v=dFealaaUthg.
Following Dreams in Cape Town (2012). http://followingdreamsincapetown.blogspot.com/2012/08.

Contemporary *Mizuko* Ritual in Japan for Aborted Children: A Proposal to Pastoral Counselling in the Christian Church

Terese Bue Kessel

Introduction

When I lived in Japan in the 1990s and some years into the new millennium, I did not pay much attention to the *mizuko kuyo* memorial services for aborted, miscarried and stillborn children,[1] which motivated me to address this practice now. I recall the small stone sculptures in the shape of a child, dressed in baby clothes and decorated with toys, lined up in some Buddhist temples. I was not aware that each of these sculptures carries a story: a story of grief and sorrow… a story of a mother's regret, of a lost child… a story of naming what was lost and giving what was lost an identity. In short, each sculpture conveys a story in some way connected to the child and seeking well-being for those in the wider family community beyond their death. The sculptures represent lost babies and reflect a significant part of Japanese religious tradition and ritual.[2] The term *mizuko* literally means 'water-child', or what LaFleur called 'liquid life'.[3] The terms 'mizu 水' and 'ko 子' refer to foetuses, both in singular and plural form, and may also refer to children who died at a young age.[4] The term *kuyo* has various meanings but often refers to rituals of ancestor worship.[5] In this chapter, *kuyo* means the memorial service for the spirits of dead foetuses.

[1] Technically, when referring to a miscarriage or abortion the term 'foetus' would be used instead of child, but since this is particularly referring to a memorial service for the 'water child', I use child here and elsewhere in the chapter.

[2] Domyo Miura, *The Forgotten Child: An Ancient Eastern Answer to a Modern Problem* (Nuffield, Henley-on-Thames, Oxon: Aidan Ellis, 1983). R.J. Zwi Werblowsky, 'Mizuko Kuyo: Notulae on the Most Important "New Religion" of Japan', *Japanese Journal of Religious Studies*, 18.4 (1991), 295-354. Helen Hardcare, *Marketing the Menacing Fetus in Japan* (Berkley: University of California Press, 1997).

[3] William R. LaFleur, *Liquid Life: Abortion and Buddhism in Japan* (Princeton: Princeton University Press, 1992).

[4] Werblowsky, 'Mizuko', 295-354.

[5] Jan-Martin Berentsen, *Grave and Gospel* (Leiden: Brill, 1985).

Scholarly publications on *mizuko kuyo* often present the perspective of the large temples that specialise in these rituals.[6] Hence, a common view is that women participate in the ritual due to the mental stress they experience after having an abortion, for fear of revenge from the spirit of the unborn, because they are naïve or as a result of the clergy's exploitation of vulnerable women.[7] However, research on this topic is incomplete, and relevant data gathered from women and their families are insufficient to establish valid generalisations.[8] Scholars who have tried to interview those who have participated in these rituals have had difficulty accessing their personal narratives. The complexity of *mizuko kuyo* and its religious foundation and connection to the spirit world, as well as issues of power, patriarchy and gender, explain to a degree why the ritual has drawn academic attention, both within and outside Japan. However, on a personal and familial level, abortion is a silent matter. Whilst abortion has been legal in the United States since 1973 and in Norway since 1978, in Japan abortion was made legal decades earlier, in 1948, through the Eugenic Protection Law. For a long time, abortion has been the safest method of contraception for Japanese women. In 1988, Smith claimed that it was 'common for women to have had at least two abortions by the time they are forty years old'.[9] Smith, who had been involved in researching *mizuko kuyo*, considered the widespread practice of abortion as a source of serious problems within Japanese society, noting that it resulted in mental stress and what he identified as 'a rupture or brokenness that tears at one's inner nature' for women.[10] Whilst abortion is common amongst all women of reproductive age in Japan, in the latter part of the 20th century, the practice decreased due to an increase in the use of other forms of contraception. However, induced abortion has increased recently amongst teenagers and adolescents, probably due to changes in sexual behaviours and a liberalised abortion law.[11]

The aim of this chapter is to contribute with a reflection on what the ritual may propose to pastoral counselling in the broader context of the Christian

---

[6] Bardwell Smith, 'Buddhism and Abortion in Contemporary Japan: *Mizuko Kuyo* and the Confrontation with Death', *Japanese Journal of Religious Studies*, 15.1 (1988), 3-24.

[7] Richard W. Anderson and Elaine Martin, 'Rethinking the Practice of *Mizuko Kuyo* in Contemporary Japan. Interviews with Practitioners at a Buddhist Temple in Tokyo', *Japanese Journal of Religious Studies* 24.1-2 (1997), 121-143.

[8] Elisabeth Harrison, 'Women's Response to Child Loss in Japan: The Case of *Mizuko Kuyo*', *Journal of Feminist Studies in Religion*, 11.2 (1995), 67-94. Georg Tanabe, 'Review of Liquid Life: Abortion and Buddhism in Japan by William R. LaFleur', *Japanese Journal of Religious Studies*, 21.4 (1994), 439-440. Werblowsky, 'Mizuko', 303.

[9] Smith, 'Buddhism and Abortion', 8.

[10] Smith, 'Buddhism and Abortion', 10.

[11] Sachiko Baba, Satoshi Tsujita and Kanehisa Morimoto, 'The Analysis of Trends in Induced Abortion in Japan: An Increasing Consequence among Adolescents', *Environ Health Preventive Medicine* 10 (2005), 9-15.

church in Japan. For centuries, pastoral counselling has been part of the worldwide church's diaconal approach,[12] in listening to the broken heart and assisting the wounded to reconcile with their own lives, with those they relate to and with God. I did not come across the pain of abortion in the relationships I was involved in as a missionary. Several colleagues from years back confirmed similar experiences. A former missionary addressed this silence and asked why women do not come to the church with this pain.[13]

The chapter is also relevant to two targets from United Nations SDG 5: Target 5.5, which is to 'ensure women's full and effective participation and equal opportunities for leadership at all levels of decision-making in political, economic and public life'[14] and Target 5c, which focuses on strengthening female empowerment. This link to the SDG targets points to a relevant meta-framing for my discussion and the embedding of the implicit gender issues. However, I do not apply the targets as theoretical lenses for my reflection.

The memorial service includes dimensions of personhood, persons in relation and contextual issues of family. Herein is a connection to the present book in which John Klaasen discusses the distinctiveness in human beings that does not mean separateness but, rather, belonging to someone else in a common humanity with implications of responsibilities. Personhood and the meaning of 'human being' in African contexts refers to the principle 'I am therefore we are, and since we are, therefore I am'.[15] The Japanese/Chinese character for a person, 人, is often interpreted as two people leaning on one another. If one falls, the other falls, too. This means that to be human is to be a person in relation to others in a community and reflects the Oriental emphasis on the interrelatedness between everything and everyone. In Japan, such mutuality and responsibility go beyond the boundaries of life and include ancestral rites.[16] In the following, I will present a selection of women's experiences with the *mizuko* ritual, relying on previous research and publications retrieved from relevant databases.

Estimating how Japanese society today is impacted by Christianity, which was introduced to the country in 1549 with the arrival of the Jesuit priest Francis Xavier, is no easy task.[17] For one reason, the Christian impact cannot be

---

[12] Berit Okkenhaug, *Når jeg ser ditt ansikt: Innføring i kristen sjelesorg* (Oslo: Verbum, 2002).

[13] Anne Berger Jørgensen, *'En av disse mine minste': Abort i Japan som utfordring for kirken* (Spesialoppgave, Stavanger: Misjonshøgskolen, 1994).

[14] https://sdgs.un.org/goals/goal5.

[15] John Klaasen, 'Personhood and Inclusive Communities: Access to Justice for All.' In *Developing Just and Inclusive Communities. Challenges for diakonia as Christian social practice and social work,* Hans Morten Haugen, Benedicte Tveter Kivle, Tony Addy, Terese Bue Kessel and John Klaasen (eds.), (Oxford: Regnum, 2022), 33-48.

[16] Berentsen, *Grave and Gospel.*

[17] Ikuo Higashibaba, *Christianity in Early Modern Japan: Kirishitan Belief and Practice* (Vol. 16; Leiden: Brill, 2001). Mark R. Mullins (ed.), *Handbook of Christianity in Japan* (Vol. 10; Leiden: Brill, 2003).

measured solely on the number of Japanese citizens who are members of Protestant and Catholic churches. Through institutions, mission schools, attractive rituals and religious traditions (such as weddings and Christmas), the Christian faith has developed a relatively distinguished reputation in Japanese society. However, the many Christian denominations do not have one unified voice in the public sphere. Rather, Christianity's significance lies in the meaning of faith and fellowship that it can offer through local churches in urban and rural areas. Thus, addressing the *mizuko* ritual and bringing it into dialogue with pastoral counselling is relevant.[18] What needs to be uncovered is what the memorial service for aborted foetuses can suggest to pastoral counselling. The chosen practice of pastoral counselling is traditionally also part of diakonia, with an implicit relation to community development. In this book, Tony Addy reflects on a person-centred approach applied to community development processes. Similarly, pastoral counselling must be understood as taking a person-centred approach in which the church has the potential to empower women and prevent mechanisms of oppression in the *mizuko* ritual that add shame and guilt. The wider relevance of the account in this chapter in view of the SDG targets is the awareness of constant bodily reproductive health issues in more severe situations globally that prevent women's full participation in community life.

Background Perspectives on the *Mizuko* Ritual

The *mizuko kuyo*, which originated in a Buddhist religious context in Japan, emerged in the late 1960s and 1970s, in the aftermath of World War II.[19] Due to the baby boom, economic challenges and the rebuilding of the country, abortion was considered a legitimate means for birth control, and still is.[20]

The memorial service takes place in Buddhist temples dedicated for this purpose. A common belief is that women participate as a result of the psychological challenges they experience after undergoing an abortion[21] because the ceremony will meet their emotional needs.[22] LaFleur stated that a sense of guilt 'is precisely why the practice of the rites for the *mizuko* arose in Japan'.[23] In the bestseller *The Forgotten Child*, Japanese Buddhist priest and author Domyo Miura argued that prayers for the spirit of the aborted child can remove

[18] Kjell Nordstokke and Lutheran World Federation, *Diakonia in Context: Transformation, Reconciliation, Empowerment: An LWF Contribution to the Understanding and Practice of Diakonia* (Geneva: The Lutheran World Federation, 2009).

[19] Elisabeth G. Harrison, 'Strands of Complexity: The Emergence of *Mizuko Kuyo* in Postwar Japan', *Journal of the American Academy of Religion*, 67.4 (1999), 769-796.

[20] Hardcare, *Menacing Fetus.*

[21] Smith, 'Buddhism and Abortion', 3.

[22] LaFleur, *Liquid,* 144.

[23] LaFleur, *Liquid,* 157.

the many problems that follow an abortion.[24] Two Japanese scholars, Hoshino and Takeda, maintained this assumption of guilt, arguing that 'the purpose of contemporary *mizuko kuyo* is one of providing comfort from the feeling of indebtedness and anxiety that comes from a fear of this curse'.[25] The ritual indicates a need to address various emotions, the need to connect to the child, the need to deal with pain and guilt and the fear of vengeance from a hostile *mizuko* spirit.[26] The collection of small stone sculptures in these Buddhist temples' entrances, gardens or backyards identify the temples' *raison d'être*.

Announcements for the ritual are made public through social media, on advertisement boards in communities, in train stations and inside trains. The ritual is also increasingly being offered through the internet.[27] Whilst the ritual is announced publicly, the abortion itself is a private and sensitive matter, which is contrary to the way it was viewed during the Edo period, and during the Tokugawa period (1603–1868), the time of Japan's isolation. At that time in traditional society, infanticide and abortion took place due to poverty, with responsibility placed in the hands of the community. Since the spirits differentiated between children and adults, people believed the child could be born again. This spared the community from feeling guilty. Today, an abortion is solely the individual's responsibility, and the fact that the burden is not shared with the community constitutes 'the basis for the feeling of indebtedness'.[28]

The term *kuyo* refers to a variety of rituals, such as a 'ritual of gratitude towards objects that have faithfully served their purpose',[29] such as chopsticks. The boundaries between the animate and inanimate are fluid. Some hospitals ask for 'wholesale *kuyo* for all the abortions performed during the year'.[30] Common for all *kuyo* is the financial aspect. Feminists, academics and the media have criticised the ritual for taking economic advantage of and exploiting vulnerable women who are experiencing feelings of guilt.

Personal *Mizuko Kuyo* Narratives

Extensive research on the ritual began in the 1980s.[31] In this section, I present several selected *mizuko kuyo* narratives, which Anderson and Martin described,

---

[24] Miura, *Forgotten Child.*

[25] Eiki Hoshino and Dosho Takeda, 'Indebtedness and Comfort: The Undercurrents of *Mizuko Kuyo* in Contemporary Japan', *Japanese Journal of Religious Studies*, 14.4 (1987), 306-320.

[26] Werblowsky, 'Mizuko' 295-297.

[27] M. Yamada and A. Shupe, 'Internet Accessibility of the *Mizuko Kuyo* (Water Child Ritual) in Modern Japan: A Case Study in Weberian Rationality', *Sociological Focus*, 46.3 (2013), 229-240.

[28] Hoshino and Takeda. 'Indebtedness and Comfort', 314.

[29] Werblowsky, 'Mizuko', 296-297.

[30] Werblowsky, 'Mizuko', 297.

[31] Smith, 'Buddhism and Abortion', 3.

based on their study, in 'Rethinking the Practice of *Mizuko Kuyo* in Contemporary Japan: Interviews with Practitioners at a Buddhist Temple in Tokyo'.[32] The authors conducted six in-depth interviews with women who regularly participated in *mizuko* rituals in a Buddhist temple in Tokyo. The clergy performed the *kuyo* once a month, in the morning and in the afternoon, with about 30 attendees at each ceremony, primarily women representing a range of ages, with most falling between 40 and 60 years old. The researchers had hoped to interview 10 people but were only able to meet with six because, as they explained, 'the process of gaining an entree to this milieu and of trying to elicit information on a topic that basically no one wanted to discuss was extremely complex'.[33] In addition to interviewing attendees, Anderson and Martin also observed the memorial service.

The monthly *mizuko kuyo* involved both formal and informal elements. The formal service lasted about one hour under the guidance of the priest, who chanted parts of the *Lotus Sutra*. Included were drum beatings by participants and a closing monologue by the priest. Afterwards, the attendees gathered for socialisation and refreshments under the charge of the priest's wife; the priest usually did not participate. Anderson and Martin proposed the following hypotheses at the beginning of their study: 1) All participants are women. 2) They attend the service only once or twice or only for a short time. 3) A close relationship possibly exists between the participants and the priest. 4) The social hour after the *kuyo* provides attendees with emotional support and works to establish support groups. The researchers had to modify most of their initial assumptions. They were partly right in that most participants were women; however, some men were also present. Moreover, participants attended the ritual rather often but did not share a close relationship with the priest.

The reasons for attending varied. Only two of the six subjects interviewed claimed to have had an abortion. Two young sisters reported they had never been pregnant and had attended because of their mother's abortion, a miscarriage their grandmother had had and for the sake of their own health. Another interviewee had lost a child in a caesarean delivery, and another attended because of two miscarriages. Different experiences pushed the attendees to participate in the ritual year after year. One had started attending 28 years after she had, at the age of 21, elected to have an abortion. At the time, 'it was an acceptable solution. But about six years ago she felt that she must do something for this *mizuko*, so she spoke with the priest at *Honpo-ji* and began attending *mizuko* services.'[34] Another began participating in rituals 12 years earlier after her second miscarriage and thereafter regularly attended 3 or 4 times a year. She planned to continue her participation. She lived in a neighbourhood where she saw 'the sign in front of the temple, felt moved, and decided to attend. She has never discussed

[32] Anderson and Martin, 'Rethinking', 121-143.
[33] Anderson and Martin, 'Rethinking', 122-123.
[34] Anderson and Martin, 'Rethinking', 126.

with the priest why she attends', however.[35] This individual said she viewed abortion as murder, especially in current times, noting 'that it was easier to understand and justify abortion at the close of World War II when times were difficult'.[36] She attended the *mizuko* ritual because she had had two miscarriages and for the sake of her daughter's health. 'Initially she felt there might be a chance for the spirits of the miscarried children to be reborn in her family, but with the passage of time her hopes have diminished.'[37] Andersen and Martin concluded that 'most women attend because they have lost a child either through abortion, miscarriage, stillbirth or infant death, but we suspect that many, or even most, of the women have had abortions' but were not willing to discuss the subject with the researchers.[38]

The *mizuko kuyo* ceremonies are held in larger temples as well as in smaller neighbourhood temples. Harrison observed such rituals for many years and has listened to the short sermons presented by the clergy, who underline that participants 'should be there not for their own sake but only for their child's'.[39] They are reminded of their obligation to mother the child that was denied birth because of their 'conscious decision or less-than-conscious carelessness' and to care for it in the afterlife. '*Mizuko kuyo* is presented as the one way she can carry out her responsibility to mother her child in whatever realm of existence it may be, to nurture and care for it as she would have done in this life.'[40]

The clergy apparently enrol women in a never-ending ritual. Berentsen addressed the dimension of continuity in ancestor worship in households and temples. Rites for ancestors are repeated in defined cycles and imply a mutual intervention, 'the living in the "life" of the dead', and 'of the dead in the life of the living'.[41] The *mizuko* ritual is not addressed in Berentsen's study; however, the need for the living to somehow connect to the dead child's spirit plays part in the contextual family structure.[42] Women play passive roles in the ritual, which reflects their invisibility in public life and in society at large. The ritual, thus, reinforces the cultural norm of female submissiveness and contradicts rituals of Christian faith that require gender inclusive involvement. A relevant consideration is whether rituals in the church can build an alternative view on women.

---

[35] Anderson and Martin, 'Rethinking', 127.
[36] Anderson and Martin, 'Rethinking', 127.
[37] Anderson and Martin, 'Rethinking', 127.
[38] Anderson and Martin, 'Rethinking', 128.
[39] Harrison, 'Response', 71.
[40] Harrison, 'Response', 71.
[41] Berentsen, *Grave and Gospel*, 81
[42] Harrison, 'Response', 71.

Giving the Dead Child a Name and a Form

Since funerals are not held for aborted children, they end up nameless. In line with the concept of life and spirits, the aborted child in contemporary Japan should be given a name. Whilst *mizuko* rituals may differ across various branches of Buddhism, common amongst all is the belief in 'giving the dead child a name and a form'.[43] The Buddhist-style death name, which signifies that the spirit is an adherent of the Buddha, is the same kind of name given to a deceased child. The naming of the dead child implies that 'its existence is being formally acknowledged'.[44]

In addition to the naming, the deceased child must be given a form, which is the representation of the lost child. 'The form given the child is often that of the deity Jizo, who in Buddhist belief freely roams the six realms of existence helping souls in need.'[45] Likenesses of the deity Jizo can be bought at temples and vary in size from the smaller stuffed forms, six centimetres long, to stone sculptures measuring about 120 centimetres that 'seem to *become* the child'.[46] Women and couples are believed to be motivated to make offerings to the images by two factors: guilt and fear. However, Anderson and Martin found that their study subjects expressed more of a sense of regret than of fear: 'Regret, remorse, and a sense of loss all play a strong role in these views; fear of vengeful spirits is not mentioned.'[47] The foetal retribution was not a matter of concern to the women in their study.

Harrison investigated women's agency and their role in the ritual and interviewed women who themselves were actively involved in developing and offering *mizuko kuyo* to women who needed a space to mourn. This contradicts the image of Japanese women as weak with little power to resist those coming for their money. Harrison, on the other hand, showed that the story of the ritual is much more complex. Before it was formalised in the 1970s, the feelings that followed unwanted pregnancies were lost, and the experiences with life and death related to fertility were invisible and silenced in a society that did not pay the matter much attention. Instead, the formalised *mizuko kuyo* now provides a space to publicly acknowledge loss and express love, demonstrated by the sculptures at the entrance of the temple.[48] The ritual is, therefore, also a story of naming what was lost and providing it with an identity.

---

[43] Harrison, 'Response', 69.
[44] Harrison, 'Response', 69.
[45] Harrison, 'Response', 69.
[46] Harrison, 'Response', 69,
[47] Anderson and Martin, 'Rethinking', 133.
[48] Harrison, 'Response', 91.

The *Mizuko* Ritual's Proposal to the Christian Church

What does the *mizuko* ritual have to contribute to a Christian church regarding those who are dealing with a deep sense of loss pertaining to relations who will never come into being? Any Christian church is struggling to identify the diaconal needs in its context and how to respond to it. What is ther to say to a church in this particular Japanese context, about how one might respond to women seeking the *mizuko* ritual?

The Christian church and its practices encounter challenges regarding the contextual framework of the individual in relation to the family in Japan. The identity of a Japanese person is entrenched in family as well as in religious life. 'Our house is Buddhist' is a common saying. The Japanese religious consciousness and values imply a fundamental clash with western Christianity that favours the nuclear family over the collective household system, which includes repetitive rites for the deceased.[49] This vacuum presents a constant challenge to the church, caused by Protestant theology in terms of the relation between the living and the dead.[50]

From the previous discussion, we can identify three dimensions of the *mizuko* abortion concerning personhood and persons in relation to family and community: i) the emotional sorrow that follows an abortion, ii) the need to somehow connect to the dead child and identify it and iii) the repetitive ritual. Smith's findings revealed a spiritual and psychological burden that follows an abortion, which implies a need for a much deeper healing process than the *mizuko* ritual can offer. As already noted, he called the experience 'a rupture or brokenness that tears at one's inner nature'.[51] The deep suffering is voiced in the repetitive adherence to the ritual. The rituals may involve a sermon and/or counselling from the priest prior to or after the service. However, Smith did not clarify how the counselling is carried out or what weight it carries. Anderson and Martin also did not identify counselling as part of the service.[52] Little emphasis appears to be placed on a person-centred approach in the ritual, and it does not include a safe space for voicing the deepest pain. The lack of a person-centred approach reinforces women's invisibility and submissiveness.

Throughout the history of the church, Christian social practices, healing processes and pastoral care and counselling have been provided to people in local communities.[53] Disability and disease, and physical and mental burden are parts

[49] Mark R. Mullins, 'Japanese Christians and the World of the Dead', *Mortality* (Abingdon: England) 9.1 (2004), 61-75.
[50] Mark R. Mullins, 'Japanese Christians', 64. Richard Fox Young, 'Abortion, Grief and Consolation: Prolegomena to a Christian Response to *Mizuko Kuyo*', *Japan Christian Quarterly* 55.1 (1989), 31-39.
[51] Smith, 'Buddhism and Abortion', 10.
[52] Anderson and Martin, 'Rethinking', 127.
[53] Okkenhaug, *Ser ditt ansikt*, 15-35.

of the biblical narratives,[54] and voicing people's pain plays a part in the global church's diaconal approach.[55] Pastoral counselling has embraced a variety of focuses. The kerygmatic approach sought to preach the gospel to the wounded so sins could be confessed, and the person could reconcile with God.[56] The authoritative biblical doctrine constituted the starting point for this approach. The therapeutic paradigm emphasised in the 1920s followed a different method, underlining the importance of listening to people's narratives.[57] It reacted against the kerygmatic model that did not sufficiently consider people's life experiences. However, the latter approach failed to identify its theological distinctiveness.[58] Eide considered new perspectives in pastoral counselling in his book, titled in Norwegian as *Forståelse og fordypning*, which I translate as 'understanding and in-depth understanding'.[59] Eide's approach was intended to fuse the kerygmatic and the therapeutic models, meaning it pertained to the confidante's ability to listen to the pain and apply appropriate biblical narratives to what is heard so that the individual receiving counsel may develop new perspectives in order to own experiences. Pastoral counselling implies a safe space where two (or more) persons, such as the counselee and the counsellor, can meet undisturbed. A safe place implies attentive listening and confidence that the story will be received without judgement.

The process of 'understanding and in-depth understanding' includes several stages. If a person who does not find healing in the *mizuko* ritual seeks counselling in the church, a twofold approach to understanding the pain may be appropriate. First, one must try to understand 'what happens' within the story that is told: What other stories can unfold from the main one? In what kind of relations within the family and community is the person involved? What kinds of interests create conflicts? What kinds of feelings influence the stories? In short, this first step of listening is about mapping the story's 'data'. The second step in this approach to understanding is the cultural contextual perspective and the question 'why does this happen'? Applied to the case in question, problems related to abortion are not unique to Japan. However, some features in society shed light on structures that prevent women from being in control of their own reproductive health. Currently, information on reproductive issues and realistic

---

54 Anna Rebecca Solevåg and Marta H. Lavik, 'Helse på kvar side? – Bibel, sjukdom og funksjonshemming', *Kirke og Kultur*, 118.2 (2013), 160-173.

55 Stephanie Dietrich, Knud Jørgensen, Kari K. Korslien and Kjell Nordstokke (eds.), *Diakonia in a Gender Perspective* (Oxford: Regnum Books, 2016). Stephanie Dietrich, Knud Jørgensen, Kari K. Korslien and Kjell Nordstokke (eds.), *The Diaconal Church* (Oxford: Regnum Books, 2019).

56 Van D. Hunsinger, *Theology and Pastoral Counseling: A New Interdisciplinary Approach* (Grand Rapids: Eerdmans,1995).

57 Charles V. Gerkin, *The Living Human Document: Re-visioning Pastoral Counseling in a Hermeneutical Mode* (Nashville: Abingdon Press, 1984).

58 Øyvind M. Eide, *Forståelse og fordypning* (Oslo: Luther, 2014), 15-20.

59 Eide, *Forståelse*.

choices in contraceptive methods appear to be lacking, which influences women's reproductive health and behaviours and also impacts the population by causing a decline in fertility rates and an increase in child abuse.[60] In 1999, Japan became the last of the industrialised countries to allow use of the oral contraceptive pill (OCP), and still few women use it.[61] Women's status in the family, in a marriage and in society is subordinate, and the literature describes the Japanese home as one filled with tension and frustration.[62] The absence of choice of contraception methods often leads to abortion, and 'the deeper causes are rooted within the whole social structure in which women have little opportunity to participate in decision-making which affects important areas of their lives'.[63] This context has led to many Japanese women experiencing induced abortions.

The counselling process of working towards gaining an 'in-depth understanding' needs to be sensitively applied, depending on the wounded person's relation to the Christian faith. The approach centres on bringing the stories of the wounded into a dialogue with biblical texts. This process refers to the counsellor's ability to reflect theologically on what was heard. How can the Christian faith relate to the life experience to develop new meanings for the story? In our case, what kind of biblical narratives may be relevant? The answers to this are many.

As already noted, the Japanese religious consciousness and values imply a fundamental clash with western Christianity. However, I suggest that an abortion story in Japan that includes dimensions of the spirit world and the hereafter, as well as issues of the identity of the unborn and repetitive rituals, can find comfort and some healing in the biblical narratives of a loving God – the God who knows us in a state that surpasses our reach. The prophet Jeremiah (1: 5) communicated these words from God: 'Before I formed you in the womb, I knew you.' Other texts, such as Psalm, confirm this special identity and trust in the creator God: 'You watched me as I was being formed in utter seclusion, as I was woven together in the dark of the womb. You saw me before I was born' (Psalm 139: 15–16a). The church has rich sources for healing processes, pastoral counselling, liturgies and rituals, prayers, and individual and communal confessions. Similar to the *mizuko* ritual, the church's sources include dimensions of personhood, of belonging to a fellowship and community. However, there is no connection to

[60] Honami Yoshida, Haruka Sakamoto, Asuka Leslie, Osamu Takahashi, Satoshi Tsuboi and Kunio Kitamura, 'Contraception in Japan: Current Trends', *Contraception*, 93.6 (2016), 475-77. Samuel Coleman, *Family Planning in Japanese Society: Traditional Birth Control in a Modern Urban Culture* (Princeton: Princeton University Press, 1983/1991).

[61] Yoshida (eds.), 'Contraception'.

[62] See women writers Enchi Fumiko and Ariyoshi Sawako on domestic life and values, fragmentation and disconnectedness.

[63] Smith, 'Buddhism and Abortion', 13.

the spirit world but rather to a God who knows us in a state that surpasses our reach.

Conclusion

I suggest that Christian social practices in Japan strive to find contextual approaches and models for pastoral counselling for persons and families with abortion experiences. The sorrow and feeling of guilt, if not dealt with in a deep sense, can cause disintegration and dysfunction in the family and in the community and can be a heavy burden for the woman to carry alone. The church has the potential to empower women beyond the *mizuko* ritual that reinforces women's invisibility and submissiveness. The person-centred approach in pastoral counselling has the potential to sustain women to engage in developing gender inclusive local communities. This could have wider implications for the public context in view of the SDG Target 5c on women and empowerment. One example from one country about women and their bodies and how they are impeded from full participation, and trapped in shame and guilt, can be generalised to more severe situations globally. This discussion leaves several questions unanswered. Therefore, further investigation into how the church can deal with abortion on a relational level to promote healing processes, not only in Japan, but also in the global context, is needed because the grief of abortion is generally silenced.

Bibliography

Anderson, Richard W. and Elaine Martin. 'Rethinking the Practice of *Mizuko Kuyo* in Contemporary Japan. Interviews with Practitioners at a Buddhist Temple in Tokyo.' *Japanese Journal of Religious Studies*, 24.1&2, 121-143 (1997).

Baba, S., Tsujita, S. & Morimoto, K. 'The Analysis of Trends in Induced Abortion in Japan: An Increasing Consequence among Adolescents.' *Environ Health Preventive Medicine*, 10. 9-15 (2005).

Berentsen, Jan-Martin. *Grave and Gospel*, Brill, 1985.

Coleman, Samuel. *Family Planning in Japanese Society: Traditional Birth Control in a Modern Urban Culture*, Princeton: Princeton University Press, 1983/1991.

Eide, Øyvind M. *Forståelse og fordypning: perspektiv på den sjelesørgeriske samtalen*, Oslo: Luther. 2014.

Gerkin, Charles V. *The Living Human Document: Re-visioning Pastoral Counseling in a Hermeneutical Mode*, Nashville: Abingdon Press, 1984.

Hardcare, Helen. *Marketing the Menacing Fetus in Japan*, Berkley: University of California Press, 1997.

Harrison, Elisabeth G. 'Women's Response to Child Loss in Japan: The Case of *Mizuko Kuyo.*' *Journal of Feminist Studies in Religion*, 11.2, 67-94 (1995).

Harrison, Elizabeth G. 'Strands of Complexity: The Emergence of *Mizuko Kuyo* in Postwar Japan.' *Journal of the American Academy of Religion*, 67.4, 769-796 (1999).

Higashibaba, Ikuo. *Christianity in Early Modern Japan: Kirishitan Belief and Practice: Vol. 16*. Leiden: Brill, 2001.

Hoshino, Eiki and Dosho Takeda. 'Indebtedness and Comfort: The Undercurrents of *Mizuko Kuyo* in Contemporary Japan.' *Japanese Journal of Religious Studies*, 14.4, 306-320 (1987).

Hunsinger, D. van D. *Theology and Pastoral Counseling: A New Interdisciplinary Approach*, Grand Rapids: Eerdmans, 1995.

Jørgensen, Anne Berger. *'En av disse mine minste': Abort i Japan som utfordring for kirkenI,* Spesialoppgave, Stavanger: Misjonshøgskolen, 1994.

Klaasen, John. 'Personhood and Inclusive Communities: Access to Justice for All', in: *Developing Just and Inclusive Communities. Challenges for Diakonia as Christian Social Practice and Social Work,* Hans Morten Haugen, Benedicte Tveter Kivle, Tony Addy, Terese Bue Kessel and John Klaasen (eds.), (Oxford: Regnum, 2022), 33-48.

LaFleur, William R. *Liquid Life: Abortion and Buddhism in Japan*, Princeton: Princeton University Press,1992.

Lutheran World Federation. *Reconciliation, Empowerment: An LWF Contribution to the Understanding and Practice of Diakonia.* Geneva: The Lutheran World Federation, 2009. https://www.lutheranworld.org/sites/default/files/DMD-Diakonia-EN-low.pdf

Mullins, Mar R. *Handbook of Christianity in Japan: vol.10*, Leiden: Brill, 2003.

Miura, Domyo. *The Forgotten Child: An Ancient Eastern Answer to a Modern Problem*, Nuffield, Henley-on-Thames, Oxon: Aidan Ellis, 1983.

Nordstokke, Kjell & Lutheran World Federation. *Diakonia in Context: Transformation.*

Okkenhaug, Berit. *Når jeg ser ditt ansikt: innføring i kristen sjelesorg*, Oslo: Verbum, 2002.

Solevåg, Anna R., & Marta H. Lavik. 'Helse på kvar side? – Bibel, sjukdom og funksjonshemming'. *Kirke og Kultur*, 118.2, 160–173 (2013).

Smith, Bardwell. 'Buddhism and Abortion in Contemporary Japan: *Mizuko Kuyo* and the Confrontation with Death.' *Japanese Journal of Religious Studies*, 15.1, 3-24 (1988).

Tanabe, Georg. 'Review of Liquid Life: Abortion and Buddhism in Japan by William R. LaFleur.' *Japanese Journal of Religious Studies*, 21.4, 437-440 (1994).

The United Nations Sustainable Development Goal (SDG) https://sdgs.un.org/goals/goal5.

Yamada, M. and Anson Shupe. 'Internet Accessibility of the *Mizuko Kuyo* (Water Child Ritual) in Modern Japan: A Case Study in Weberian Rationality.' *Sociological Focus*, 46.3, 229-240 (2013).

Yoshida, Honami, Haruka Sakamoto, Asuka Leslie, Osamu Takahashi, Satoshi Tsuboi & Kunio Kitamura. 'Contraception in Japan: Current Trends'. *Contraception*, 93.6, 475–477, 2016.

Young, Richard Fox. 'Abortion, Grief and Consolation: Prolegomena to a Christian Response to *Mizuko Kuyo.' Japan Christian Quarterly,* 55.1, 31-39 (1989).

Werblowsky, R.J. Zwi. '*Mizuko Kuyo*: Notulae on the Most Important "New Religion" of Japan.' *Japanese Journal of Religious Studies*, 18:4,295-354 (1991).

Parenting Strategies to Prevent Risks for Adolescents in Urban Neighbourhoods

Silje Hole Hirsch

Introduction

Parenting adolescents involves supporting their development between childhood and adulthood and avoiding their exposure to risks.[1] This chapter investigates parents' perceived risks and strategies to prevent risks for adolescents in urban communities. Parenting reflects and affects the family's context.[2] Therefore, strategies for preventing risks may vary depending on the communities the families live in and the characteristics of the individual parents.[3] Parents are crucial elements of any community. To build just and inclusive communities, actors in community development need knowledge about parents' everyday experiences and how structural inequality and processes of inclusion and exclusion affect parenting.[4]

It may be more challenging to parent in neighbourhoods with an accumulation of social problems,[5] and parents with low educational, occupational, and income levels may experience more stressors in their parenting and fewer options for support.[6] Moreover, changes in contexts because of migration and immigration

---

[1] G. Wolfe, P.G. Jaffe, and C.V. Crooks, *Why Teens Experiment and Strategies to Keep Them Safe* (Yale University Press, 2006).
[2] M. Solem, 'Understanding Parenting as Situated in the Larger Socio-Cultural Context in Clinical Social Work', *Child & Adolescents Social Work Journal*, 30:1 (2013), 61-78.
[3] R. Ceballo and N. Hurd, 'Neighbourhood Context, SES, and Parenting: Including a Focus on Acculturation among Latina Mothers', *Applied Developmental Science*, 12:4 (2008), 176-80.
[4] Addy, T., Approaches to Community Development in H. M. et.al. (eds.), *Developing Just and Inclusive Communities. Challenges for Diakonia as Christian Social Practice and for Social Work* (Oxford, Regnum, 2022), 15-32.
[5] G. H. Brody, R. Conger, F. X. Gibbons, X. Ge, V. McBride Murry, M. Gerrard, and R. L. Simons, 'The influence of Neighborhood Disadvantage, Collective Socialisation, and Parenting on African American Children's Affiliation with Deviant Peers', *Child Development*, 72:4 (2003), 1231-46.
[6] D. E. Kohen, T. Leventhal, V. S. Dahinten, and C. N. McIntosh, 'Neighborhood Disadvantage: Pathways of Effects for Young Children', *Child Development*, 79:1 (2008), 156-69. See also B. A. Kotchick & R. Forehand, 'Putting Parenting in

may mean that some parents lack knowledge regarding the environments of their adolescents.

To buffer risk, parents may adopt specific parenting strategies in response to threats and opportunities in their neighbourhoods.[7] Moreover, a parent's local community may be essential for preventing social problems and facilitating the families' overall good health. A well-functioning local community with high social cohesion and conviviality may relieve the stress for vulnerable parents.[8]

More research is needed on the coping strategies used by parents to prevent risks for adolescents. That is particularly important when parents have an immigrant background and also experience challenging living conditions.[9] Therefore, I investigated what parents perceived as risks and what strategies they used to prevent risks, asking the following research questions:

- What parental strategies do parents with immigrant backgrounds use to prevent risks for their adolescents?
- How are different strategies related to parents' perceptions of their neighbourhoods?

I sought to answer these questions through an empirical project involving parents with immigrant backgrounds parenting teenagers in three local communities and parents from a parental guidance course in Oslo, Norway. In this chapter, I discuss some of the findings using theories of 1) parenting strategy and 2) theories about the characteristics of neighbourhoods: social cohesion and conviviality.

Despite an extensive universalistic welfare state in Norway, the inequality in socio-economic status between different neighbourhoods of Oslo is significant.[10] That may cause different conditions for parenting. I concentrated on parents with relatively shorter education, lower occupational levels, and lower Norwegian language skills compared to the average population. These conditions may place them in a vulnerable position which, in turn, may affect their parenting.

To understand families' needs, I investigated the ecological influences on parenting and how conditions in different levels of their surroundings

---

Perspective: A Discussion of the Contextual Factors that Shape Parenting Practices', *Journal of Child and Family Studies*, 11:3 (2002), 255-69.

[7] R. L. Jarrett and S. R. Jefferson, '"A Good Mother Got to Fight for Her Kids": Maternal Management Strategies in a High-Risk, African-American Neighborhood', *Journal of Children and Poverty*, 9:1 (2003), 21-39.

[8] N. Sletteland and R. M. Donovan, *Helsefremmende lokalsamfunn* (Oslo: Gyldendahl Forlag, 2012). See also A. Wise and G. Noble, 'Convivialities: An Orientation', *Journal of Intercultural Studies*, 37:5 (2016), 423-431.

[9] Q. G. Jiao, A. J. Onwuegbuzie, and K. M. Collins (eds.), *Toward a Broader Understanding of Stress and Coping: Mixed Methods Approaches* (Charlotte, NC: IAP, 2010).

[10] Toft, M. and Ljunggren J. 'Geographies of Class Advantage: The Influence of Adolescent Neighbourhoods in Oslo,' *Urban Studies*, 53:14 (2016), 2939-2955.

(individual, local, and structural) are interconnected.[11] That meant exploring how social and material conditions, cultural background,[12] neighbourhood quality and family dynamics interact with parenting practices.[13]

Parenting Strategies to Prevent Risks

Parents who perceive their neighbourhood as negative for the social outcomes of their children may try to protect them from these influences. The literature presents different strategies available for parents, and two types of strategies are the *protective* and the *promotive* parenting strategies.[14]

The protective parenting strategy restricts teenagers from interacting with people and being in places perceived by the parents as inappropriate or destructive influences; parents may buffer children from dangers in the neighbourhood. There are two versions of this strategy: *monitoring* and *isolation*.[15] Monitoring refers to a parent's knowledge of their child's whereabouts and activities, seeking to protect adolescents from engaging in risky behaviours. Isolation refers to keeping teenagers at home to 'shield' them from physical dangers, negative role models, 'deviant' peers, and harmful activities. Monitoring does not reduce their connections with social networks in the same way isolation does.

When using the promotive strategy, parents promote their teenagers' educational, cultural, and social skills.[16] One promotive strategy is the *similarity seeking* strategy, where parents try to find 'appropriate' people and places for their teenagers through building social networks.[17] Another promotive strategy is the *selective* strategy, which draws on resources inside and outside a family's neighbourhood.

Social Cohesion and Conviviality in Neighbourhoods

Parenting practices may be influenced by the parents' involvement in their neighbourhood networks and whether they experience social support and

---

[11] T. Luster and L. Okagaki, *Parenting: An Ecological Perspective*, vol. 2 (New York: Routledge, 2006).

[12] Solem, 'Understanding Parenting'.

[13] K. W. Pizarro, P.J. Surkan, and I.V. Bustamante, 'The Social Ecology of Parental Monitoring: Parent–Child Dynamics in a High-Risk Peruvian Neighborhood', *Family Process*, 60:1 (2021), 199-215.

[14] Jarrett and Jefferson, 'A Good Mother'.

[15] Jarrett and Jefferson, 'A Good Mother'.

[16] Jarrett and Jefferson, 'A Good Mother'.

[17] Visser, K., Bolt, G., & van Kempen, R., 'A Good Place to Raise Your Children? The Diversity of Parents' Neighbourhood Perceptions and Parenting Practices in a Low-income, Multi-ethnic Neighbourhood: A Case Study in Rotterdam', *Geoforum*, 64 (2015), 112-120, 117.

informal social control from these networks.[18] Structural characteristics such as poverty and instability may affect social cohesion in a neighbourhood and the level of informal social control.[19] The level of social cohesion – social bonds and interdependence – can, in turn, affect the level of stress and vulnerability amongst parents living there.[20] In neighbourhoods where parents lack trusting relationships with other community members,[21] they have fewer occasions to receive parenting advice from others.[22] That may leave parents more isolated in handling their parenting duties, causing increased stress and making positive parenting more challenging.[23]

Social connections and social support between neighbours are usually perceived to improve the functioning of the family,[24] as well as reducing fear and parenting stress.[25] That may, in turn, make it easier for parents to engage in positive parenting even in disadvantaged neighbourhoods or neighbourhoods perceived as dangerous.[26] In diverse communities, interconnectedness and social support depend on the capacity of the community to live convivially. That means people live with and relate to one another in everyday life, regardless of their differences, and can negotiate and transcend these differences.[27]

Methodological Approaches

This chapter builds on data from an empirical study which was undertaken in two phases: 1) three group interviews with mothers of Somali background who were parenting teenagers, and 2) participatory observations in a parental

---

[18] Visser et el., 'A Good Place'; see also A-M. Isola, I. Roivainen, and H. Hiilamo, 'Lone Mothers' Experiences of Poverty in Finland: A Capability Approach', *Nordic Social Work Research* (2020), 1-14.

[19] R. J. Sampson, 'How Do Communities Undergird or Undermine Human Development? Relevant Contexts and Social Mechanisms', in: A. Booth & A. C. Crouter (eds.), *Does It Take a Village? Community Effects on Children, Adolescents, and Families* (Psychology Press, 2001), 3-30.

[20] M. Franco, L. J. K. Pottick, and C. C. Huang, 'Early Parenthood in a Community Context: Neighborhood Conditions, Race–Ethnicity, and Parenting Stress,' *Journal of Community Psychology*, 38:5 (2010), 574-90.

[21] J. Cuellar, D.J. Jones, and E. Sterrett, 'Examining Parenting in the Neighborhood Context: A Review,' *Journal of Child and Family Studies*, 24:1 (2015), 195-219.

[22] J. M. Beyers, J. E. Bates, G.S. Pettit, and K.A. Dodge, 'Neighborhood Structure, Parenting Processes, and the Development of Youths' Externalising Behaviors: A Multilevel Analysis,' *American Journal of Community Psychology*, 31:1 (2003), 35-53.

[23] Cuellar et al., 'Examining'.

[24] Kohen et al., 'Neighborhood'.

[25] D. J. Kruger, T. M. Reichl, and G. C. Gee, 'Neighborhood Social Conditions Mediate the Association Between Physical Deterioration and Mental Health', *American Journal of Community Psychology*, 40:3-4 (2007), 261-71.

[26] Cuellar et al., 'Examining'.

[27] Wise and Noble, 'Convivialities'.

guidance course, where the participants had children of different ages (about half included teenagers).[28] Combining data from these two phases provides a broad understanding of the phenomena and reveals variation in the material studied.

The study was exploratory and qualitative methods were used to investigate and interpret the meaning parents attached to their experiences of parenthood.[29] I interpreted these experiences through theoretical concepts and others' empirical research. As a researcher, I interpreted how the informants interpreted their experiences – thus conducting double hermeneutics.[30]

For the group interviews, parents with immigrant backgrounds were recruited through 'co-creators' with similar immigrant backgrounds as the participants.[31] These co-creators were members of networks providing relevant acquaintances and knowledge about the relevant groups of parents, and they had higher education levels than the participants. They conveyed the necessary information in the parents' mother tongues, recruited those willing to participate in the study, and were present during the interviews. An adult education centre selected the participants for the parental guidance course. The course leaders were social entrepreneurs with immigrant backgrounds who had grown up in Norway and had education at the university level. Before the interviews and the parental guidance course, each participant received an informational letter in Norwegian translated orally at the beginning of the course. I then received written consent from each participant.

I conducted group interviews with a colleague (in December 2018, March 2019, and May 2019).[32] We used an open interview style that aimed to guide the participants' conversation as little as possible[33] and asked a few open-ended questions so that the parents could speak freely. The interviews were transcribed verbatim. I conducted participatory observations during a parental guidance course once a week for 12 weeks during the fall of 2020, making notes about the interactions between course leaders and participants, and participating in conversations. In this chapter, only data from spoken words are included. At the end of the parental guidance course, I interviewed the participants through an interpreter. All quotations used are de-identified, as required by the Norwegian Data Protection Services (NSD).

---

[28] For more details on the methodological perspectives, see B. M. T. Kivle and S. M. H. Hirsch, 'Participation in Research: Experiences from Collaborating with Co-creators During a Study among Mothers of Teenagers with Immigrant Backgrounds in Oslo', *Diaconia*, 10:2 (2020), 141-159.

[29] J. W. Creswell, *Research Design* (Los Angeles: SAGE Publications, 2014), 4.

[30] J. A. Smith, P. Flowers, and M. Larkin, *Interpretative Phenomenological Analysis: Theory, Method and Research* (London: SAGE, 2009).

[31] Kivle and Hirsch, 'Participation'.

[32] Kivle and Hirsch, 'Participation'.

[33] A. Tjora, *Kvalitative forskningsmetoder i praksis* (2nd vol) (Oslo: Gyldendal Akademisk, 2012).

The mothers with Somali backgrounds who took part in the group interviews lived in city districts in Oslo with an accumulation of welfare problems and a high proportion of immigrants. The parents from the parental guidance course lived in various city districts of Oslo with more variations in living conditions. All participants, however, lived in neighbourhoods with a diverse or so-called super-diverse population.

Participants of group interviews	27 mothers
Country of origin	Somalia
Reason for immigration	Refugees or family reunification
Age	39–57
Number of children	2–9
Age of children	5–32 years old (all mothers had teenagers)
Children born and raised	Somalia or Norway (majority Norway)
Education in Norway	Norwegian courses to upper secondary level
Everyday activity	Homemaking, education, traineeship, or work
Marital status	Single mothers or married
Years of stay in Norway	12–26 years

Table 1

Participants of parental guidance course	19 parents
Country of origin	Somalia, Iraq, Syria, Pakistan, Vietnam, Morocco
Reason for immigration	Refugees or family reunification
Age	32–60
Number of children	2–7
Age of children	3–31 years (half of them teenagers)
Children born and raised	Country of origin or Norway
Education in Norway and everyday activity	Primary education for adults combined with homemaking or traineeship
Years of stay in Norway	4–24 years
Marital status	Single parents or married
Norwegian skills	Relatively low

Table 2

Thematic analysis was applied[34] to identify and analyse patterns and themes of the data. In the first readings, I found that all parents identified strategies for preventing risk for their teenagers in their local communities. In the next phase,

[34] V. Braun and V. Clarke, 'Using Thematic Analysis in Psychology,' *Qualitative Research in Psychology*, 3:2 (2006), 77-101.

I asked questions to the data material such as: 'What do they perceive as risks?'; 'What do they say about their parenting strategies to prevent risks?' and 'What does the community mean for their parenting strategies?' Subsequently, I reread the interviews and field notes and compared the topics within and across them to look for patterns. During this phase, I identified the perceived risks and strategies to prevent risks that emerged from the material. In the next phase, I blended empirical and theoretical investigation of the data.

Results

First, I present findings related to the parents' perceived risks, followed by strategies to prevent these risks.

Perceived Risks

When newly arrived, the parents expressed insecurity and fear which, for some, decreased when becoming more familiar with society. For others, the feeling of unsafety remained after many years in Norway. When having adolescents, the parents experienced less contact with other parents and the schools than when they had younger children; they also reported that social support was more challenging to obtain. Furthermore, the parents reported less understanding of where their teenage children were and with whom.

The parents, particularly those living in the most disadvantaged areas, feared that their teenagers would experience risks. They talked about their continuous monitoring efforts to prevent risks and discussed the best ways to protect their teenagers. An essential premise in their narratives was that teenagers differ from one another and cannot all be treated in the same way. Parents indicated that some follow their parents' norms more than others and that girls were easier to handle than boys. Some had teenagers already in risky situations as part of 'delinquent' youth communities, and their focus was on strategies to remove them from the risks. Other parents indicated that their teenagers were doing fine, but they had heard stories about teenagers in risky situations 'going the wrong way'. The parents used various strategies, depending on their perception of their neighbourhood, the parents' and the teenager's personalities, and what types of risks they perceived; they also indicated that their strategies had changed over time.

The parents recognised different kinds of risks: 1) Some of the perceived risks were what parents with teenagers generally fear, such as too much gaming and social media, 'bad friends', social withdrawal or failing in school. 2) Some were related to existing risks in the parents' neighbourhoods, sometimes reflected in crime rates, such as fear of delinquent activities. 3) They also expressed fear related to their minority position, such as fear of discrimination, and 4) related to the families' religious backgrounds (mainly Muslim), and a fear that their teenagers would violate religious or cultural norms.

The recognised risks were also affected by perceived risks in the parents' networks and parents' lack of knowledge about their neighbours and the Norwegian society. Objective conditions of the neighbourhood were also important: Level of perceived risks, level of social cohesion, and whether teenagers were in risky situations or simply had the potential to be in risky situations.

One mother from a neighbourhood she perceived as unsafe expressed that the problem was not that she lacked knowledge but that teenagers listen more to their peers than to her. She experienced that the youth community, therefore, had more influence. Some worried that the adolescents had too few extracurricular activities and places to stay, making them hang out in the streets. Because this neighbourhood was situated near the city centre, it also attracted youth from all over the city, increasing the neighbourhood's delinquent situation. Some of the parents had teenagers involved in delinquent activities and described parenting in these neighbourhoods as particularly challenging, and even more so for single parents with little material resources, little education, low Norwegian skills, and little familiarity with the Norwegian welfare system. For some, the perceived risks were related to their relatively low socio-economic position and a fear that their adolescents, to be able to afford what other adolescents have, would be easier to exploit to do delinquent activities. On the other hand, one of the mothers said that her son had similar challenges despite having two parents with stable economic status. The local youth community was the same regardless of the parents' living conditions.

Parents in the same community with teenagers *not* involved in delinquent activities feared that their teenagers would be involved in or be victims of others' delinquent activities. Some of the parents also experienced that their sons, because of their minority status, were often controlled by the police, despite having no criminal record, making them feel labelled as criminals.

Parenting Strategies

In the following section, I will present the parenting strategies used to prevent risks for adolescents. Two sub-strategies were identified: strategies for setting boundaries and strategies for participation in the community.

Setting Boundaries

Some said that the parenting strategies they were raised with did not always function in Norway and they found it challenging to understand how to set boundaries for their teenagers. For example, the parents indicated that they had more defined roles in their family hierarchies in their countries of origin. However, once in Norway, these parents experienced the reality that more communication was expected between parents and children. The teenagers, on the other hand, were more influenced by the expectations from the Norwegian context, which led to a lack of mutual understanding and increased conflict and distance between parents and children. The parents described the reality as being that some teenagers, who viewed their parents' upbringings as too strict, sought acceptance and community outside the family. The parents indicated that this might make them vulnerable to negative influences. In other cases, parents reported that their teenagers took advantage of their parents' insecurity in their monitoring and went so far as to threaten calling child-welfare services if they did not get what they wanted. Because the parents fear such child-welfare intervention, some expressed that they 'give in' to what the teenagers want: '… the control goes out… no boundaries'. Some indicated taking a passive role concerning their teenagers, expressed feeling powerless and often waited for hours for their teenagers to call or come home in the evenings. Not all struggled with setting boundaries, however. Some encouraged the other parents to set boundaries early and continue throughout childhood, making sure the children understand that 'no is no'.

In addition to a 'hierarchic', a 'permissive' and a 'consistent boundaries' approach, some parents described a fourth way of setting boundaries. These parents are what I would call *communicators*. When describing how they communicated with their adolescents, they used words such as 'meeting them in the middle', 'meeting them where they are', or 'we should not use coercion'. Some also wanted to be role models for their adolescents and support and motivate them. Others informed them about the consequences of different actions. Several participants had attended parental guidance courses or received help from child-welfare services to learn how to communicate effectively with their teenagers. Others said that Islam had inspired them not to coerce their teenagers: 'Their destiny is in Allah's hands', they said, and indicated that they felt they could not 'force it'. Referring to the Somali parenting tradition, one of the mothers described the teenage period as the period where parents are supposed to make friends with their children. Others believed that not being too strict or controlling was necessary, as doing otherwise could cause teenagers to do what their parents did not want them to or avoid disclosing problems they might have to their parents.

The parents indicated that they know what is essential to give their children a 'good upbringing', but they expressed a lack of knowledge about raising children in 'two different cultures'. The more knowledge they have, the steadier the boundaries they feel they can set. One mother said: 'If Mom and Dad know what is right and wrong in Norway, the situation becomes calmer.' The parents sought knowledge on what is expected of parents in Norway and what constitutes legal and illegal parenting. They sought to establish well-functioning communication methods in the Norwegian context, encouraging their teenagers to follow the parents' norms without creating a vast and lasting conflict.

Participation in the Community

The parents' involvement and their processes of inclusion and exclusion in the local community varied. I identified the various strategies as follows: *the active, the support-seeking*, *the distancing*, *the avoiding*, and *the passive* strategies.

The active: One way that parents tried to protect teenagers was by *actively participating* in the local community. In our study, mothers from communities they perceived to be dangerous or disadvantaged reported wandering through the neighbourhood streets in the evenings to protect their children and other teenagers and indicated that the adolescents listened more to someone from similar backgrounds. Some expressed the desire to know the teenagers' friends, where their children were and what they did, or encouraged their adolescents to attend extracurricular activities. They also attended meetings in their communities organised by the police or the welfare services to ask for help and advice.

The support-seeking: Some parents used a parenting strategy that I describe as *support seeking*. They sought support and advice for their parenting from their surroundings: school, neighbours, friends, the mosque, and parents with majority background. They also organised support through networks in Norway with people from similar backgrounds that gave each other advice in their parenting and ensured 'no one is left alone when facing the welfare services'. However, some parents found the advice from this kind of network caused too much interference, and found it difficult to disclose their challenges even to those with similar backgrounds because they worried that the other parents would share their personal information. Fear of child-welfare services may also make it more difficult to tell others about their challenges or seek help. For some parents, this fear was related to personal experiences with child-welfare services, whilst others had heard 'stories' about children taken away from their parents.

The parents also reported trying to participate in the fellowship of the local community with parents and neighbours of immigrant and Norwegian backgrounds. For some, this provided valuable support in their parenting. Some spoke of good relationships with neighbours, noting that they ask them for advice, visit each other and give each other food.

Some parents sought help from the welfare services. They sought guidance from courses or child-welfare services on parenting teenagers. In severe cases, they sought help to place the adolescent in another part of Norway for some months to decrease influences from a 'delinquent' youth community. Conversely, one of the mothers encouraged the welfare services to help the entire local youth community, follow them up more closely and involve the adolescents in creating solutions. Others requested the local welfare services to provide more extracurricular activities for adolescents or sought economic support to give the teenagers 'what other teenagers have'. They also requested the police not to discriminate against the adolescents.

The distancing: Other parents maintained a *distance* in relationships with the welfare services and people in their community of Norwegian backgrounds. Some parents in the study indicated that parents with Norwegian backgrounds did not speak to them at gatherings for parents and their children's classmates. Some experienced neighbours who did not reply when the parents greeted them or turned their faces away when they passed. This created a feeling of social exclusion. Another mother said that her family also kept some distance from the local community because they were unfamiliar with the Norwegian culture. They were worried about what would happen to their children if they visited neighbours and, for instance, feared that their children might receive food that is not halal or would see their classmates' parents drinking alcohol. Some also found it difficult to approach new people when they did not know the Norwegian language well. However, they noted that the distance decreased when they became more acquainted with their neighbours: 'Getting to know each other can change the world. Then the prejudice disappears.'

The avoiding: Another parenting strategy is one I will describe as the *avoiding.* These parents expressed that they actively tried to keep their teenagers out of danger by avoiding risk situations. Some parents reported living in disadvantaged neighbourhoods that they believed were not safe for their teenagers. Therefore, the parents tried to keep their children at home as much as possible to avoid them hanging out with 'delinquent' youth. One participant indicated that this involved telling her teenagers to go directly home from school and not talk to anyone hanging out in the streets. She called them if they took too long on their way home and complained about other parents letting their teenagers be outside unsupervised. Others gave their teenagers a PlayStation or expensive clothes to make them stay away from the streets. These parents were concerned with ensuring their teenagers avoided having 'bad friends', as they believed it would 'infect' their children. Some indicated asking their teenagers to 'cut' their connections with friends that the parents believed had immoral values or were a 'bad influence'; others made their children change schools to remove them from a community perceived as risky. Some knew parents who 'threw their teenagers out' due to fear that the delinquent behaviour would spread to the child's siblings.

The passive: Some parents were *passive* in their communities and found it challenging to contribute to them because they had 'lost faith' as parents after losing some of their children to child-welfare services.

Discussion

This study investigated parenting strategies that immigrant parents used to protect their teenagers from risks in their neighbourhoods regarding the sub-strategies *setting boundaries* and *participation in the neighbourhood.*

Risk and protective factors are unequally distributed in society.[35] The parents in this study had less privileged positions, and some faced severe parenting stressors in their neighbourhoods. However, my findings showed that the parents creatively strived to solve their parenting dilemmas. Moreover, although they had similar educational and occupational levels, and some also belonged to the same ethnic group, the participants differed in parenting strategies.

The connection between perceived risks and parenting strategies is complex. Some strategies were connected to preventing specific risks, such as avoiding the streets to shield adolescents from delinquency or keeping a distance from the community to avoid violating religious and cultural norms. However, the same type of risk may also be met by various strategies by the same parent, or different parents making different choices of strategies. For instance, they nearly used all the strategies mentioned above to prevent delinquency. They used the communicating, distancing, and avoiding strategies to prevent violating cultural and religious norms. They varied between support seeking, active and passive strategies to prevent discrimination and failure in school. Some strategies were also used to prevent risks in general.

The strategies were also related to the neighbourhoods where they lived. The participants' perceptions of their neighbourhoods ranged from sceptic attitudes and feelings of unsafety to experiencing them as safe spaces. This variety in experience led some parents to employ isolation or strict monitoring, whilst others searched for social support and communication in their parenting. These findings are consistent with Visser and colleagues, who argue that parenting practices vary according to the parents' levels of involvement in their neighbourhoods and how they perceive them.[36] The strategies in this study, related to participation in the community, also corresponded with Visser and colleagues' parenting strategies.[37] The promotive strategy corresponds with the active and the support-seeking strategies; the protective strategy corresponds with the distancing and avoiding strategies.

As newcomers in Norway or living in neighbourhoods perceived as unsafe, the parents in our study mainly used a protective strategy (avoiding and distancing). The level of fear in parenting differed amongst and within the various neighbourhoods, and the parents in the most disadvantaged neighbourhood, perceived as unsafe, appeared more worried than the other parents. The participants living in this neighbourhood with teenagers not at risk seemed to employ the isolation or avoidance strategies most often. They were also the parents who seemed to monitor their teenagers more strictly. In my interpretation, the isolation and avoiding strategies were not the most favourable options. However, they were used due to a lack of alternative strategies or resources.

---

[35] Solem, 'Understanding', 86.

[36] Visser et al., 'A Good Place'.

[37] Visser et al., 'A Good Place'.

Parenting strategies are dynamic and may be changed and modified over time based on increased experience. When the parents perceived their neighbourhoods as safe, and experienced social cohesion, conviviality, and inclusion, they seemed to shift towards a more promotive and support-seeking strategy, even in disadvantaged communities. When having a trusting relationship with the child-welfare services or seeing no other options for help, they also actively involved them. One mother changed from a hierarchic and avoiding strategy to a communicating and actively participating strategy during her time in Norway. She described how her sceptical attitude towards the surroundings when she arrived in Norway affected her relationship with her daughter. However, her monitoring changed when she became more familiar with Norwegian society. She reported that the insecurity in her parenting decreased over time because she actively participated in society through education, work, and learning the Norwegian language. These actions made her feel safer in her surroundings, less controlling in her monitoring, and more secure in her self-efficacy as a mother.

Parents with challenging living conditions may be in most need of well-functioning social cohesion in their communities and social support surrounding their parenting. However, these parents may also be those who have little social support.[38] Whether the parents in this study used a support-seeking strategy by building networks with neighbours of different backgrounds did not necessarily depend on the level of disorganisation of the neighbourhood, as Sampson describes.[39] Instead, it may depend on the parents' experiences of social distance or social connection to these neighbours. That, in turn, depended on whether the parents felt included, experienced racism, had close friendships, and whether they trusted that their neighbours would respect their religious standards. Most parents used selective strategies[40] by receiving support from parents of similar backgrounds, both within and outside their neighbourhoods.

Conclusion and Implications for Practice and Further Research

This study shows that for parents to strengthen their capacity to handle risks, it may be helpful to have increased knowledge about society and adequate communication methods with adolescents in a Norwegian context. However, interventions that target only one parent or one family at a time is not sufficient. Actors in community development need to understand how parenting is related to the families' context. They need to build support structures around and relationships amongst parents and strengthen the networks and relationships that parents already have. Efforts towards mutual inclusion, trust-building and decreasing stereotypes amongst neighbours are essential to enhance conviviality

---

38 Beyers et al., 'Neighborhood'.

39 Sampson, 'How Do'.

40 Visser et al., 'A Good Place'.

and social cohesion. These efforts may, in turn, ensure that parents are less vulnerable.[41] In community work, it is also crucial to listen to the parents' perceptions of their perceived risks and parental strategies, and involve them in finding solutions. However, efforts to strengthen families and their networks must also be followed by efforts on the structural level: to improve living conditions, decrease structural inequalities in society, create safer local environments and, by this, make parenting less challenging.

In this study, I had access to the parents' perspectives only. Further research is needed on the effects of various strategies for preventing risks to adolescents and the adolescents' perceptions of their parents' strategies.

Bibliography

Addy, T., Approaches to Community Development in H. M. et al. (eds.), *Developing Just and Inclusive Communities. Challenges for Diakonia as Christian Social Practice and for Social Work* (Oxford, Regnum, 2022).

Beyers, J. M., Bates, J. E., Pettit, G. S., & Dodge, K. A. 'Neighborhood Structure, Parenting Processes, and the Development of Youths' Externalising Behaviors: A Multilevel Analysis', *American Journal of Community Psychology*, 31:1 (2003).

Braun, V., & Clarke, V. 'Using Thematic Analysis in Psychology', *Qualitative Research in Psychology*, 3:2 (2006).

Brody, G. H., Conger, R., Gibbons, F. X., Ge, X., McBride Murry, V., Gerrard, M., & Simons, R. L. 'The Influence of Neighborhood Disadvantage, Collective Socialisation, and Parenting on African American Children's Affiliation with Deviant Peers', *Child Development*, 72:4 (2001).

Ceballo, R., & Hurd, N. 'Neighbourhood Context, SES, and Parenting: Including a Focus on Acculturation among Latina Mothers.' *Applied Developmental Science*, 12:4 (2008).

Cuellar, J., Jones, D. J., & Sterrett, E. 'Examining Parenting in the Neighborhood Context: A Review', *Journal of Child and Family Studies*, 24:1 (2015).

Creswell, J. W. *Research Design* (Los Angeles: SAGE Publications, 2014).

Franco, L. M., Pottick, K.J., & Huang, C.C. 'Early Parenthood in a Community Context: Neighborhood Conditions, Race–Ethnicity, and Parenting Stress.' *Journal of Community Psychology*, 38:5 (2010).

Isola, A-M., Roivainen I., & Hiilamo H. 'Lone Mothers' Experiences of Poverty in Finland: A Capability Approach.' *Nordic Social Work Research* (2020).

Jarrett, R. L., & Jefferson, S. R. '"A Good Mother Got to Fight for Her Kids": Maternal Management Strategies in a High-Risk, African-American Neighborhood', *Journal of Children and Poverty*, 9:1 (2003).

---

[41] Wise and Noble, 'Convivialities'; see also Beyers et al., 'Neighborhood'.

Jiao, Q. G., Onwuegbuzie, A. J., & Collins, K. M. (eds.), *Toward a Broader Understanding of Stress and Coping: Mixed Methods Approaches* (Charlotte, NC: IAP, 2010).

Kivle, B. M. T., & Hirsch, S. M. H. (2020). 'Participation in Research: Experiences from Collaborating with Co-creators During a Study among Mothers of Teenagers with Immigrant Backgrounds in Oslo', *Diaconia*, 10:2 (2008).

Kohen, D. E., Leventhal, T., Dahinten, V. S., & McIntosh, C. N. 'Neighborhood Disadvantage: Pathways of Effects for Young Children.' *Child Development*, 79:1 (2008).

Kotchick, B. A., & Forehand, R. 'Putting Parenting in Perspective: A Discussion of the Contextual Factors that Shape Parenting Practices.' *Journal of Child and Family Studies*, 11:3 (2002).

Kruger, D. J., Reischl, T. M., & Gee, G. C. 'Neighborhood Social Conditions Mediate the Association Between Physical Deterioration and Mental Health.' *American Journal of Community Psychology*, 40: 3-4 (2007).

Luster, T., & Okagaki, L. *Parenting: An Ecological Perspective* (volume 2) (New York: Routledge, 2006).

Pizarro, K. W., Surkan, P. J., & Bustamante, I. V. 'The Social Ecology of Parental Monitoring: Parent–Child Dynamics in a High-Risk Peruvian Neighborhood.' *Family Process*, 60:1 (2021).

Sampson, R. J., 'How Do Communities Undergird or Undermine Human Development? Relevant Contexts and Social Mechanisms'. *Does it Take a Village? Community Effects on Children, Adolescents, and Families*. Eds. A. Booth & A. C. Crouter (Mahwah, NJ: Lawrence Erlbaum, 2011).

Sletteland, N., & Donovan, R. M. *Helsefremmende lokalsamfunn* [Health-promoting communities] (Oslo: Gyldendal Akademisk, 2012).

Smith, J. A., Flowers, P., & Larkin, M. *Interpretative Phenomenological Analysis. Theory, Method and Research* (London: SAGE, 2009).

Solem, M. 'Understanding Parenting as Situated in the Larger Socio-cultural Context in Clinical Social Work', *Child & Adolescents Social Work Journal*, 30:1 (2013).

Tjora, A. *Kvalitative forskningsmetoder i praksis* (2. vol), [Qualitative research methods in practice] (Oslo: Gyldendal Akademisk, 2012).

Toft, M. and Ljunggren J. 'Geographies of Class Advantage: The Influence of Adolescent Neighbourhoods in Oslo', *Urban Studies*, 53:14 (2016).

Visser, K., Bolt, G., & van Kempen, R., 'A Good Place to Raise Your Children? The Diversity of Parents' Neighbourhood Perceptions and Parenting Practices in a Low-income, Multi-ethnic Neighbourhood: A Case Study in Rotterdam', *Geoforum,* 64 (2015), 112-120.

Wise, A., & Noble, G.' Convivialities: An Orientation', *Journal of Intercultural Studies*, 37:5 (2016), 423-431.

Wolfe, G., Jaffe, P. G., & Crooks. *Why Teens Experiment and Strategies to Keep Them Safe* (New Haven CT: Yale University Press, 2006).

Part Four

Learning, Social Innovation and Leadership

Ministerial Formation of Former 'Mission Churches' in South Africa: 'Missional Consciousness' as an Enabler for Community Development

Eugene Baron

Introduction

The former mission churches in South Africa were ushered into a new dispensation when the country moved into a new phase in terms of its political landscape. Since 1990 and the release of former President Nelson Mandela, the churches were called to reflect on their position within the new South Africa. Churches that were for an extended period constituted along racial lines have held discussions to amalgamate. Some became structurally one denomination in April 1994.[1] Some of these include the Uniting Reformed Church in Southern Africa (URCSA), and the Uniting Presbyterian Church in Southern Africa (UPCSA), as well as other 'mission churches'[2] embarking on such a journey. However, this chapter provides a critical reflection on these churches as 'mission churches' in South Africa. It remains to be seen if the challenge for witness in the world through community development is indeed based on available resources, forming partnerships with their white counterparts, or a matter of consciousness from within the 'mission churches' themselves and specifically in ministerial formation processes – those of ministerial candidates.

In South Africa, the social development approach is articulated in the White Paper on Social Development and highlights the following components:

---

[1] This has reference to the Dutch Reformed Mission and Church (coloured congregations) and the Dutch Reformed Church in Africa (DRCA) (African members) that became the Uniting Reformed Church in Southern Africa (URCSA). However, the 'white church", namely, the Dutch Reformed Church (DRC) did not yet become united with the two former mission churches. The Uniting Presbyterian Church in Southern Africa (UPCSA) is the amalgamation between the white church, the Presbyterian Church of Southern Africa (*PCSA*), and the black (mission) church, Reformed Presbyterian Church in Southern Africa (*RPCSA*).

[2] The reference to mission church in the paper, refers to those churches that were often established by missionaries of foreign churches. These churches were often supervised by the white missionaries, ministers and by those 'mother churches', though they operated separately.

'participation, empowerment, equity, accountability, accessibility and partnership'.[3] It is crucial for the development process in post-apartheid South Africa to empower the citizenry. In this regard, the church has become a space where members are trained to become agents of change in their respective communities.[4] The issue of 'empowerment' is close to the notion that the author propagates in this chapter.

The argument in this chapter will be structured in the following way: first, a conceptual discussion on what the author understood by these concepts and how they will function in this chapter, namely, 'mission churches', 'missional consciousness', 'ministerial formation' and 'community development'. Secondly, it will discuss the challenges that some scholars argue emerge within the churches' participation in community development. The author therefore introduces the important gap within the discussions – to add ministerial formation as a salient critical element to such a discourse. Thirdly, the author continues to scaffold the argument to contend that within such a ministerial formation process, specifically in the former mission churches, the core function should be the establishment of a 'missional consciousness'. Fourthly, the author reflects on the ministerial formation processes of two former mission churches, namely, the URCSA and UPCSA, and discusses the challenges and processes of ministerial formation in these churches. The author thereafter concludes and argues for a 'missional consciousness' as an enabler for community development.

A Conceptual Discussion

Through various mission work done in South Africa by way of mission agencies, the establishment of 'mission churches' happened sporadically. At the same time, through segregation in South Africa, the black (African coloured, Indian), and white churches operated separately. In most cases the white churches had the oversight function and guardianship over the 'non-white' churches in South Africa during apartheid. Moreover, the former mission churches were also largely dependent on these mother churches in terms of community development initiatives, leadership and projects, and would not take ownership completely of matters, events, and projects but would await the cue from the white churches. In this sense the white churches were often referred to as the 'mother' churches, and the mission churches as the 'daughter' churches. However, it is from here that the author draws his argument – that it remains important to venture on a

[3] Government of South Africa, White Paper for Social Welfare: Principles, Recommendations, Guidelines, Proposed Policies and Programmes for Developmental Social Welfare in South Africa (1997).

[4] A Nieman, 'Churches and Social Development in South Africa', in: I Swart (eds.), *Religion and Social Development in Post-apartheid South Africa. Perspectives for Critical Engagement* (Stellenbosch: Sun Press, 2010), 37.

road of psychological liberation of members, ministers and prospective ministers within the 'mission churches' (black ministers) from a dependency and paternalistic relationship and, rather, nurture a missional consciousness. Though there are numerous academic responses on fleshing out such a dependency syndrome, not much is articulated in terms of such a shift in 'consciousness'.

The notion of missional consciousness can be derived from the missional movement in North America, followed by a similar movement in South Africa,[5] which describes the church as 'missionary' in nature, being itself an agent of God in the world.[6] However, the notion does not only have significance for institutional churches, but also for individuals within the churches as witnesses of God in the world. Therefore, the notion of missional consciousness is indeed a notion coined by Baron in which he argues that people who have previously understood themselves to be sent by the church should also imagine themselves to be 'sent ones' of God.[7] Many churches found it difficult to understand themselves to be agents of God in the world when their experiences were full of external control, supervision, and the leadership of the white 'mother' churches, whereas their self-agency and self-development was stifled in the process.[8]

The 'mission churches' had their own ministerial formation processes before 1994, but mostly under supervision of the 'mother churches'. After becoming independent, they embarked on informal agreements with their white counterparts in terms of joint ministerial processes. These processes were not entirely successful for multiple reasons. Hence, whilst partnership was achieved, a shift of consciousness within the former mission churches did not fully come into its own. This also plays a role in 'community development' processes and ownership that remain a challenge for the churches in post-apartheid South Africa.

Community development is defined by Swanepoel and De Beer[9] as the concern of the church with societal or community challenges, not individual ones, but it needs 'communities' to solve the issues. Van Schalkwyk makes the distinction between development and community development: 'Whereas development is a process of directed social change, community development is

---

[5] See, for instance, Marais in Burger, C, Marais, F & Mouton, D (eds.), *Cultivating Missional Change. The Future of Missional Churches and Missional Theology* (Wellington, Bybelkor, 2017), 20–34.

[6] DL Guder, *Missional Church. A Vision for the Sending of the Church in North America* (Michigan: WB Eerdmans, 1998).

[7] See his articles, E. Baron, 'The Call for African Missional Consciousness through Renewed Mission Praxis in URCSA', *Studia Historiae Ecclesiasticae*, 45:3 (2020), 1-19; E. Baron and M.S. Maponya, 'The Recovery of the Prophetic Voice of the Church: The Adoption of a "Missional Church" Imagination', *Verbum Et Ecclesia* 41:1 (2020), 1–9.

[8] Baron, 'The Call'.

[9] H. Swanepoel and F. De Beer, *Community Development. Breaking the Cycle of Poverty,* Fifth edition (Parow: Juta, 2011), 2.

one method of planned change within the broader development framework....'[10] Community development is a process that is initially planned and organised by a local community. They identify the needs, the goals, and the strategic plan, to ensure sustainable development. Therefore, in terms of the above conceptual discussion the author argues that it would be salient to engender a 'missional consciousness' within ministerial processes in the former mission churches in the quest to address the participation of prospective ministers of former mission churches to initiate, lead and influence their members towards the creation, initiation, development, planning and participation in community development.

Church, Community Development and Ministerial Formation

Swart has argued that the modern paradigm repudiates the values that exist in African societies. Therefore, it has always been 'backward, inferior, in conflict with progress'.[11] But this attitude has not assisted community development at all because from such a premise there is nothing that the African societies can contribute unless they would allow for the westernised methodologies to be utilised. Therefore, African knowledge about their environment and society and its working has been lost. This concurs with Katongole,[12] arguing that the story for Africa from the west is that there is nothing good in Africa. He states that as long as Africans believe in that narrative and adopt the 'nation-state' narrative (modern paradigm), it will be a misfit for African communities. He calls for a different narrative that should be embraced by postcolonial society.

Moreover, there has to be a shift of consciousness for both rich and poor,[13] because development should also be viewed through the lenses of 'class' and not exclusively by 'race' as is often the case in South African development discourse.[14] The problem, however, is not often the influence of the church in the west, or colonisation, but also the ministers that have often been so removed from their context for quite some time (academia) that their circumstances and their status (class) has changed dramatically, from being a member of a congregation to becoming a minister of the church. During such a transition they often become insensitive to some of the realities faced by congregants, the community and congregations which they serve and, therefore, conscientisation

---

[10] A. Van Schalkwyk, 'The Church, Community Development, and Liberation', *Missionalia*, 24:1 (1996), 40-62, 49.

[11] I Swart, 'Church, Mission and Development. Revisiting the Pragmatic Debate', in Swart, I. et al. (eds.) *Religion and Social Development in Post-apartheid South Africa. Perspectives for Critical Engagement*. Pretoria: Sun Press, 2010) 243-259, 249.

[12] EM Katongole, *The Sacrifice of Africa. A Political Theology for Africa* (Grand Rapids, Michigan: WMB Eerdmans, 2011), 121

[13] Swart, 'Church', 249.

[14] Swart states: 'Conscientisation for development involves a double entry point in which the rich and powerful are to be brought to an alternative consciousness determined by the interests and point of view of the poor.'; Swart, 'Church', 249.

is also needed for ministers of the Word, broader than a racial analysis, but also in terms of class. It is often the case that their 'conversation partners' (interlocutors) have changed since being enrolled as a student at university.

However, Swart makes a further analysis in which he argues that often the focus is on the poor when interrogating the influence of class on development. The church's analysis should also be on the rich and the privileged.[15] It would therefore be important for ministers to develop a consciousness about the relationship between the rich and the poor, as well as their own consciousness that might have changed during their studies. An alternative consciousness is required even in the confines of the church. Whilst ministers have moved to a different class in society, they are still confronted with a congregation that is trapped in paternalism. The ministers need to provide spiritual guidance to break those strongholds.

The discussion of consciousness has to do with the question, 'Who am I, and what must I do?'[16] It becomes, therefore, more than only an issue of involvement as a community within development activities. However, it becomes personal and reflexive. It is to develop a consciousness of one's own praxis as God's agent in the world. Kritzinger calls for 'reflexive praxis' as a necessary approach of agents in mission.[17] This would entail an awareness of who I am, but also who the other is through our encounter with one another that would be crucial for the shifting of consciousness in community development projects as well. This has been slightly differently posited by Swart who argues in terms of class interaction, as the poor challenges the 'consciousness' and the ideological life worlds of the rich.[18]

It is in terms of a 'shift of consciousness' that Swart would argue that the black churches would be able to contribute immensely because of being an exponent of a 'pedagogy of the oppressed' that would be able to make a meaningful contribution in terms of the need for 'personal change, spirituality, values and ethics in order to achieve systemic change – in the language of the pragmatic debate, the need for liberation, a spiritual renewal, a conversion of the rich and powerful and their lifeworlds.'[19] Swart argues that the church should become in its nature missional – which in community development will imply that it becomes an extended community that will be able to draw 'outsiders to participate and share in its activities of renewal.'[20] In terms of linking community development with a 'missional ecclesiology' Swart argues that the church is the place where the poor and oppressed are finding the 'transformative' action and

---

[15] Swart, 'Church', 252.

[16] J. Klaasen, 'The Role of Personhood in Development: An African Perspective on Development in South Africa', *Missionalia*, 45.1 (2017), 29-44, 33.

[17] JNJ Kritzinger, 'Faith to Faith – Missiology as Encounterology', *Verbum Et Ecclesia*, 29:3 (2008), 764-790.

[18] Swart, 'Church', 253.

[19] Swart, 'Church', 253.

[20] Swart, 'Church', 254.

life, from which subsequently, the church participates and collaborates with the rich, not as 'dependent' but as co-creators and collaborators of the transformation of structures in society.[21]

Therefore, it is crucial for a minister to understand their role in the church, but also inter-relationships within the church, as this will be key in terms of 'empowerment' or 'disempowerment'.[22] In this sense a minister as a 'missional leader' would be pivotal. He must address 'domination' and power relationships that stifle the empowerment of the poor in their midst. Klaasen emphasises 'self-development', where the person understands themselves as 'created in the image of God', as part of the 'whole of creation',[23] referring to Desmond Tutu's notion of 'interdependence'.[24] MacIntyre affirms: 'Where interdependence, the mutual giving and receiving, is exercised, there is no room for politics of competing interests. Care results in the narrowing of the gap between rich and poor.'[25]

Why Are Ministers Not Involved in Community Development?

Despite the collaborative activities and projects between former 'mission churches' and their white counterparts, there seems not to be a shift in consciousness. As the former mission churches were previously in a subservient relationship with their white counterparts or 'mother churches', it remains questionable whether collaboration projects are sufficient. It was the mother churches that normally took the initiative for the 'daughter churches' (mission churches), therefore it could not be argued that there was agency of the 'mission churches' during apartheid in South Africa. Van Schalkwyk states that during apartheid the 'mother church'(es) (such as the Dutch Reformed Church) did well in terms of development, building of educational and health service, but without 'local participation'.[26]

It has always been conceded that Christian ministers should be sensitive, aware, act prophetically and develop strategies to address social development challenges in their respective communities of which they form part.[27] Kritzinger echoes those pointing to the absence of the churches and their apparent insufficient engagement with the present challenges of South Africa.[28] Makofane and Botha agree, but do present some emerging signs of the churches' re-

---

[21] Swart, 'Church', 255.
[22] Swart, 'Church', 250.
[23] Klaasen, 'The role', 44.
[24] Klaasen, 'The Role', 37-38.
[25] A. MacIntyre, Dependent Rational Animals. Why Human Beings Need the Virtues. (London: Duckworth, 1999), 144-145.
[26] Van Schalkwyk, 'The Church', 44.
[27] Baron and Maponya, 'The Recovery'.
[28] JNJ Kritzinger, 'Overcoming Theological Voicelessness in the New Millennium', *Missionalia*, 40:3 (2012), 233–250.

engagement with the public.[29] However, in their engagements the church is understood as the 'institutional' church, not the engagement of all members within the churches, especially the disempowered, and the average church attender.

When analysing the engagement and disengagement of the church in South Africa in the public sphere, several reasons for the silence are given, all affecting the inability of the post-apartheid church to read its context.[30] Hence, the nurturing of 'missional consciousness' within the former mission churches; particular ministers of the Word in these churches were not prioritised.[31] This calls for some reflection on how the ministerial formation processes of such churches has, through its programmes, methodologies and theological content, been able – or not – to reform the praxis of black ministerial candidates and infuse a 'missional consciousness' for its members. However, the call for 'missional consciousness' of ministers does not mean the stifling of the agency of the laity, but, indeed, a consciousness of ministers would mean that they would understand their role as clergy as being different; that the clergy and the laity are co-workers in addressing the challenges of the community.[32]

Kritzinger, involved in the ministerial formation process in URCSA,[33] provides certain suggestions on how to deal with the 'voicelessness' of the church.[34] He focuses widely on ministerial processes.[35] However, he stresses that course modules presented at the universities should always be aimed at contributing towards the common good.[36] This could be done through a concept he uses as a metaphor: 'roots and wings'. His approach asks for good self-identification but respectful engagement with others. The issue of 'self-identification' should be part and parcel of the process of ministerial formation but more specifically, a reflection on the effects of the apartheid past on their

---

[29] K. Makofane and N. Botha, 'Christianity and Social Transformation in Post-apartheid South Africa: From Prophetic Quietism to Signs of Prophetic Recovery', *Acta Theologica*, 28:6 (2019), 88–103.

[30] Kritzinger, 'Overcoming', 234-236, the reasons listed are shock, inferiority, guilt, apathy, friendship (with those in power), world-view and (too strong) admiration.

[31] See particular Baron's (2019) article on the URCSA and its history as a 'mission church' which has still to cultivate a missional consciousness and get rid of the system of paternalism.

[32] H.J. Hendriks, 'Missional Theology and Social Development', HTS Theological Studies 63.3 (2007), 1008.

[33] Kritzinger, JNJ, Maponya, MS and Mokoena, KK. '25 Years of Ministerial Formation Praxis in the Uniting Reformed Church in Southern Africa: How Belharic Have We Become?' Studia Historiae Ecclesiasticae 45:3 (2019). All authors are at the Northern Theological Seminary (NTS) as the formation centre for URCSA.

[34] Kritzinger, 'Overcoming', 249.

[35] See his article, Kritzinger, JNJ. 2010. 'Ministerial Formation Praxis in the Uniting Reformed Church in Southern Africa: In Search of Inclusion and authenticity', *Missionalia*, 38 (2): 211-234.

[36] Kritzinger, 'Overcoming', 248.

future actions in ministry. Without reading too much into what Kritzinger proposes for ministerial formation, he does in his own way address the issue of 'missional consciousness' in which the former mission churches would allow students to come to a self-consciousness.[37]

Makofane and Botha suggest a transformation of Christianity itself:

> One fairly clear issue is that the essential transformation of Christianity is not more doctrine or more confessions, but a conversion of Christianity to particular categories of people in society, including women, children, the disabled, and the working-class people, in general, as well as those affected most by socio-economic inequality, unemployment and poverty.[38]

They argue that because the churches are not reflecting together on the situation of the poor, and *not* being at the margins, they have not been able to transform themselves.[39] The abuses of religion show the symptoms of a church that is no longer conscious of the 'downtrodden', the 'marginalised' the unemployed and the needy.[40]

Baron and Maponya also argue for the prophetic voice of the church in the context of social transformation and development.[41] According to their argument, the challenge lies in the 'ecclesial imaginations' which is related to the consciousness of members within the church becoming a context in which members will re-imagine themselves and the church as an agent of God's mission on earth. This is the core of a missional consciousness.

In Quest of a Missional Consciousness in Two Former 'Mission Churches'

(a) The Uniting Reformed Church in Southern Africa (URCSA)

The history of URCSA's ministerial formation was one of dependency on the DRC for infrastructure funding for its training 'centres'. However, at URCSA's 1997 synod after the establishment of URCSA in 1994, it declared that the training of ministers of URCSA would from then be the responsibility of URCSA.[42] This could facilitate a shift of consciousness among students who would enter such URCSA ministerial formation centres. However, this decision from URCSA General Synod is not adequate to ensure that those graduating have a shift in consciousness.

---

[37] Kritzinger, 'Overcoming', 248.
[38] Makofane and Botha, 'Christianity', 94.
[39] Makofane and Botha, 'Christianity', 96.
[40] Makofane and Botha, 'Christianity', 96.
[41] Baron and Maponya, 'The Recovery'.
[42] They stated, 'Die opleiding van sy bedienaars van die Woord is die verantwoordelikheid van die Verenigende Gereformeerde Kerk'; see VGKSA, *Agenda en Handelinge* (Belhar: Lusboek, 1997), 154.

Kritzinger argues that what the students learn during the formal curriculum at university should be aligned with practice,[43] and this is where he also sees the role that the ministerial formation centres of the church should play. He explains at great length the practical skills[44] that prospective URCSA ministers should acquire in the process and how it could not be divorced from the epistemology they are exposed to at the still predominantly white DRC influenced universities,[45] and therefore, during the five years of ministerial formation and training (the prerequisite time of study before being ordained as a minister), it is important to cultivate a certain 'consciousness'.

Taking the URCSA as a whole, four central factors are identified as pivotal for URCSA:[46] a consciousness of 'self-reliance'; strengthening patterns of responsibility; developing its own curriculum; and legitimising African epistemologies in the curriculums. Overall, URCSA and its ministerial formation centre need to become equal partners with the DRC's already well-functioning ministerial formation structures, and that will rid them from the shackles of paternalism.

One important institution is the Northern Theological Seminary (NTS),which is part of URCSA. It has adopted the motto 'African and Reformed' which makes African values part of the formation process, exposing students to various contexts, and allowing them to place their studies and ministry within the African context.

Finally, one purpose of ministerial formation should be to train prospective ministers as trainers of their members in the congregations.[47] Hence, ministers can cultivate a new consciousness amongst their congregants of the churches to which they would be called. These strategies will establish also a 'missional consciousness' amongst the prospective ministers which would make future relationships ones of interdependency rather than dependency.

(b) The Uniting Presbyterian Church in Southern Africa (UPCSA)

Turning to ministerial formation of the UPCSA, a slightly smaller church than the URCSA, an assessment of the process to have one ministerial formation is

---

[43] JNJ. Kritzinger, 'Ministerial Formation Praxis in the Uniting Reformed Church in Southern Africa: In Search of Inclusion and authenticity', *Missionalia*, 38:2 (2010), 211-234.

[44] The ministerial formation for URCSA students involved one hundred hours' practical work in an URCSA congregation per year. For the five years of studies at the University the ministerial candidates should also have acquired five hundred hours of practical work during their ministerial formation at a congregation, and through a mentor (ministers) that was assigned by URCSA.

[45] Kritzinger, 'Ministerial Formation'.

[46] Kritzinger, 'Ministerial Formation'.

[47] Kritzinger et al., '25 Years', 12.

revealing.[48] The main institution for UPCSA is the University of Pretoria (UP), but this is not the only university available for those seeking to become UPCSA ministers.

The tendency is that white theology students of the church prefer other universities to UP. Therefore, it is still a challenge to produce a formation process in which both black and white students would participate as equal partners: 'As it stands at the moment, it is not healthy for a united church that its black candidates for ministry are training at UP, whilst their white counterparts train in other institutions…'[49] There is every reason to agree with this.

Using similar arguments as Kritzinger, the authors call for 'reconstructive discourse promoting authentic African epistemologies.'[50] They also call for a 'spirituality of inclusion' as being crucial in promoting a missional consciousness.[51] Including these vital elements as part of the ministerial formation process must be considered crucial for the UPCSA congregations' role in community development.

The Need for Missional Consciousness in Ministerial Formation

Whilst the chapter has not analysed all aspects of community development, there are obvious relationships between ministerial formation processes and the ability of the churches to be active partners in community development. Missional consciousness seems imperative to strengthen both and the future relationship between the two.

Hendriks made the link between mission and development when he argues for a paradigm shift in missiology.[52] He argues that one should think not in terms of the old missionary (clerical) paradigm.[53] One element of such ecumenical thinking could be to learn from African Independent Churches (AIC).[54] They initiate credible associations and small businesses, whilst the previous mission churches' ministers were inextricably dependent on the white churches for subsistence. Those conditions of paternalism are still prevalent – though on a

[48] M. Mogashoa and K Makofane, 'Challenges Facing the Ministerial Formation in Uniting Presbyterian Church in Southern Africa: A Critical Reflection', *HTS Theological Studies*, 73:3 (2017), 1-9.
[49] Mogashoa and Makofane, 'Challenges', 4.
[50] Mogashoa and Makofane, 'Challenges', 6; On reconstruction, see J. Mugambi, 'From Liberation to Reconstruction.' In EM Katongole (ed.), *African Theology Today* (Oregon: Wipf & Stock, 2000), 189-206, 200.
[51] Mogashoa and Makofane, 'Challenges', 8.
[52] Hendriks, 'Missional', 1000.
[53] This is the author's own word.
[54] A. Nieman, 'Churches and Social Development Debate in South Africa, in: I Swart, H. Rocher, S. Green and J. Rasmus (eds.), *Religion and Social Development in Post-apartheid South Africa. Perspectives for Critical Engagement* (Stellenbosch: Sun Press, 2010), 37-43.

different scale – in various congregations in South Africa. In such circumstances, it becomes easy to trade one's values for continued paternalism.

Ministers themselves need to be empowered to be able to empower others and create such spaces for empowerment. Kritzinger, Maponya and Mokoena[55] argue that how a church 'trains' or 'forms' its ministers provides them with a glimpse of the future church. Therefore, in line with the critical observations by Nieman and Swart,[56] we should ask: How would the above conditions materialise when this is not addressed during ministerial formation? It is often addressing the 'psychological feelings of degradation and dependency'[57] but is not specifically related to ministers of the Word who would have to empower others, whilst they themselves are not psychologically, and spiritually and theologically prepared to transform church spaces as contexts of empowerment towards social development.

The question needs to be asked whether, within ministerial formation itself, candidate ministers have become aware of their agency, or are they more exposed to scholarships and grants, 'hand-outs' and foreign funding without being exposed to self-reliance and self-support? In most former mission churches, money is still received from outside donors, and the local congregations only act as local agents and administrators. This has been the case in various ministerial formation centres. This surely does not lead to a socially just community but might lead to a reduced conscience of one's 'spirit of dependency'.[58]

In addition to the inclusion of postcolonial, black and liberation theologies as a core part of curriculums for ministerial formation,[59] the 'reconstruction' of African epistemologies seems relevant.[60] This would be a crucial debate to allow ministerial candidates to enter into a creative discussion on the two paradigms (liberation and reconstruction) as both are still imperative in the neo-colonial contexts – such as South Africa. Within 'reconstruction' theologies it becomes important to search for African values, norms, and standards.

However, how this can be done varies from institution to institution. Missiology has been introduced with a theological method, the praxis cycle, that aims at providing students with an instrument to analyse their context, and agency that would be geared towards a structural analysis of society, the analysis of power relationships, the addressing of conditions of the poor and the marginalised, inspired by a contextual reading of biblical texts. However, it should state that denominations have adopted the 'practical' phase in

[55] Kritzinger et al., '25 Years', 2.
[56] Nieman, 'Churches'; Swart, 'Church'.
[57] Nieman, 'Churches', 40.
[58] Swart, 'Church', 245
[59] Swart, 'Church'.
[60] Mogashoa and Makofane, 'Challenges', 8; Mugambi, 'From Liberation'.

congregations, some as the penultimate one and others as a continuous one throughout their studies.

Nevertheless, despite the development in South African academia, this has often not been the case at ministerial formation centres in South Africa. Though this is one example when a praxis of 'missional consciousness' is emerging, there are also other ministerial formation contexts in which there are some sparks of a new approach. The author believes that this should be fully developed within the ministerial formation process as a process of 'shifting the consciousness' of ministerial candidates.

Bibliography

Baron, E., 'The Call for African Missional Consciousness through Renewed Mission Praxis in URCSA', *Studia Historiae Ecclesiasticae*, 45:3 (2020), 1-19.

Baron, E and Maponya, MS., 'The Recovery of the Prophetic Voice of the Church: The Adoption of a "Missional Church" Imagination', *Verbum Et Ecclesia*, 41:1 (2020), 1-9.

Bosch, DJ. *Transforming Mission. Paradigm Shifts in Theology and Mission*, Maryknoll: Orbis Books, 1991.

Government of South Africa, White Paper for Social Welfare, Principles, Recommendations, Guidelines, Recommendations, Proposed Policies and Programmes for Developmental Social Welfare in South Africa (1997); https://www.gov.za/sites/default/files/gcis_document/201409/whitepaperonsocialwelfare0.pdf.

Guder, DL. Missional Church. *A Vision for the Sending of the Church in North America*, Michigan: WB Eerdmans, 1998.

Hendriks, HJ., 'Missional Theology and Social Development', *HTS Theological Studies*, 63:3 (2007), 999-1016.

Katongole, EM., *The Sacrifice of Africa. A Political Theology for Africa* (Grand Rapids, Michigan: WMB Eerdmans, 2011).

Klaasen, J. 'The Role of Personhood in Development: An African Perspective on Development in South Africa', *Missionalia*, 45:1 (2017), 29-44.

Kritzinger, JNJ. 'Faith to Faith: Missiology as Encounterology', *Verbum Et Ecclesia*, 29:3 (2008), 764-790.

Kritzinger, JNJ. 'Ministerial Formation Praxis in the Uniting Reformed Church in Southern Africa: In Search of Inclusion and Authenticity.' *Missionalia*, 38:2 (2010), 211-234.

Kritzinger, JNJ. 'Overcoming Theological Voicelessness in the New Millennium', *Missionalia*, 40:3 (2012), 233–250.

Kritzinger, JNJ., Maponya, MS. and Mokoena, KK., '25 Years of Ministerial Formation Praxis in the Uniting Reformed Church in Southern Africa: How Belharic Have We Become?', *Studia Historiae Ecclesiasticae*, 45:3 (2019), 1-15.

MacIntyre, A., *Dependent Rational Animals. Why Human Beings Need the Virtues* (London: Duckworth, 1999).
Marais, F. 'The History and Challenge of the Missional Movement in South Africa. Perspectives from an Insider', in: Burger, C, Marais, F & Mouton, D (eds.), *Cultivating Missional Change. The Future of Missional Churches and Missional Theology* (Wellington: Bybelkor, 2017), 20–34.
Makofane K and Botha, N., 'Christianity and Social Transformation in post-apartheid South Africa: From prophetic quietism to signs of prophetic recovery', *Acta Theologica*, 28:6 (2019), 88–103.
Mogashoa, M. and Makofane, K., 'Challenges Facing the Ministerial Formation in Uniting Presbyterian Church in Southern Africa: A Critical Reflection', *HTS Theological Studies*, 73.3 (2017), 1-9.
Mugambi, J., 'From Liberation to Reconstruction.', in: EM Katongole (ed.), *African Theology Today* (Oregon: Wipf & Stock, 2000), 189–206.
Nieman, A., 'Churches and Social Development in South Africa', in: I Swart, H. Rocher, S. Green and J. Rasmus (eds.), *Religion and Social Development in Post-apartheid South Africa. Perspectives for Critical Engagement* (Stellenbosch: Sun Press, 2010), 37–43.
Swanepoel, H. and De Beer, F., *Community Development. Breaking the Cycle of Poverty*. Fifth edition (Parow: Juta, 2011).
Swart, I., 'Church, Mission and Development. Revisiting the Pragmatic Debate', in I. Swart, H. Rocher, S. Green and J. Rasmus (eds.), *Religion and Social Development in Post-apartheid South Africa. Perspectives for Critical Engagement* (Pretoria: Sun Press, 2010), 243–259.
Van Schalkwyk, A., 'The Church, Community Development, and Liberation', *Missionalia*, 24:1 (1996), 40-62.
VGKSA, *Agenda en Handelinge* (Belhar: Lusboek, 1997).

Faith-based Organisations and Social Innovation for Just and Inclusive Communities? A Scoping Review

Dag Håkon Eriksen and Annette Leis-Peters

Introduction

In the momentous 2030 Agenda for Sustainable Development, the United Nations (UN) stresses that we live in a time of 'immense challenges to sustainable development, but also, however, in a time of immense opportunity'.[1] Faith-based organisations (FBOs) responding to the 2030 Agenda face these challenges, opportunities and changes as they strive to develop just and inclusive communities.[2] As Ledwith says, 'This is not the time to feel defeated: It is an exciting opportunity for change, and we need to be bold'.[3]

Christian development organisations, diaconal institutions and initiatives and churches (which we include in the term FBO) have a longstanding tradition of social service and community development, in service provision and the development of new approaches and methods in diaconal action.[4] In the face of these challenges, it is appropriate to enquire critically about this tradition to see if and how FBOs, in their involvement in community development, contribute to innovation and change.

This article presents a scoping review on empirical research done in the intersections of FBOs, community development and innovation. It will enquire what material this research is based on, which concepts are used, and which results are discussed in the included studies. This chapter summarises current knowledge on FBOs, innovation and community development helpful for practitioners and decision-makers, and points to some avenues for further research.

---

[1] United Nations, Transforming Our World: The 2030 Agenda for Sustainable Development, A/RES/70/1 (2015).

[2] Carlos E. Ham, 'The Church Responding to the Agenda 2030', in Stephanie Dietrich, Knud Jørgensen, Kari Korslien, and Kjell Nordstokke (eds.), *The Diaconal Church* (Oxford UK: Regnum Books International, 2019), 185-198.

[3] Margaret Ledwith, *Community Development: A Critical Approach* (Bristol: Policy Press, 2020).

[4] Stephanie Dietrich, Knud Jørgensen, Kari Korslien, and Kjell Nordstokke, 'Introduction', in Stephanie Dietrich et al. (eds.), *The Diaconal Church* (Oxford: Regnum Books International, 2019), 1-11, 2.

Methodological Approach

The search for and analysis of relevant research literature were performed through a scoping review. According to Levac *et al.*, scoping reviews are useful 'to examine the nature, range and extent of research activity' and to 'clarify a complex concept'.[5] A scoping review can thus reveal the most important approaches and findings at the intersection of research on FBOs, social innovation and community development.

We follow Levac *et al.*'s six-stage model: 1. Formulate a clear research question and purpose; 2. Plan a review process that secures a comprehensive range of studies that is also practicable; 3. The process of selecting studies is iterative and should be done via a team; 4. Organise articles in overviews according to their approaches, topics and results; 5. Thematic analysis, in which the articles and their texts become the material scrutinised. In this stage, we also drew on a qualitative meta-ethnography approach, particularly in steps 3 to 5: read the studies, identify communalities and connections, translate the studies to each other, synthesise the translations and write the results from this process in a summary;[6] and 6. Discuss the results with experts and practitioners to ensure their relevance to the field of practice. Reflections from such a consultation are included here in this chapter.

Purpose, Research Question and Scoping Process

In a time of both 'immense challenges to sustainable development, but also, however in a time of immense opportunity', the purpose of our study is to provide an overview of the current empirically based knowledge on factors and processes relating to FBOs and innovation and community development that is helpful for practitioners and researchers.

Our research question is: What is the current state of empirical knowledge on the relationship between FBOs, innovation and community development? Sub-questions exploring different aspects of this relationship are as follows: What empirical data are studied, and which concepts are used? What external factors influence this relationship? What organisational factors hinder or enhance innovation? How is the connection between faith and innovation characterised? What factors related to leadership are described as important? How do these studies portray different innovation processes? What do these studies find regarding the results of innovation?

---

[5] D. Levac, H. Colquhoun, and K.K O'Brien, 'Scoping Studies: Advancing the Methodology', *Implementation Science*, 5:69 (2010), 1-9.

[6] G.W. Noblit, 'Meta-Ethnography: Adaptation and Return', in: *Cultural Constructions of Identity: Meta-Ethnography and Theory*, ed. Luis Urrieta Jr. and George W. Noblit (Oxford: Oxford University Press, 2018), 34-50.

Figure 1. Key concepts of the scoping process

We searched four databases and developed a search using thesaurus terms and keywords related to our research focus. One challenge with the scoping process was the multitude of terms used for each of the three key concepts in different disciplines and research areas. For instance, we found no less than 35 ways of naming what could be faith-based non-governmental organisations (NGOs). The term 'innovation' has gained popularity in research about health and welfare services and the third sector during the last decades but is not similarly widespread in all research fields. In theology and religious studies, other terms (e.g., change or renewal) are more widespread.

Against this background, we conducted our search twice. In the first round, we received 645 hits. We complemented this with a manual search by exploring references in key studies, searching in Google Scholar and key journals, and consulting other scholars and librarians. When analysing these results, we realised that many key articles did not appear in our initial search. It was striking that the first search provided only limited studies on the intersection of FBOs, innovation and community development. This is an interesting finding that points to the need for more research in this area. Therefore, we conducted a second search and obtained a better selection of studies, which enabled us to keep our original focus and primarily, to include studies relating to all three of our key concepts: Innovation, FBOs and Community development.

A protocol with the research question, several search criteria and keywords, and inclusion and exclusion criteria guided this review. After refinement according to relevant database categories and applying formal exclusion and inclusion criteria, we got a total of 5,943 hits. Then, we combined this with a search for community development and got an additional 193 hits (i.e., 6,136 total hits). Our initial findings confirmed that few studies have focused on innovation and community development in FBOs compared to other NGOs.

Selection Process

Due to the many hits, we needed to perform a thorough selection process to decide which studies to include in our research. One tool for this was refining the inclusion and exclusion criteria (see Table 2).

Inclusion Criteria	Exclusion Criteria
Studies in English, German, Danish, Swedish and Norwegian	
Empirical studies	
Studies published in the year 2000 and later	
Studies published in scientific, peer-reviewed journals	
Studies that focus on FBOs involved in local innovation and development, particularly in the field of community development	Studies primarily focusing on how to scale social innovation
Studies that discuss innovation and organisational change in and by FBOs and secondarily, NGOs related to a local context	Studies primarily focusing on diffusion or adaption of social innovation
Studies about innovation and organisational change that focus on FBOs operating in local contexts but, secondary, also other NGOs if the link to community development is strong	Studies on innovation and organisational change that neither focus on FBOs or NGO-based local community development
Studies that highlight the importance of leadership in innovation and change, in and by FBOs related to a local context and, secondary, for other NGOs if the link to community development is strong	Studies on the link between leadership and innovation/change that neither focus on FBOs nor NGO-based local community development
Studies on social entrepreneurship in NGOs with a focus on local development and local welfare and, secondary, for other NGOs if the link to community development is strong	Studies on social entrepreneurship that neither focus on FBOs nor NGO-based local community development

Table 1. Inclusion and exclusion criteria

Using these criteria, we reduced the material for the analysis to 60 articles.

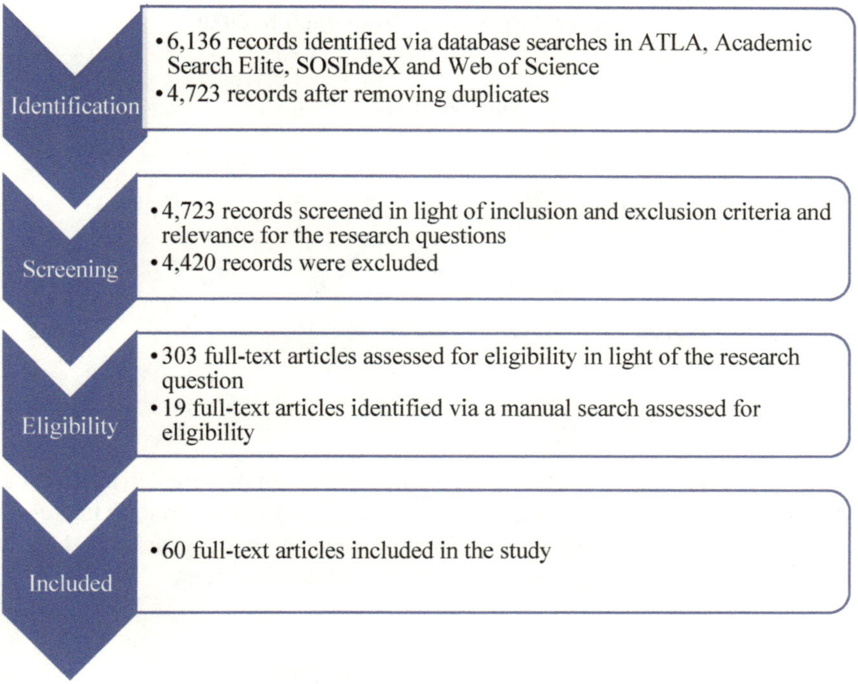

Figure 2. The process of inclusion

Extracting and Analysing the Findings from the Studies

We then began the analysis by extracting the data from the studies. The authors met several times to discuss a data chart and emerging categories, metaphors and themes related to the focus of the study. The process included a descriptive numerical summary; a qualitative thematic analysis inspired by qualitative meta-ethnography; an identification of connections between themes in the different studies; and a comparison of the concepts and metaphors. The last step was synthesising the results by elaborating on overarching interpretations, with the results of each of the studies in mind.

Overview of the Studies Included in the Review

In this section, we present how the selected studies disperse over time, over different countries on the globe and different methodological approaches, disciplines and research areas. These numerical overviews give a first impression of the nature and complexity of the research field, which we will continue to discuss in later sections of the article on a content level. The 60 studies are marked by a * in the reference list at the end of the chapter.

Temporal Spreading from 2000 to 2020

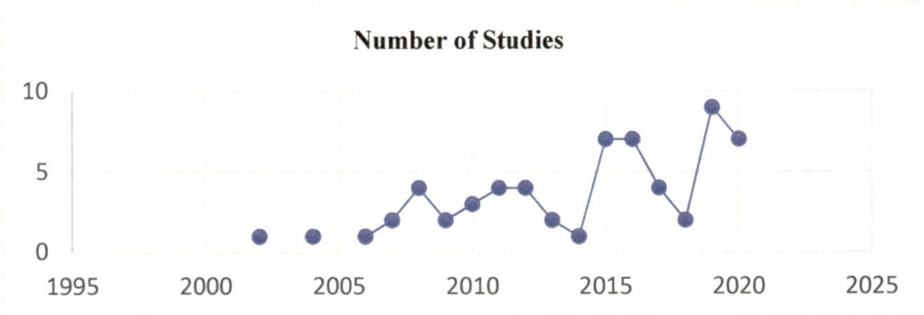

Figure 3. Number of studies per year of publication

The overview illustrates that there are fluctuations in the research interest, but the downs tend to not last long and are followed by an even stronger interest in subsequent years. Interest in this research field is growing and the highest number of studies has been published during the last five years.

Geographical Distribution

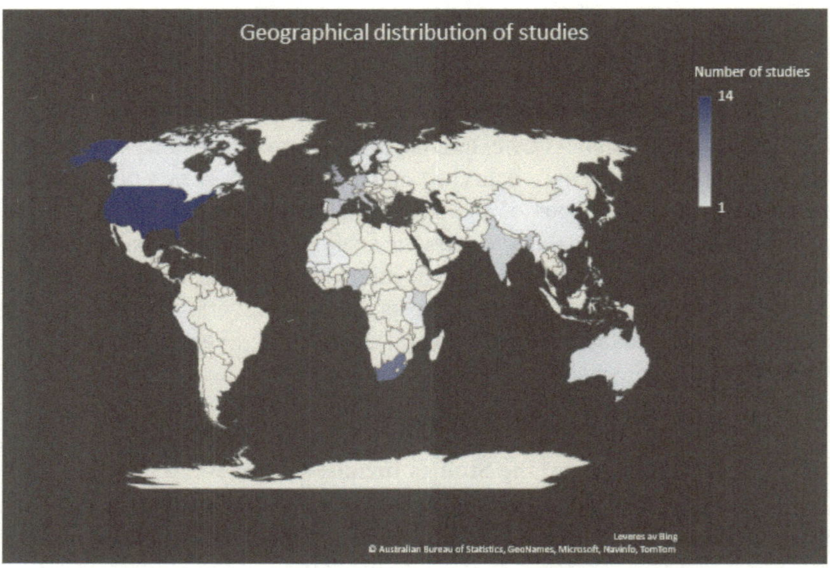

Figure 4. Geographical representation of the studies

This map shows two tendencies: First, geographical spreading indicates global interest in this area. Second, some countries could be called centres in this research field. This applies to the U.S. and, to a lesser degree, South Africa. This concentration would have appeared even more pronounced if the analysis had been based on the institutional origins of the authors of the included studies. A considerable share of the studies on Africa or Asia was written by researchers from academic institutions in the U.S., even if some might have a background of Africa or Asia.

Thus, the geographical tilt actualises critical questions. Both the U.S. and South Africa have systems for academic publications based on rated journals that appear in large (often commercial) academic databases. Thus, is only certain research likely to be found in searches of established international databases?

Initially, we included more languages in the searches but found an overwhelming majority of studies published in English. We expected to find more studies from Latin America – particularly Brazil – France and French-speaking African countries, and German-speaking countries where an intense research and practice debate is focusing on developments in the 'Sozialraum' (social room). It is an open question as to whether the language bias in our hits was caused by publication routines or insufficient translation functions of the databases. Nevertheless, 60 studies from about 30 countries on five continents represent a diversity of contexts.

Methodological Approaches

Many of the studies write only in very general terms about the methods used. This explains the contradictions in the sector diagram, which mentions both qualitative methods in general and more specific approaches in methods that can be classified as qualitative methods.

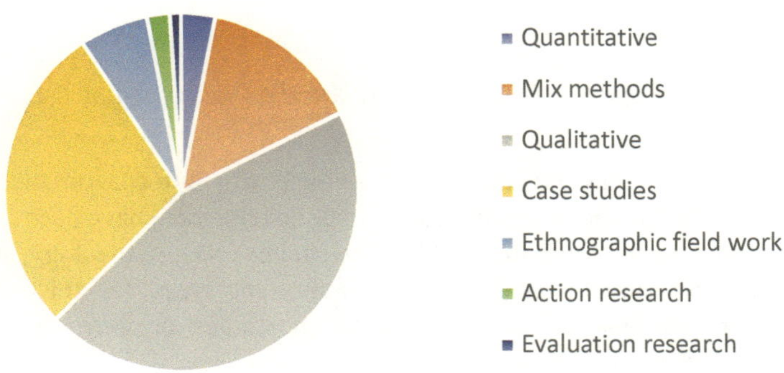

Figure 5. Representation of methods

The majority of the 60 studies are qualitative. Most of the case studies are also qualitative and could be included in the large number of qualitative studies. What is striking is the small number of quantitative studies and limited articles based on action or evaluation research.

Research Areas

Studies from many disciplinary contexts constitute the empirical knowledge base for this review. In the figure below, we illustrate the interdisciplinary character of the research discourse by summarising the disciplinary affiliation of the selected articles, based on the journals in which they are published.

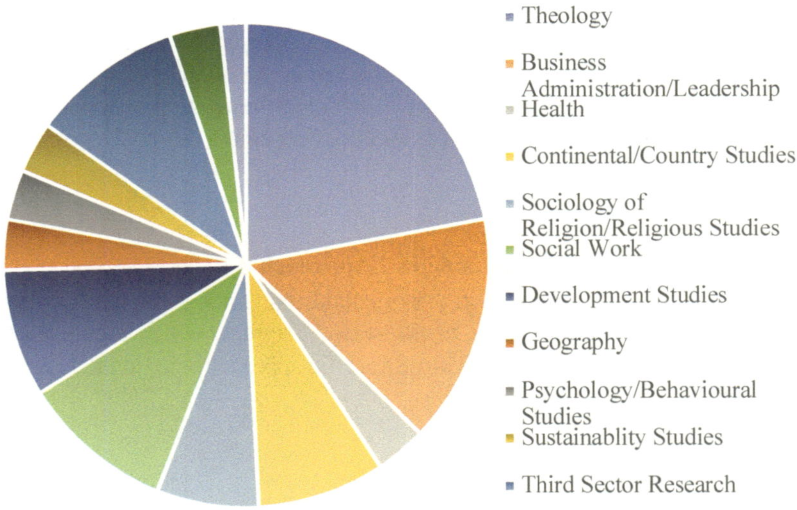

Figure 6. Research areas based on scientific journals

This sector diagram shows that studies with a focus on the connection between FBOs, innovation and community development have been conducted in 14 research areas. More than 25% of the studies relate to theology, sociology of religion or religious studies. Other important areas for this research are management, business and administration studies or third sector research. Overall, this is an interdisciplinary field.

Research on the intersection of FBOs, social innovation and community development is gaining momentum, is conducted globally – with some noticeable hotspots – is overwhelmingly qualitative and comes from a plurality of disciplines and research areas in social sciences and humanities.

Materials and Concepts

Before we address the key terms in the 60 articles and the specific aspects of the relationship between them, we present the material on which they are based. This helps us evaluate existing knowledge and research gaps that need to be filled.

Materials

The studies have a broad range of contexts, including rural and urban contexts. The empirical material related to FBOs stems largely from Christian contexts, including Catholic, mainline Protestant, Pentecostal, and independent churches. A few studies from Muslim contexts are also included.

Most articles about how FBOs work with innovation and community development, that come from theology, are based on a vision for community development and innovation, discussed against the example of illustrative (small) cases rather than a completed case study. Most contributions from the social sciences are interview studies, many of which are combined with ethnographic studies (i.e., observations and document studies). The quantitative studies that are included in the sample often do not fit the exact focus of our study but represent interesting findings.[7]

The selected articles include some evaluation studies but fewer than could be expected in scientific empirical research about innovation and community development. Most of the studies are methodologically rather conventional, with only a few examples of action research elements or a participative approach. Many give snapshots of small cases and how innovation and community development are perceived by leaders or professionals.

Most striking is the focus on explorative ethnographic and case studies. Some of these work with the operationalisation of key concepts, such as change, innovation or community development, whilst others presuppose there exists a common understanding regarding these concepts. Whilst the factors of innovation have been discussed in several studies, only a few have discussed or provided indicators for innovation or community development. This coincides with a lack of longitudinal studies of innovation or community development over time, and points to the need for more research.

---

[7] R. Dakung and T. Soemunti, 'Entrepreneurial Behaviour among Catholic Christians in Plateau State-Nigeria', *World Journal of Entrepreneurship Management and Sustainable Development*, 12:2 (2016), 176-192.

Use of Concepts

Various terms were used regarding the key concepts of our study. Regarding the denotation of the organisations involved in community development and innovation, the terminology differs between disciplines and geographical contexts. Many variations can be explained by the level of abstraction that the researchers have in relation to their material. Whilst our starting point was to focus on faith-based organisations and FBOs as NGOs in the non-profit sector, studies exploring Christian FBOs are in the clear majority amongst the studies in our sample. Therefore, not surprisingly, theologians and religious scholars call the objects of their research churches (often specific churches) or congregations. Sometimes, more general terms, such as faith communities, Christian organisations, or congregation-based organisations (CBO), are used. Some social scientists study FBOs but call them NGOs or human service organisations (HSOs). The few Muslim FBOs included in the sample used rather distanced ways of denotation, such as NGOs or faith-based NGOs. If researchers focus on the involvement of organisations in community development, they may be called community-based enterprises or faith-based community organisations (FBCOs). This shows how disciplines, the relation to the studied organisations and the focus of the research impact the terminology.

When it comes to community development, the terminology applied is somewhat more congruent. The variations reveal different accents when discussing community development: grassroots development, community-based, bottom-up approaches, asset-based community transformation or holistic community development. Most studies we included in the review relate to a concrete location, although some reflect on communities that transcend geographical limitations. In general, we did not include articles about renewal processes in regional and national churches in this sample but incorporated interesting examples, such as the study of an unsuccessful innovation in the Scottish Episcopal Church.[8]

The 60 studies in the sample describe innovation for the most part in well-known categories often borrowed from business studies.[9] The change that innovations represent is often represented in a range from incremental to radical, and the outcomes are generally categorised as product, process, and socially transformative innovations. The first type includes developing new and more inclusive services, adapting existing services or including new groups into services. The second type depicts new ways of operating or new organisational practices, processes, and structures. The third type seeks holistic community

[8] M. Brown, 'Entrepreneurial Leadership and Cultural Change in a Faith-Based Organization', *International Journal of Entrepreneurship and Innovation*, 10:2 (2009), 125-135.

[9] B. Kang and K. Jaskyte, 'Congregational Leaders' Perceptions of Organizational Innovation', *Administration in Social Work*, 35:2 (2011), 161-179, 165.

transformation by, for example, advocacy work influencing public policy or community empowerment.

These concepts are used somewhat differently in the studies of the sample, depending on whether they focus on innovation *in* or *by* FBOs.[10] The concept of product innovation is not referred to frequently in the sample, which indicates that this type of innovation is rare amongst FBOs involved in community development. In turn, terms related to incremental innovations related to process and socially transformative innovation are prevalent. This implies that innovation in FBOs involved in community development is usually related to new ways of working, organising, communicating, cooperating, engaging stakeholders, and functioning as a community. The impetus for innovation is both connected to external or internal sources and to bottom-up and top-down approaches, with bottom-up approaches being the most common.

In the next section we explore different aspects of the relationship between FBOs, community development and innovation as we address the sub-research questions: What external factors influence this relationship? What organisational factors hinder or enhance innovation? What is the role of faith in this relationship? What factors related to leadership are described as important? How are the different innovation processes conducted and described? How are the results of these innovation processes described?

The Current State of Knowledge About the Relationship Between FBOs, Innovation and Community Development

External Factors

Most studies in the sample link innovation to changes in context, such as the emergence of new social problems, new groups in need, new needs amongst service recipients and increased demands for services.[11] Change is often described in general terms, including the demographic, social, technological, political and economic transformations in a globalised world. In some contexts, the speed of change appears overwhelming or as complex dynamics and crises that provoke responses. External factors can be on micro, meso and macro levels, for example, requirements from donors, institutional pressures, geographic location, economic development, or national culture. They are drivers for innovation, as FBOs respond to new challenges and needs or exploit emerging opportunities.

---

[10] Evans *et al.*, 'Promoting'. Allen, Jennifer D. et al. 'Enhancing Organizational Capacity to Provide Cancer Control Programs among Latino Churches', *BMC Health Services Research*, 15:147 (2015), 1-12.

[11] J. Shin and Y.K. Choi, 'Organizational Innovativeness and Its Determinants in South Korean Nonprofit Human Service Organizations', *Nonprofit Management & Leadership*, 30:1 (2019), 51-68.

A recurring question is whether innovations are primarily driven by external or (internal) organisational factors. Three articles illustrate the span of this debate. An Australian study about how non-profit organisations (NPOs) in the disability sector responded to a major national reform is especially insightful as it shows nuanced and diverse dynamics between external and internal.[12] A comparative study from the UK and a study from South Korea claim that all NGOs have a variable organisational capacity that is dependent on institutional and policy environments.[13] From this, it seems that innovations are influenced by external factors, but internal organisational factors may enhance or modify the process. The question is, then, what organisational factors hinder or enhance innovation?

Organisational Factors

In the sample, no clear relationship between an organisation's age, size or structure and innovation can be seen, perhaps because most of the included studies are qualitative case studies and lack the easily measurable variables of quantitative surveys. The qualitative studies in our sample highlight organisational factors, such as culture, procedures and policies and intrinsic factors, such as values and spirituality, as an impetus for change. Faith and shared religious beliefs,[14] values, visions, feelings or love for a community can be motivation for change.[15] Values considered particularly supportive of innovation include forgiveness (allowing people to make mistakes), spirituality, the ability to take advantage of opportunities, and openness and willingness to listen to other people's ideas.[16] Other studies have underlined the importance of having space for improvisation.[17] In line with qualitative studies, a quantitative study in the sample underlines organisational characteristics such as creativity, willingness to take risks, openness to change, future orientation, proactivity,

---

[12] R. Taylor, N. Torugsa, and A. Arundel, 'Social Innovation in Disability Nonprofits: An Abductive Study of Capabilities for Social Change', *Nonprofit and Voluntary Sector Quarterly*, 49:2 (2020).

[13] Shin and Choi, 'Organizational'; S. P. Osborne, C. Chew, and K. McLaughlin, 'The Once and Future Pioneers? The Innovative Capacity of Voluntary Organisations and the Provision of Public Services: A Longitudinal Approach', *Public Management Review*, 10:1 (2008), 51-70.

[14] S. Krige, 'Towards a Coherent Vision for Faith-Based Development', *Journal of Theology for Southern Africa*, 132 (2008) 16–37; Kang and Jaskyte, 'Congregational'.

[15] Stella Darby and Paul Chatterton, 'Between and Beyond Social Entrepreneur and Activist: Transformative Personas for Social Change', *ACME: An International E-Journal for Critical Geographies*, 18:3 (2019), 724-750.

[16] Kang and Jaskyte, 'Congregational'.

[17] Kapp, 'I'll Think'.

learning orientation, trust, local roots, community relations and accountability as factors that enhance innovation.[18]

Organisational innovativeness includes the capability to recognise new opportunities, exploit and internalise new knowledge from external sources to network and listen to stakeholders.[19] Fear of loss of finances, members or social recognition can, with slow decision-making processes, strict procedures and strong leaders' attitudes, be hindrances to innovation.[20] In addition, innovation is also dependent on individuals who are creative, willing to take calculated risks, work autonomously, take responsibility for large-scale impacts, and can see opportunities and act on them.[21] One especially helpful study by Evans et al emphasises that organisations working for community development must themselves be carriers of the same values.[22] This highlights the relationship between FBOs, innovation and community development.

Faith and Innovation

Thirty-five studies, which means more than half of the 60 studies, link faith and innovation to each other but in distinctive ways. As we state in the presentation of the findings, some of the theological studies are characterised by conceptual, normative, and theological reflections that use empirical cases as examples. A common pattern amongst the 11 studies in this category in our sample is that they carve out the capability of churches in general or in specific churches (e.g., Pentecostal, Catholic and mainstream Protestant) to contribute to innovation in general and in local communities in particular.

---

[18] C.S. Marques *et al.*, 'Facets and Outcomes of Healthcare Service Innovation: A Study of Catholic Service Providers in Northern Portugal', *International Journal of Innovation and Learning*, 18:1 (2015), 23-44.

[19] A. Antonites, W.J. Schoeman, and W.F. J. van Deventer, 'A Critical Analysis of Social Innovation: A Qualitative Exploration of a Religious Organisation', *Hervormde Teologiese Studies*, 75:4 (2019), 1-12.

[20] Kang and Jaskyte, 'Congregational'.

[21] M. Nandan, M. London, and T. Bent-Goodley, 'Social Workers as Social Change Agents: Social Innovation, Social Intrapreneurship, and Social Entrepreneurship', *Human Service Organizations Management Leadership & Governance*, 39:1 (2015), 38-56.

[22] Evans *et al.*, 'Promoting'.

The studies see innovative potential in churches and FBOs because they promote (community) transformation,[23] social entrepreneurship,[24] (social) development[25] or social capital.[26] Other perspectives on their innovative ability are that they work with social critique,[27] meet social needs in practical ways,[28] have philanthropic activities[29] or provide poverty alleviation.[30] Many of the studies point to theology as the basis of innovative potential, either existing theology or that which should be developed. Outward-looking theologies are mainly identified as stimulating social innovation.[31]

The second-largest group amongst the studies with a focus on faith and innovation are those about cases evaluated from the perspective of social innovation. These studies show that FBOs' specific resources, amongst other things expressed in their theology, can contribute to being on the frontline of innovation,[32] give marginalised groups access to resources[33] or strengthen the ability to improvise.[34] Other case studies point to external factors, such as the dependence of institutional settings and the objectives of cooperation partners, not least in the field of development aid. This is illustrated well by an ethnographic study of faith-based HIV/AIDs programmes in South Africa pointing to the tension between a donor-driven technocratic civil society logic

---

[23] S.O. Akanbi and J. Beyers, 'The Church as a Catalyst for Transformation in the Society', *Hts Teologiese Studies-Theological Studies*, 73:4 (2017), 1-8; Timothy Van Aarde, 'Equipping the Poorest of the Poor to Become Agents of Community Transformation: A Case Study of Milk as a Catalyst in Burundi', *In die Skriflig*, 51:1 (2017), 1-11.

[24] K.J. Alderson, 'At the Crossroads: Social and Faith-Based Entrepreneurship', *Thunderbird International Business Review*, 54:1 (2012), 111–116; Manyaka-Boshielo, 'The Role'.

[25] I. Swart, 'Churches as a Stock of Social Capital for Promoting Social Development in Western Cape Communities', *Journal of Religion in Africa*, 36:3/4 (2006); Krige, 'Towards'.

[26] J.W. Beukes, 'Leveraging Social Capital of the Church for Development: A Case Study of a Farming Community in Wellington', *Hervormde teologiese studies*, 75:4 (2019) 1-10; Swart, 'Churches'.

[27] J. Delehanty, 'Social Critique as Religious Formation: Relational Practices in Faith-Based Activism', *Liturgy*, 35:2 (2020), 25-32.

[28] Musa A. B. Gaiya, 'Charismatic and Pentecostal Social Orientations in Nigeria', *Nova Religio: The Journal of Alternative & Emergent Religion* 18:3 (2015), 63-79.

[29] J. Katapura, 'Philanthropic Organizations and Community Development', *Asian Journal of Social Science* 43:4 (2015), 400-434.

[30] C. Schliesser, 'On a Long Neglected Player: The Religious Factor in Poverty Alleviation: The Example of the So-Called 'Prosperity Gospel' in Africa', *Journal of Religion in Africa,* 46(1) (2016) 116-117.

[31] Gaiya, 'Charismatic'.

[32] T.A. Wolfer and K. Del Pilar, 'Ten Thousand Villages: Partnering with Artisans to Overcome Poverty', *Social Work & Christianity*, 35:4 (2008), 449-472.

[33] G. Deacon, 'Pentecostalism and Development in Kibera Informal Settlement, Nairobi', *Development in Practice*, 22:5/6 (2012), 663-674.

[34] Kapp, 'I'll Think'.

and the expression of specific religious beliefs in the everyday practice of the programmes.[35]

Three studies asked leaders or key persons of FBOs in interviews how they perceive and handle change or innovation. These studies find that strategic leadership, teamwork and trust in FBOs are important preconditions for successful change,[36] and that religious leaders' understanding of innovation and of supporting or inhibiting factors for change conform with those of leaders in other fields.[37] Some of the interview studies aim to raise awareness of particular churches, such as independent churches in Africa, as innovative actors for social development that have been largely neglected.[38]

One study from the field of health studies explores the roles of churches as participants and contributors to innovation projects designed by health services with no interest in faith itself but in the spaces that FBOs can provide. It is one of the few articles based on quantitative research about FBOs and innovation and thus an example for an important development direction for future research.[39] Only three studies focus on Muslim FBOs (and none on FBOs from other religions). They all mention religion as a barrier, for example, in the case of an Islamic NGO in Bangladesh that faced Islamophobia. This article is worth reading both because of its focus on Muslim FBOs and its portrayal of the ambiguity of the role of religion in innovation processes.[40] The issue of faith as a hindrance has not been discussed in studies about Christian FBOs, which all stress the huge potential of FBOs. Altogether, the studies show that faith, on individual and organisational levels, can be an important factor for innovation in a community. This deserves more research attention, not least in religions other than Christianity.

Leadership and Innovation

In many studies, the role of leadership is addressed either directly or indirectly as important for innovation and community development, but only nine focus specifically on the role of leadership in various types of organisations. According to these studies, leaders, and their personalities either support or hinder innovation. Some leadership attitudes and practices are identified as particularly

---

[35] M. Burchardt, 'Faith-Based Humanitarianism: Organizational Change and Everyday Meanings in South Africa', *Sociology of Religion*, 74:1 (2013), 30-55.

[36] Noel J. Pearse, 'Effective Strategic Leadership: Balancing Roles During Church Transitions', *Hervormde Teologiese Studies*, 67:2 (2011), 1-7.

[37] Kang and Jaskyte, 'Congregational'.

[38] B. Bompani, 'Religion and Development from Below: Independent Christianity in South Africa', *Journal of Religion in Africa*, 40:3 (2010), 307-330.

[39] Allen *et al.*, 'Enhancing'.

[40] Shofiqur Chowdhury, Rezaul Islam and Haris Abd Wahab. 'Challenges of Faith-Based NGO Intervention in Community Development: A Case Study in Bangladesh', *Global Social Welfare*, 7 (2020), 301–313.

important, such as trust in employees and volunteers, encouragement of creative ideas, openness to advice and criticism, understanding of people's concerns and forgivingness for making mistakes.[41]

Constellations of collective or group leadership are likely to affect cultural change.[42] Other studies stress that relational work is vital for engaging different people at all levels in leadership processes.[43] In a thought-provoking study of church leaders' narratives, Simpson argues that it can be fruitful for leaders to engage with the experience of not knowing. Rather than perpetuating the leader-as-hero myth, it is helpful to view leaders as persons not with all the answers but with a responsibility to engage in difficult situations and to find a resolution with and through others.[44] Another major challenge for leaders is managing resistance. Pearse underlines that it is important for church leaders to balance different patterns of leadership that challenge and strengthen the sense of community in periods of organisational change.[45]

Leaders of innovation processes must pave the way for cooperation across disciplines, professions, agencies, sectors and levels.[46] Some studies imply that leaders' innovative efforts are most needed in organisations with unstable financial resources and legitimacy. In such contexts, externally oriented, dynamic and competitive leaders who are 'vision setters and task masters' are significant preconditions for innovation.[47] Even if the number of studies that specifically highlight the role of leadership in innovation in community development is limited, these articles argue strongly for not underestimating leadership in this context.

The Process of Innovation

In most of the studies, a process was reflected on, and 24 articles specifically addressed this issue. Some focused on specific intended methods and processes such as T-teams,[48] Human Centred Design,[49] the LIN model of participatory

[41] Evans *et al.*, 'Promoting'. Kang and Jaskyte, 'Congregational'.; Pearse, 'Effective'.; Shin and Choi, 'Organizational'.
[42] Brown, 'Entrepreneurial'.
[43] Taylor et al, 'Social'.
[44] P. Simpson, 'Complexity and Change Management: Analyzing Church Leaders' Narratives', *Journal of Organizational Change Management*, 25:2 (2012), 283-296.
[45] Pearse, 'Effective'.
[46] Langer, 'Social'.
[47] Shin and Choi, 'Organizational'.
[48] Evans *et al.*, 'Promoting'.
[49] M. Nandan, K. Jaskyte, and G. Mandayam, 'Human Centered Design as a New Approach to Creative Problem Solving: Its Usefulness and Applicability for Social Work Practice', *Human Service Organizations: Management, Leadership & Governance*, 44:4 (2020), 1-7.

community development,[50] asset-based community transformation[51] and the 'relationship-driven process' of community transformation,[52] whilst other researchers studied unintended changes, for example, the decision to offer breakfast to homeless people, which led to radical change in a church and its environment.[53] Altogether, the studies show that processes are related to contextual and organisational factors and no one fixed method can be applied in all circumstances.[54] It seems favourable if processes are community embedded[55] and based on trust.[56]

Innovation processes in community development often have bottom-up approaches, but sometimes also hybrid approaches in which the government, NGOs and local communities work together and thus combine top-down and bottom-up logic.[57] The joint response of external and local stakeholders to a complex social problem is another form of hybrid approach.[58] The roles of NGOs in innovation processes can be to mobilise a community, introduce change, represent a community and advocate on its behalf, and deliver services to a community.[59] NGOs can also inspire communal change that promises a better future through communication and storytelling.[60]

---

[50] Doan-Bao *et al.*, 'Catalysing Social Change in Ho Chi Minh City, Vietnam: Evaluating the Lin Model', *Community Development Journal*, 54:3 (2019), 519–540.
[51] Van Aarde, 'Equipping'.
[52] Huff, 'Operationalizing'.
[53] D.A. Plowman *et al.*, 'Radical Change Accidentally: The Emergence and Amplification of Small Change', *Academy of Management Journal*, 50:3 (2007), 515-543.
[54] O.S. Crocco and M. Cseh, 'Learning, Development and Change in a Community-Based Enterprise in Myanmar', *European Journal of Training and Development*, 45:4/5 (2020), 436-448.
[55] Langer, 'Social'. 186.
[56] Bompani, 'Religion'.; S. Patel and S. Bartlett, 'Reflections on Innovation, Assessment, and Social Change: A Sparc Case Study', *Development in Practice*, 19:1 (2009), 3-15; R. Perkons and N. Brown, 'Intercultural Organisational Development', *Systemic Practice & Action Research*, 23:1 (2010); Swart, 'Churches'.
[57] Meredith and MacDonald, 'Community-Supported'.
[58] Tello-Rozas, 'Inclusive'.
[59] Perkons and Brown, 'Intercultural'.; S.C. Prasad, 'Innovating at the Margins: The System of Rice Intensification in India and Transformative Social Innovation', *Ecology & Society*, 21(4):7 (2016), 595-603.; Holly Ritchie, 'Unwrapping Institutional Change in Fragile Settings: Women Entrepreneurs Driving Institutional Pathways in Afghanistan', *World Development*, 83© (2016), 39-53; Chowdhury, *et al.*, 'Challenges'.
[60] R.A. Smith *et al.*, 'Communal Innovations: Inspiring Neighborhoods of Hope and Advocacy', *Journal of Health Communication*, 25:5 (2020), 444–453.

FBO's take on different roles, and many actors are involved in processes of social innovation such as institutional entrepreneurs,[61] users,[62] leaders,[63] community members,[64] grassroots organisations,[65] transformative teams,[66] churches[67] and external actors.[68] Collaboration across sectors and between different organisations and actors seems to be an important factor.[69] Different organisations have different strengths and challenges in community development.[70]

Processes of innovation should be inclusive and imply structures that facilitate reflection, learning and action.[71] Such processes need leadership to ensure inclusiveness and a balance between processes and outcomes, and internal and external dynamics. They can be reactive or proactive but are often triggered by massive and accelerating changes. The process should correspond to the anticipated change.[72] The descriptions of the processes of innovation in the articles included in our sample underline the interrelatedness of leadership,

---

[61] Ritchie, 'Unwrapping'; Patrick Valeau, 'Stages and Pathways of Development of Nonprofit Organizations: An Integrative Model', *Voluntas: International Journal of Voluntary & Nonprofit Organizations*, 26:5 (2015), 1894–1919.

[62] Taylor et al, 'Social'.

[63] D.J. Kapp, 'I'll Think of Something: Improvisation in Small Church Service Programs', *Review of Religious Research*, 54:2 (2012), 197-215.

[64] S. Tello-Rozas, 'Inclusive Innovations through Social and Solidarity Economy Initiatives: A Process Analysis of a Peruvian Case Study', *Voluntas: International Journal of Voluntary & Nonprofit Organizations*, 27:1 (2016), 61–85.

[65] J. Kirwan *et al.*, 'Grassroots Social Innovations and Food Localisation: An Investigation of the Local Food Programme in England', *Global Environmental Change*, 23:5 (2013), 830-837.

[66] S.D. Evans *et al.*, 'Promoting Strengths, Prevention, Empowerment, and Community Change through Organizational Development: Lessons for Research, Theory, and Practice', *Journal of Prevention & Intervention in the Community*, 39:1 (2011), 50-64.

[67] S.J. Manyaka-Boshielo, 'The Role of a Missional Social Entrepreneurial Church in a Township Community', *HTS Teologiese Studies / Theological Studies*, 74:1 (2018), 1-8; Joel A. Tejedo, 'Pentecostal Civic Engagement: How Ilocano Pentecostal Churches Build Poor Communities in the Philippines', *Asian Journal of Pentecostal Studies*, 13:1 (2010), 41-64.

[68] A. Langer & J. Eurich, 'Social Innovations as Opportunities: How Can Innovations in Social Services Be Stimulated and Managed?', *Diaconia. Journal for the Study of Christian Social Practice*, 7:2 (2016), 174-190.

[69] T. Meredith and M. MacDonald, 'Community-Supported Slum-Upgrading: Innovations from Kibera, Nairobi, Kenya', *Habitat International*, no 60 (February 2017), 1-9.

[70] J.D. McCarthy and E.T. Walker, 'Alternative Organizational Repertoires of Poor People's Social Movement Organizations', *Nonprofit and Voluntary Sector Quarterly*, 33:3 (2004), 97-119.

[71] Tello-Rozas, 'Inclusive'.

[72] Evans *et al.*, 'Promoting'.

external and organisational factors, and faith, which can all hinder or enhance changes and community development. The study by Huff is a useful example.[73]

Results of Innovations

The articles report the types and results of innovations related to community development in various ways that confirm categories identified by earlier research on social innovation: new services/products, new ways of working and partnering, new forms of resourcing, new forms of evaluation, new forms of governance and new forms of communicating or transformative change in the context.[74]

The results from the innovations reported in the studies range from changes in the situation of women in Afghanistan[75] and improvement of critical infrastructure in slums[76] to how fair-trade initiatives changed attitudes amongst consumers in the west and provided a fair wage for artisans in Asia, thus changing their communities.[77] Innovation also influences FBOs internally by creating team spirit, employee satisfaction and organisational performance.[78]

Other studies indicate changes in the socioeconomic structures of a community through development aid and education and how the poorest of the poor could break free of dependency and create a better future through a holistic, asset-based community transformation. The longitudinal study by Katapura is a good example.[79] Another example of this is Meredith and MacDonald's study on community-supported slum upgrading in Nairobi, where a settlement executive committee was created to foster unity amongst slum dwellers and stakeholders and to ensure that the views and interests of slum dwellers were taken care of throughout the project phase.[80]

Not all innovation processes succeed,[81] and it is difficult to evaluate the results of innovation processes with qualitative research dominating the articles due to the complex dynamics and changes in the context. Some articles underline that the evaluation of innovation should ideally be connected to reference points, such as values and human rights. When trying to develop just and inclusive communities, not all innovations are helpful, and it is important to be cautious regarding innovation for innovation's sake. Before starting innovation processes,

---

[73] Huff, 'Operationalizing'.
[74] O. H. Angell, 'Diakonia as Innovation: A Political and Organisational Perspective', *Diaconia*, 7:2 (2016), 142–158; Langer and Eurich, 'Social'.
[75] Ritchie, 'Unwrapping'.
[76] Meredith and MacDonald, 'Community-Supported'.
[77] Wolfer and del Pilar, 'Ten Thousand'.
[78] Marques *et al.*, 'Facets'.
[79] Katapura, 'Philanthropic'.
[80] Van Aarde, 'Equipping'.
[81] Brown, 'Entrepreneurial'.

FBOs should thus ask: What is innovation for my organisation? For what and why do I want to innovate?[82]

Results from the Consultations with Practitioners and Experts

In line with the method for conducting a scoping review, we consulted with experts and practitioners from the field of community development and presented our study and findings. Together, this group of about 15 people represents experiences and perspectives from different countries in Europe, Africa and Asia.

The response from the consultation supports the impression that the term 'innovation' is perceived as a somewhat new or foreign term in the field of community development. Some comments underline the need to specify the focus on social innovation. They expressed that social innovations do take place in and by FBOs in community development: 'most projects are doing new things' but that terms other than innovation are used to describe them. This might point to a widespread understanding that links innovation with new technological products being introduced into the market. In contrast, this scoping review shows that most social innovations conducted within and by FBOs involved in community development are incremental and related to service, process, or transformative innovation. In our search, we used many synonyms, such as (organisational) change, transformation and even renewal, so we do believe that most variations in the use of terms related to social innovation are included.

Another focus in the response was on the term 'faith-based organisation' (FBO). Some expressed concerns about whether this term is related primarily to larger organisations, excluding grassroots organisations and churches involved in community development. This confirms the impression we got during our search that terms for these kinds of organisations are fragmented and diversified. Our use of synonyms in the search facilitated the inclusion of smaller community-based organisations of different kinds and churches.

Conclusion

This scoping review documents an emerging and growing interest in academia about the intersection of FBOs, innovation and community development. The many contributions from theology and religious studies illustrate the desire to know about how innovation and community development can be related to (everyday) practice in FBOs. The fact that researchers from many disciplines and research areas study innovation and community development related to FBOs indicates that FBOs are perceived as important for innovation and community development.

[82] L. Nader and J. G.F. de Campos, 'Five Reasons to Fear Innovation', *Sur: International Journal on Human Rights*, 13:23 (2016), 211-221.

Most of the empirical knowledge in the reviewed studies is based on qualitative research, some with limited validity. This confines how the studies' findings can be generalised beyond the cases on which they focus. The review also points to a lack of studies in languages other than English. However, 60 empirical studies from about 30 countries on five continents provide some knowledge about how the connection between innovation and community development can be understood globally.

The model below (see Figure 7) illustrates the main components of the results of the included studies. Common to most is the interest in the process of innovation or FBOs' capacity to contribute to innovation. Many analyse the external and internal factors that trigger innovation. It seems that the most common types of innovation in the context of FBOs and community development are incremental process innovations and transformational innovations. Radical product innovations are less common.

The review shows that more knowledge is needed for empirical-based claims that FBOs create innovation through community development (and vice versa) and if so, how they achieve this. More quantitative and longitudinal (evaluation) studies and studies about hindrances and failures could address this research gap.

Research on innovation in and by FBOs is still rare compared to the for-profit field.[83] Qualitative studies could focus on exploring the roles of FBOs in innovation and/or community development and how they can be interpreted. If what most studies in this review suggest is correct, namely, that FBOs have the potential to contribute to innovation and community development, there is a pressing demand for more development in this field. This will help to understand future tasks for FBOs in creating just and inclusive societies.

[83] Kang and Jaskyte, 'Congregational'.

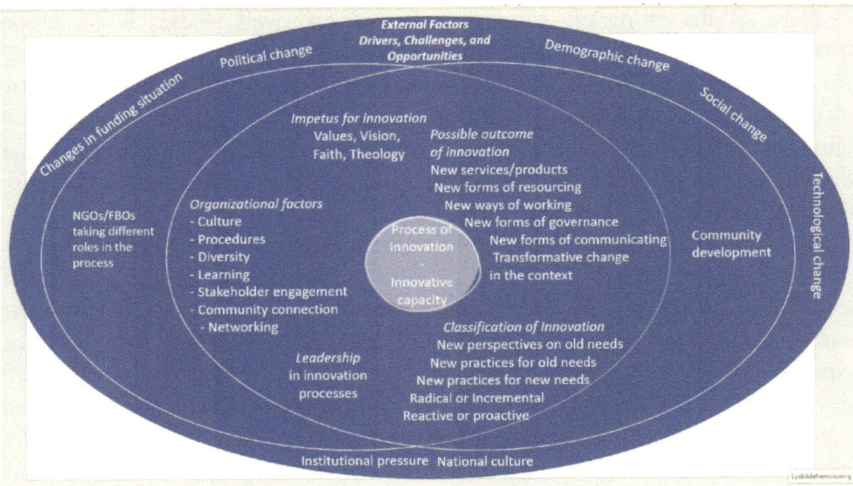

Figure 7. Model of the possible connections between FBOs, innovation and community development

Bibliography

An asterix indicates publications from the scoping review.

Akanbi, S. and J. Beyers. 'The Church as a Catalyst for Transformation in the Society', *HTS Teologiese Studies/Theological Studies*, 73:4 (2017), 1-8.*

Alderson, Keanon J. 'At the Crossroads: Social and Faith-Based Entrepreneurship', *Thunderbird International Business Review*, 54:1 (2012), 111–116.*

Allen, Jennifer D., Maria Torres, Laura Tom, Sarah Rustan, Bryan Leyva, Rosalyn Negron, Laura Linnan, Lina Jandorf, and Hosffman Ospino. 'Enhancing Organizational Capacity to Provide Cancer Control Programs among Latino Churches', *BMC Health Services Research*, 15:147 (2015), 1-12.*

Angell, Olav. 'Diakonia as Innovation: A Political and Organisational Perspective', *Diaconia*, 7:2 (2016), 142–158.

Antonites, Alex, Wentzel Schoeman, and Willem van Deventer. 'A Critical Analysis of Social Innovation: A Qualitative Exploration of a Religious Organisation', *Hervormde Teologiese Studies*, 75:4 (2019), 1-12.*

Beukes, Jacques. 'Leveraging Social Capital of the Church for Development: A Case Study of a Farming Community in Wellington', *Hervormde Teologiese Studies*, 75:4 (2019), 1-10.*

Bompani, B. 'Religion and Development from Below: Independent Christianity in South Africa', *Journal of Religion in Africa*, 40:3 (2010), 307-330.*

Brown, Mary. 'Entrepreneurial Leadership and Cultural Change in a Faith-Based Organization', *International Journal of Entrepreneurship and Innovation*, 10:2 (2009), 125-135.*

Burchardt, Marian. 'Faith-Based Humanitarianism: Organizational Change and Everyday Meanings in South Africa', *Sociology of Religion*, 74:1 (2013), 30-55.*

Chowdhury, Shofiqur, Rezaul Islam and Haris Abd Wahab. 'Challenges of Faith-Based NGO Intervention in Community Development: A Case Study in Bangladesh', *Global Social Welfare*, 7 (2020), 301–313.*

Crocco, O., and M. Cseh. 'Learning, Development and Change in a Community-Based Enterprise in Myanmar', *European Journal of Training and Development* 45:4/5 (2020), 436-448.*

Dakung, R., and T. Soemunti. 'Entrepreneurial Behaviour among Catholic Christians in Plateau State-Nigeria', *World Journal of Entrepreneurship Management and Sustainable Development*, 12:2 (2016), 176-192.*

Darby, Stella, and Paul Chatterton. 'Between and Beyond Social Entrepreneur and Activist: Transformative Personas for Social Change', *ACME: An International E-Journal for Critical Geographies*, 18:3 (2019), 724-750.*

Deacon, Gregory. 'Pentecostalism and Development in Kibera Informal Settlement, Nairobi', *Development in Practice*, 22:5/6 (2012), 663-674.*

Delehanty, Jack. 'Social Critique as Religious Formation: Relational Practices in Faith-Based Activism', *Liturgy*, 35:2 (2020), 25-32.*

Dietrich, Stephanie, Knud Jørgensen, Kari Korslien, and Kjell Nordstokke. 'Introduction'. *The Diaconal Church*, Stephanie Dietrich, Knud Jørgensen, Kari Korslien, and Kjell Nordstokke Eds. (Oxford: Regnum Books International, 2019), 1-11.

Doan-Bao, Chau, Evangelia Papoutsaki, and Giles Dodson. 'Catalysing Social Change in Ho Chi Minh City, Vietnam: Evaluating the Lin Model', *Community Development Journal*, 54:3 (2019), 519–540.*

Evans, Scotney D., Ora Prilleltensky, Adrine McKenzie, Isaac Prilleltensky, Debbie Nogueras, Corinne Huggins, and Nick Mescia. 'Promoting Strengths, Prevention, Empowerment and Community Change through Organizational Development', *Journal of Prevention & Intervention in the Community*, 39:1 (2011), 50-64.*

Gaiya, Musa. 'Charismatic and Pentecostal Social Orientations in Nigeria', *Nova Religio: The Journal of Alternative & Emergent Religion*, 18:3 (2015), 63-79.*

Ham, Carlos. 'The Church Responding to the Agenda 2030'. *The Diaconal Church*, Stephanie Dietrich, Knud Jørgensen, Kari Karsrud Korslien and Kjell Nordstokke Eds. (Oxford, UK: Regnum Books International, 2019), 185-198.

Huff, James. 'Operationalizing Opportunities and Creating Publics in Salvadoran Churches: Findings from an Ethnographic Process Evaluation', *NAPA Bulletin*, 33:1 (2010), 105-125.*

Kang, Byungdeok, and Kristina Jaskyte. 'Congregational Leaders' Perceptions of Organizational Innovation', *Administration in Social Work*, 35:2 (2011), 161-179.*

Kapp, D. 'I'll Think of Something: Improvisation in Small Church Service Programs', *Review of Religious Research*, 54:2 (Jun 2012), 197-215.*

Katapura, Jose. 'Philanthropic Organizations and Community Development. The Case of the Bettiah Christians in India', *Asian Journal of Social Science*, 43:4 (2015), 400-434.*

Kirwan, James, Brian Ilbery, Damian Maye, and Joy Carey. 'Grassroots Social Innovations and Food Localisation: An Investigation of the Local Food Programme in England', *Global Environmental Change*, 23:5 (2013), 830-837.*

Krige, Skip. 'Towards a Coherent Vision for Faith-Based Development', *Journal of Theology for Southern Africa*, 132 (2008), 16-37.*

Langer, Andreas and Johannes Eurich 'Social Innovations as Opportunities: How Can Innovations in Social Services Be Stimulated and Managed?' *Diaconia. Journal for the Study of Christian Social Practice*, 7:2 (2016), 174-190.*

Ledwith, Margaret. *Community Development: A Critical Approach* (Bristol: Policy Press, 2020).

Levac, Danielle, Heather Colquhoun, and Kelly O'Brien. 'Scoping Studies: Advancing the Methodology', *Implementation Science, 5:*69 (2010), 1-9.

Manyaka-Boshielo, Semape. 'The Role of a Missional Social Entrepreneurial Church in a Township Community', *HTS Teologiese Studies/Theological Studies*, 74:1 (2018), 1-8.*

Marques, C.,C. Marques, F. Nogueira, C. Gerry, and S. Andrade. 'Facets and Outcomes of Healthcare Service Innovation: A Study of Catholic Service Providers in Northern Portugal', *International Journal of Innovation and Learning*, 18:1 (2015), 23-44.*

McCarthy, J., and E. Walker. 'Alternative Organizational Repertoires of Poor People's Social Movement Organizations', *Nonprofit and Voluntary Sector Quarterly*, 33:3_suppl (Sep 2004), 97S-119S.*

Meredith, Thomas, and Melanie MacDonald. 'Community-Supported Slum-Upgrading: Innovations from Kibera, Nairobi, Kenya', *Habitat International*, 60 (February 2017), 1-9.*

Nader, Lucia, and José de Campos. 'Five Reasons to Fear Innovation', *Sur: International Journal on Human Rights*, 13:23 (2016), 211-221.*

Nandan, M., M. London, and T. Bent-Goodley. 'Social Workers as Social Change Agents: Social Innovation, Social Intrapreneurship, and Social Entrepreneurship', *Human Service Organisations: Management Leadership & Governance*, 39:1 (2015), 38-56.*

Nandan, Monica, Kristina Jaskyte, and Gokul Mandayam. 'Human Centered Design as a New Approach to Creative Problem Solving', *Human Service Organisations: Management, Leadership & Governance*, 44:4 (2020), 1-7.*

Noblit, G.W. 'Meta-Ethnography: Adaptation and Return'. *Cultural Constructions of Identity: Meta-Ethnography and Theory*, Luis Urrieta Jr. and George Nobilt Eds. (Oxford: Oxford University Press, 2018), 34-50.

Osborne, S., C. Chew, and K. McLaughlin. 'The Once and Future Pioneers? The Innovative Capacity of Voluntary Organisations and the Provision of Public Services: A Longitudinal Approach', *Public Management Review*, 10:1 (2008), 51-70.*

Patel, Sheela, and Sheridan Bartlett. 'Reflections on Innovation, Assessment and Social Change: A Sparc Case Study', *Development in Practice*, 19:1 (2009), 3-15.*

Pearse, Noel. 'Effective Strategic Leadership: Balancing Roles during Church Transitions', *Hervormde Teologiese Studies*, 67:2 (2011), 1-7.*

Perkons, R., and N. Brown. 'Intercultural Organisational Development', *Systemic Practice & Action Research*, 23:1 (2010), 47-71.*

Plowman, D., L. Baker, T. Beck, M. Kulkarni, S. Solansky, and D. Travis. 'Radical Change Accidentally: The Emergence and Amplification of Small Change', *Academy of Management Journal*, 50:3 (2007), 515-543.*

Prasad, Shambu. 'Innovating at the Margins: The System of Rice Intensification in India and Transformative Social Innovation', *Ecology & Society*, 21(4):7 (2016), 595-603.*

Ritchie, Holly. 'Unwrapping Institutional Change in Fragile Settings: Women Entrepreneurs Driving Institutional Pathways in Afghanistan', *World Development*, 83© (2016), 39-53.*

Schliesser, Christine. 'On a Long Neglected Player: The Religious Factor in Poverty Alleviation: The Example of the So-Called 'Prosperity Gospel' in Africa', *Journal of Religion in Africa,* 46(1) (2016) 116-117.*

Shin, J., and Y. Choi. 'Organizational Innovativeness and Its Determinants in South Korean Nonprofit Human Service Organisations', *Nonprofit Management & Leadership*, 30:1 (Sep 2019), 51-68.*

Simpson, P. 'Complexity and Change Management: Analyzing Church Leaders' Narratives', *Journal of Organizational Change Management*, 25:2 (2012), 283-296.*

Smith, Rachel, Youllee Kim, Stephen Matthews, Eleanore Sternberg, Dimi Doudou, and Matthew Thomas. 'Communal Innovations: Inspiring Neighborhoods of Hope and Advocacy', *Journal of Health Communication*, 25:5 (2020) 444-453.*

Swart, Ignatius. 'Churches as a Stock of Social Capital for Promoting Social Development in Western Cape Communities', *Journal of Religion in Africa*, 36:3/4 (2006), 346-378.*

Taylor, R., N. Torugsa, and A. Arundel. 'Social Innovation in Disability Nonprofits: An Abductive Study of Capabilities for Social Change', *Nonprofit and Voluntary Sector Quarterly*, 49:2 (2020), 399-423.*

Tejedo, Joel. 'Pentecostal Civic Engagement: How Ilocano Pentecostal Churches Build Poor Communities in the Philippines', *Asian Journal of Pentecostal Studies*, 13:1 (2010), 41-64*

Tello-Rozas, Sonia. 'Inclusive Innovations through Social and Solidarity Economy Initiatives: A Process Analysis of a Peruvian Case Study', *Voluntas: International Journal of Voluntary & Nonprofit Organizations*, 27:1 (2016), 61-85.*

United Nations, *Transforming Our World: The 2030 Agenda for Sustainable Development, A/RES/70/1* (2015).

Valeau, Patrick. 'Stages and Pathways of Development of Nonprofit Organizations: An Integrative Model', *Voluntas: International Journal of Voluntary & Nonprofit Organizations*, 26:5 (2015), 1894-1919.*

Van Aarde, Timothy. 'Equipping the Poorest of the Poor to Become Agents of Community Transformation: A Case Study of Milk as a Catalyst in Burundi', *In die Skriflig*, 51:1 (2017), 1-11.*

Wolfer, Terry and Katrina del Pilar. 'Ten Thousand Villages: Partnering with Artisans to Overcome Poverty', *Social Work & Christianity*, 35:4 (2008), 449-472.*

Leading towards Inclusion in Communities – Unity and Diversity when Leading towards Inclusiveness

Benedicte Tveter Kivle and Beate Jelstad Løvaas

In this chapter, the authors present a theoretical framework for community leaders to better understand how to lead towards inclusive communities. They combine known indicators of inclusion in organisations with theoretical elements of leadership and place them according to the theoretical divide between diversity and unity. They suggest specific leadership strategies that can make inclusion a reality for participants and members in community organisations by balancing the need for unity and diversity.

Introduction

Leadership plays a crucial role in developing communities[1] and for including individuals in community organisations. Developing inclusive communities can be described as the effort to shape, uphold, and disturb communities towards 'a society for all in which every individual, each with rights and responsibilities, has an active role to play'.[2] Organisations hold important mechanisms for inclusion and/or exclusion in communities.[3] Leaders in community organisations play an important part in this effort through managing volunteers and leading community members.

The question guiding this chapter is: How can community leaders lead towards inclusiveness? We seek an answer to this by drawing on already known insights on indicators for inclusion in organisations and combining this knowledge with established leadership principles from the theory of Transformational Leadership (TFL). We present a table to show the theoretical divide between unity and diversity, where we also distinguish between

---

[1] Kirk, P., & Shutte, A. M., 'Community Leadership Development', *Community Development Journal*, 39:3 (2004), 234-251.

[2] UN DESA, *Creating an Inclusive Society: Practical Strategies to Promote Social Integration* (2009), 8; https://www.un.org/esa/socdev/egms/docs/2009/Ghana/inclusive-society.pdf.

[3] Dobusch, L., 'How Exclusive are Inclusive Organizations?', *Equality, Diversity and Inclusion: An International Journal*, 33:3 (2014), 220-234.

leadership strategies on the collective and individual levels. We encourage researchers to further explore the proposed theoretical model through empirical inquiry.

Inclusive societies and local communities are highlighted within the UN's sustainable development goal (SDG) 11.[4] However, the concept of inclusion has a divided and disputed understanding and connotation within the community development literature.[5] As defined by a UN expert group:

> An inclusive society is a society that… ensures inclusion, equality of opportunity as well as capability of all members of the society to determine an agreed set of social institutions that govern social interaction.[6]

Whilst this definition emphasises the agreement of common institutions as the inclusive mechanism, the level of *disagreement* and even conflict is not addressed. However, one may find common ground in the fact that the consequences of failing to create inclusive communities are severe; inequalities and economic suffering are, in many cases, connected to the lack of inclusive communities. Processes of exclusion and marginalisation push some of us away from access to certain qualities of life, such as fulfilling a career dream, the chance to create a family, and pursuing creative talents. Exclusion is simultaneously pushing some of us into situations of despair and a lack of hope for the future. We also know that the road to radicalisation almost always includes experiences of exclusion and a lack of belonging to someone or something in the local or wider society, and then finding a sense of belonging within groups with radical ideas.

We know from early social theory the risks for social exclusion connected to systematic mechanisms (such as barriers in the labour market for certain groups), and the possibilities for inclusion connected to structures (securing legal and civil rights) in society are issues that force political discussions.[7] However, we still know little about how the informal mechanisms connected to internal norms, values, and habits towards inclusion within local communities' work,[8] and even less about how leaders may play a role in the creation, upholding, or changing of these cultural mechanisms. By combining established knowledge on transformational leadership principles with more specific knowledge on inclusion in organisations, we suggest how specifically first-level leaders in community organisations can influence the level of inclusion in the groups they

[4] UN DESA, SDG 11 (undated); https://sdgs.un.org/goals/goal11.
[5] UN DESA, *Creating.*
[6] Quoted in UN DESA, *Creating*, 8.
[7] Bynner, J., *Risks and Outcomes of Social Exclusion Insights from Longitudinal Data* (Paris: OECD, 2000). P.9; Sciortino, Giuseppe. 'A Blueprint for Inclusion: Talcott Parsons, the Societal Community and the Future of Universalistic Solidarities.' *The American Sociologist*, 52, no. 1 (2020): 159-77.
[8] Dobusch, 'How Exclusive', 224.

lead, and how, through this, they might play a role in preventing exclusion of their members, firstly as included members of the organisation, but secondly towards a sense of inclusion and acceptance within the local community.

Community is defined and structured in numerous ways.[9] A local community is, in this chapter, understood as a neighbourhood or a district within a town or city. It is something between a block and a town in size. The only thing people may have in common is the sharing of public spaces. However, in communities, there are most often locally based organisations: organised units on a meso level, sport associations, faith-based organisations, local libraries, and social work organisations with one or more expressed goal(s) or purpose(s). In these organisations, people from the community come together for different activities. In the pursuit of creating and upholding inclusive communities, community organisations play a crucial role, not least because they enhance the possibility to lead collective actions and establish collective norms, habits, and values.

What does it mean for a leader in a community organisation to promote inclusion? What contradictions may the leader face? And what are the possibilities for balancing these contradictions?

In other words, *how can community leaders lead towards inclusiveness?* We address these questions below using three steps. We start by presenting recent insights on inclusion in organisations, based on Dobusch's developed categorisation.[10] Next, we present some chosen and well-established principles for transformational leadership and develop a model where we combine the two. We then apply this model and discuss it within the context of community organisations.

First, however, we give a brief introduction to our two illustrative examples of typical community leaders.

Two Illustrative Cases

Who are the community leaders?

The football coach for a children's soccer team is, in a Norwegian context, a typical community leader on the first level. There are about 20,000 children's soccer teams in Norway,[11] with members between the ages of 4 and 16 years old. The coaches are either minimally paid youths or parents who are given symbolic compensation for the hours they spend during their recreational time coaching children in soccer. Often, but not always, the coach has a personal engagement in building a safe space for children in the community through playing soccer. Organised sports clubs have the inherent risk of excluding those of us who lack money for tuition and equipment; however, the local sports associations are still

---

[9] Dominelli, L., *Introducing Social Work. Short Introductions* (Cambridge: Polity Press, 2009).

[10] Dobusch, 'How Exclusive'.

[11] Norges fotballforbund, Statistikk (2021).

looked upon as tools for inclusion, and strategies for covering tuition and equipment when needed are seen as important elements for including children from all different backgrounds.

Home-Start is a toolbox developed by Home-Start Worldwide, incorporated by community organisations in 22 countries to meet the needs of families with small children below school age. The purpose of Home-Start is to help families that for a period need extra support, due to, for example, twin birth, illness in the family, single parenthood, or the lack of a support network.[12] The work is organised through idealistic organisations or public services. In Norway, there are 47 coordinators across the country employed to recruit, train, and lead volunteers to visit and help families in their homes for two to four hours per week for a period of six months. The volunteers are adults with experience in dealing with small children. Ideally, the group of volunteers should reflect the diversity amongst the families they cater to. The Home-Start coordinator reports in interviews that they have an outspoken goal, wish, or strategy for including volunteers with varied socio-economic backgrounds, genders, ages, or professions to accommodate the varied needs amongst the families. It is challenging to recruit enough male volunteers and volunteers with immigrant backgrounds.[13]

Inclusive Communities and Community Development

Inclusion is at the core of community development. The literature on community development often disagrees on the understanding of 'community' and 'development',[14] being more concerned with how solidarity and agency can develop and how one could counteract the forces that erode solidarity and agency.[15] According to the UN, community development is 'a process where community members come together to take collective action and generate solutions to common problems'.[16]

There is one descriptive and one comprehensive side of community. In this chapter, we understand 'community' first descriptively, in line with Poland and Maré, to be 'a lasting group of people living and belonging to a defined territorial

---

[12] Home-Start report 2019.

[13] Home-Start report 2019 p.63.

[14] Addy, T., 'Seeking Conviviality as a Core Concept of Community Development', In Haugen+++ (Eds.), *Developing Just and Inclusive Communities* (Oxford: Regnum Books, 2022); Dinnie, E., & Fischer, A., 'The Trouble with Community: How 'Sense of Community' Influences Participation in Formal, Community-led Organisations and Rural Governance', *Sociologia Ruralis*, 60:1 (2020), 243-259.

[15] Bhattacharyya, J., 'Solidarity and Agency: Rethinking Community Development', *Human Organization*, 54:1 (1995), 60-69; Lund, V., & Juujärvi, S., 'Residents' Agency Makes a Difference in Volunteering in an Urban Neighbourhood' *Voluntas*, 29 (2018), 756-769.

[16] UN Terms, Community Development.

area'.[17] Firstly, we localise communities to geographical spaces. Secondly, we take a more comprehensive understanding of the concept, seeing (the *sense* of being) community as a defined 'state of deeply shared identity and code of conduct'.[18] This sense of community may be experienced, or it may be something desirable in contexts where people interact. An ideal state of a geographical community was characterised by Bhattacharyye in 1995 as 'justice for all included, inclusiveness and solidarity and a common identity and code of conduct'.[19] This comprehensive sense of community adheres largely to the understanding of inclusive society, since the sense of community and common identity is a central part of an inclusive society. Inclusiveness may be present to a variable degree within a locally defined area, just as the sense of community may vary. People feel bound together by a common identity in sharing the same name of place and shared interests for living – or not.

An *inclusive* community is an ideal (not realistic) state where a 'community… values all its members and helps them to meet their basic needs so that they can live with dignity, engage actively, and contribute to their community'.[20] In geographic communities, inhabitants must interact or coexist, willingly, or reluctantly, and share space with each other.

In the ideal state of an inclusive community, people are welcomed and accepted with their individual differences and needs. No communities have actually reached this state, at least not for a prolonged period. The literature on inclusive communities has, for example, shown how people outside the 'hetero-physical ability-norm' often experience that their life conditions are left out of the planning and mindset of those in power within the community.[21] The culture of inclusive communities is characterised by high trust amongst the members. Where trust is high, people are, not surprisingly, more willing to interact, assist each other, and support each other both as friends and strangers.[22]

What happens in communities where inclusiveness and trust are lacking? In local communities with *little* trust amongst the community members, people tend to keep to themselves within households, locking doors and feeling annoyed by other people's interruptions to their day. People feel the need to guard their

---

[17] Poland, M., & Maré, D. C., 'Defining Geographic Communities', Motu Working Paper No. 05-09 (2005).

[18] Bhattacharyya, 'Solidarity'.

[19] Bhattacharyya, 'Solidarity'.

[20] Burnaby City 'Burnaby City Social Sustainability Strategy' 2011, Retrieved from: chrome-extension://efaidnbmnnnibpcajpcglclefindmkaj/viewer.html?pdfurl=https%3A%2F%2Fwww.cip-icu.ca%2FFiles%2FAwards%2FPlanning-Excellence%2FBurnaby-Social-Sustainability-Strategy-Report-2011.aspx&clen=4778440&chunk=true.

[21] Azzopardi, A., & Grech, S., *Inclusive Communities: A Critical Reader* (Rotterdam: Sense Publishers, 2012).

[22] Marsh, Robert. 'Social Trust in Japan and Taiwan: A Test of Fukuyama's Thesis.' In *Trust in Contemporary Society*, edited by Masamichi Sasaki, 42:210–30. Brill, 2019.

property and family, and energy is put into security and defence strategies, but also, there is often high solidarity and mutual trust amongst members of subgroups or families. The causes for lack of trust in communities vary. Our assumption is that exclusion occurs when inclusive forces are getting out of balance.[23] For those who work to strengthen inclusiveness, the challenges are, therefore, many.

Knowledge of Inclusion

What are the central indicators of inclusion within organisations? Inclusion, exclusion, and diversity in organisations are under-researched themes, although inclusion in leadership has been given increasing interest.[24] A search of the academic literature for 'inclusion' and 'diversity' shows a domination of empirical inquiries for inclusion, primarily within health services, education, and work-life contexts. Whilst research on diversity management has mainly focused on supporting minority individuals, inclusion shifts attention to creating an organisational context in which everybody feels like an insider.[25]

Structural inclusion mechanisms secure equal access to resources and responsibilities in a society. Parsons mentioned civil rights as the most important structural mechanisms for securing the inclusion of all citizens in a society.[26] He also acknowledged that the range of structural mechanisms is limited and relies on cultural mechanisms to fully function, exemplified by the case of black Americans in the USA.

Organisations are given the responsibility for creating accepting, inclusive climates amongst organisational members but also as being a meso-level actor in contributing to an inclusive society.[27]

To become an 'inclusive organisation', leaders are encouraged to adopt not only diversity-blind strategies but also diversity-conscious strategies.[28] In her literature review on inclusive organisations, Dobusch sums up that the two strategies of diversity blindness and diversity consciousness seem to be the analytical distinction that distinguishes inclusion from exclusion in organisational work life. A diversity-blind approach implies that all organisational members are treated equally irrespective of their group

---

[23] Dobusch, 'How Exclusive'.

[24] Mor Barak, Michàlle E., Gil Luria, and Kim C. Brimhall. 'What Leaders Say versus What They Do: Inclusive Leadership, Policy-Practice Decoupling, and the Anomaly of Climate for Inclusion.' *Group & Organization Management* (May 2021). https://doi.org/10.1177/10596011211005916.

[25] Janssens, M., & Zanoni, P., *What Makes an Organization Inclusive? Organizational Practices Favoring the Relational Inclusion of Ethnic Minorities in Operative Jobs,* paper presented at the 21st IACM Conference, Chicago, IL, 3-6 July (2008).

[26] Kivisto, P., 'Inclusion: Parsons and beyond', *Acta Sociologica,* 47:3 (2004), 291-297.

[27] Gilbert and Ivancevich, quoted in Dobusch, 'How Exclusive', 9.

[28] Dobusch, 'How Exclusive', 9.

identification. A diversity-conscious approach explicitly addresses those of us who find ourselves in minority positions. To exclusively emphasise one of the strategies is associated with failing to create an inclusive organisation. A manoeuvring between these two approaches, however, creates space for acceptance and belonging without being pressured towards assimilation.[29]

The specific indicators that characterise an inclusive organisation are suggested by Dobusch, and Janssens and Zanosi:[30]

(1) Spontaneous formation of groups with participants from different backgrounds
(2) Humorous relationships between minority and majority employees
(3) Expressions of interest for minorities
(4) Commonly accepted expressions of distinctive cultural practices by minority employees

The four approaches have the advantage that they are easily operationalised, whilst they maintain the theoretical complexity of diversity and unity approaches. They point to the importance of spontaneity and humour as well as sincere interest and acceptance towards what is different. All characteristics are institutional features of the organisation.

	Unity	***Diversity***
Indicators for inclusion in organisations	Spontaneous formation of groups (1) Numerous relationships between minority and majority employees (2)	Expressions of interest for minority cultures (3) Acceptance for expressions of distinct cultural practices (4)

Table 1. Classifying indicators for inclusion according to unity and diversity

This insight on inclusion in operational businesses in Belgium[31] teaches us about the importance of balancing the sense of *unity*, with the acknowledgement of *diversity* in work organisations. In the following, we explore the relevance of transformational leadership theory for leading towards inclusive community organizations.

Leaders, Followers, and Situations

Leadership theories give understanding, guidance, and tools for leaders in leadership positions. Agency, understood as the ability of people to order their world and 'to act otherwise',[32] is traditionally understood as an ability initiated

[29] Dobusch, 'How Exclusive' 9; Janssens & Zanoni, *What Makes*, 14-16.
[30] Dobusch, 'How Exclusive' 9; Janssens & Zanoni, *What Makes*, 14-16.
[31] Janssen and Zanoni, *What makes*, 3.
[32] Bhattacharyya, 'Solidarity'.

and managed by the leader, within what we call a traditional and oligarchic leader perspective. Polyarchic leadership theories assume that leadership and agency rely on followers and context just as much as the one in a leadership position. However, organisational researchers have recognised that leadership in practice has features from both oligarchic and polyarchic perspectives.[33] Leadership is acted both through leadership positions and through the dynamic triangle of leader, follower, and situation.[34] Kirk and Shutte describe, from a South African context, how the understanding of Ubuntu as a polyarchic principle and the local chief as a representative of oligarchic positioning draws on this dualistic assumption of leadership. They state that leadership is 'a relational activity between role holders in a system, and this allows for some roles to have wider remits than do others'.[35] Leaders will, because of their position, have some responsibility, although not entire control, for the climate in a group. Instead of making all decisions and providing all information to the followers, the leaders are the ones responsible for the processes rather than the product.[36]

Transformational Leadership

In this chapter, we build our conceptual construction of leadership on the theory of transformational leadership.[37] TFL is becoming a well-established framework for practitioners as well as researchers, emphasising the informal and institutional aspects of organisation and leadership. Being a mainstream leadership theory developed for hierarchical structured organisational contexts, transformational leadership assumes an oligarchic role of leadership. The theory emphasises more or less one-sidedly the leader's performance of leadership on a group of followers. TFL does, however, include some polyarchic elements, through the emphasis on processes for involving all participants.

TFL is contrasted with transactional leadership, which implies exchange processes and contractual relations.[38] TFL aims at guiding leaders towards developing supportive relationships with members and building commitment to a common purpose in a group or organisation.[39] Such leadership behaviour seems to be an appropriate approach when leading towards inclusive communities,

---

[33] Kirk & Shutte, 'Community'.

[34] Bolden, R., 'Distributed Leadership in Organizations: A Review of Theory and Research', *International Journal of Management Reviews: IJMR* 13, no. 3 (2011): 251-69.

[35] Kirk & Shutte, 'Community'.

[36] Kirk & Shutte, 'Community'.

[37] Bass, B. M., *Leadership and Performance beyond Expectations* (New York: Free Press, 1985); Bass, B. M., & Riggio, R. E., *Transformational leadership*, 2nd edn. (Mahwah, NJ: Erlbaum, 2006).

[38] Ibid.

[39] Riggio, Bass, & Orr (2004).

where meeting the members' needs for purpose and motivation is essential. In addition, the changing society in which the community organisations operate requires leaders to pay attention to these changes, and transformational leadership behaviour is seen as appropriate when leading change,[40] such as in the case of aiming to increase the level of inclusion in the community organisation. Hence, we argue that TFL theory has the potential to provide relevant guidance for leadership efforts in community organisations. To what extent transformational leaders embrace both diversity and unity as the characteristics of inclusiveness in organisations will be discussed later in this chapter, after a short presentation of the four dimensions of the theory.

The four dimensions that characterise TFL theory are: inspirational motivation, idealised influence, intellectual stimulation, and individualised consideration.[41]

Inspirational motivation signifies that the leader provides the employees with a clear purpose, vision, or mission. This is done when the leader motivates and inspires, amongst other things, by communicating the meaning of the work tasks and by paying attention to the organisational vision. Optimism and enthusiasm are idealised characteristics of such leaders, and good team spirit is the desired outcome.

Idealised influence implies that the leader serves as a role model for ethical conduct. The leader lives by the organisation's vision and values and is willing to risk something to defend those values.[42]

Intellectual stimulation reflects that the leader motivates their employees to examine the traditional and common ways of solving problems and encourages them to question the methods they use to improve them. The leader facilitates creativity and innovation by asking for new ideas, challenging intellectually, and involving employees in finding solutions to existing problems. New ideas are not criticised, and creativity is stimulated.

Individualised consideration means that the leader focuses on understanding the needs of each employee and works continually to develop their employees' full potential. TFL is contrasted with transactional leadership, which implies exchange processes and consists of contingent rewards.

The four dimensions within TFL theory represent tools available for leaders who wish to transform the culture, motivation, and actions of the followers or participants within a group. When we take a closer look at these dimensions through the lens of unity and diversity, we may find that the tools implicitly point towards unity and diversity amongst the followers. We will, therefore, use these

---

[40] Bommer, W. H., Rubin, R. S., & Baldwin, T. T., 'Setting the Stage for Effective Leadership: Antecedents of Transformational Leadership Behavior', *The Leadership Quarterly*, 15, no. 2 (2004): 195-210.

[41] Bass (1985); Bass & Riggio (2006).

[42] Bass & Riggio, *Transformational*.

four approaches as steppingstones when we discuss what tools are available for leaders when working towards inclusion.

Discussion: How can Unity and Diversity be Balanced by Transformational Leadership?

In Table 2, we present our interpretation of how the four dimensions in TFL relate to unity and diversity within organisations. We elaborate further by examining unity and diversity at the collective and individual levels.

		Unity (A)	***Diversity (B)***
Approaches in transform-ational leadership	Collective level (1)	Inspirational motivation (1/A)	Intellectual stimulation/involving followers in new ideas (1/B)
	Individual level (2)	Idealised influence (2/A)	Individual considerations (2/B)

Table 2. Leadership approaches related to diversity and unity dimensions

The table shows how TFL can inform leaders along the axis of unity and diversity and at both the collective and individual levels. More specifically, the four approaches indicated by the squares of the table above may represent different leadership tools to promote indicators for inclusion.

Inspirational motivation at a collective level (square 1/A): The leader has the opportunity and responsibility for providing followers with a larger sense of purpose for their specific tasks. For example, in a football team, the coach may set the vision that all players should get the chance to score during the season. Visions like these go beyond the goal of winning or losing the next game. The vision may give the players motivation and purpose, particularly if the team begins to lose a lot of matches during a season. In Home-Start, the coordinator reminds the volunteers about the purpose of visiting the families every week. Even if each visit may not seem particularly engaging and important, the coordinator keeps the spirit alive and the sense of fellowship amongst the volunteers by reminding them about their purpose of providing crucial services for young families who are struggling with life. These collective, inspirational visions are not only motivational, they also have the indirect effect of establishing the higher unit where all members belong and have a share .

Idealised influence on an individual level (square 2/A): The leader contributes to a sense of unity by being a role model for their followers. The leader also acts according to the common values of the organisation when the actions involve sacrifices. For example, a football coach can promote unity when they enact fair play on the football field, respecting the referee's decisions, talking positively about other teams, and holding back players on the team in solidarity towards a competing team. Ethical conduct like this may create dignity and pride within the group; it may promote similar actions from members and unite the members/participants on a deeper level than their common goal of winning the match can do. The common inclusive patterns of moral conduct strengthen the shared commonness that binds the group members together. The individual differences connected to background and habits fade, replaced with an emphasis on the shared values strengthened by the role modelling leader.

Intellectual stimulation on a collective level (square 1/B): Whilst leaders are encouraged to emphasise unity within the group, TFL also emphasises the need for uplifting diversity amongst the followers. Through establishing and practising mechanisms for involvement and the sharing of ideas, the unique qualities of members within the group are shown and consequently, in time, the diversity within the group may become more accepted and appreciated. For example, the way a football coach makes decisions that concern the whole team shows how accepting they are towards different perspectives. TFL encourages the leader to find mechanisms that make spaces for promoting ideas from all members. In Home-Start, there is a challenge in recruiting male volunteers. To find a solution to this recruitment problem, it might be possible to specifically invite men to participate in a project group to share ideas on how to attract male volunteers. On a collective level, the community leader might look for decision-making strategies where they include alternative ways to find the answers. However, intellectual stimulation is also achieved through the informal arenas that the community leaders create. The coach and coordinator have positions for encouraging connections across social boundaries within the groups, even if they cannot direct the actions of the participants.

Individual considerations on an individual level (Square 2/B): The leader has a special responsibility for considering the personal and individual needs of each follower. In a football team, different situations at home may have a severe influence on the members' attendance in the team. If a player is going through a family crisis, for example, the coach might be a significant person, calling and asking about how things are. Often, this informal relationship building is crucial for keeping sports teams together and for youth who are in danger of falling out of organised sports. In Home-Start, the job of connecting the right families with the right volunteers has been shown to be one of the most important elements of the Home-Start coordinator's work and for the successful outcome of the arrangements.

The Balance between Unity and Diversity in Leadership

TFL points towards collective and individual strategies for promoting unity and diversity. Table 2 highlights some paradoxes that will be discussed and nuanced. How can leaders balance the need for diversity within unity? What are the limitations of the presented framework? There may be a number of paradoxes, but for now we point to two in particular: the dynamics of inclusion and exclusion, and the limitation in leading towards spontaneity and a sincere interest in diversity.

Inclusion and exclusion imply a dualism that is understood both as opposites and in a continuum.[43] The underlying normativity of promoting inclusion as the desired state and exclusion as the undesired state also drives this chapter and our 'model' (Table 2). On the other hand, a more analytical approach towards inclusion/exclusion acknowledges that all inclusion also involves exclusion to some degree.[44] You cannot include someone without excluding someone or something else. How, then, do leaders balance inclusion and exclusion mechanisms? When a community leader includes specific members and their opinions in decision-making, they simultaneously run the risk of excluding other members and their perspectives. All members of a team or organisation, whether they take the form of a soccer team or a group of Home-Start volunteers, bring with them specific experiences, perspectives, opinions, and interests. By giving attention in one direction, the leader risks unconsciously contributing to the exclusion of other members of the group. There are, however, tools available for dealing with this challenge. Leaning towards the theoretical framework of TFL, one approach would be to look for the collective focus on diversity (approach 2) – creating a mechanism for welcoming a broad variety of perspectives and ideas on a collective level, such as establishing listening rounds. The dynamic between the mechanisms of inclusion and exclusion will always be present and something a sensitive leader must balance.

To lead towards inclusion can never be a top-down process guided by an oligarchic leader. Inclusion is identified by spontaneous and even humorous relations and constellations across minority/majority groups and identities (Table 1). These processes cannot be directed since the directive nature in itself will erode the spontaneity. Leaders do, however, play a crucial role in facilitating processes for inclusive practice and have tools available for promoting unity across the differences when emphasising the vision and common purpose of their group's activities (Table 2). The value of diversity can in itself be a common platform to create unity within the group. The football coach must be on board and accept or even show an interest in the players' backgrounds and individual personalities. On the other hand, over time, the players will adapt to the coach's example and promotion of vision and unity and their sense of sensitivity towards diversity, depending on whether or not the coach has gained the players' trust and respect.

---

[43] Dobusch, 'How Exclusive'.

[44] Dobusch, 'How Exclusive'.

Conclusion

The work on inclusion and accepting diversity is important and challenging. The community leader takes on a complex task when they wish to promote an inclusive culture amongst community members within organisations. It is not enough to embrace diversity, nor to act as if differences do not exist. In this chapter, we have shown how leading towards inclusion means simultaneously upholding a sense of unity and acknowledging and welcoming diversity. We have pointed to some dilemmas that may occur, and we have also implied some of the limitations a leader faces in the role of facilitating towards an inclusive culture.

Characteristics of leadership towards inclusiveness in communities means balancing both unity and diversity within a group or organisation.[45] The leader will benefit from being sensitive towards what it is that binds members together, but also from acknowledging differences and diversity within the group. The differences may be connected to the members' affiliations towards minority or majority cultures, or to specific personal situations and needs. The approaches highlighted within transformational leadership indirectly address the issue of unity and diversity, and we suggest this framework as a useful tool for leaders pursuing inclusion within their organisations.

The knowledge we have presented here could have an impact beyond the context illustratively described. By creating space for minority perspectives in community organisations, the more general processes of inclusion within hyper-diverse and multifaceted communities could be strengthened. Future research could examine empirically whether the elements highlighted here actually are the ones characterising leaders who wish to promote inclusion and whether there are other, yet undiscovered, approaches that could lead to a deeper understanding of how to lead towards inclusive communities.

Bibliography

Addy, T., 'Seeking Conviviality as a Core Concept of Community Development', In Haugen et al., *Developing Just and Inclusive Communities* (Oxford: Regnum, 2022).

Azzopardi, A., and Grech, S., *Inclusive Communities: A Critical Reader* (Rotterdam: Sense Publishers, 2012). DOI: 10.1007/978-94-6091-849-0.

Barak, M. E. M., Luria, G., and Brimhall, K. C., 'What Leaders Say Versus What They Do: Inclusive Leadership, Policy–Practice Decoupling, and the Anomaly of Climate for Inclusion', *Group & Organization Management* (2021), DOI: 10.1177/10596011211005916.

Bhattacharyya, J., 'Solidarity and Agency: Rethinking Community Development', *Human Organization*, 54:1 (1995), 60-69.

[45] Dobusch, 'How Exclusive'.

Bass, B. M., *Leadership and Performance beyond Expectations* (New York: Free Press, 1985).

Bass, B. M., and Riggio, R. E., *Transformational Leadership* (2nd edn.) (Mahwah, NJ: Erlbaum, 2006).

Bolden, R., 'Distributed Leadership in Organizations: A Review of Theory and Research', *International Journal of Management Reviews*, 13:3 (2011), 251-69.

Bommer, W. H., Rubin, R. S., and Baldwin, T. T., 'Setting the Stage for Effective Leadership: Antecedents of Transformational Leadership Behavior', *The Leadership Quarterly*, 15:2 (2004), 195-210.

Burnaby City 'Burnaby City Social Sustainability Strategy'(2011). chrome-extension://efaidnbmnnnibpcajpcglclefindmkaj/viewer.html?pdfurl=https%3A%2F%2Fwww.cip-icu.ca%2FFiles%2FAwards%2FPlanning-Excellence%2FBurnaby-Social-Sustainability-Strategy-Report-2011.aspx&clen=4778440&chunk=true.

Bynner, J., *Risks and Outcomes of Social Exclusion Insights from Longitudinal Data* (Paris: OECD, 2000). https://www.oecd.org/education/innovation-education/1855785.pdf.

Dinnie, E., and Fischer, A., 'The Trouble with Community: How 'Sense of Community' Influences Participation in Formal, Community-led Organisations and Rural Governance', *Sociologia Ruralis*, 60:1 (2020), 243-59.

Dobusch, L., 'How Exclusive are Inclusive Organizations?' *Equality, Diversity, and Inclusion: An International Journal*, 33:3 (2014), 220-234.

Dominelli, L., *Introducing Social Work. Short Introductions* (Cambridge: Polity Press, 2009).

Janssens, M., and Zanoni, P., 'What Makes an Organization Inclusive? Organizational Practices Favoring the Relational Inclusion of Ethnic Minorities in Operative Jobs', paper presented at the 21st IACM Conference, Chicago, IL, 3-6 July (2008), https://papers.ssrn.com/sol3/papers.cfm?abstract_id=1298591.

Kirk, P., and Shutte, A. M., 'Community leadership development', *Community Development Journal*, 39:3 (2004), 234-251.

Kivisto, P., 'Inclusion: Parsons and beyond', *Acta Sociologica*, 47:3 (2004), 291-297.

Lund, V., and Juujärvi, S., 'Residents' Agency Makes a Difference in Volunteering in an Urban Neighbourhood' *Voluntas*, 29 (2018), 756-769, https://doi-org.ezproxy.vid.no/10.1007/s11266-018-9955-4.

Mor Barak, Michàlle E., Gil L., and Brimhall K.C. 'What Leaders Say versus What They Do: Inclusive Leadership, Policy-Practice Decoupling, and the Anomaly of Climate for Inclusion.' *Group & Organization Management* (May2021). https://doi.org/10.1177/10596011211005916.

Norges fotballforbund, Statistikk (2021), https://www.fotball.no/tema/om-nff/statistikk-og-historikk/statistikk/#140539.

Poland, M., and Maré, D. C., *Defining Geographic Communities*, Motu Working Paper No. 05-09 (2005), https://papers.ssrn.com/sol3/papers.cfm?abstract_id=911070.

Riggio R. E., Bass B. M., and Orr, S. S., 'Transformational Leadership in Nonprofit Organizations', Riggio R.E., and Orr S.S. (Eds.), *Improving Leadership in Nonprofit Organizations* (San Francisco, CA: Jossey-Bass; 2004), 49-62.

Sciortino, Giuseppe. 'A Blueprint for Inclusion: Talcott Parsons, the Societal Community and the Future of Universalistic Solidarities.' *The American Sociologist*, 52, no. 1 (2020): 159-77.

Smircich, L., and Morgan, G., 'Leadership: The Management of Meaning', *The Journal of Applied Behavioural Science*, 18:3 (1982), 257-273.

UN DESA, *Creating an Inclusive Society: Practical Strategies to Promote Social Integration* (2009). https://www.un.org/esa/socdev/egms/docs/2009/Ghana/inclusive-society.pdf.

UN DESA, *SDG 11* (undated); https://sdgs.un.org/goals/goal11.

UN Terms (2014) Community Development. http://unterm.un.org/DGAACS/unterm.nsf/8fa942046ff7601c85256983007ca4d8/526c2eaba978f007852569fd00036819?OpenDocument.

Part Five

Social Inclusion, Gender, Disability and Diversity

Ruth the Moabite: A Story about an Immigrant and Her Struggle for Identity

Tiana Bosman

Introduction

Hidden within the pages of the Old Testament (OT) we find the well-known story of Ruth. It recounts the narrative of a foreign Moabite woman who, during the time of ancient Israel, immigrated to Bethlehem in Judah. She did so by accompanying her Israelite mother-in-law, Naomi, who returned to Bethlehem, her town of birth, after the death of her husband and two sons. Whilst many biblical scholars and pastors regard this short story as a very 'charming' story in the OT, a story in which blessings are bestowed and *hesed* ('kindness'/'loyalty') is shown to a foreigner,[1] a close reading of the text shows that Ruth's attempt to assimilate into the host culture of her mother-in-law happened with great struggle and sacrifice.

My contribution to this book comes from the context of a biblical scholar who specialises in the translation and interpretation of OT texts. Whilst I am not a practical theologian with expertise in diaconal work, I do have a keen interest in this field, and I hope that my reading of the ancient narrative in the Book of Ruth (RB) can serve readers who are engaged in diaconal work to see that the common problem of exclusion is nothing new; it can be seen throughout history as illustrated in this ancient Bible story. When working towards just and inclusive communities, the biblical texts do not always provide the best examples to follow.

Setting of the Book of Ruth and Its Ancient Audience

Whilst set in the time of the Judges when the Israelites did not yet have a king, the RB was written much later, during the post-exilic time. Right through the Israelite history in the OT, there has always been a strong nationalistic tendency

[1] Kristin Moen Saxegaard, '"More than Seven Sons": Ruth as Example of the Good Son,' *Scandinavian Journal of the Old Testament*, 15.2 (2001), 257.

and the people were known to be extremely exclusivist, generally.[2] This seems to have become even more important in the post-exilic time. In the Books of Ezra and Nehemiah, particularly, we see radical actions taken against mixed marriages and these books 'end by the dissolving of mixed marriages and the expulsion of the foreign wives and their children'.[3] Originating from this context, the RB would have served as a counter-text, a text that wanted to tell the story of once upon a time long ago when an influential Israelite did indeed go against the custom and married a foreign woman. He did not marry just any foreign woman but one from Moab(!) and, as the end of the story attests to, all turned out well for the people of Israel since this woman was the ancestor of King David. The story wanted to provide proof that it is not always bad to include foreigners; in fact, sometimes it can be very beneficial.

Reading the Book of Ruth Today

Today this OT narrative is still read and retold with an appreciative lens. Popular sermon topics include 'loyalty', 'hope', 'daring to act' and 'new life'.[4] The Contextual Bible Study on the RB by the Ujamaa Centre also fails to engage with this text critically.[5] This study guide views the 'whole Book of Ruth as a story of redemption'.[6]

An in-depth reading of the biblical Hebrew text together with the voices of some critical scholars, shows us that reading the text and casting the story in such a positive light, as if it provides a wonderful example of how we should act towards the strangers in our midst, may not be the best way of engaging with this narrative. Rather, this interpretation comes from a superficial reading of the text and does not take the ancient culture and language nuances into account. Whilst this narrative may have been a critique of the ancient society and their exclusion of strangers, it was nevertheless set within a deeply patriarchal society and, for the most part, it still played by the rules of that society. As faith communities of the 21st century, we are challenged by the detail of the text not to apply this

---

[2] Gerda de Villiers, 'The "Foreigner in Our Midst" and the Hebrew Bible', *HTS Theological Studies*, 75.3 (2014), 2.
[3] De Villiers, 'The "Foreigner"', 3.
[4] A sermon series by Schifferdecker with these themes appears on the website workingpreacher.org (Kathryn Schifferdecker, 'Commentary on Ruth 1:1-4:22,' *Working Preacher*, 2014). It is meant as a tool to assist preachers with their sermon preparation. In this particular series on Ruth the sermon messages are very positive and nothing is said about Ruth's struggles as an immigrant.
[5] Ellen Davis, Femi Adeleya, *et al*, 'Study Guide: Ruth', in *Contextual Bible Studies on Various Themes* (2016), Ujamaa Centre, University of KwaZulu-Natal.
[6] Davis, Adeleya, *et al*., 'Study Guide', 8.

narrative too readily to our contemporary contexts but, rather, to engage with it critically and learn how *not* to treat immigrants.[7]

In my exposition of the RB I will convey my findings from reading and translating the Hebrew text. I will employ narrative exegesis,[8] taking the plot, the narrator and the characters into account. I will also consider language markers in the ancient text, especially repetitions and omissions of certain words and phrases. I will glean mostly from the work of women biblical scholars such as De Villiers (2014, 2016, 2019), Fewell (2015), Saxegaard (2010), Sharp (2014), Trible (1976) and Van Wolde (1997) who, like me, challenge the normative interpretations of ancient biblical texts.

In the next section, I will attend to specific themes in the RB that highlight the challenges that Ruth faced in her attempt to settle in a foreign country and assimilate into a new community.

Challenges That Ruth Faced in Her Struggle for Identity in Bethlehem

I have identified three main themes that highlight Ruth's struggle, namely *stereotyping immigrants*, *excluding immigrants* and *putting a price on an immigrant's value*. These struggles all relate to the ancient context that forms the backdrop of the story.

Stereotyping Immigrants

Stereotyping immigrants denotes the negative evaluation of immigrants because they are foreigners.[9] A study on immigrants in South Africa shows that the stereotypes attached to immigrants are often unfounded.[10] Not all immigrants are stereotyped in the same way. In South Africa, for example, 'those who reject or dislike foreigners are not necessarily anti-immigrant; they are anti-black immigrant'.[11]

Southwood states that 'the most obvious marker of otherness in the RB is the repetition of the epithet 'the Moabite' throughout the narrative.'[12] This epithet so often accompanies the name of Ruth that we need to ask the question: Why?

---

[7] Whilst this chapter focuses on the plight of immigrants, other groups who are often regarded as outsiders and excluded from their host communities can also be added.
[8] See David Miller Gunn and Danna Nolan Fewell, *Narrative in the Hebrew Bible* (Oxford: Oxford University Press, 1993) for a discussion on narrative theory.
[9] De Villiers 'The "Foreigner"', 2, explains how this way of stereotyping happens in contemporary societies and links it to how foreigners were treated in the Old Testament times.
[10] Lawrence Schlemmer, 'Immigrants in South Africa: Perceptions and Reality in Witbank, a Medium-sized Industrial Town' (abridged version), *The Centre for Development and Enterprise*, 9 (2006), 7.
[11] Savo Heleta, 'High Fences and Unworthy Foreigners: Anti-poor Immigration Plans and Rhetoric in South Africa', *The Mail and Guardian*, 22 March 2018.
[12] Katherine Southwood, 'Will Naomi's Nation Be Ruth's Nation?: Ethnic Translation

As a rule, the Israelites did not place a high value on the Moabites.[13] They believed that this nation originated from the incestuous behaviour that was initiated by Lot's daughters when they made him drunk and had sex with him (Gen 19:31-38). Both daughters fell pregnant after sleeping with their father. The eldest daughter's son was called Moab (who became the ancestor of the Moabites), whilst the name of the youngest daughter's son was Ben-Ammi (the ancestor of the Ammonites). Another incident that added to the negative perception of the Moabites is when king Balak of Moab hired Balaam to curse Israel (Numbers 22-24). Deuteronomy 23:4 suggests that this was one of the reasons why Moabites were excluded from the community of Yahweh.[14] Furthermore, in Numbers 25:1 we read that the Israelite men allowed themselves to be profaned by having sex with Moabite women. It is clear that the Moabites, especially Moabite women, were not viewed in high regard by the Israelites.

This stereotype can be seen throughout the RB. As soon as Ruth sets foot within the gates of the city of Bethlehem (1:22) where her status officially becomes that of a foreigner, she is most often referred to as 'Ruth the Moabite'. It is remarkable how the narrator, by repetition, really brings the point of Ruth's foreign identity across in Ruth 1:22: 'So Naomi returned, and *Ruth the Moabite*, her daughter-in-law, with her, the one who came back *from the fields (region) of Moab*.'[15] The focus on Ruth's Moabite status is underscored repeatedly in the further unfolding of the plot, both by the narrator as well as by other male characters in 2:2, 6, 21; 4:5 and 4:10.

On the day that Ruth started gleaning in Boaz's field, he visits the field and enquires from his servant about the young woman. Typical to the patriarchal context, he does not ask about the woman's personal identity, but wants to know who she belongs to – Who is her father? Who is her husband?[16] The servant replied: 'She is *the Moabite girl*, the one who came back with Naomi *from the fields of Moab*'. Whilst the servant uses Naomi's name (since, in her widowed status, she does not belong to another man anymore), he does not include Ruth's name when he describes who she is. Trible aptly states: 'Her name he does not give. Her identity he derives from her own strangeness and from another woman.'[17]

---

as a Metaphor for Ruth's Assimilation within Judah' *Humanities*, 3.2 (2014), 111.

[13] Gerda de Villiers and Jurie le Roux, 'The Book of Ruth in the Time of the Judges and Ruth, the Moabitess', *Verbum et Ecclesia*, 37.1 (2016), 4; Danna Nolan Fewell and David Miller Gunn, '"A Son is Born to Naomi!": Literary Allusions and Interpretation in the Book of Ruth,' *Journal for the Study of the Old Testament*, 40 (1988), 106.

[14] De Villiers and Le Roux, 'The Book of Ruth', 4.

[15] In this chapter all translations from the RB are the author's own direct translations.

[16] Frederic Bush, *Ruth-Esther* (Word Biblical Commentary, Vol 9 Dallas: Word, 1996), 113.

[17] Phyllis Trible, 'Two Women in a Man's World: A Reading of the Book of Ruth,' *Soundings: An Interdisciplinary Journal*, 59.3 (1976), 261.

Together with many other scholars,[18] I argue that the repetitive reference to Ruth as 'Ruth the Moabite' attests to how she was labelled with the negative stereotype that Moabites triggered for the Israelite people. We can call it an act of naming and shaming.

Excluding Immigrants

This section deals with how immigrants often suffer exclusion from the host community. Even though Ruth voices her determination to become a member of the Israelite community in Ruth 1:16 – and in doing so renounces her own religion and takes up the Israelite religion[19] – there are multiple instances where she is excluded from this very community. Sometimes this exclusion is done covertly (as if she is invisible to the host community) and at other times overtly; sometimes it is the narrator who excludes Ruth, at other times it is the other characters.

As soon as Elimelech dies in Ruth 1:3, Naomi becomes the main character.[20] When her two sons who were married to Ruth and Orpah died, 'the woman was left without her two sons and without her husband' (1:5b). Here the narrator only acknowledges Naomi's loss. No mention is made of the two daughters-in-law who were also 'left without' their husbands. It is therefore not surprising that Fewell and Gunn describe the book as a story about Naomi rather than Ruth.[21]

When Naomi heard that the famine in Israel was over, she decided to move back to Bethlehem. She encouraged her daughters-in-law to return to their mothers' houses, trying very hard to persuade them. This, however, goes against the custom of the ancient Israelite context. Widows did not become the responsibility of their birth parents after their husbands passed away. They still belonged to their family-by-marriage and it was this family's responsibility to find a new husband for them or take care of them.[22] Since Naomi's husband died, the responsibility to take care of her daughters-in-law now fell on her.[23] Whilst

---

[18] De Villiers and Le Roux, 'The Book of Ruth', 4; Fewell and Gunn, '"A Son is Born"', 106;
Danna Nolan Fewell, 'Space for Moral Agency in the Book of Ruth,' *Journal for the Study of the Old Testament*, 40.1 (2015), 86; Tod Linavelt, 'Narrative and Poetic Art in the Book of Ruth,' *Interpretation* (2010), 119;
Agnethe Siquans, 'Foreignness and Poverty in the Book of Ruth: A Legal Way for a Poor Foreign Woman to Be Integrated into Israel,' *Journal of Biblical Literature*, 128.3 (2009), 447.

[19] Gerda de Villiers, 'Interpreting Texts and the Matter of Context: Examples from the Book of Ruth.' *Verbum et Ecclesia*, 40.1 (2019), 4, 6.

[20] Saxegaard, '"More than Seven Sons",' 258, 273.

[21] Fewell & Gunn, '"A Son is Born"', 99-108.

[22] Also see Genesis 38 where Tamar remains the responsibility of her father-in-law after her husband died.

[23] Saxegaard, '"More than Seven Sons",' 260.

it might have been easier for the daughters-in-law to return to their Moabite families, this would be against the custom of the time.

Orpah was persuaded to return, but Ruth would not let go. In 1:15 Naomi urges Ruth once more: 'Look, your sister-in-law has returned to her people and her gods. Follow your sister-in-law and (also) return home.' Here we hear Naomi saying 'Go back to where you belong'. This message is unsettling, especially if we consider the fact that Ruth – even when widowed – did not primarily belong to her family of origin anymore, but with her in-laws. Furthermore Naomi, together with her late husband and two sons, did not stay away from Moab, a country where they did not belong, when they went looking for greener pastures during the famine in Judah. They lived off the land in Moab for about ten years until the famine was over (1:4-6).

Upon realising that Ruth was determined to accompany her, Naomi 'ceased to talk to her' (1:18). Fewell and Gunn rightfully ask how Ruth's famous speech is heart-touching for so many preachers and congregations over the centuries, but it does not seem to move Naomi?[24] I add my voice to those of Fewell and Gunn who interpret Naomi's silence in a negative light as 'resentment, irritation, frustration, unease. Ruth the Moabite is to her an inconvenience'.[25]

Ruth's resolution to not abandon her mother-in-law is met by disregard; Naomi ignores her.[26] This becomes even clearer upon their arrival in Bethlehem where we see a second silence on the side of Naomi. According to 1:19 'the whole city went wild because of *them*, and the women asked: "Can this be Naomi?"' From the text it is clear that the women recognise only Naomi (remembering her from years before); however, they did notice Ruth by her side as well. Naomi's bitter reply conveys her sense of loss: 'Do not call me Naomi, but call me Mara, because Shaddai caused great bitterness for me. I have gone away full but with empty hands I have returned' (1:20a). Whilst it is true that Naomi suffered great loss, she did not return empty. She returned with her loyal daughter-in-law by her side. Sadly, as noted by Sharp,[27] it appears that Ruth is invisible to Naomi, or, if not invisible, certainly not someone who brings comfort in her distress. Saxegaard argues that 'Naomi considers Ruth as unimportant when telling her story to the women of the city'.[28] Fewell and Gunn have an even stronger view, arguing that Naomi perhaps saw Ruth as an embarrassment and a

---

[24] Fewell & Gunn, '"A Son is Born"', 100.

[25] Fewell & Gunn, '"A Son is Born"', 104.

[26] In Saxegaard's view "Naomi refuses to talk to Ruth because of the latter's disobedience". Saxegaard, '"More than Seven Sons",' 261.

[27] Sharp further remarks that 'Ruth is entirely ignored as Naomi rejoins her community'. Carolyn Sharp, 'Feminist Queries for Ruth and Joshua: Complex Characterization, Gapping and the Possibility of Dissent,' *Scandinavian Journal of the Old Testament*, 28.2 (2014), 242.

[28] Saxegaard, '"More than Seven Sons",' 264.

liability, another woman to worry about besides herself, and this other woman being a Moabite of all people.[29]

Towards the end of the story Boaz calls the community as witnesses when he accepts the responsibility to act as Ruth's redeemer. In their response (a blessing) the elders name Rachel, Leah and Tamar, but when it comes to Ruth, they simply call her 'this woman' (4:11) and 'this young woman' (4:12). Why is it that Ruth's name is not included in the blessing? Tamar, who was from Canaan and thus also a foreigner, is included, but the name of the Moabite woman is omitted.

This exclusion of Ruth reaches a climax right at the end where the women of the town also do not speak her name. When speaking to Naomi they call Ruth 'your daughter-in-law, who loves you' (4:15). Even after Ruth is married to Boaz, even after she has given birth to a son, still she has not assimilated successfully into her host community. Whilst the people value her display of love towards her mother-in-law and the fact that she could give birth to a son, it is clear that, except perhaps for Boaz, they never see her as 'Ruth'. If she is not 'the Moabite', then she is 'the daughter-in-law'. Despite the fact that Ruth gave birth to a son, she is not acknowledged as his mother. The women sing praises as if Naomi is the boy's mother; Naomi takes the boy and places him on *her* lap. It is the women of the neighbourhood who gave the boy his name, saying: 'A son has been born to *Naomi*', after which the narrator comments: '*They* (the women, not Boaz or Ruth) named him Obed' (4:17). Ruth is as invisible here at the conclusion of the narrative as she was at the beginning upon her arrival in Bethlehem.[30]

It is clear that Ruth's desire to assimilate did not lie solely in her determination, but was very dependent on the host community's reaction towards her, a reaction that oftentimes spoke of exclusion rather than inclusion.

Putting a Price on an Immigrant's Value

This section explores the instances where Ruth is valued in terms of what she had (or did not have) to offer to her host or host community.

Naomi's Changed Attitude when Ruth Becomes a Gleaner

Shortly after their arrival in Bethlehem, Ruth[31] said to Naomi that she wanted to go to the field and gather grain behind someone who allows her to do so, and Naomi reacted positively: 'You may go, my daughter' (2:2). Here, we notice a shift in Naomi's treatment of Ruth.[32] She who ignored her daughter-in-law

[29] Fewell & Gunn, '"A Son is Born"', 100-101, 104.

[30] Ellen van Wolde, 'Texts in Dialogue with Texts: Intertextuality in the Ruth and Tamar Narratives,' *Biblical Interpretation*, 5.1 (1997), 27-28.

[31] The text reads 'Ruth the Moabite' (2:2). Yet again the narrator sees it fit to remind the readers that this woman was from Moab.

[32] Also see Trible, 'Two Women', 260.

suddenly takes notice of her. This only happens when it appears that Ruth may perhaps be of value if she can manage to find a field where she may gather grain.

The fact that Naomi, back in her homeland, values her Moabite daughter-in-law in terms of what she can bring to the table rather than who she is as a person, becomes even clearer when Ruth returns that evening with thirty pounds of barley as well as what she saved over from lunchtime (2:18-20). In 2:18 the text says nothing about Naomi noticing *Ruth* when she returns from the field. More important to her is the food that she brings with her. Naomi wants to know where Ruth gathered grain, where she worked, who took notice of her (2:19). When Ruth then recounts the day's events and tells Naomi that she worked in the field of Boaz, there is another shift in Naomi's attitude towards Ruth. Amongst other things, she says 'to her daughter-in-law: "This man is a close relative of *ours*, he is *our* redeemer"' (2:20). Here, Naomi starts to use inclusive language, including Ruth in the family in Bethlehem.[33] It seems that, from Naomi's perspective, Ruth earned her way into the family.[34]

When Ruth informs Naomi that Boaz invited her to glean in his field until the end of the barley season and to stay alongside his servants, Naomi replies: 'It is good, my daughter that you should go out with his female servants. (In this way) you will not be harmed (as could happen) in another field' (2:22). Why is it that Naomi expressed no concern when Ruth went out to glean in the morning, but now that Ruth has returned with a huge profit to show, Naomi suddenly cares for her safety? I propose two reasons: Ruth has shown herself to be beneficial to Naomi and Naomi is therefore concerned that she stays safe, and Naomi wants Ruth to remain in Boaz' field lest she goes to another field and perhaps meets another man there who does not have family ties with Naomi. Ruth's safety is not Naomi's primary concern. Naomi's own future is her main concern and she tries to secure this future as best as possible.[35]

Naomi Sends Ruth to the Threshing Floor

In Ruth 3, Naomi approaches Ruth with a plan. She wants to find Ruth 'a home and a husband', meaning her goal for Ruth is to get married, so that 'it will go well' with Ruth.[36] She unpacks her plan in detail: Ruth must bath, rub herself in oils and get dressed in preparation for a secret midnight meeting with Boaz at the threshing floor where he will sleep after a hard day's work of winnowing and an evening of eating and drinking with the men. After he has gone to sleep, Ruth must uncover his feet and lie down. Then she must wait for Boaz to tell her what to do (3:1-4).[37]

---

[33] Trible, 'Two Women', 263.

[34] It is noteworthy that, immediately after this utterance where Naomi includes Ruth in her family, the narrator reminds the readers again that Ruth is still a Moabite.

[35] See Fewell & Gunn, '"A Son is Born"', 105 for further support of this argument.

[36] Bush, *Ruth-Esther*, 147.

[37] The sexual overtones in this plan are clear.

But what is it exactly that Naomi is asking of Ruth, and does her plan really have Ruth's well-being at heart or perhaps rather her own?[38] It is important to notice that Naomi is asking Ruth to put herself in a very dangerous situation. Sharp argues that Naomi is expecting Ruth to act like a prostitute by paying a midnight visit to a man at the threshing floor.[39] Especially given the background of the stereotypical Israelite stories about Moabite women and the possibility that Ruth could run the risk of being accused of living up to the Moabite reputation, it makes one question Naomi's plan. Ruth is asked to put not only her reputation on the line, but also her life (in case some of the other men might see her). Whilst Naomi asks Ruth to do this in order to stand a chance to secure her own future, we know that Naomi's future is also in the balance here. For the sake of Naomi it is important that Ruth must marry Boaz, since Boaz was the man who had family connections with Elimelech. Whilst Ruth was asked to take this incredibly risky action, the mastermind behind the plan, Naomi, remained safe at home 'distancing herself from culpability (not to mention danger)'.[40]

The events that transpired upon Ruth's return to Naomi's house the next morning are a further indication that Naomi valued Ruth's worth to her more than Ruth's personal safety. When she returned home, Naomi inquired about her status rather than her safety: 'Who are you, my daughter?'[41] she asks Ruth (3:16), not 'How are you? Did you manage to stay safe?' Since Naomi is using the epithet 'my daughter', she is clearly not asking about Ruth's identity, but about her possible change of status: 'Are you [as good as] Boaz's wife?'[42] This question exposes Naomi's main concern – was Ruth successful in securing a marriage proposal and, in doing that, a secure future that included Naomi?[43]

Naomi was prepared to put her immigrant daughter-in-law's life at risk for her personal benefit.[44]

The Women of the Town View Ruth as 'Better to Naomi Than Seven Sons'

After Boaz took Ruth to be his wife, she conceived and gave birth to a son (4:13). The women celebrated with Naomi (4:14) and, according to Trible, their

---

[38] Fewell and Gunn, '"A Son is Born"', 106, argues that Naomi's plan has entrapment as the goal. 'Sexual intercourse, if not pregnancy, will enforce either marriage or a pay-off'. Ruth's subsequent request in 3:9 ('Spread your wing over your servant') can also be interpreted as a marriage proposal. Also see Linavelt, 'Narrative and Poetic Art', 122; Van Wolde, 'Texts in Dialogue', 21-22; and Trible, 'Two Women', 266.

[39] Sharp, 'Feminist Queries', 244.

[40] Fewell & Gunn, '"A Son is Born"', 104.

[41] Robert L. Hubbard, *The Book of Ruth* (New International Commentary of the Old Testament, Grand Rapids: Eerdmans, 1988), 223-224 & Bush, 'Ruth-Esther', 184-185, for a discussion on this literal translation of the text.

[42] Bush, *Ruth-Esther*, 184-185 and Fewell, 'Space for Moral Agency', 92.

[43] Saxegaard, '"More than Seven Sons",' 264 and Van Wolde, 'Texts in Dialogue', 26.

[44] Fewell and Gunn, '"A Son is Born"', 105.

celebration culminates in 'the exultation of Ruth'.[45] Trible refers here to the women's words in Ruth 4:14-15 where they say to Naomi:

> Blessed is the Lord, for He has not left you without a redeemer (a guardian) today!
>
> His (the boy's) name will be proclaimed in Israel! He will become a restorer of life for you and he will provide for you in your old age, for your daughter-in-law, who loves you, has given birth to him. She is better to you than seven sons! (Ruth 4:14-15)

I disagree with Trible's interpretation for three reasons. Firstly, the women exclude Ruth from their celebration by not addressing her directly, but only speaking about her. Secondly, they do not bother to call her by her name but merely refer to her in terms of her relationship with Naomi as 'your daughter-in-law'. And lastly, their high regard for her lies in the value that she has contributed to Naomi's life by giving birth to a boy and thus securing Naomi's future. The focus is never on Ruth, but on Naomi. According to Fewell and Gunn the women regard Ruth merely as a surrogate for Naomi.[46] All they care about is that Ruth, having given birth to a baby boy for Naomi, added value and future security to Naomi's life. Sharp speaks of the 'erasure of Ruth at the end of the story, when the kinship structure between Ruth and her son Obed is reconfigured as Naomi appropriates the infant.'[47]

> Naomi took the boy and placed him on her lap; she became his nurse (caregiver). The women of the neighbourhood named him, saying: 'A son has been born to Naomi.' They named him Obed. He was the father of Jesse (who was) the father of David. (Ruth 4: 16-17)

The immigrant Ruth has served her purpose in the host community by securing Naomi's future and after having done so she disappears tragically into the background.

Immigrants in South Africa

The stereotyping, exclusion and evaluation of immigrants in terms of their worth is still happening today. Literature about the mistreatment of immigrants (especially women) in my country, South Africa, attests to these three challenges that immigrants still face.[48] There are also stories of hope where communities are

---

[45] Trible, 'Two Women', 277.
[46] Fewell & Gunn, '"A Son is Born"', 107.
[47] Sharp, 'Feminist Queries', 242.
[48] On stereotyping: Heleta, 'High Fences'. On exclusion: Alex Farley, 'South African Migration Policy: A Gendered Analysis', *Policy Insights*, 70 (2019), 6; Alex Farley, 'Refugee Legislation in South Africa: A Feminist Foreign Policy Analysis – Part 1', *Centre for Feminist Policy* (15 June 2019) and 'The Exclusion of Migrant Women in

getting involved in creating spaces and opportunities for welcoming immigrants into the community and where they are taught skills to help them settle permanently.[49] Klaasen[50] and Settler & Mpofu[51] are amongst South African scholars who advocate for spaces of hospitality that focus on the recognition of the 'Other' in a way that will not alienate immigrants but recognise and include them.

Conclusion

This chapter investigated the well-known story in the RB, highlighting the immigrant woman Ruth and her struggle to be accepted in her host community whilst never managing to be fully accepted. As this chapter presented a critical reading of the RB which is generally read in a positive light, diaconal workers are challenged to not only engage in projects that are aimed at creating hospitable and inclusive spaces for immigrants to have a new start on life, but also to stand back and continually re-evaluate the work that they are doing.

Bibliography

Bush, Frederic W. Ruth-Esther. Word Biblical Commentary, Vol 9. Dallas: Word, 1996.

Chalumbira, Nomvelo. 'WATCH: NGO Empowers Refugee and Migrant Women with Hairdressing and Beauty Courses', News24 (13 Feb 2021), <https://www.news24.com/news24/Video/SouthAfrica/News/watch-ngo-empowers-refugee-and-migrant-women-with-hairdressing-and-beauty-courses-20210213> (accessed 14.8.21).

Africa/Access to the Labour Market', *Scalabrini Institute for Human Mobility in Africa* (2021).
On exploiting immigrants, specifically women, by underpaid labour: 'Migration Dynamics of Women, Children and the Elderly in South Africa', *Statistics South Africa*, Report 03.51.04 (Pretoria: Statistics South Africa, 2020), vi.

[49] For examples see: Nomvelo Chalumbira, 'WATCH: NGO Empowers Refugee and Migrant Women with Hairdressing and Beauty Courses', News24 (13 Feb 2021); Kate Pond, 'Refugees in South Africa Share Acts of Kindness with their Hosts', *The UN Refugee Agency* (13 October 2020) and Farley, 'South African Migration Policy', 8-10.

[50] John Klaasen, 'Identity and Immigration in Post-apartheid South Africa: The Retelling of the Christian Open-Ended Narrative as Service to the Church and the World', *Diaconia*, 8 (2017), 152-165. See also Klaasen, John. 'Personhood and Inclusive Communities: Access to Justice for All', in Hans Morten Haugen, Benedicte Tveter Kivle, Tony Addy, Terese Bue Kessel and John Klaasen (eds.), *Developing Just and Inclusive Communities. Challenges for Diakonia as Christian Social Practice and Social Work* (Oxford: Regnum, 2022), 33-48.

[51] Federico Settler & Buhle Mpofu, 'Social Responsibility with Respect to Religion and Migration in South Africa', *Journal for the Study of Religion*, 30:2 (2017), 12-31.

Davis, Ellen; Adeleya, Femi *et al*. 'Study Guide: Ruth'. Contextual Bible Studies on Various Themes (2016), Ujamaa Centre, University of KwaZulu-Natal, <http://ujamaa.ukzn.ac.za/Libraries/manuals/2-Ruth.sflb.ashx> (accessed 24.4.21).

De Villiers, Gerda. 'The "Foreigner in Our Midst" and the Hebrew Bible.' HTS Theological Studies 75:3 (2014), 1–7.

De Villiers, Gerda and Jurie le Roux. 'The Book of Ruth in the Time of Judges and Ruth, the Moabitess.' Verbum et Ecclesia 37:1 (2016), 1–6.

De Villiers, Gerda. 'Interpreting Texts and the Matter of Context: Examples from the Book of Ruth.' Verbum et Ecclesia 40:1 (2019), 1-7.

Farley, Alex. 'South African Migration Policy: A Gendered Analysis', Policy Insights 70 (South African Institute of International Affairs) (2019), 1-19.

Farley, Alex. 'Refugee Legislation in South Africa: A Feminist Foreign Policy Analysis – Part 1', Centre for Feminist Policy (15 June 2019), <https://centreforfeministforeignpolicy.org/journal/2019/6/3/refugee-legislation-in-south-africa-a-feminist-foreign-policy-analysis-part-1> (accessed 14.8.21).

Fewell, Danna Nolan, and David Miller Gunn. '"A Son Is Born to Naomi!": Literary Allusions and Interpretation in the Book of Ruth.' *Journal for the Study of the Old Testament*, 40 (1988), 99–108.

Fewell, Danna Nolan. 'Space for Moral Agency in the Book of Ruth.' *Journal for the Study of the Old Testament*, 40:1 (2015), 79-96.

Gunn, David Miller and Fewell, Danna Nolan. Narrative in the Hebrew Bible. Oxford: Oxford University Press, 1993.

Heleta, Savo. 'High Fences and Unworthy Foreigners: Anti-poor Immigration Plans and Rhetoric in South Africa', The Mail and Guardian, 22 March 2018, <https://mg.co.za/article/2018-03-22-high-fences-and-unworthy-foreigners-anti-poor-immigration-plans-and-rhetoric-in-sa/> (accessed 1.8.21).

Hubbard, Robert L. The Book of Ruth. New International Commentary on the Old Testament. Grand Rapids: Eerdmans, 1988.

Klaasen, John 'Identity and Immigration in Post-apartheid South Africa: The Retelling of the Christian Open-Ended Narrative as Service to the Church and the World.' *Diaconia*, 8 (2017), 152-165.

Klaasen, John. 'Personhood and Inclusive Communities: Access to Justice for All', in: *Developing Just and Inclusive Communities. Challenges for Diakonia as Christian Social Practice and Social Work,* Hans Morten Haugen, Benedicte Kivle Tveter, Tony Addy, Terese Bue Kessel and John Klaasen. (eds.) (Oxford: Regnum, 2022), 33-48.

Linavelt, Tod. 'Narrative and Poetic Art in the Book of Ruth.' *Interpretation* (2010), 117-129.

'Migration Dynamics of Women, Children and the Elderly in South Africa', Statistics South Africa Report 03.51.04 (Pretoria: Statistics South Africa, 2020).

Pond, Kate. 'Refugees in South Africa Share Acts of Kindness with Their Hosts', The UN Refugee Agency (13 October 2020).

<https://www.unhcr.org/afr/news/stories/2020/10/5f7ec0574/refugees-south-africa-share-acts-kindness-hosts.html> (accessed 14.8.21).

Saxegaard, Kristin Moen. '"More than Seven Sons": Ruth as Example of the Good Son.' *Scandinavian Journal of the Old Testament*, 15:2 (2001), 257-275.

Schifferdecker, Kathryn M. 'Commentary on Ruth 1:1-4:22.' Working Preacher (2014), <https://www.workingpreacher.org/commentaries/narrative-lectionary/preaching-series-on-ruth/commentary-on-ruth-11-22-21-23-31-18-41-22> (accessed 24.8.21).

Schlemmer, Lawrence. 'Immigrants in South Africa: Perceptions and Reality in Witbank, a Medium-sized Industrial Town' (abridged version), *The Centre for Development and Enterprise*, 9 May 2006: 1-12.

Settler, Federico & Mpofu, Buhle. 'Social Responsibility with Respect to Religion and Migration in South Africa.' *Journal for the Study of Religion*, 30:2 (2017), 12-31.

Sharp, Carolyn J. 'Feminist Queries for Ruth and Joshua: Complex Characterization, Gapping and the Possibility of Dissent.' *Scandinavian Journal of the Old Testament*, 28:2 (2014), 229-252.

Siquans, Agnethe. 'Foreignness and Poverty in the Book of Ruth: A Legal Way for a Poor Foreign Woman to Be Integrated into Israel.' *Journal of Biblical Literature*, 128:3 (2009), 443-452.

Southwood, Katherine. 'Will Naomi's Nation Be Ruth's Nation?: Ethnic Translation as a Metaphor for Ruth's Assimilation within Judah.' *Humanities*, 3:2 (2014), 102-131.

'The Exclusion of Migrant Women in Africa / Access to the Labour Market', Scalabrini Institute for Human Mobility in Africa (2021), <https://sihma.org.za/Blog-on-the-move/the-exclusion-of-migrant-women-in-africa-access-to-the-labour-market> (accessed 14.8.21)

Trible, Phyllis. 'Two Women in a Man's World: A Reading of the Book of Ruth.' *Soundings: An Interdisciplinary Journal*, 59:3 (1976), 251-279.

Van Wolde, Ellen. 'Texts in Dialogue with Texts: Intertextuality in the Ruth and Tamar Narratives.' *Biblical Interpretation*, 5:1 (1997), 1-28.

Gender Responsive Organisations and the 2030 Agenda

Marit Breen

Introduction

The UN states that gender equality is the accelerator for achieving the sustainable development goals (SDG), and that ensuring equal participation of women and men in decision-making processes is crucial.[1] SDG goal 5 calls for achieving gender equality, but this remains only a fantasy unless women's representation in decision-making is addressed. SDG Target16.7 empasises responsive, inclusive, participatory and representative decision-making at all levels.[2] Only then can institutions and societies deliver justice and protect individuals against human rights violations. Therefore, it is crucial to have knowledge about how institutions – actors in civil society – can contribute to building inclusive societies by being gender responsive. To be gender responsive means to create an environment that reflects an understanding of the realities of men and women's lives and respond to their strengths and challenges, including the issues of women.[3] Amongst others, where women are underrepresented, this will include advancing women's participation and their effective representation in decision-making bodies. This means enabling women to have the power to use their voices to influence the outcomes of organisational decisions, so that outcomes benefit both genders.[4]

How can institutions and organisations – actors of civil society – be gender responsive and create an environment that enables a contribution for building inclusive societies by strengthening women's agency? Key to being gender

---

[1] UNDP, UN Women, 'Gender Equality as an Accelerator for Achieving the Sustainable Development Goals', Discussion paper (New York: United Nations Development Programme 2018), 9.

[2] United Nations Goal 16, Promote just, peaceful and inclusive communtiies (no date), section 'Goal 16 targets' https://www.un.org/sustainabledevelopment/peace-justice/, 'Peace, Justice and Strong Institutions: Why they matter' (United Nations, 2020).

[3] Barbara E., Bloom & Stephanie S., Covington, 'Gendered Justice: Programming for Women in Correctional Settings', Paper presented to the American Society of Criminology. (San Francisco, CA 2000), p.11.

[4] Susan Franceschet and Jennifer M. Piscopo, 'Gender Quotas and Women's Substantive Representation: Lessons from Argentina', *Politics and Gender*, 4:3 (2008), 393-425.

responsive is to be aware of how gender and gender relations play a role in the works of the organisation and influence outcomes. This chapter will give insights to how efforts that are aimed at gender responsive organisational change are influenced by the gendered organisational context, which affects gendered power relations and the nature of women's empowerment. The context represents both supporting factors and obstacles to advancing women's positions and representation. By presenting qualitative data from interviews and focus group discussions that were conducted with women and men in the Free Pentecost Fellowship in Kenya (FPFK) and the FPFK Tuinuane Women's project in 2016, and by applying theories of empowerment, gender and development – and organisational change – the following research question is investigated in this chapter: *How does the gendered context influence gender-sensitive organisational change and women's empowerment?*

By responding to the research question, we will provide a deeper understanding of why it is important to have knowledge about the relationship between the gendered context and women's empowerment when seeking to advance women's representation as part of the agenda to build inclusive communities. This is important knowledge for the church and faith-based organisations that have influential positions in society. With a call to be a witness through diaconal action, the church as an institution and its members included, must critically reflect upon whether its own affairs and its members' actions advocate Gods love and justice to both men and women.[5]

The methodology from the field study is presented below, followed by a presentation of FPFK and the Tuinuane project. Theories are then presented along with the data before the analysis and discussion that will result in the response to the research question. How women can exercise agency within a patriarchal structure where they might appear to not have any is particularly highlighted by presenting the concept of 'silent power'. The analysis will result in the suggestion of a viable avenue for gender responsive organisational change with a potential for churches and faith-based organisations to be better equipped to influence the wider community and thus contribute to building inclusive societies.

Methodology

For three weeks, 14 semi-structured in-depth interviews were conducted with 16 respondents from FPFK. Excluding one woman, all respondents were FPFK members and 11 Tuinuane members (8 females, 3 males), all of whom were members of one local congregation where the fieldwork was conducted. Nine of

[5] Rudolf von Sinner, 'The Diaconal Church in the Public Sphere', in Dietrich S., Jørgensen K., Koslien K.K., Nordstokke K. (eds), *The Diaconal Church* (Regnum Books International 2018), 171; Penelope J. Plowman, 'Organisational change from two perspectives', *Development in Practice*, 10:2 (2000), 190.

these held leadership positions. The interviews focused on the respondents' narratives about their experiences. Reflections around their roles and power in relation to the processes of organisational change were revealed. A focus was particularly on the nature of the participants' agency and gendered relations. Two focus group discussions were also conducted: one men's group and one women's group.

Broader themes were identified by applying a thematic content analysis of the data after transcribing each interview and group discussion.[6] Alongside reviewing relevant organisational documents, literature and concepts, coding of transcripts enabled the finding of key themes that provided an overview used to guide the analysis.

FPFK and the Tuinuane Women's Project

At the time of the study, the female population in FPFK comprised 80%. According to the FPFK gender analysis from 2012, no women were represented in the National Board, and female pastors numbered 11 out of 357.[7] According to two of my respondents, the local church boards represented the highest number of women, although no data was available to verify this.[8] Furthermore, in 2013, no women were represented in the regional councils of the church, but in 2015, 16 out of the 27 councils had women represented and 26 out of the 270 council members were women.[9] This situation was a starting point for the organisational change process that FPFK embarked upon, whilst one of the aims of the conducted study was to make their structure more inclusive for women.

Tuinuane is one of FPFK's development projects, initiated in 2005 and funded by Norad. Its aim is to enhance 'Kenyan poor women's ability to secure a better livelihood for themselves and their families by offering them access to savings and loans through credit associations'.[10] Beyond improving socio-economic aspects of the Tuinuane members' lives, improvements in gender relations at a family level and women's leadership capacity are also outcomes of the project.[11] The Kenyan Institute of Economic Affairs states that a main factor in women's lack of access to resources is the patriarchal organisation of society where men control most resources.[12] Increasing women's access to resources became a focus of Tuinuane.

---

[6] Alan Bryman, 'Social Research Methods'. (Oxford: Oxford University Press, 2012).
[7] FPFK Gender Analysis of Free Pentecostal Fellowship in Kenya (2012).
[8] From interviews with the FPFK General Secretary and a male pastor.
[9] From interviews with the FPFK General Secretary and a male pastor.
[10] Doreen Kwarimpa-Atim, Tuinuane Women's Project End of Project Evaluation Final Report, 2015 (FPFK, PYM, 2015), 2.
[11] Kwarimpa-Atim, Tuinuane Evaluation Final Report.
[12] Institute of Economic Affairs Kenya (IEA) (2008). Profile of Women's Socio-Economic Status in Kenya.

The Tuinuane groups consist of women, both from the FPFK congregations and outside. They meet for monthly fellowship and prayer and bring their savings. Each woman has her savings book for personal saving and she also contributes a share to the group joint account, which generates loans. In this way, the groups are self-sustained, only receiving technical support from the project staff.[13] In 2017, the project had reached 27 FPFK regions, having 1,215 active groups with a total membership of 40,249: 97% female and 3% male.[14]

Since Tuinuane is implemented through the local churches, part of the grassroots of FPFK is represented through its members in Tuinuane. As such, Tuinuane is seen as a place where norms and values are challenged, and constituencies that 'demand change' within the church can be created – resulting in change instigated from the bottom up.[15] The project therefore served as a case study to investigate what drives organisational change in terms of advancing women's representation in decision-making bodies.

GAD and the Gendered Organisation

The Gender and Development (GAD) discourse, which frames this study, provides us with the necessary gender lens to approach organisational change, which is crucial to achieve gender equality and, particularly, to enable institutions to be inclusive, deliver justice and ensure rights. Presenting GAD in relation to this study also includes my understanding of gender and organisational change from a gender perspective.

GAD explains women's subordinate status by the unequal power relationship between the sexes.[16] Unless a redistribution of power in social relations takes place, women are less likely to enjoy increased access to various resources and rights, including decision-making.[17] In order to understand women's representation and position, gender relations and the power dynamics of these must be investigated.[18] Goetz's conceptualisation of the gendered nature of organisations in development provides an approach to investigate from a feminist perspective. Feminists in the GAD field have asserted that there is little

[13] Everlyne Nairesiae, Final Evaluation report of Tuinuane project (2017) 7.

[14] Nairesiae, Final Evaluation report, 7.

[15] Maitrayee Mukhopadhyay, 'Mainstreaming Gender or "Streaming" Gender Away: Feminists Marooned in the Development Business'(IDS Bulletin, 35(4), 2004), 95–103.

[16] Sally, Baden and Anne Marie, Goetz, 'Who Needs [Sex] When You Can Have [Gender]?: Conflicting Discourses on Gender at Beijing', *Feminist Review*, 56:1 (1997), 3–25; Shahrashoub Razavi, and Carol Miller, 'From WID to GAD: Conceptual Shifts in the Women and Development Discourse' (Geneva: United Nations Research Institute for Social Development, 1995).

[17] Naila Kabeer, *Reversed Realities: Gender Hierarchies in Development Thought* (London and New York: Verso, 1994).

[18] Anne Marie, Goetz, *Getting Institutions Right for Women in Development* (New York: Zed Books, 1997).

theoretical and empirical work available to illuminate gendered features of organisations and their links to unsatisfactory outcomes.[19] This served as a rationale for the study, and its findings contribute a better understanding of how organisations and societies can deliver satisfactory outcomes so that they can deliver justice and ensure rights for men and women alike. The GAD approach is helpful when addressing structural issues that are obstacles to achieving gender equality.[20]

The notion of the 'gendered organisation' has its roots in feminist critiques of organisational theory.[21] According to Acker's theory of the gendered organisation,[22] previous attempts to theorise gender and organisations failed to address gender in relation to organisational structure because organisations were assumed to be gender neutral. Only when we acknowledge that organisations are not gender neutral can analyses truly deal with gender and problems of gender segregation and discrimination, as noted by Acker.[23]

In the following, I present the gendered context by which FPFK and the Tuinuane project operate and are influenced. Does the context represent both supporting factors and obstacles to advancing women's positions? The study identified three themes that influence FPFK in terms of their work to advance women's position and representation: 1) African culture and tradition; 2) development; and 3) religious ideology.

African Culture and Tradition

When reflecting upon gender norms many respondents referred to this theme by saying 'African' with a sense of generalisation. The Kenyan society was described as patriarchal in nature, where men are the household heads providing for the family and women are homemakers taking care of the household and children. This divide has implications for women's ability to participate in matters outside the home and their access to control resources.[24]

The FPFK and Tuinuane members will naturally reflect the context in which they live and be influenced by this in various ways. Bue Kessel's research on Femmes pour Christ, the women's association in the Lutheran Church in Cameroon, confirms the significance of how contextual patterns are embedded in the association to such extent that women are not empowered to question

[19] Goetz, *Getting Institutions Right*.
[20] Sandra, Fredman, Beth Goldberg, Discussion Paper, Gender Equality and Human Rights No 4 (UN Women, 2015).
[21] Marta B. Calas and Linda Smircich, 'From The Woman's Point of View: Feminist Approaches to Organisation Studies', in: Stewart R. Clegg et al. *Handbook of Organization Studies (*London: Sage, 1996).
[22] Joan Acker, 'Hierarchies, Jobs, Bodies: A Theory of Gendered Organizations', *Gender and Society* 4|:2 (1990), 139–158.
[23] Acker, Hierarchies, Jobs, Bodies.
[24] IEA, Profile of Women's Socio-Economic Status.

gender oppression at the home.[25] She finds that women may maintain a self-perception provided by the context, which is to be subordinate to men, and also that weak family economy is a factor that contributes to excluding women from full participation in society. The latter relates to the situation that informed the initiation of the Tuinuane project in 2005. The following is a series of quotes from some of my male and female respondents, that reflect such influence of the patriarchal 'African culture and tradition':

> 'Women must serve their husbands'; 'women in Africa marry very young'; 'Kikuyu men don't go to the kitchen'; 'They don't care, African men… you came there to get children, and to work – to produce…'; 'men are breadwinners'; 'women are slaves… men believe they are the king'; 'if we are in Africa… I mean letting the power from the man is a process'.

The following quote reflects some of the implications the above-mentioned views and practices may have on the matter of women's position and representation in FPFK:

> The process in the grass root in electing and appointing the pastor is still [blocking women to reach to the top leadership] because I must come from a church, and if I come from a church from a man who is pastor who is not a feminist he will not allow me whatsoever to participate, and you will never have a change (Female respondent).

The quote relates to the structural practice within FPFK, which says that the congregations shall appoint the members of the church's national board. One of the criteria for being a member is several years of leadership experience, which is likely only to apply to men. However, in an attempt to bring change, FPFK has decided to apply the two-third gender principle, which is also justified in the Kenyan Constitution. This principle aims at allowing women to take up at least one-third of all appointive or elective leadership opportunities,[26] and is crucial to the changes that are taking place within FPFK. However, introducing gender quotas are not enough. Since the members of FPFK are those who elect and appoint people for representation, there must also be a growing will to appoint and elect women. The views presented above prevent both women and men from voting for women leaders in the church. The work of Tuinuane is observed as important in challenging such views and attitudes.

[25] Terese B. Kessel, *Between God's Sharing Power and Men's Controlling Power: A Quest for Diaconal Empowerment and Transformation in Femmes pour Christ in Cameroon* (Stavanger: Misjonshøgskolens Forlag, 2014).
[26] Federation of Women Lawyers (FIDA): Factsheet on Gender Rule.

The Development Discourse

Has the development discourse influenced FPFK's agenda on gender?

According to one of the FPFK development workers, development projects in FPFK play a role in terms of women's empowerment within FPFK.[27] The General Secretary (GS) confirmed the projects' influence, for example, in relation to the process of developing the gender policy in FPFK. The policy development enabled them to identify gaps which resulted in initiatives aiming to advance women's participation. One such initiative was 'campaigns to change the mindsets of people', and the changing of the name 'church elder' to 'local church board'.

> We realised that "an elder" in an African perspective is an old man with grey hair, and so we said now, that shall be called church board so that it can be inclusive also of the other gender, so that it is not just masculine when you say elder (GS).

The campaigns consisted of dialogues and advocacy work with regional councils, local church leaders and pastors, and motivating women to embrace leadership positions and run for election.[28] One of the themes drawn upon is that of religious ideology.

Religious Ideology

This theme appeared to hold elements that are both constraining and enabling in terms of women's position and representation. The following quotes from FPFK members reflect this tension. The quotes reveal underlying attitudes and gender norms that may affect the organisation and its members in different ways, depending on the level of influence of the people who hold the views, and as such they demonstrate the role and power of the gendered context.

> Because we are in God's business, we count each other as equal, mainly (male respondent).
>
> Outside there, where men just see women as they have no value, in the church they are recognised as men of God. Despite being a lady, they are respected as men of God. And so we equally do things, we equally bring up matters and they are heard as equal (female respondent).
>
> In general, the body of Christ, the entire Body of Christ, to be accepted and for men to gather something good coming out of that woman that is not easy (female respondent).

---

[27] The final evaluation from 2017 also confirms that Tuinuane has economically transformed the lives of rural and urban low-income women and their families.

[28] The FPFK project evaluation of Tuinuane from 2015 confirms that trainings from these campaigns influenced positive gender relations.

Advancing Interests in Civil Society

According to Goetz and Hassim, the nature of civil society is one of the factors that the success of gender equity interests in policy making depends on.[29] *Gender equity interests* refer to 'those oriented to transforming gender relations in the direction of justice and equity between the sexes'.[30] Civil society defined as 'all manner of self-chosen group-based activities that grow out of interest divisions in society, and which are not formally part of the state',[31] would include FPFK and the Tuinuane project. Civil society is described as 'the key proving ground for establishing the legitimacy of gender equity policy goals, and for building a feminist constituency'.[32] It can therefore be argued that Tuinuane could act as a place that creates constituencies for a women's agenda in the FPFK and thus a place where awareness of gender justice is developed and, potentially, also where injustice is challenged. The outcome of this is mutually influenced by the gendered context presented above and the constituencies' level of empowerment.

Empowerment

According to Kabeer, empowerment is 'the process by which those who have been denied the ability to make strategic life choices acquire such ability'.[33] 'The ability to make choices' incorporates three dimensions of choice: *resources, agency* and *achievements*.[34] The choices of importance are strategic life choices, which relate to identity and status.

Agency is 'the ability to define one's goals and act upon them',[35] which encompasses the meaning, motivation and purpose that individuals bring to their activity, their sense of agency, or the 'power within'.[36] *Resources* are understood as both material and non-material, including human and social resources such as position, authority and status.[37] *Achievements* are the outcomes of the use of resources and agency.[38] The reason why women often cannot translate their resources and agency into achievements relates to gender ideologies and culture.[39]

---

[29] Anne Marie Goetz and Shireen Hassim (ed), *No Shortcuts to Power: African Women in Politics and Policy Making* (London: Zed Books, 2003), 37.
[30] Goetz and Hassim, *No Shortcuts*, 27.
[31] Goetz and Hassim, *No Shortcuts*, 42.
[32] Goetz and Hassim, *No Shortcuts*, 42.
[33] Naile Kabeer, 'Resources, Agency, Achievements: Reflections on the Measurement of Women's Empowerment', *Development and Change*, 30:3 (1999), 435-464, 435.
[34] Kabeer, Resources, Agency, Achievements, 436.
[35] Kabeer, Resources, Agency, Achievements, 438.
[36] Kabeer, Resources, Agency, Achievements, 438.
[37] Kabeer, Resources, Agency, Achievements, 438.
[38] Kabeer, Resources, Agency, Achievements. 438.
[39] Kabeer, Resources, Agency, Achievements, 438.

All respondents who are Tuinuane members equally emphasised the importance of economic empowerment which, according to Goetz and Hassim, is one of the factors that affects women's positions in social relations and thus their capacity to advance their interests in civil society.[40] The ability to translate increased resources into achievements, however, depends on the nature of agency and power, and the extent to which these can be exercised to overcome the constraints caused by gendered power relations. To reveal such agency in relation to Tuinuane and increased access to resources, the nature of power within the three levels where it operates, as proposed by Rowlands, was investigated.[41] Empowerment at a personal level is a condition to empowerment at the relational and collective level. Here, the latter two are presented through the description of 'silent power'.

Empowerment at a Personal Level

The ability to dress well and gain weight are powerful signs of wealth in Kenya, and something most of the women refer to as an achievement. It provides a boost in self-esteem, which increasingly enables socialisation with others; exposure to new ideas and the opportunity to develop and act on ideas; gaining respect; going to places that they previously found intimidating (especially the bank); and contributing and participating in activities they previously would not have encountered. These data point to the power money has to increase a woman's position in the home, in society and in the church – with great implications on her life – mainly starting with gaining respect and recognition.[42]

Some of the women leaders expressed self-confidence, proudly sharing how their skills and qualities are used in church. One woman described Tuinuane as a school of leadership where they practise how to stand before a big crowd; learn how to speak up; and administer and manage books for loans and savings.[43]

'Silent Power'

Some respondents referred to a form of 'silent power', which they would use deliberately in certain situations. It is a form of power which does not include violence or an overt conflict that could prevent them from getting what they want. One woman shared how she identifies herself in relation to her husband as 'the neck who is controlling the head'. She explained how women must make sure the men believe they are 'the man of the house' but, at the same time, the women have strategies to control 'the head'. This entails showing love and

---

[40] Goetz and Hassim, *No Shortcuts*, 35.

[41] Jo Rowlands, 'A Word of the Times, but What Does it Mean? Empowerment in the Discourse and Practice of Development', *Women and Empowerment* (1998), 11–34.

[42] Nairesiae, Final Evaluation report of Tuinuane, 17-18.

[43] The FPFK, End of project evaluation from 2015 also concluded similar findings: FPFK, End of Project Evaluation, 25.

serving food that he likes until she gets an opportunity to speak her mind: 'It prevents him from getting annoyed and beating you'.

Through certain strategies, the women manage to use their power to influence and achieve goals despite the constraining gender relations they may be in. From the outside, these women may appear disempowered by 'submitting' to their husbands but, as the data reveal, there is a significant level of power and agency with a potential to transform social circumstances.[44] The question is whether a similar nature of agency can be used to influence decision-making within the congregation and, potentially, at higher levels in FPFK as an organisation?

As a collective, Tuinuane women seem to undertake similar strategies of 'silent power' in the church. One example is through the contribution of money to buy things they want:

> If you go there and tell them, we want women to put water and electricity, they will refuse, because you are overtaking them, we are the one to overtake, so… we request; please, we'd like to… We have a little money and we want to… but then we brought the money we brought 125,000 (KSH)! (The men) are amazed. But we were requesting… (Female respondent).

The women had further plans to invest in the church, but these were on hold currently because the men disagreed and told them to use the money for something that the men had planned instead. The women's response to this was:

> We are refusing, silently… we don't talk those things again… and we stay with our money, and then… we tell them, when you finish your things, then you tell us. Silently, without violently, without making a lot of noise, that's how it is….

These strategies show that when women act as a collective, they can achieve goals within given structures and potentially influence outcomes. Another female leader described women as 'the changers' – 'the drivers': they can 'push things to happen in the church, push issues and move fast, then men support them'. This resembles findings from Stewart-Thomas's study on how women's agency in religious organisations can be exercised collectively in ways that can bring about structural change despite the 'stained glass ceiling'.[45] By taking risks through manoeuvres within given structures, and by supporting other women in religious leadership, they are able to bring across their agenda.[46]

---

[44] Derek Layder, *Understanding Social Theory*. (London: Sage Publications, 2006), 177.

[45] Michelle, Stewart-Thomas, Gendered Congregations, Gendered Service: The Impact of Clergy Gender on Congregational Social Service Participation, *Gender, Work and Organization*, 17:4 (2010), 406-432.

[46] Jimi, Adams. Stained Glass Makes the Ceiling Visible: Organizational Opposition to Women in Congregational Leadership, *Gender and Society*, 21:19 (2007), 80-105.

Conclusion: Organisational Change Pushed from Below

This chapter set out to provide deeper knowledge of elements crucial to developing a gender responsive organisation relevant to the church and faith-based organisations so that they can be better equipped to influence and contribute to building inclusive communities by advancing women's participation. Through presenting data from the case study and from applying relevant theories to analyse these data, the chapter has achieved its objective by showing that efforts aimed at gender responsive organisational change are influenced by the gendered context, which affects gendered power relations and the nature of women's agency.

The data show that agency and gender relations mutually influence one another through social practice – reproducing aspects of a gender regime that excludes women and, at the same time, produces gender norms that support women's position and potential effective representation. Women are empowered through the activities of Tuinuane, and their ability to exercise their agency depends on whether there is a conducive environment to push for change or not. In Tuinuane, we have seen that small changes take place when women are empowered to exercise agency, especially through applying their 'silent power' either individually or collectively. More women exercise leadership skills within the groups and thus gain more confidence potentially to apply these also beyond the groups – either in church or the community. Women's self-perception and confidence are changed when resources increase, and they are increasingly being recognised for their ability to participate and contribute. At the same time, they are limited by views and attitudes embedded in the patriarchal African context and the religious discourse that represent obstacles to advancing women's position.

A conducive environment for a women's agenda is created by structural changes that are put in place from 'above'; for example, through introducing gender quota to advance women's representation in decision-making bodies. Another example is to change the practice such that only members who have several years of leadership experience are eligible to be elected for the church board. However, the advocacy for such changes can only come from the constituencies, who we have seen are influenced by the gendered context. They can either support the changes or perpetuate the status quo, depending on their ability to exercise power.

Of importance to this study is the women's ability to influence decisions and the ongoing change processes in the organisation. Shifting gendered power relations is crucial to such a process, results of which are evidenced in Tuinuane, and from evaluations; women do influence through their interactions with men in the home, in the church and on the church board where decisions are made.[47] These shifts seem to derive from a place whereby women's leadership is recognised through practice, coming from a place of personal transformation and

[47] Nairesiae, Final Evaluation report, 33.

consciousness-raising, which results from participating in the groups. On this basis, such a personal process, deriving from the nature of women's empowerment and agency, and generated from Tuinuane, holds a potential for the creation of constituencies for gender equality and thus organisational change. Through exercising agency and mobilising collective action to achieve common goals, women's agenda is pushed from the bottom up.[48]

A bottom-up approach to change implies local participation, empowerment, agency, advocacy, capacity building and awareness raising,[49] elements that are all observed in Tuinuane. Top-down initiatives such as affirmative action, if implemented, will then speed up a process already established through empowerment and changed gendered relations generated at the grassroots level. This means that the organisation is facilitating places and platforms where the roles of women can be put to meaningful use. Only then can women translate their resources and agency into achievements – in this case as leaders. My data does not evidence enough of the outcomes from the shifting gendered power relations that are observed but, supported by theory, the analysis indicates that the potential to push for a women's agenda from the bottom up continues due to the empowerment in Tuinuane and the changing environment for the exercise of their agency. Knowledge about how the gendered context represents both support and obstacles to such intended change is crucial and must guide the process. A woman's project aiming to empower women economically, resulting in agency that is exercised both individually and in collective action formed around common goals of advancing women's position and representation, can contribute significantly towards the building of a gender responsive organisation and more inclusive communities. Faith-based organisations often have a unique infrastructure where such platforms for women at the grassroots level can be facilitated and created easily. Furthermore, it is likely that within their fellowships, there are individuals – men and women – who are supportive of change. Allying with these and gathering a joint force will further broaden and strengthen constituencies who can exercise collective agency that will push for change in other areas related to women's positions in society. Advancing women's representation is only the beginning.

---

[48] Franceschet and Piscopo, 'Gender Quotas and Women's Substantive Representation, 402.

[49] Baden and Goetz, Who Needs [Sex] When You Can Have [Gender]?; Frank Ellis and Stephen Biggs, 'Evolving Themes in Rural Development' 1950s-2000s, *Development Policy Review*, 19:4 (2001), 437–448; Robert Chambers, *Whose Reality Counts?: Putting the First Last* (London: Intermediate Technology, 1997).

Bibliography

Acker, J., 'Hierarchies, Jobs, Bodies: A Theory of Gendered Organizations'. *Gender and Society*, 4(2) (1990).

Adams, J. (2007). Stained Glass Makes the Ceiling Visible: Organizational Opposition to Women in Congregational Leadership. *Gender and Society*, 21(1) (2007).

Baden, S, Goetz, A.M., 'Who Needs [Sex] When You Can Have [Gender]? Conflicting Discourses on Gender at Beijing'. *Feminist Review*, 56(1) (1997).

Bloom, B. and Covington, S. Gendered justice: Programming for Women in Correctional Settings; Paper presented to the American Society of Criminology, San Francisco, CA 2000.

Bryman, A. *Social Research Methods*, Oxford: Oxford University Press, 2012.

Calas, M.B., Smircich, L., 'From the Woman's Point of View: Feminist Approaches to Organisation Studies', in: Stewart R. Clegg et al. *Handbook of Organization Studie*. (London: Sage, 1996).

Chambers, R. *Whose Reality Counts?: Putting the First Last* (London: Intermediate Technology, 1997).

Ellis, F. and Biggs, S. 'Evolving Themes in Rural Development' 1950s–2000s. *Development Policy Review*, 19:4 (2001).

Federation of Women Lawyers (FIDA), Factsheet on Gender Rule; https://www.genderinkenya.org/publication/fact-sheet-on-gender-rule-by-the-federation-of-women-lawyers-fida/.

Free Pentecostal Fellowship in Kenya. Gender Analysis of Free Pentecostal Fellowship in Kenya (2012). Available via author.

Franceschet, S. and Piscopo J.M., 'Gender Quotas and Women's Substantive Representation: Lessons from Argentina'. *Politics and Gender*, 4:3 (2008), 393-425.

Fredman, S., Goldberg, B., Discussion Paper, Gender Equality and Human Rights, No 4, July 2015. UN Women (2015);https://www.unwomen.org/en/searchresults?keywords=gender%20equality%20and%20human%20rights.

Goetz A.M., *Getting Institutions Right for Women in Development* (New York: Zed Books, 1997).

Goetz, A.M. and Hassim, S. (ed), *No Shortcuts to Power: African Women in Politics and Policy Making*. London: Zed Books, 2003.

Institute of Economic Affairs Kenya (IEA). Profile of Women's Socio-Economic Status in Kenya. Nairobi (2008).

Kabeer, N., 'Resources, Agency, Achievements: Reflections on the Measurement of Women's Empowerment'. *Development and Change*, 30:3 (1999), 435-464.

Kabeer, N., *Reversed Realities: Gender Hierarchies in Development Thought,* London and New York: Verso, 1994.

Kessel, B.,K., Between God's Sharing Power and Men's Controlling Power: A Quest for Diaconal Empowerment and Transformation in Femmes pour

Christ in Cameroon (Misjonshøgskolens Forlag, 2014) Resultat #1725999 – Between God's Sharing Power and Men's Controlling Power: A Quest for Daiconal Empowerment and Transformation in Femmes Pour Christ in Cameroon – Cristin.

Kwarimpa-Atim, D., Tuinuane Women Project (TWP), End of Project Evaluation Final Report (FPFK, PYM 2015); tuinuane-women-project-twp-end-of-project-evaluation.pdf (norad.no).

Layder, D., *Understanding Social Theory.* London: Sage Publications, 2006.

Mukhopadhyay, M., 'Mainstreaming Gender or "Streaming" Gender Away: Feminists Marooned in the Development Business'. IDS Bulletin, 35:4 (2004), 95-103.

Nairesiae, E., *Final Evaluation Report; FPFK, End of Project Evaluation* (2017); https://www.norad.no/globalassets/publikasjoner/publikasjoner-2017/sivsa-evalueringer/final-evaluation-report-of-tuinuane-project.pdf.

Plowman, P.J., 'Organisational Change from Two Perspectives'. *Development in Practice*, 10:2 (2000), 189-203.

Razavi S. and Miller, C., 'From WID to GAD: Conceptual Shifts in the Women and Development Discourse' (Geneva: United Nations Research Institute for Social Development, 1995).

Rowlands, J., 'A Word of the Times, but What Does it Mean? Empowerment in the Discourse and Practice of Development'. *Women and Empowerment* (1998), 11-34.

Von Sinner, R., 'The Diaconal Church in the Public Sphere', in Dietrich S., Jørgensen K., Koslien K.K., Nordstokke K. (eds), *The Diaconal Church* (Oxford: Regnum Books International, 2018).

Stewart-Thomas, M., Gendered Congregations, Gendered Service: The Impact of Clergy Gender on Congregational Social Service Participation. *Gender, Work and Organization*, 17:4 (2009), 406-432.

UNDP, UN Women, Gender Equality as an Accelerator for Achieving the Sustainable Development Goals, Discussion paper. New York: United Nations Development Programme (2018); https://www.undp.org/content/undp/en/home/librarypage/womens-empowerment/gender-equality-as-an-accelerator-for-achieving-the-sdgs.html.

United Nations, Goal 16: Promote just, peaceful and inclusive societies (no date); https://www.un.org/sustainabledevelopment/peace-justice/.

The Use of Asset-Based Approach as a Tool for the Inclusion of Persons with Disabilities: Case Study of HANDICARE in Ngaoundéré – Cameroon

Amos Ounsoubo

Introduction

My background of specialised teacher for deaf people and professional of development created in me a great interest in the inclusion of persons with disabilities (PwD) from the development perspective. Most of the time, the inclusion of PwD is envisaged from the perspective of their vulnerability and weakness, neglecting the fact that they are also full of competencies and can be actors instead of mere 'receivers' and 'beneficiaries'. This chapter aims to discuss the process of the inclusion of PwD from the perspective of their strengths. It assumes that a just and inclusive society should enable the full participation of all its members. It is based mainly on a master's thesis in Community Development and Social Innovation within the specialisation 'Diakonia, Community Development, and Christian Social Practice', and entitled 'The use of Diaconal Asset-Based Approach as a tool for the inclusion of persons with disabilities: Case study of the Association HANDICARE's work with the hearing-impaired youth in Ngaoundéré, Cameroon'. Acknowledging that neither methods for collecting data nor the insights gained through the work with the master's thesis can be adequately presented in this chapter, it will answer the research question: In which way can an asset-based approach be a tool for the inclusion of PwD?

The chapter will present overall approaches used in the process of inclusion of PwD, particularly through the lens of the *Use Your Talents* (UYT) approach (the main concept of this chapter) which is referred to as an asset-based congregational community development approach[1] and four other concepts: Seeking Conviviality, Empowerment, Social Innovation, and Disability-Inclusive Development (DID), which will support the analysis mainly as complementary to the UYT concept. The *twin-track* approach will constitute a

---

[1] Zo Ramiandra Rakotoarison, Stephanie Dietrich, and Heikki Hiilamo, 'Tackling Poverty with Local Assets: A Case Study on Congregational Asset-Based Community Development in a Lutheran Church in Madagascar,' *Diaconia*, 10:2 (2019), 119-140.

framework that will summarise the findings. Space does not provide for an in-depth discussion on how this framework is applied by HANDICARE. The above-named master's thesis provides this analysis.[2]

Three core terms are crucial too:

Inclusion: This is about taking into account all members of the society in all spheres of social life in terms of rights and effective participation; it refers to a process encouraging interaction between people with different relevant attributes or an impersonal institutional mechanism of opening up access to participation of all in all spheres of social life.[3]

Diakonia: This refers to the expression of the Christian faith by deed and words, manifesting thus the nature of the Church in daily life through compassion, inclusive communities, responsible stewardship of creation, and the struggle for justice.[4]

Asset-Based Community Development (ABCD): This refers to a process of acting collectively for the improvement of a community in any or all the spheres of their lives (physical, environmental, cultural, social, political, economic …) focusing on their strengths and already existing resources by building capacity within that community.[5]

Background and Context

The study was conducted in the town of Ngaoundere, the capital city of the Adamawa Region of Cameroon. According to the last General Population and Housing Census (GPHC),[6] conducted in 2005 and released in 2010, there were

---

[2] Amos Ounsoubo, *The Use of Diaconal Asset-Based Approach as a Tool for the Inclusion of Persons with Disabilities: Case Study of the Work of the Association HANDICARE with Hearing-impaired Youth in Ngaoundéré – Cameroon',* Master's thesis (Oslo: VID Specialiazed University, 2021).

[3] Hilary Silver, *The Contexts of Social Inclusion, UN-DESA Working Paper No. 144* (2015).

[4] Lutheran World Federation, *Diakonia in Context: Transformation, Reconciliation, Empowerment: An LWF Contribution to the Understanding and Practice of Diakonia* (Geneva: The Lutheran World Federation, 2009), 28.; Norwegian Church Aid, *Together for a Just World: Norwegian Church Aid's Statement of Principles* (Oslo: Norwegian Church Aid, 2008), 7.

[5] Rhonda Phillips and Robert Pittman, 'A Framework for Community and Economic Development,' in: *An Introduction to Community Development*, ed. Rhonda Phillips and Robert Pittman (London: Routledge, 2009), 3-21, 8; Anna Haines, 'Asset-based Community Development', in: *An Introduction to Community Development*, ed. Rhonda Phillips and Robert Pittman (London: Routledge, 2009), 38-48, 39-40.

[6] BUCREP, http://bucrep.cm/index.php/fr/recensements/3eme-rgph/resultats assessed on 27-10-2020.

close to 900,000 inhabitants.[7] The population of PwD was then 8602 out of which 3045 were hearing impaired.

The context of PwD in the Adamawa region is quite similar to the rest of the country. They are in a situation of marginalisation which explains the huge need for their inclusion as expressed by the UN-DESA.[8] Despite an increasing attention to inclusive education, many children with disabilities are yet to benefit from their educational and social rights.[9] The number of hearing-impaired children who fulfilled their secondary school and university studies is very low (close to zero).[10]

Due to discrimination, fewer PwD are employed in Cameroon compared to those without disability,[11] because disability reduces the chance to participate in the labour market and thus represents a barrier to employment.[12] However, education, professional training, and household-head status increase the possibility of being employed. Consequently, PwD mainly operate in the informal sectors such as agriculture and small-scale business with a negligible income, hence being amongst the poorest in society.[13]

Despite all the laws, conventions, and rules set by the State, the marginalisation and exclusion of PwD are often rooted in their own families,[14] since they are perceived as a 'social overload', leading to fears, rejection and shame. Moreover, the little consideration given to PwDs often rather results in a dependence mentality and an auto-negation of their dignity characterised by the

---

[7] There are many divergences in the figures presented by various studies consulted. As a choice, the statistics from the 3rd General Population and Housing Census (GPHC) conducted in 2005 and released in 2010 are the official reliable data collected from the field. This might be explained by the socio-political situation of Cameroon.

[8] UN-DESA, *Disability and Development Report: Realizing the Sustainable Development Goals by, for and with Persons with Disabilities, 2018* (New York: United Nations Publications, 2019).

[9] Lynn Cockburn et al., 'Realizing the Educational Rights of Children with Disabilities: An Overview of Inclusive Education in Cameroon,' *Journal of Education and Practice*, 8:6 (2017), 1-11.

[10] Ignace Edgar Mbom, 'Déterminants familiaux de la non scolarisation des enfants vivant avec un handicap au Cameroun entre 2001 et 2007' (Master Thesis, University of Yaounde II, 2012), 50.

[11] Arlette Simo Fotso, Christian Marie Zamo Akono, and Roger Tsafack Nanfosso, "Disability and Labour Force Participation in Cameroon," in: *Inclusive Growth in Africa: Policies, Practice, and Lessons Learnt*, ed. Steve Kayizzi-Mugerwa et al. (2016).

[12] C. Zamo-Akono, 'Disability and Labour Force Participation in Cameroon,' *International Journal of Human Resource Studies*, 3 (2013).

[13] Zamo-Akono, 'Disability and Labour Force'.

[14] Benedict Venance Mope, 'Précarité de l'environnement familial et perturbation du parcours scolaire des élèves déficients auditifs nés de parents entendants. Cas des élèves de l'ESDA à Ngaoundéré' (Diplôme de Professeur Spécialisé pour Déficients Auditifs Monograph, FEPPDA, 2017).

refusal to believe in their abilities.[15] However, PwDs consider this picture of themselves as worthless and without capacity for exclusion.[16] This is how a PwD from the town of Buea (Southwest Region) expressed it:

> It is very sad that our own people don't believe in us. They see us as worthless persons who can't support the family in any way. I have suffered this all my life and I'm now used to it. It hurts my soul to hear people say "what can he do?"[17]

This expression captures the context of life for a PwD in Cameroon and is important to keep in mind when introducing a diaconal organisation devoted to them.

Introducing HANDICARE

HANDICARE is an association founded in July 2017 and located in the town of Ngaoundere, with the motto: 'Breaking Barriers'. Their global objective is stated as 'promote the well-being and socio-professional development of people with disabilities' and their specific objectives are: (i) fighting against the marginalisation of PwD; (ii) contributing to the psychosocial and medical care of PwD; (iii) contributing to the emancipation, empowerment and inclusion of PwD; (iv) promoting the protection of PwD's rights; and (v) contributing to literacy, training, and socio-professional integration of PwD.

These objectives are carried out through literacy programmes, pedagogic support courses, learning of sign language, debates and educational talks, practical trainings, and sport and leisure.

The participants are around 30 hearing-impaired youths aged between 17 and 35, males and females. There are nine members of staff at HANDICARE. To achieve their mission, they are working in collaboration with the parents of the youths, with professionals, and with decision-makers.

HANDICARE is an outcome of the Specialised School for Hearing-Impaired Pupils of Ngaoundere (ESDA), a diaconal work of the Evangelical Lutheran Church of Cameroon. The association is expanding the Church's work through individuals' initiatives and is embedded in Christian and biblical values.

---

[15] Association Vaincre le Handicap, La situation sociale de la personne handicapée au Cameroun (no date). http://vhandicap.net/La-situation-sociale-de-la.html.

[16] Maxwell Opoku, Wisdom Mprah, Judith McKenzie, Bernard Sakah, and Eric Badu, 'Lives of Persons with Disabilities in Cameroon after CRPD: Voices of Persons with Disabilities in the Buea Municipality in Cameroon,' *International Journal on Disability and Human Development*, 16: (2016), 67-75.

[17] Opoku et al., 'Lives', 4.

Theoretical Framework

Two frameworks are relevant: disability-inclusive development (DID) and the twin-track approach.

Disability-Inclusive Development. DID implies that the development process through all its stages is inclusive of and accessible to PwD; it demands equal access for all persons to all the development sectors.[18]

Inclusive development can be defined as development which boosts people's well-being through equality of opportunity for all with a special care for the poor, the vulnerable and the disadvantaged groups.[19] It also supports empowerment, which enables PwD to become resource groups and development actors in society, rather than being categorised as 'vulnerable persons' that should be assisted.[20] Thus, PwD will not be a burden to families and society; rather, they will be contributors and actors. From this point, DID can be presented as a good framework that would allow the use of an asset-based method since it is intended to empower PwD to stand as self-advocates in order to ensure their full participation in all development processes and emergency responses. It works to tackle the barriers hindering their access and participation.[21] DID appreciates disability in the sense of diversity and as an aspect of daily human experience.[22]

The main elements (not exhaustive) of DID are: (i) inclusive education; (ii) inclusive health services; (iii) decent work and employment; and (iv) social protection.[23]

The Twin-Track Approach. This is the most commonly used approach in the realisation of DID.[24] It consists of a double-wing (twin-track) intervention: (i) Providing initiatives for the empowerment of PwD that ensure the full participation of PwD; and (ii) mainstreaming disability (disability-sensitiveness) in all processes (design, implementation, monitoring and evaluation of policies and programmes).[25]

The two tracks of this approach to inclusion are intrinsically bound to each other; to ensure successful outcomes for people with disabilities, both tracks should be activated as complementary elements. One track cannot secure good results and the approach would no longer be a twin-track one.[26]

---

[18] UN-DESA, *Toolkit on Disability for Africa: Disability-Inclusive Development* (2016), 3.

[19] Eiji Kozuka, 'Inclusive Development: Definition and Principles for the Post-2015 Development Agenda,' *Perspective on the Post-2015 Development Agenda* (2014), 110.

[20] UN-DESA, *Toolkit*, 4.

[21] Kathy Al Ju'beh, *Disability Inclusive Development Toolkit: CRPD Influencing Everything We Do*, ed. Christian Blind Mission (J2017), 48.

[22] Christian Blind Mission, 'Inclusion Made Easy: A Quick Program Guide to Disability in Development (*Melbourne: CBM Australia*, 2012), 18.

[23] Christian Blind Mission, 'Inclusion Made Easy', 4.

[24] Al Ju'beh, *Disability Inclusive*, 55.

[25] UN-DESA, *Toolkit*, 9-12.

[26] Al Ju'beh, *Disability Inclusive*, 55.

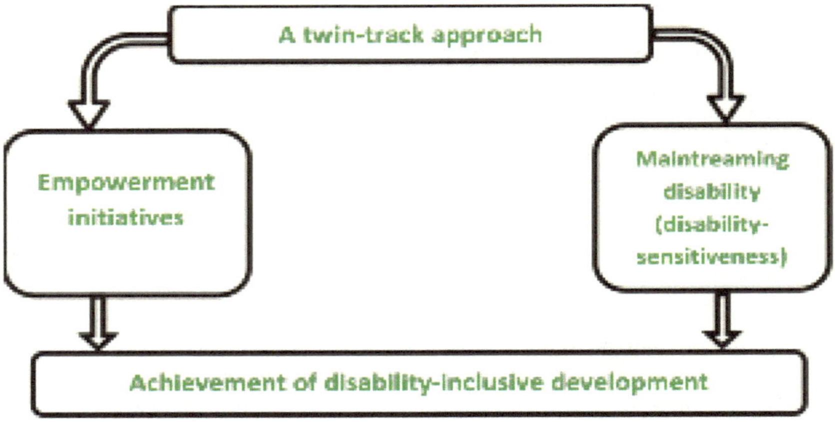

Figure 1. The twin-track approach. Source: UN-DESA[27]

Diaconal Approaches: Using Your Talents, Seeking Conviviality, Social Innovation and Empowerment

According to Margaret Ledwith, community development has as a vision of a just and sustainable world, married with social and environmental justice principles, embedded in values such as equality, dignity, trust, mutuality and reciprocity, processing through practical projects led by critical consciousness, going from local projects to movements for change.[28]

In line with this, ABCD focuses on a community strength and already existing resources by building capacity within that community.[29] Here, assets can be defined as valuable qualities, persons and things as well as advantages and resources – all of these referring to gifts, skills and capacities of individuals, associations, institutions and organisations.[30]

From a diaconal perspective, one should remember that as *faith-based* and *rights-based*, and the connection between the two,[31] diakonia stands for people in need and fights for justice for the helpless.

Use Your Talents (UYT). UYT is a diaconal ABCD approach developed within an African context with the aim of making the congregation a primary development agent putting a high emphasis on the use of each member's resources.[32] It is also referred to as a congregational asset-based community

---

[27] UN-DESA, *Toolkit*, 9.

[28] Margaret Ledwith, *Community Development in Action: Putting Freire into Practice* (Bristol: Policy Press, 2016), 5.

[29] Haines, 'Asset-based Community Development,' 39-40.

[30] Haines, 'Asset-based Community Development,' 40-41.

[31] World Council of Churches, *Ecumenical Diakonia* (2017), 3.

[32] Galunde Waketa Warotte, '"Use Your Talents" Concept: An Evolving Complementary or Alternative Approach to Development Work,' in *Use Your Talents:*

development.[33] Here, the congregational character comprises the actions and initiatives made by all of the Christians on their own. Thus, UYT assumes that every Christian should take an active part in the development of the community in which they live.

In UYT, the word 'talents' represents people's skills and knowledge in a broader way, their relationships to others, and their 'belongings, such as land, houses and money.'[34] There are tangible and intangible assets.[35] Hence, 'talent' can be seen as a synonym of 'asset'.

The UYT approach is characterised by seven elements:[36] (i) start with the available resources; (ii) seeing all as actors;[37] (iii) integrated in congregations; (iv) based on voluntary work; (v) networking; (vi) sustainability; and (vii) ownership. We will return to UYT below.

Seeking Conviviality. Seeking Conviviality is an ABCD approach developed within countries from Eastern and Central Europe. Whilst this chapter cannot provide an in-depth analysis,[38] conviviality refers to 'the art and practice of living together.'[39] It is about 'living together in solidarity, in sharing resources and in the joint struggle for human dignity and sustainable community life.'[40]

The Congregation as Primary Development Agent, ed. Sigurd Haus (Oslo: Digni, 2017), 148-159, 156.

[33] Sigurd Haus (ed), *Use Your Talents: The Congregation as Primary Development Agent* (Oslo: Digni, 2016).

[34] Sigurd Haus, 'Use Your Talents' knowledge development project, in Sigurd Haus (ed), *Use Your Talents: The Congregation as Primary Development Agent* (Oslo: Digni, 2017), 17-21, 18.

[35] Kjell Nordstokke, 'Mapping Out and Mobilising Diaconal Assets,' in *Diakonia as Christian Social Practice: An Introduction*, ed. Stephanie Dietrich et al. (2015), 214, 225, 217-220.

[36] Sigurd Haus, 'Use', 20-21.

[37] On this actorship, see Beatrice Nekesa Johanson, 'Use Of Talents: A Way to Transform and Develop Communities in Kenya Through Congregations, master's thesis (Oslo: VID Specialiazed University, 2017), iii.

[38] Tony Addy, '"Seeking Conviviality" as a Core Concept for Community Development', in: Hans Morten Haugen, Benedicte Kivle, Tony Addy, Terese Bue Kessel and John Klaasen (eds), *Developing Just and Inclusive Communities. Challenges for Diakonia as Christian Social Practice and for Social Work* (Oxford: Regnum, 2022), 79-94.

[39] Lutheran World Federation and interdiac, *Seeking Conviviality: Re-forming Community Diakonia in Europe* (Geneva: Lutheran World Federation, 2013), 4; see also Tony Addy, 'New approaches to Community-based Work, Social Service, and Diaconia Challenges from the CABLE Approach,' *Diaconia*, 4:2 (2013), 194-215, 195.

[40] Lutheran World Federation and interdiac, *Seeking*, 4; see also Lutheran World Federation and interdiac, *Towards a Convivial Economy. The Contribution of a Re-formed Community Diakonia in Europe* (Geneva: Lutheran World Federation, 2017).

The efforts should focus first on the togetherness and then on services.[41] Therefore, *Seeking Conviviality* is grounded in daily life in Church and society,[42] where people's creativity in addressing their situation is actively encouraged.[43]

In that perspective, diakonia is understood as '"Gospel in action" and as a mark of and task for the whole church, it is not simply for specialists or a specific group of volunteers.'[44] Thus, diaconal work should be carried out in the everyday life by the entire Church, highlighting the great importance of voluntary work.

Social Innovation. William Voorberg *et al.* define social innovation as the creation of long-lasting outcomes that aim to address societal needs by fundamentally changing the relationships, positions and rules between the involved stakeholders, through an open process of participation, exchange and collaboration with relevant stakeholders, including end-users.[45]

Social innovation is also described by Howaldt *et al.* as 'a new combination or configuration of practices in areas of social action… by using existing practices'.[46]

Considering the inclusion of PwD, social innovation will encourage stakeholders (PwD being the first) to actively use practices and a combination of practices that would lead to a social change where PwD will feel fully part of the community.

Empowerment. In brief, empowerment is about moving from powerlessness, understood as 'lack of means to gain control… '[47] to power, that is 'intrinsically linked to participation… '[48]

Stephanie Dietrich defines empowerment as:

> A multi-dimensional social process by which people gain ability to decide over aspects of their lives and take part in the community with dignity; it is a process

---

[41] Tony Addy, '"Seeking Conviviality": A New Core Concept for Diaconal Church,' in *The Diaconal Church*, ed. Stephanie Dietrich et al. (Oxford: Regnum Books, 2019), 158-170, 160-61.

[42] Addy, '"Seeking Conviviality": A New Core', 160-61.

[43] Lutheran World Federation and interdiac, *Seeking*, 4.

[44] Lutheran World Federation and interdiac, *Seeking*, 4.

[45] William Voorberg, Victor Bekkers, and Lars Tummers, 'A Systematic Review of Co-creation and Co-Production: Embarking on the Social Innovation Journey,' *Public Management Review*, 17:9 (2014), 1333-1357, 1334.

[46] Jürgen Howaldt, Ralf Kopp, and Michael Schwarz, 'Social Innovations as Drivers of Social Change: Exploring Tarde's Contribution to Social Innovation Theory Building,' in *New Frontiers in Social Innovation Research*, edited by Alex Nicholls, Julie Simon, and Madeleine Gabriel (Basingstoke: Springer Nature, 2015) pp. 29-51, 30.

[47] John Lord and Peggy Hutchison, 'The Process of Empowerment: Implications for Theory and Practice,' *Canadian Journal of Community Mental Health*, 12:1 (1993), 5-22, 6.

[48] Nadine Bowers Du Toit, 'The Elephant in the Room: The Need to Re-discover the Intersection between Poverty, Powerlessness and Power in "Theology and Development" Praxis,' *HTS Theological Studies*, 72:4 (2016), 1-9, 5.

> that enables people to gain power for acting on issues they define as important concerning their own lives, their communities, and the society in which they are living.[49]

In line with this, Charles Elliot asserts that to empower the poor and marginalised 'is to give them decision-making power.'[50]

In fact, empowerment is a process of change at three levels: personal, small group, and community.[51] This is affirmed by Taylor *et al.*, asserting: 'Empowerment is human energy.'[52]

In a community development perspective, Margaret Ledwith explains that empowerment is built on principles of participatory democracy and encourages people to question their reality which is the basis of collective action.[53] Furthermore, she argues that empowerment is a commitment to social justice which leads to 'believing in people to such an extent that they believe in themselves!'[54] It leads to an engagement in movements that challenges disadvantage, exclusion, and oppression that the specific community is facing.[55]

An Integrated Model of UYT as a Method for the Inclusion of Persons with Disabilities

According to Kjell Nordstokke, members of local congregations can manifest a sort of 'diakonia from below' and 'self-empowerment' as an energy from within, grounded in their daily experiences and the vision of their faith.[56] This represents an implementation of the UYT approach.

The whole process of UYT is grounded in empowerment which is seen as the 'diakonia from the margins' which is prophetic, transformative and justice-seeking.[57] From its principles UYT, as an instrument of inclusion and

---

[49] Stephanie Dietrich, 'Reflections on Core Aspects of Diaconal Theory,' in: Stephanie Dietrich Knud Jorgensen, Kari Karsrud Korslien and Kjell Nordstokke (eds), *Diakonia as Christian Social Practice. An Introduction* (Oxford: Regnum, 2014), 13-27, 21.

[50] Charles Elliott, *Comfortable Compassion?: Poverty, Power and the Church* (Londo: Hodder and Stoughton, 1987), 78.

[51] Lord and Hutchison, 'The Process,' 7.

[52] Taylor *et al.*, *Empowerment*, 65.

[53] Margaret Ledwith, *Community Development: A Critical Approach* (Bristol: Policy Press, 2011), 2-3.

[54] Ledwith, *Community Development in Action*, 23.

[55] Ledwith, *Community Development: A Critical Approach*, 13.

[56] Kjell Nordstokke, 'Empowerment in the Perspective of Ecumenical Diakonia,' *Diaconia*, 3:2 (2012), 185-95, 186.

[57] World Council of Churches, *Ecumenical Diakonia*, 28-29.

participation, is seeing PwD as fully part of the community and holding talents with which they can contribute to the development of that community.[58]

Merging the questions '*how can diakonia contribute to people living together?*' from *Seeking Conviviality* and '*what can we do with what we have here and now?*' from UYT would enable a good implementation of the twin-track method in ensuring the disability-inclusive development.

Additionally, asking the question '*What kind of economic and social policies support living together?*', expressed in the Seeking Conviviality approach, would strengthen mainstreaming the disability aspect in everything done towards the common action as it will require policies that would integrate the specificities of all. Thus, the inclusion of PwD would be integrated in the daily life of the community as all the social groups would be taken into account.

However, in all of the UYT literature, none mentioned a clear and strong perspective of this approach in addressing root causes of injustice. This could be presented as a limit of UYT as a diaconal asset-based method for the inclusion of PwD. That could be interpreted as working on just one track of the twin-track approach (the empowerment branch). Though the gender sensitiveness is quite developed in the UYT approach,[59] there is a need to widen and scale up this sensitiveness to all kinds of marginalisation, and enhance awareness of power asymmetries.[60] However, UYT as an empowering approach does not yet adequately address power dynamics in its implementation. Therefore, elements from Seeking Conviviality, such as the struggle for justice, could contribute to scaling up the rights-based perspective of UYT as a diaconal approach since diakonia should link faith to rights.[61] This would comply with Voorberg et al.'s definition of social innovation which implies 'changing the relationships, positions and rules… '[62] Such changes might foster the inclusion of PwD.

Main Findings on HANDICARE's Achievements

This section is based on the findings of my master's thesis.[63] Three main approaches are implemented by HANDICARE: promoting inclusion, fostering a diaconal ABCD and contributing to less discrimination in competencies.

---

[58] Zo Ramiandra Rakotoarison, 'Women, Use Your Talents', in: *Use Your Talents: The Congregation as Primary Development Agent*, ed. Sigurd Haus (Oslo: Digni, 2017), 62-68, 65, 67.

[59] Currently, there is a gender guideline in the process of being edited. This guideline has been made with the intension of mainstreaming all of the activities within the UYT project framework.

[60] Johannes Nissen, 'Towards a Transformation of Power: New Testament Perspectives on Diaconia and Empowerment,' *Diaconia*, 3:1 (2012), 26-43.

[61] World Council of Churches, *Ecumenical Diakonia*, 3.

[62] Voorberg *et al.*, 'A Systematic Review', 1334.

[63] Ounsoubo, 'The Use'.

Promoting Inclusion: According to the field information, the expression of exclusion as experienced by hearing-impaired youths is mostly presented as a language barrier and cultural perceptions. Eight of the 10 youths interviewed explicitly pointed to the language barrier as their major experience of exclusion and five experienced it from home. Concerning the cultural cause of exclusion, the interviews revealed that many people think that disability is a curse and a cause of shame (this is mentioned by all of the parents).

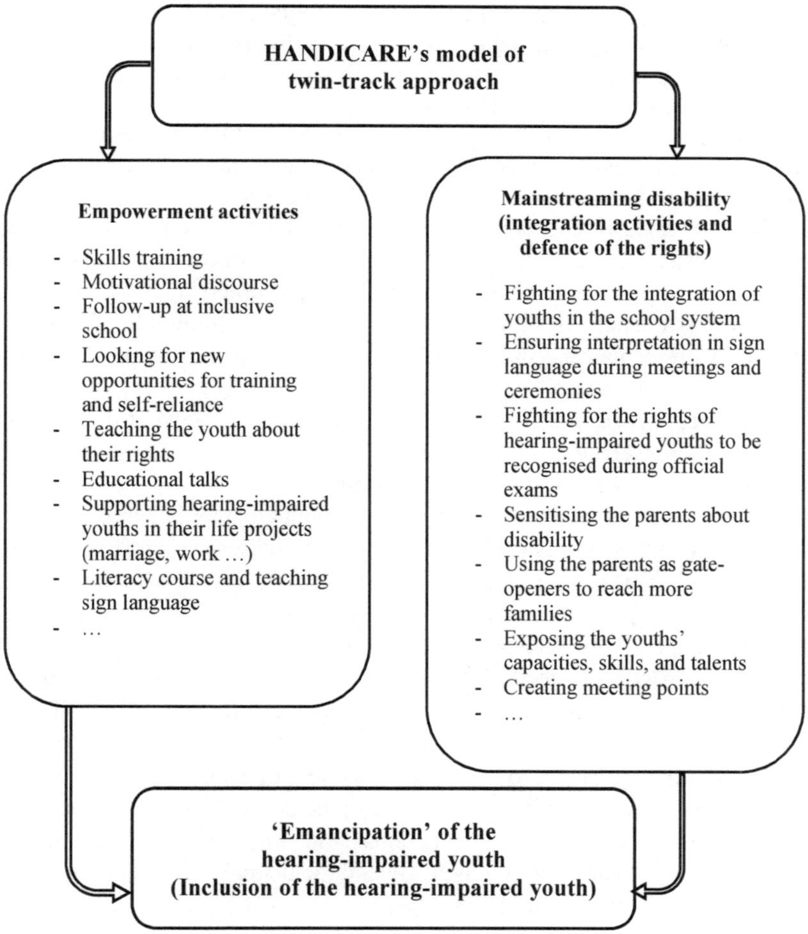

Figure 2. The twin-track approach – the HANDICARE model
Source: Amos Ounsoubo[64]

[64] Ounsoubo, 'The Use'.

This can explain the formulation of HANDICARE's motto: "breaking barriers!" HANDICARE promotes empowerment and restoration of the dignity of PwD (termed 'emancipation') and works with the community through what they call 'integration and the defence of the rights' of hearing-impaired youths. Those are the two branches of the *twin-track* approach.

Empowerment is carried out through the training at various levels that HANDICARE is organising, and the integration or mainstreaming of disability sensitiveness is done through exposing youths' talents and skills to the community, through common activities such as sports and official ceremonies, and the defence and popularisation of the rights of PwD at all levels. This represents a new way of using existing practices by using the skills of the youth for their integration which creates a sustainable solution for the youth, giving them a new position and participation.[65]

This is how one informant expressed it: 'HANDICARE teaches us that we are not less than the hearing people, we are equal. Everything the hearing people can do, we too can do it. We can work equally like hearing people.'

This strong statement represents the effectiveness of the inclusion driven by an asset-based method. From the expression of the hearing-impaired youth, it can be noticed that this feeling of 'being like all the others' created an emulation in the youths and helped them assume their social lives through funding a family, seeking a job or making use of the skills acquired in HANDICARE, such as starting a small business.

Fostering a Diaconal ABCD: Two of the three interviewed parents clearly made a link between the actions of HANDICARE and their Christian faith. This presents the work of HANDICARE as diaconal.

HANDICARE's motivation and service model are mainly based on their will to demonstrate their faith through 'transmitting to others the love [they] received from Christ' (Founder of HANDICARE) which is also the foremost goal of UYT. This perspective aligns with the definition of diakonia as 'faith into action',[66] and could be seen as 'Gospel by deeds'.[67]

HANDICARE is concentrating on the assets/resources of hearing-impaired youths to work on their inclusion. As the leader and founder of HANDICARE asserts it: 'Everything we are doing is based on what those youth can do.'

The seven approaches of UYT are applied in HANDICARE's methods. HANDICARE uses what is at their disposal, including the founder's homeplace, the members' money, their connections, and all kinds of opportunities, to promote the rights of PwD and their societal inclusion by exposing the potential and talents of hearing-impaired youths.

---

[65] Voorberg *et al.*, 'A Systematic Review', 1334.

[66] Norwegian Church Aid, *Together*.

[67] Lutheran World Federation, *Diakonia in Context: Transformation, Reconciliation, Empowerment: An LWF Contribution to the Understanding and Practice of Diakonia*, 40.

Moreover, HANDICARE fosters empowerment through discourse and training, based on the skills and talents of hearing-impaired youths. The founder and leader of HANDICARE explains: 'I keep on telling them that they are as skilled as the others.... They understand that discourse.' This discourse galvanises the youths and they become more involved in the training.

Contributing to Less Discrimination in Competencies: Persons trained at HANDICARE face less discrimination regarding the performance of their competencies and talents. Moreover, parents become less pessimistic and stand as strong advocators and propagators of the inclusion of those youths.

Conclusion

The method used by HANDICARE in working for the inclusion of hearing-impaired youths is diaconal asset-based.[68] In line with the findings from my master's thesis, for inclusion to be effective, the UYT approach must integrate a 'rights-based' approach, which is done by HANDICARE, integrating the fight for the rights of PwD as a key element of their method.

Hence, whilst UYT is an ABCD essential for empowering PwD, rights-based elements should be fully included in order for UYT to be a method for the real inclusion of PwD.

Bibliography

Addy, Tony. 'New Approaches to Community-Based Work, Social Service, and Diaconia Challenges from the Cable Approach', *Diaconia*, 4:2 (2013): 194-215.

Addy, Tony. 'Seeking Conviviality: A New Core Concept for Diaconal Church'. *The Diaconal Church.* Stephanie Dietrich, Knud Jørgensen, Kari Karsrud Korslien and Kjell Nordstokke Eds. (Oxford: Regnum Books, 2019), 158-70.

Addy, Tony. '"Seeking Conviviality" as a Core Concept for Community Development'. *Developing Just and Inclusive Communities. Challenges for Diakonia as Christian Social Practice and for Social Work.* Hans Morten Haugen, Benedicte Tveter Kivle, Tony Addy, Terese Bue Kessel and John Klaasen Eds. (Oxford: Regnum, 2022), 79-94.

Al Ju'beh, Kathy. *Disability Inclusive Development Toolkit: CRPD Influencing Everything We Do.* Edited by Christian Blind Mission (2017). https://www.cbm.org/fileadmin/user_upload/Publications/CBM-DID-TOOLKIT-accessible.pdf.

Association Vaincre le Handicap, La situation sociale de la personne handicapée au Cameroun (no date). http://vhandicap.net/La-situation-sociale-de-la.html.

[68] On inclusion in UYT; see Rakotoarison, 'Women'.

Bowers Du Toit, Nadine. 'The Elephant in the Room: The Need to Re-Discover the Intersection between Poverty, Powerlessness and Power in "Theology and Development" Praxis' *Herv. Teol. Stud* 72:4 (2016), 1-9. https://doi.org/10.4102/hts.v72i4.3459.

BUCREP. *3e Recensement Général De La Population Et De L'habitat: Situation Socio-Économique Des Personnes Vivant Avec Un Handicap.* Ministère de l'Economie, du Plan et de l'Aménagement du Territoire (Yaoundé, Cameroon: 2010). http://bucrep.cm/index.php/fr/ressources-et-documentations/telechargement/category/42-analyses-thmatiques?download=83:tome-13-situation-socio-economique-des-personnes-vivant-avec-un-handicap.

Christian Blind Mission. 'Inclusion Made Easy: A Quick Program Guide to Disability in Development.' *Melbourne: CBM Australia* (2012). https://www.cbm.org/fileadmin/user_upload/Publications/cbm_inclusion_made_easy_a_quick_guide_to_disability_in_development.pdf.

Cockburn, Lynn, Goli Hashemi, Christian Noumi, Allison Ritchie, and Kimberly Skead. 'Realizing the Educational Rights of Children with Disabilities: An Overview of Inclusive Education in Cameroon.' *Journal of Education and Practice*, 8:6 (2017), 1-11.

Dietrich, Stephanie. 'Reflections on Core Aspects of Diaconal Theory'. *Diakonia as Christian Social Practice.*

An Introduction. Stephanie Dietrich, Knud Jørgensen, Kari Karsrud Korslien and Kjell Nordstokke Eds. (Oxford: Regnum, 2014), 13-27.

Elliott, Charles. *Comfortable Compassion?: Poverty, Power and the Church* (London: Hodder and Stoughton, 1987).

Fotso, Arlette Simo, Christian Marie Zamo Akono, and Roger Tsafack Nanfosso. 'Disability and Labour Force Participation in Cameroon'. *Inclusive Growth in Africa: Policies, Practice, and Lessons Learnt*, Steve Kayizzi-Mugerwa Abebe Shimeles, Angela Lusigi, Ahmed Moummi Eds. (London: Routledge, 2016), 22-36.

Haines, Anna. 'Asset-Based Community Development'. *An Introduction to Community Development.* Rhonda Phillips and Robert Pittman Eds. (London: Routledge, 2009), 38-48.

Haus, Sigurd (ed), *Use Your Talents: The Congregation as Primary Development Agent* (Oslo: Digni, 2017).

Howaldt, Jürgen, Ralf Kopp, and Michael Schwarz. 'Social Innovations as Drivers of Social Change: Exploring Tarde's Contribution to Social Innovation Theory Building'. *New Frontiers in Social Innovation Research*, Rhonda Phillips and Robert Pittman Eds. (Basingstoke: Springer Nature, 2015), 29-51.

Kozuka, Eiji. 'Inclusive Development: Definition and Principles for the Post-2015 Development Agenda'. *Perspective on the Post-2015 Development Agenda*, Hiroshi Kato Ed. (Tokyo: JICA Ogata Sadako Research Institute for Peace and Development 2014), 109-122.

Ledwith, Margaret. *Community Development: A Critical Approach* (Bristol: Policy Press, 2011).

Ledwith, Margaret. *Community Development in Action: Putting Freire into Practice* (Bristol: Policy Press, 2016).

Lord, John, and Peggy Hutchison. 'The Process of Empowerment: Implications for Theory and Practice.' *Canadian Journal of Community Mental Health*, 12:1 (1993), 5-22.

Lutheran World Federation. *Diakonia in Context: Transformation, Reconciliation, Empowerment: An LWF Contribution to the Understanding and Practice of Diakonia* (Geneva: The Lutheran World Federation, 2009).

Lutheran World Federation and interdiac. *Seeking Conviviality: Re-forming Community Diakonia in Europe* (Geneva: Lutheran World Federation, 2013).

Lutheran World Federation and interdiac. *Towards a Convivial Economy. The Contribution of a Re-formed Community Diakonia in Europe* (Geneva: Lutheran World Federation, 2017).

Mbom, Ignace Edgar. *Déterminants Familiaux De La Non Scolarisation Des Enfants Vivant Avec Un Handicap Au Cameroun Entre 2001 Et 2007. Master's Thesis, University of Yaounde II*, 2012.

Mope, Benedict Venance. *Précarité De L'environnement Familial Et Perturbation Du Parcours Scolaire Des Élèves Déficients Auditifs Nés De Parents Entendants. Cas Des Élèves De L'esda À Ngaoundéré.' Diplôme de Professeur Spécialisé pour Déficients Auditifs Monograph* (Yaoundé: FEPPDA, 2017).

Nekesa Johanson, Beatrice. *Use of Talents: A Way to Transform and Develop Communities in Kenya through Congregations. Master's Thesis* (Oslo: VID Specialiazed University, 2017).

Nissen, Johannes. 'Towards a Transformation of Power: New Testament Perspectives on Diaconia and Empowerment', *Diaconia*, 3:1 (2012), 26-43. https://doi.org/10.13109/diac.2012.3.1.26.

Nordstokke, Kjell. 'Empowerment in the Perspective of Ecumenical Diakonia', *Diaconia*, 3:2 (2012), 185-95.

Nordstokke, Kjell. 'Mapping out and Mobilising Diaconal Assets'. *Diakonia as Christian Social Practice: An Introduction*. Stephanie Dietrich, Knud Jorgensen, Kari Karsrud Korslien and Kjell Nordstokke Eds. (Oxford: Regnum, 2014), 214-225.

Norwegian Church Aid. *Together for a Just World: Norwegian Church Aid's Statement of Principles* (Oslo: Norwegian Church Aid, 2008). https://fabo.org/pluginfile.php/32990/mod_resource/content/1/NCAs%20Statement%20of%20Principles.pdf.

Opoku, Maxwell, Wisdom Mprah, Judith McKenzie, Bernard Sakah, and Eric Badu. 'Lives of Persons with Disabilities in Cameroon after CRPD: Voices of Persons with Disabilities in the Buea Municipality in Cameroon', *International Journal on Disability and Human Development*, 16:1 (2016), 67-75. https://doi.org/10.1515/ijdhd-2016-0009.

Ounsoubo, Amos. *The use of Diaconal Asset-Based Approach as a Tool for the Inclusion of Persons with Disabilities: Case Study of the Work of the*

Association HANDICARE with Hearing-impaired Youth in Ngaoundéré, Cameroon, Master's Thesis (Oslo: VID Specialized University, 2021).

Phillips, Rhonda, and Robert Pittman. 'A Framework for Community and Economic Development'. *An Introduction to Community Development.* Rhonda Phillips and Robert Pittman Eds. (London: Routledge, 2009), 3-21.

Rakotoarison, Zo Ramiandra. 'Women, Use Your Talents', in Sigurd Haus (ed), *Use Your Talents: The Congregation as Primary Development Agent* (Oslo: Digni, 2017), 62-68.

Rakotoarison, Zo Ramiandra, Stephanie Dietrich, and Heikki Hiilamo. 'Tackling Poverty with Local Assets: A Case Study on Congregational Asset-Based Community Development in a Lutheran Church in Madagascar.' *Diaconia*, 10:2 (2019), 119-40. https://doi.org/10.13109/diac.2019.10.2.119.

Silver, Hilary. *The Contexts of Social Inclusion. UN-DESA Working Paper No. 144* (2015).

Taylor, Daniel C., Carl E. Taylor, and Jesse O. Taylor. *Empowerment on an Unstable Planet: From Seeds of Human Energy to a Scale of Global Change* (Oxford: Oxford University Press, 2011). doi:10.1093/acprof:osobl/9780199842964.001.0001.

UN-DESA. *Disability and Development Report: Realizing the Sustainable Development Goals by, for and with Persons with Disabilities, 2018.* (New York: United Nations Publications, 2019).

UN-DESA. *Toolkit on Disability for Africa: Disability-Inclusive Development.* Toolkit on Disability for Africa. Edited by DSPD-DESA (New York: UN-DESA, 2016.

Voorberg, William, Victor Bekkers, and Lars Tummers. 'A Systematic Review of Co-Creation and Co-Production: Embarking on the Social Innovation Journey.' *Public Management Review*, 17:9 (2014). 1333-1357.

Warotte, Galunde Waketa. '"Use Your Talents" Concept: An Evolving Complementary or Alternative Approach to Development Work'. *Use Your Talents: The Congregation as Primary Development Agent*, Sigurd Haus Ed. (Oslo: Digni, 2017), 148-59.

World Council of Churches. *Ecumenical Diakonia. Revised Draft, 21.04.2017* (2017). https://kirken.no/globalassets/kirken.no/smm/dokumenter/2019/wcc-ecumenical-diakonia-study-document.pdf.

Zamo-Akono, C. 'Disability and Labour Force Participation in Cameroon.' *International Journal of Human Resource Studies*, 3:1 (2013): 1-13.

Developing Just and Inclusive Communities

Tony Addy, John Klaasen, Terese Bue Kessel, Benedicte Tveter Kivle and Hans Morten Haugen

Challenges for Community Development and Diakonia as Christian Social Practice

The contributors to this book see social exclusion as a major factor requiring a critique of conventional approaches to development, including some approaches to community development. Dominant, emergency or short-term development approaches, donor–recipient approaches and binary approaches are challenged as exclusive and discriminatory. Sensitivity to gender identity, disability and diversity heighten awareness about these limited approaches. From these chapters we can discern guidelines for the inclusion of marginalised people such as migrants, refugees and people with disabilities as well as for gender inclusivity. It is hoped that this book will inspire new approaches to community development as well as to diakonia as Christian social practice, as we seek for the creation of just and inclusive communities.

The book is intended to be a resource for both academic teaching and learning and for those who are practising community development. Community development is investigated from a diversity of disciplinary perspectives, including social work, theology and religion, ethics and human rights. The different scholars therefore represent a number of disciplines, and their approaches arise from different perspectives, including grassroots practice, social analysis and theological reflection. Apart from the different disciplines, the international geography of the scholars and their contextual focus adds to the richness and depth of the book.

The development of just and inclusive communities is examined through three interrelated themes which are united around the contribution of place-based work to the sustainable development goals, especially SDG 16.7: 'Ensure responsive, inclusive, participatory and representative decision-making at all levels.' The three related themes, which are all linked to practice are:

- Approaches to community development work and the contribution of concepts such as conviviality and Ubuntu to an enriched understanding of practice, rooted in diverse contexts.

- Theological and ethical reflection on personhood, agency and community in relation to community development and Christian social practice.
- Diversity and community including themes related to gender identity, migration, race and disability.

These three themes and the contribution to theory and practice in relation to SDG 16.7 make this research contextual, relevant and universal, even though the chapters are rooted within different geographical, national and local settings. Therefore, the particularity of the chapters related to a specific context does not negate the universal relevance of each contribution.

Community is an important overarching concept, and the different conceptualisations of community are indicative of the positioning of the person in the collective context. Within each world region, community is a contested phenomenon and the relationship between person and community shifts according to the dominant view, emphasising the person or the community. This is explored in a number of chapters and related to different contexts. An important issue is the way in which the assertion of similarity of identity as a basis for community life is used as a mechanism to exclude those who are different. Again, this is an issue which affects all regions and international perspectives. The underlying question which guides the various discussions is, 'How do we develop just and inclusive communities?' All of the chapters discuss the need for communities that are more inclusive, whether looking at this from a research, practical or theoretical perspective. The principles and values of inclusive communities are highlighted in many of the articles.

Community development work and diakonia and are defined both in general terms and through discipline-specific terminologies. The primary objective relates to the contribution that an analysis of actual communities and development makes to practices and theories of social and community development work and diakonia. This is the core significance of the contribution this resource makes to the discourse of community development and diakonia as Christian social practice.

The structure of the book reflects both the diverse approaches and expertise of the contributors. The introductory chapters introduce important concepts such as community, development, personhood and human rights. These concepts form a basis for the linkages between the remaining chapters and provide a lens through which the different contributions can be read. The introductory chapters also provide a clustering of the variety of approaches to community development, highlighting both the strengths and limitations of the approaches that are dominant within recent practice and research.

Concepts such as personhood and human rights provide innovative ideas for the continued study of community development and Christian social practice, both for the broader religious landscape and for secular approaches. These concepts elicit new paths that may result in new trends and approaches to community development which have implications for diakonia as Christian social practice.

Personhood draws from the long tradition of the Christian doctrine of imago Dei to investigate the role that identity plays in the development of communities. This theoretical and abstract approach presents linkages and markers such as responsibility, relationships and power dynamics within approaches of development that fosters more inclusive and just communities. These three – responsibility, relationships and power dynamics – form a matrix for growth, participation, and the agency of persons.

The importance of inclusive decision-making in line with human rights cannot be overestimated. Such inclusive decision-making can, of course, be practised without having to consider the legal sphere represented by human rights. Recently, different development theories have shifted the overall focus from the macro level to the local and even personal level. What is unique within the framework of human rights is that it makes clear the explicit state obligations for fostering such inclusive decision-making. States are also, however, the main obstacle for such inclusion in several parts of the world. Preservation of the status quo is prioritised above fostering empowerment. Restrictions on the work of human rights organisations might also impede processes of community development. Churches are often in a position to respond to these authoritarian tendencies but maintaining order and a good relationship with the authorities is also prioritised, hence limiting this transformative potential.

The book joins current debates about different approaches to community development because it is important to distinguish those approaches which effectively contribute to long-term change. There is a danger that a focus on local community development provides a cover for the reduction in social, educational and other provision by governments. In other contexts, where the social state is not so developed, it is important that the model of community development is able to lead to advocacy or campaigning for the state to take its rightful responsibility. This means the contribution to governance of people on or near the margins is vital for ensuring full representation. The various chapters in the book enable reflection on this issue in order to inform the choice of approach being followed.

Ubuntu, 'seeking conviviality' and 'leaving no one behind' are explorations of new perspectives on community development for inclusive and just communities. These concepts seek to expand theory and practice beyond social, religious and political boundaries to create peaceful and just communities. The normativity of essentialism is challenged and the perspectives from different nations and communities are brought into an active and participatory discussion between the Global North and Global South. This is one important focus of the chapter on Ubuntu whereas the practice of seeking conviviality challenges the dominance of national or regional identity and similar notions to the understanding of community in the face of diversity. Therefore, the understanding of migrant identities and super diversity become key issues for development of inclusive and just communities and structures. 'Leaving no one behind' introduces a shift of power relations from a dominant centre to an approach which begins from the margins and emphasises processes which start 'from below'. The margins are reconfigured and the agency of people and communities on the margin is affirmed as a key factor for community development. Drawing from a liberation hermeneutic, this approach critiques the dominant, excluding and exploitative methods which often underly classic approaches to development. Instead, the liberal and neo-liberal approaches towards the agency of marginalised communities are shifted towards approaches which recognise the expertise and agency of people themselves. This approach supports local innovation and political action towards structural transformation.

One section of the book is devoted to elements for development, change, innovation and learning related to community development. The three chapters highlight how space for change is created and understood within or between communities. Mechanisms of change are seen both in the historical development of educational structures through a literature review, and through moulding conceptual models for inclusive leadership. The section contributes to the understanding of how exclusion and injustice can be counteracted by continually learning from the past, and by creating innovative practice.

The four chapters under the heading 'Social Practice and Diakonia' which arise from different geographical contexts discuss selected communal and personal lived experiences of the role of churches and religious communities, faith-based organisations, and urban contexts in building sustainable majority and minority communities. The investigations range from experiences with the dominant faith community of the Church of Norway to diaconal approaches to the underprivileged in some suburbs in Cape Town; reproductive health issues in family life in Japan; and parenting strategies by refugee parents in urban Oslo. The discussions build on qualitative research methods and secondary literature analysis to expand the understanding of macro and micro social work beyond religious, diaconal, familial, and spiritual boundaries. Whilst a study of congregations within the Church of Norway reveals that the historic church tradition and the church building contribute to community formation in urban contexts, informants in Cape Town express the understanding that tangible hope is experienced through diaconal engagement with marginalised neighbourhoods. On a familial level, structural challenges of reproductive health prevent gender inclusive communities in Japan, and the response of Buddhist communities presents a challenge to the practice of the Christian church. Starting with a different issue facing families, parents with refugee background in Oslo navigate between identified risks and lean on strategies for setting boundaries and for participation within the community.

There is no doubt that this book has identified a number of gaps in community development theory and practice. Therefore, further research is needed to maximise the potential impact of community development on work with poor and marginalised people and localities, minority groups and oppressed and dominated people. Community development has an important role to play in addressing the issues faced by the parts of our societies that do not have access or have limited access to resources, relevant policies, laws and skills that can foster greater equity, inclusivity and development.

Although the authors of this volume come from different parts of the world, work in different disciplines and have different perspectives of community development, there is a thread that makes this book a unique resource for practitioners, students and academics of community development. The value of inclusivity, the indispensability of understanding the context, and the constant re-imaging of new theoretical frameworks that the authors of this book offer are intended to contribute to new directions in the discourse and practice of community development and diakonia as Christian social practice.

The consistent reference to and application of the sustainable development goals is a constant reminder that this resource is not limited to academic and scholarly ideas, but rather that it aims to strengthen the impact on the practical and actual difference that community development makes to marginalised communities across the world. This resource is inspired by the common human care for people and the environment. It is within the spirit of Ubuntu that this book contributes to the flourishing of the whole of humanity through inclusive communities.

Contributors

Editors

Tony Addy, University of Manchester, MA (Theol), University of St. Andrews (PGDip). Ordained, Community Minister, South Leeds (1971-76), Executive Secretary, Division of Community affairs, British and Irish Council of Churches (1976-80), Director, William Temple Foundation (1980 -91), General Secretary, European Contact Group on Urban Industrial Mission and Work and Economy Network (1991-2004), Consultant on Globalisation, World Council of Churches (1998-2000), Head of International Education, Diaconia University of Applied Sciences (2005-12), Chairperson, International Society for the Study and Research of Diaconia and Christian Social Practice (2012-16), Member, Editorial Team 'Diaconia, Journal for the Study and Research of Diaconia and Christian Social Practice' (2010-), Head of Education, interdiac, Czech Republic (2008-), Consultant, Lutheran World Federation, 'Re-forming Community Diakonia in Europe' (2012-), Research Associate, University of Pretoria (2020-), Lecturer, VID Specialized University (2021-). Published on community development, diakonia, work, economy and more recently on conviviality as a core concept for diakonia.

Hans Morten Haugen is Professor in International Diakonia at VID Specialized University, Norway. Dr. philos (political science 2022) Dr. juris (2006), both from University of Oslo. He was Senior Executive Officer on International Affairs and Human Rights in Church of Norway (CoN) 1996-2002 and Representative in Jerusalem for Norwegian Church Aid 2005-2006. Trough CoN he was member of World Council of Churches' Ecumenical Team at two UN conferences: Geneva 2000 and Financing for Development 2002. Chair of the Norwegian 'Crossroads' movement 2006-2009; Chair of Oslo Diocese (CoN) Green Church Resource Group 2004-2019, still member. He has also chaired the association Norwegian Constitution Section 112 (on environmental protection), still board member. His two English books are (short version): *The Right to Food and the TRIPS Agreement* (2007) and *Technology and Human Rights* (2012). He has written extensively on inclusive development, including the societal role of churches, and law and justice issues, focusing on patent rights, conflicts over land & resources and accountability for corporations.

Terese Bue Kessel is Associate Professor in Practical Theology with work experience as pastor and missionary in Japan for the Norwegian Mission Society. Her research interest is in the role of the church in community development regarding gender issues and women empowerment. She has written several articles on diakonia/pastoral counselling in cross-cultural contexts, and on questions regarding Christian teaching to children and young people in Church of Norway. Her PhD dissertation is an exploration of the diaconal work carried out by the semi-rural women in a context of the Evangelical Lutheran Church in Cameroon and their quest for personal and collective empowerment and transformation processes. From 2016 until today Kessel is the Head of the Department of Theology at VID Specialized University, Stavanger, Norway.

Benedicte Tveter Kivle, Associate Professor in Sociology and Values-based leadership, VID Specialized university, Oslo, Norway. Defended her PhD from Institute for Health Management, Medical Faculty, University of Oslo in 2009. The thesis was titled "From student to professional – experiences from medical Interns in Hospitals". Was a Leader for the Church City Mission in Kragerø, 2010-2013. Associate professor in Social Work and later in Values-based leadership from 2014. Program responsible for Master in Community Development and Social Innovation at VID Specialized University, Oslo, Norway since 2021. She has previously published articles and chapters on Trust-based Leadership, Participatory Research and Discourse analysis. This book is the first she has co-edited.

John Klaasen is Professor at The University of the Western Cape in Cape Town, South Africa. He is Head of the Department of Religion and Theology. His research interests are in practical theology and he is currently part of a number of international research projects including Religion and Community Development, Religion and Migration, Narrative theology and Development, and International Religion and Transformation Group. He is also a Visiting Professor at VID Specialized University, Norway, where he lectures in the Master in Community Development and Social Innovation, highlighting theology and development. He is part of VID's ReconTrans research project which investigates models of reconciliation within South Africa, Nordic countries and Canada. He is also part of the management committee of the NORPART partnership project which include VID, Chancellor College, Malawi and The University of the Western Cape. Klaasen is an ordained minister and serve as Canon and Dean of Studies in the Anglican Church. He also serves as a board member of FGLouw Village for the frail and aged and a board member of the Ecumenical Foundation of South Africa.

Contributors

Silje Kivle Andreassen is an ordained minister in The Church of Norway, currently serving in Holmlia church in a suburb of Oslo. She is also Adjunct Assistant Professor (PT) at MF Norwegian School of Theology, Religion and Society. Together with her co-writer Silje Kivle Andreassen, she received in 2020 a scholarship from the Bishops Conference in Church of Norway to do a study on how two local churches within CoN interact with the urban communities they are located in.

Benson Anofuechi is a doctorate candidate at the University of the Western Cape, South Africa, supervised by Professor John Klaasen. He teaches Theological Education by Extension College, Johannesburg, English for Education Development, and Graduate Lecturing Assistant at the Department of Religion and Theology, UWC. He is a member of the All Saints Anglican Church in South Africa. His research field includes Ethics, Development, and Practical Theology.

Eugene Baron is Senior Lecturer in the Department of Practical and Missional Theology at the University of the Free State in South Africa, specialising in black theologies of Liberation, Reconciliation, Church and Identity. Among his recent publications are 'Mission studies at South African Higher Education institutions: An ethical and decolonial perspective in the quest to "colour" the discipline', HTS Theological Studies, 76.1 (2020), (co-authored) 'The recovery of the prophetic voice of the church. The adoption of a "missional church" imagination', Verbum et ecclesia 41.1 (2020) and 'Die Ligdraer as a Grassroot Engagement on URCSA's Unification and Reconciliation between 1990–1997', Missionalia 48.1 (2020).

Tiana Bosman holds a PhD in Biblical Languages and is a senior lecturer at the University of the Western Cape, South Africa. Her field of specialization is the translation and interpretation of Old Testament texts. Before her appointment at UWC, she was appointed at the University of Stellenbosch and also served as a minister in the Dutch Reformed Church, where she was involved in the fight against gang violence and drug abuse on the Cape Flats.

Marit Breen is PhD fellow at VID, Specialized University, Oslo, Norway; MA in Gender Analysis in International Development, University of East Anglia, UK; MA in Global Studies, School of Mission and Theology (MHS; now VID), Stavanger, Norway; Gender Advisor in Norwegian Mission Society, whereas five years based in Ethiopia (2012-2018); Assistant professor in science of religion and culture at MHS (2012); Deputy leader at a center for asylum seekers in Sandnes, Norway (Hero, 2009-2010); various consultancies for the teaching and production of information materials on HIV/AIDS, general North/South issues, youth work, mission and life skills. She has published an article in the

Regnum Edinburgh Centenary Series, and a chapter in Dietrich, et al. (2016) Diakonia in a Gender Perspective. Breen is currently working on her PhD project about the Coptic Orthodox church's response to gender injustice in Egypt.

Stephanie Dietrich, Dr. theol., is Professor of diaconal studies at VID Specialised University in Oslo, Norway. She has co-edited the three earlier volumes of the Regnum series on diakonia. Dietrich is member of the WCC Faith and Order Commission and of the International Lutheran-Orthodox Dialogue Commission and has been involved in ecumenical cooperation and dialogue both in Norway and globally. She has broad teaching- and research experience within the field of diakonia and community development. She is the leader of the interdisciplinary research group on diaconal community development at VID called CODE; the co-chair of PARI, a Romanian-Norwegian research project on Participatory approach in Roma inclusion; and also the chair of the board of Digni, an umbrella organisation for 19 Norwegian mission societies and churches engaged in long-term development cooperation.

Dag-Håkon Eriksen, Assistant Professor and a Phd Fellow at VID Specialized University, Norway. Eriksen has extensive international experience from working with faith-based organizations involved in community development. Now he is doing a Phd on leadership and organizational innovation in faith-based organizations. Eriksen teaches courses on value-based leadership, social innovation, and sustainability at VID, and conducts leadership development programs for different NGOs. Eriksen is also a visiting scholar to Oxford Center for Mission Studies in 2022.

Silje Hole Hirsch is a sociologist and PhD Fellow at the Centre for Diaconia, Values and Professional Practice at VID Specialized University, where she previously worked as an assistant professor at the Faculty of Social Work. She also has experience from research, development work, and facilitation within the field of equity in health and welfare services.

Annette Leis-Peters is Dr. theol and Professor of the Sociology of Religion and Diaconal Studies at VID Specialized University in Norway. She is academically responsible for the PhD programme in Diakonia, Values and Professional Practice. Her research interests lie in the intersection between religion, civil society, welfare and migration. Within this field she has been involved in several Nordic and European research projects and published various articles in peer-reviewed journals and books. She is also editor-in-chief of the interdisciplinary journal Diaconia: Journal for the Study Christian Social Practice.

Beate Jelstad Løvaas is an associate professor at VID Specialized University in Oslo at the master's program in values-based leadership. She holds a PhD in management from the Norwegian School of Economics (NHH). She has a master of Science degree from the Norwegian University of Life Sciences and a European master's degree from the University of Kiel in Germany. She has published on leadership and organization with an emphasis on the third sector. Her research interests include meaningful work, motivation, supervision and the role of group reflection processes, relations, values and volunteering.

Kjersti Gautestad Norheim is an ordained minister in Church of Norway, currently serving in Birkeland, a congregtion located in an urban community on the outskirts of the city of Bergen. She is also part of the editorial team of Luthersk Kirketidene, a journal published by MF Norwegian School of Theology, Religion and Society. Together with her co-writer Silje Kivle Andreassen, she received in 2020 a scholarship from the Bishops Conference in Church of Norway to do a study on how two local churches within CoN interact with the urban communities they are located in.

Amos OUNSOUBO has studied Community Development and Social Innovation at VID Specialised University in Norway within the specialisation 'Diakonia, Community Development and Christian Action'. He is currently working in the Norwegian Mission Society as advisor within the 'Use Your Talents Institutional Development Project' which aims at developing and promoting a diaconal asset-based community development called 'Use Your Talents'. He has an experience in training congregations and FBOs in conceiving and carrying out their development philosophy.

Jeremy Gregory Wyngaard holds a PhD in Practical Theology and Missiology from Stellenbosch University and is the founder of Life Zone Ministries International, a faith-based organization in Factreton and Kensington, Cape Town, South Africa. Teaches youth ministry and development studies at various theological tertiary institutions. Main area of research and publication over the past years have been in the field of community development and youth development. Appointed as Director of Moravian Theological Centre in Cape Town in January 2022.

Index